Learn SQL Database Programming

Query and manipulate databases from popular relational
database servers using SQL

Josephine Bush

BIRMINGHAM - MUMBAI

Learn SQL Database Programming

Commissioning Editor: Brandon D'Abreo
Acquisition Editor: Reshma Raman
Content Development Editor: Nazia Shaikh
Senior Editor: Ayaan Hoda
Technical Editor: Utkarsha S. Kadam
Copy Editor: Safis Editing
Project Coordinator: Aishwarya Mohan
Proofreader: Safis Editing
Indexer: Manju Arasan
Production Designer: Jyoti Chauhan

First published: May 2020

Production reference: 1290520

Published by Packt Publishing Ltd.
Livery Place
35 Livery Street
Birmingham
B3 2PB, UK.

ISBN 978-1-83898-476-2

www.packt.com

Packt.com

Subscribe to our online digital library for full access to over 7,000 books and videos, as well as industry leading tools to help you plan your personal development and advance your career. For more information, please visit our website.

Why subscribe?

- Spend less time learning and more time coding with practical eBooks and Videos from over 4,000 industry professionals

- Improve your learning with Skill Plans built especially for you

- Get a free eBook or video every month

- Fully searchable for easy access to vital information

- Copy and paste, print, and bookmark content

Did you know that Packt offers eBook versions of every book published, with PDF and ePub files available? You can upgrade to the eBook version at www.packt.com and as a print book customer, you are entitled to a discount on the eBook copy. Get in touch with us at customercare@packtpub.com for more details.

At www.packt.com, you can also read a collection of free technical articles, sign up for a range of free newsletters, and receive exclusive discounts and offers on Packt books and eBooks.

Contributors

About the author

Josephine Bush has over 10 years of experience as a Database Administrator. Her experience is extensive and broad-based, including in financial, business, and energy data systems using MySQL, SQL Server, Oracle, and PostgreSQL. She is a Microsoft Certified Solutions Expert: Data Management and Analytics. She holds a BS in Information Technology, an MBA in IT Management, and an MS in Data Analytics.

I would like to acknowledge my husband, Jim, who provided support and encouragement at every step, and gave me especially useful baseball insights.

About the reviewers

Starting out with the Microsoft stack, **Frank Solomon** gradually focused on SQL Server and database development. He then extended to writing and technical writing. He writes for SQL Shack, he blogs at Bit Vectors, and he had the lead co-author role for The SQL Workshop, a Packt book. Find Frank at LinkedIn, and reach out to him with writing / technical writing/development opportunities. He levers sharp software development and writing skills to build awesome products. He has plenty of remoting experience, and he uniquely relies on the active voice to build high-quality writing products.

Awni Al Saqqa is a Microsoft Technology Specialist in MS SQL Server and a certified solutions developer since 2007. He has over a decade of experience with database development and administration on SQL Server, Oracle, and MySQL. He is a solutions architect, who is hands-on in many enterprise projects for different business sectors, such as education, hospitality, retail, manufacturing, marketing, and more, which has given him the perfect combination between business and technical experience. Awni is also the Lead Author for The SQL Workshop book which is published by Packt

Packt is searching for authors like you

If you're interested in becoming an author for Packt, please visit `authors.packtpub.com` and apply today. We have worked with thousands of developers and tech professionals, just like you, to help them share their insight with the global tech community. You can make a general application, apply for a specific hot topic that we are recruiting an author for, or submit your own idea.

Table of Contents

Section 3: Advanced SQL Querying

Section 4: Presenting Your Findings

Preface

SQL is a powerful querying language used to store, manipulate, and retrieve data, and is one of the most popular languages used by developers to query and analyze data efficiently. If you're looking for a comprehensive introduction to SQL, *Learn SQL Database Programming* will help you to get up to speed with using SQL to streamline your work in no time. Starting with an overview of relational database management systems, this book will show you how to set up and use MySQL Workbench and design a database using practical examples. You'll also discover how to query and manipulate data with SQL programming using MySQL Workbench. As you advance, you'll create a database, query single and multiple tables, and modify data using SQL querying. This SQL book covers advanced SQL techniques, including aggregate functions, flow control statements, error handling, and subqueries, and helps you process your data to present your findings. Finally, you'll implement best practices for writing SQL and designing indexes and tables.

By the end of this SQL programming book, you'll have gained the confidence to use SQL queries for retrieving and manipulating data.

Who this book is for

This book is for business analysts, SQL developers, database administrators, and students learning SQL. If you want to learn how to query and manipulate SQL data for database administration tasks or to simply extract and organize relevant data for analysis, you'll find this book useful. No prior SQL experience is required.

What this book covers

Chapter 1, *Introduction to Relational Database Management Systems*, introduces the concepts required to understand the basics of relational database management systems. It introduces foundational topics such as understanding SQL, the relational model, data integrity, database normalization, and the various types of relational database management systems. It gives you fundamental knowledge about SQL and databases that will be required throughout the book.

Chapter 2, *Installing and Using MySQL Workbench,* covers how to install MySQL Workbench on Windows and Mac, including step-by-step instructions to help you walk through each part of the installation process. The instructions also include the configuration of MySQL Workbench on both Windows and Mac. We will walk through some examples of connecting to your local MySQL and also setting up connections to other MySQL servers. We conclude with a step-by-step explanation of how to restore a database to MySQL.

Chapter 3, *Understanding Data Types,* covers what data types are and how they are used. You will learn about specific data types and what data can be stored in each of them. The data types include string, numeric, and date and time. String data types include char and varchar, binary and varbinary, blob, enum, and text. Numeric data types include bit, int, float, double, and decimal. Date and time data types include date, time, datetime, timestamp, and year. You will learn from the perspective of MySQL data types, but where there are differences versus SQL Server, Oracle, and PostgreSQL, those differences will be noted. We will also go through some examples of types and values of data to see how to assign them correctly to data types, including an explanation of why you need to be careful when selecting a data type and how it can impact database performance.

Chapter 4, *Designing and Creating a Database,* introduces you to designing and creating a database. We'll walk through the guidelines for naming conventions and understand SQL code errors. You will learn how to format SQL code for readability and apply data types and data integrity to our tables. You will also learn about the different types of table relationships and how to build entity-relationship diagrams. Going further, we will discuss the concept and usage of indexing. You will gain an understanding of how indexing helps database performance. Finally, you will learn how to create a table in a database.

Chapter 5, *Importing and Exporting Data,* introduces you to importing and exporting data. There are many ways to import and export data in MySQL. You will learn how to import and export data using MySQL Workbench via table data from/to CSV files. We will also cover importing and exporting via SQL data with SQL scripts. An additional way to export data via result data and query results will also be covered. The final topic discussed is using SQL syntax to import and export data.

Chapter 6, *Querying a Single Table,* covers how to use the basic SQL SELECT statement and the FROM, WHERE, and ORDER BY clauses. This chapter also covers how to tell which index your query is using and whether you may need additional indexes. By the end of this chapter, you will understand how to query data using the SELECT statement and the FROM clause. You will also learn how to limit results with a WHERE clause, how to use ORDER BY to return results in a specified order, and how to see information about what indexes are being used or may be needed.

Chapter 7, *Querying Multiple Tables*, covers how to use SQL joins to join two or more tables together, including INNER, OUTER (LEFT, RIGHT, and FULL), and advanced joins (the cross and self joins). You will learn about set theory and how to combine queries using UNION and UNION ALL, and how to get the differences and intersections of different queries. Lastly, you will learn how to optimize queries when they contain multiple tables.

Chapter 8, *Modifying Data and Table Structures*, goes through how to modify data in tables. This includes learning how to use INSERT, UPDATE, and DELETE statements. You will also learn about SQL transactions, which help to control the modification of data. Finally, you will learn how to modify a table structure.

Chapter 9, *Working with Expressions*, covers how to use literals, operators, columns, and built-in functions to create expressions. You will learn about the different types of built-in functions, including string, numeric, date and time, and advanced functions, which include casting and converting to other data types. You will learn how to use statistical functions, including how to get and use variance and standard deviation. Finally, you will learn how to create a generated column based on an expression.

Chapter 10, *Grouping and Summarizing Data*, covers how to use aggregate functions to group and summarize data. Aggregate functions include math functions such as AVG, SUM, COUNT, MIN, and MAX. You will also learn how to use the GROUP BY and HAVING clauses in conjunction with the aggregate functions. Finally, you will learn how MySQL executes your query clauses.

Chapter 11, *Advanced Querying Techniques*, covers how to use two different kinds of subqueries, correlated and non-correlated. Then, you will learn about two different types of common table expressions, recursive and non-recursive. You will learn about query hints and how to choose which index your query will use. Finally, you will learn about isolation levels and concepts relating to how data is read from and written to tables.

Chapter 12, *Programmable Objects*, covers how to create and use views, which includes selecting data from views, and inserting, updating, and deleting data using views. You will learn how to create and use variables, which includes how to declare and assign values to variables. You will also learn how to create and use stored procedures, including how to use variables and parameters in stored procedures, as well as how to control flow and error handling. In addition to all that, you will learn how to create and use functions, triggers, and temporary tables.

Chapter 13, *Exploring and Processing Your Data*, covers how to explore and process data. By the end of this chapter, you will understand how to get to know data by creating a statistical identity, you will have learned how to detect and fix anomalous and missing values, and will know how to use regular expressions to match data value patterns.

Chapter 14, *Telling a Story with Your Data*, teaches you how to find a narrative, including what types of stories you can tell with data and how to use the statistical identity of your data to determine a story. You will also learn about knowing your audience, including deciding who they are and what would be a compelling presentation for them. Then, you will learn how to identify a presentation framework, including explaining the question, answer, and methodology. Finally, you will learn how to use visualizations in your presentations.

Chapter 15, *Best Practices for Designing and Querying*, covers database best practices for database design, indexing, and querying and modifying data. You learned about these topics in the previous chapters, and this chapter will summarize and give additional tips for best practices. This chapter will also provide a way for the more experienced among you to quickly reference best practices instead of having to go through each chapter.

Chapter 16, *SQL Appendix*, covers the SQL commands discussed, which are outlined for quick reference. It includes the syntax for querying data, modifying data, and designing databases and tables. This chapter will help you by providing a quick reference guide, so you won't have to go back through all the chapters to check the syntax, but if you require more details about how the syntax works, you can refer to the specific chapter for that information.

To get the most out of this book

For this book to be useful, you either need access to MySQL Workbench and the ability to query a MySQL Server, or the ability to install them. To install them yourself, you will need elevated permissions. Installations for MySQL Workbench are found at `https://dev.mysql.com/downloads/workbench/` and installations for MySQL server are found at `https://dev.mysql.com/downloads/mysql/`. If you don't want or don't have MySQL installed, you can follow along in most chapters with SQL code that will work in Oracle, PostgreSQL, or SQL Server, as well.

If you are using the digital version of this book, we advise you to type the code yourself or access the code via the GitHub repository (link available in the next section). Doing so will help you avoid any potential errors related to the copying and pasting of code.

Download the example code files

You can download the example code files for this book from your account at www.packt.com. If you purchased this book elsewhere, you can visit www.packtpub.com/support and register to have the files emailed directly to you.

You can download the code files by following these steps:

1. Log in or register at www.packt.com.
2. Select the **Support** tab.
3. Click on **Code Downloads**.
4. Enter the name of the book in the **Search** box and follow the onscreen instructions.

Once the file is downloaded, please make sure that you unzip or extract the folder using the latest version of:

- WinRAR/7-Zip for Windows
- Zipeg/iZip/UnRarX for Mac
- 7-Zip/PeaZip for Linux

The code bundle for the book is also hosted on GitHub at https://github.com/PacktPublishing/learn-sql-database-programming. In case there's an update to the code, it will be updated on the existing GitHub repository.

We also have other code bundles from our rich catalog of books and videos available at https://github.com/PacktPublishing/. Check them out!

Download the color images

We also provide a PDF file that has color images of the screenshots/diagrams used in this book. You can download it here: https://static.packt-cdn.com/downloads/9781838984762_ColorImages.pdf.

Conventions used

There are a number of text conventions used throughout this book.

CodeInText: Indicates code words in text, database table names, folder names, filenames, file extensions, pathnames, dummy URLs, user input, and Twitter handles. Here is an example: "BINARY is like CHAR, but stores byte strings instead of character strings."

A block of code is set as follows:

```
<books>
  <book>
    <name>Learn SQL Programming</name>
    <author>Josephine Bush</author>
  </book>
</books>
```

Any command-line input or output is written as follows:

```
SELECT * FROM lahmansbaseballdb.appearances;
```

Bold: Indicates a new term, an important word, or words that you see onscreen. For example, words in menus or dialog boxes appear in the text like this. Here is an example: "Click **Download** on the DMG Archive."

 Warnings or important notes appear like this.

 Tips and tricks appear like this.

Get in touch

Feedback from our readers is always welcome.

General feedback: If you have questions about any aspect of this book, mention the book title in the subject of your message and email us at customercare@packtpub.com.

Errata: Although we have taken every care to ensure the accuracy of our content, mistakes do happen. If you have found a mistake in this book, we would be grateful if you would report this to us. Please visit www.packtpub.com/support/errata, selecting your book, clicking on the Errata Submission Form link, and entering the details.

Piracy: If you come across any illegal copies of our works in any form on the Internet, we would be grateful if you would provide us with the location address or website name. Please contact us at copyright@packt.com with a link to the material.

If you are interested in becoming an author: If there is a topic that you have expertise in and you are interested in either writing or contributing to a book, please visit authors.packtpub.com.

Reviews

Please leave a review. Once you have read and used this book, why not leave a review on the site that you purchased it from? Potential readers can then see and use your unbiased opinion to make purchase decisions, we at Packt can understand what you think about our products, and our authors can see your feedback on their book. Thank you!

For more information about Packt, please visit packt.com.

Section 1: Database Fundamentals

The objective of this section is to introduce you to relational database management systems, how to set up and use MySQL Workbench, how to use data types, how to design and create a database, and how to import and export data.

This section comprises the following chapters:

- Chapter 1, *Introduction to Relational Database Management Systems*
- Chapter 2, *Installing and Using MySQL Workbench*
- Chapter 3, *Understanding Data Types*
- Chapter 4, *Designing and Creating a Database*
- Chapter 5, *Importing and Exporting Data*

1

Introduction to Relational Database Management Systems

This chapter introduces the concepts required to understand the basics of **relational database management systems** (**RDMS**). It will introduce foundational topics such as SQL, the relational model, data integrity, database normalization, and the types of relational database management systems. It will provide you with fundamental knowledge about SQL and databases that will be required throughout this book.

In this chapter, we will cover the following topics:

- Understanding SQL
- Understanding databases
- Understanding data integrity
- Understanding database normalization
- Types of RDMS

Understanding SQL

Structured Query Language, or **SQL** (pronounced *see-quel*), is the language that is used for querying and manipulating data and defining structures in databases. Initially developed at IBM in the early 1970s, SQL became an ANSI and ISO standard in 1986.

SQL is a powerful, yet simple language, and can do many things, such as execute queries, retrieve, insert, update, and delete data, create databases and tables, and much more.

These types of activities can be grouped into different subdivisions of SQL: **Data Definition Language (DDL)**, **Data Manipulation Language (DML)**, and **Data Control Language (DCL)**:

- Use DDL commands to specify database schema:
    - CREATE: This is used to create a new database or objects in a database.
    - ALTER: This is used to alter a database or objects in a database.
    - DROP: This is used to delete a database or objects in a database.
    - TRUNCATE: This is used to remove all data from a table instantaneously.
- Use DML commands to query and modify data:
    - SELECT: This is used to retrieve data from a database.
    - INSERT: This is used to insert data into a database.
    - UPDATE: This is used to update data in a database.
    - DELETE: This is used to remove data from a database.
- Use DCL commands to control permissions and translations:
    - GRANT: This is used to give access to a user.
    - REVOKE: This is used to take access away from a user.
    - COMMIT: This is used to save changes in a transaction.
    - ROLLBACK: This is used to remove the saved changes in a transaction.

 You won't learn about GRANT and REVOKE in this book. To get more information on granting and denying permissions, please visit https://dev.mysql.com/doc/refman/8.0/en/grant.html and https://dev.mysql.com/doc/refman/8.0/en/revoke.html.

Elements of SQL

The SQL language comprises several elements that will be explained in more depth in subsequent chapters. These elements include the following:

- Queries that retrieve data based on specific criteria.
- Clauses that are components of statements or queries.
- Predicates that are logical conditions that evaluate to true or false. These help you to narrow down the results of your queries.
- Expressions that produce either scalar values or tables of columns and rows. Expressions are a part of predicates.

- Statements that are queries run against a database, comprised of clauses and, optionally, expressions and predicates.
- White space that is generally ignored in SQL statements and queries, making it easier to format for readability because you don't have to worry so much about particular spacing for the SQL to run correctly.

The following diagram shows you the components of a SQL statement, which is also called a SQL query:

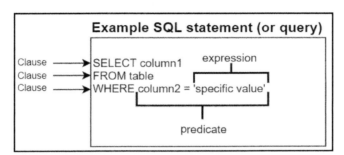

In the preceding diagram, you can see the different elements of a SQL statement. Each line in the preceding statement is considered a clause. Clauses use SQL keywords. Keywords are reserved words that have special significance in the SQL language—SELECT, FROM, and WHERE are just some of the keywords that are used. More information on keywords is provided in Chapter 4, *Designing and Creating a Database*. The preceding diagram also shows an expression and predicate. A predicate helps you to narrow down your query results. The expression is a piece of a predicate that sets the value. The diagram also helps to illustrate the use of white space. You could write out your entire query on one line, but it's much easier to read when you add carriage returns and spaces. The details of the different elements of queries will be covered more in future chapters of this book.

Understanding databases

A **database** is a collection of data. You store databases in a **relational database management system (RDMS)**. The RDMS is the basis for modern database systems like MySQL, SQL Server, Oracle, PostgreSQL, and others. These will be covered in more detail later in this chapter.

Tables

In an RDMS, objects called **tables** store data. Tables are a collection of related data stored in columns and rows. The following screenshot is a cross-section of a table that contains data about baseball players' appearances in all-star games:

playerID	yearID	gameNum	gameID	teamID	lgID	GP	startingPos
aaronha01	1955	0	NLS195507120	ML1	NL	1	NULL
aaronha01	1956	0	ALS195607100	ML1	NL	1	NULL
aaronha01	1957	0	NLS195707090	ML1	NL	1	9
aaronha01	1958	0	ALS195807080	ML1	NL	1	9
aaronha01	1959	1	NLS195907070	ML1	NL	1	9

A **NULL** value in a table is a value that appears to be blank. It doesn't represent a string of blank spaces, zero, or a zero-length character string: it's a missing or unknown value.

The data has been sourced from http://www.seanlahman.com/baseball-archive/statistics/ with a CC BY-SA 3.0 license.

Fields

A **field** is an intersection of a row and a column. This field could be any type of data, including a yearID, teamID, or a playerID field (using our example). Each red arrow in the following screenshot points to a value in a column that is considered a field:

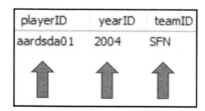

Records or rows

A **row** contains values in a horizontal division of data. In this example case, it's a row or record from a table:

aaronha01	1955	0	NLS195507120	ML1	NL	1	NULL

Columns

A **column** contains values in a vertical division of data. In this example case, it's the `gameID` column from a table:

gameID
NLS195507120
ALS195607100
NLS195707090
ALS195807080
NLS195907070

To ensure that the data in your tables is consistent and accurate, you will need to understand data integrity. You will learn about data integrity in the next section.

Understanding data integrity

Data integrity refers to the consistency and accuracy of the data. It is typically enforced by the procedures and guidelines in the database design phase. In RDMS, keys enforce data integrity. A key is user-defined and forces values in a table to conform to a specified standard. This standard will allow only certain kinds of values to be in the database.

Types of integrity

Data integrity refers to the consistency and accuracy of data and table relationships. The following table lists the types of integrity you can use:

Entity integrity	Referential integrity	Domain integrity
Unique constraint	Foreign key	Check constraint
Not null constraint		Default constraint
Primary key		

Each type of integrity and how each relates to one another is discussed in the following sections.

Entity integrity

To ensure that each row in a table is identifiably unique, you use **entity integrity**. This is done with a few different types of keys or constraints, including unique, not null, and primary key constraints.

Unique constraints

To ensure that all values in a column or columns are different from each other, you use a unique constraint. This type of key can be applied to any data type and is used to avoid duplicate data. You can apply a unique constraint to multiple columns so that it creates a unique value across those multiple columns. It can contain null values.

If you create a unique constraint on one column, it will force the table to have unique values in that specific column. If they are not unique, then the row will not be able to be inserted or updated.

In the following screenshot, the `parkkey` constraint is unique. All the other fields can have duplicate information as long as the `parkkey` unique constraint isn't violated:

parkkey	parkname	city	state	country
ALB01	Riverside Park	Albany	NY	US
ALT01	Columbia Park	Altoona	PA	US
ANA01	Angel Stadium of Anaheim	Anaheim	CA	US
ARL01	Arlington Stadium	Arlington	TX	US
ARL02	Rangers Ballpark in Arlington	Arlington	TX	US
ATL01	Atlanta-Fulton County Stadium	Atlanta	GA	US
ATL02	Turner Field	Atlanta	GA	US
ATL03	Suntrust Park	Atlanta	GA	US
BAL01	Madison Avenue Grounds	Baltimore	MD	US
BAL02	Newington Park	Baltimore	MD	US
BAL03	Oriole Park I	Baltimore	MD	US

If you create a unique constraint on a combination of columns in a table, it will force the table to have unique values in the combination of those columns in the unique constraint. If they are not unique, the row will not be able to be inserted or updated.

The following screenshot shows an example of a composite, unique constraint. In this case, `playerID`, `yearID`, and `teamID` would need to be unique for the row to be acceptable:

playerID	yearID	teamID	lgID	W	L	G
aardsda01	2004	SFN	NL	1	0	11
aardsda01	2006	CHN	NL	3	0	45
aardsda01	2007	CHA	AL	2	1	25
aardsda01	2008	BOS	AL	4	2	47
aardsda01	2009	SEA	AL	3	6	73
aardsda01	2010	SEA	AL	0	6	53
aardsda01	2012	NYA	AL	0	0	1
aardsda01	2013	NYN	NL	2	2	43
aardsda01	2015	ATL	NL	1	1	33
aasedo01	1977	BOS	AL	6	2	13
aasedo01	1978	CAL	AL	11	8	29

Not null constraints

To ensure that all values in a column are not null, you use a *not null* constraint. This type of key can be applied to any data type and is used to avoid missing data. If you create a not null constraint on a column, it will force the table to have values in that specific column. If the values are null, then the row will not be inserted or updated.

In the following screenshot, you can see that the `birthYear` constraint is set to not null. The `deathYear` constraint would allow nulls since not all people have a year of death:

playerID	birthYear	birthCountry	deathYear
aardsda01	1981	USA	NULL
aaronha01	1934	USA	NULL
aaronto01	1939	USA	1984
aasedo01	1954	USA	NULL
abadan01	1972	USA	NULL
abadfe01	1985	D.R.	NULL
abadijo01	1850	USA	1905
abbated01	1877	USA	1957
abbeybe01	1869	USA	1962
abbeych01	1866	USA	1926
abbotda01	1862	USA	1930

The primary key

The **primary key** is used to ensure that all values in a column are not null and unique. This key combines the unique and not null constraint properties into one key. This type of key can be applied to any data type and is used to avoid missing and duplicate data. You can only have one primary key per table.

If you create a primary key on a table, it will force the table to have unique, not null values in that specific column. If the values don't comply, then the row will not be able to be inserted or updated. You can also create a primary key on multiple columns. This is considered a composite key. In this case, the composite key would have to be unique for each row, otherwise the row could not be inserted or updated.

In the following screenshot, the `playerID` constraint would be the primary key because it's unique and not null for every row in the table:

playerID	birthYear	birthMonth	birthDay	birthCountry	birthState	birthCity
aardsda01	1981	12	27	USA	CO	Denver
aaronha01	1934	2	5	USA	AL	Mobile
aaronto01	1939	8	5	USA	AL	Mobile
aasedo01	1954	9	8	USA	CA	Orange
abadan01	1972	8	25	USA	FL	Palm Beach
abadfe01	1985	12	17	D.R.	La Romana	La Romana
abadijo01	1850	11	4	USA	PA	Philadelphia
abbated01	1877	4	15	USA	PA	Latrobe
abbeybe01	1869	11	11	USA	VT	Essex
abbeych01	1866	10	14	USA	NE	Falls City

In the following screenshot, the `playerID`, `yearID`, and `teamID` constraints could be the composite primary key because the combination of those three columns is unique and not null for every row in the table:

playerID	yearID	teamID	g	ab	r	h	rbi
aardsda01	2004	SFN	11	0	0	0	0
aardsda01	2006	CHN	45	2	0	0	0
aardsda01	2007	CHA	25	0	0	0	0
aardsda01	2008	BOS	47	1	0	0	0
aardsda01	2009	SEA	73	0	0	0	0
aardsda01	2010	SEA	53	0	0	0	0
aardsda01	2012	NYA	1	0	0	0	0
aardsda01	2013	NYN	43	0	0	0	0
aardsda01	2015	ATL	33	1	0	0	0
aaronha01	1954	ML1	122	468	58	131	69
aaronha01	1955	ML1	153	602	105	189	106

Referential integrity

Referential integrity refers to the consistency and accuracy between tables that can be linked together. By having a primary key on the parent table and a foreign key on the child table, you achieve referential integrity. A foreign key on the child table creates a link between one or more columns in the child table and the primary key on the parent table. When a foreign key is present, it must reference a valid, existing primary key in the parent table. This way, the data in both tables can maintain a proper relationship. You will learn more about this in the following example.

If you don't set up referential integrity, you wind up with orphaned records. For example, let's say that you delete a player from the first table here:

playerID	birthYear	bats	throws	
aardsda01	1981	R	R	
abreubo01	1974	L	R	This row is deleted

Now let's say that you didn't delete the corresponding record in the second table here. In this case, the second table's records would be orphaned:

PlayerID	salary	year	
aardsda01	2750000	2010	
aardsda01	4500000	2011	
abreubo01	10600000	2004	This row is orphaned
abreubo01	13100000	2005	This row is orphaned

If there was a foreign key constraint on the `salary` column, then the player could not be deleted from the parent table without first deleting the corresponding salary rows in the salary table. By having a foreign key constraint, we will also prevent users from adding rows to the child table without a corresponding parent row or changing values in a parent table that would result in orphaned child table records.

You won't get an error if there is incomplete data when you lack referential integrity constraints. It's basically like your records are lost in the database since they may never show up in reports or query results. This can cause all kinds of problems, such as strange results, lost orders, and potentially life-and-death situations where (for example) patients don't receive proper treatments.

When creating a foreign key constraint, the foreign key must reference a column in another table that is the primary key. It can be any data type and accept duplicate and null values by default. The foreign key constraint can maintain three types of table relationships (covered in more detail in `Chapter 7`, *Querying Multiple Tables*):

- **One-to-one**: This type of relationship is when one table has just one corresponding row in another table. An example of this could be a table with employees and computers. Each employee has one computer.
- **One-to-many**: This type of relationship is when one table has none, one, or many corresponding rows in another table. An example of this could be a table with adults and children. An adult table row may have none, one, or many rows in the child table.
- **Many-to-many**: This type of relationship is when many rows in one table correspond to many rows in another table. An example of this could be the `customers` and `products` tables. Customers can purchase many products.

In the following screenshots, the primary key would be on the first table as `playerID`. The second table would have a foreign key reference to `playerID` on the first table. In this case, there would be a one-to-many relationship between the first and second tables because there is one player in the first table and none, one, or many rows corresponding to that player in the second table.

If you had a foreign key setup on `playerID` in the second table, then you would not be able to delete the `playerID` value from the first table unless you deleted it in the second table beforehand. This key setup maintains the referential integrity and ensures that you won't have orphaned records in the second table:

playerID is the primary key in this table

playerID	birthYear	birthMonth	birthDay	birthCountry	birthState	birthCity
aardsda01	1981	12	27	USA	CO	Denver
aaronha01	1934	2	5	USA	AL	Mobile
aaronto01	1939	8	5	USA	AL	Mobile
aasedo01	1954	9	8	USA	CA	Orange
abadan01	1972	8	25	USA	FL	Palm Beach
abadfe01	1985	12	17	D.R.	La Romana	La Romana
abadijo01	1850	11	4	USA	PA	Philadelphia
abbated01	1877	4	15	USA	PA	Latrobe
abbeybe01	1869	11	11	USA	VT	Essex
abbeych01	1866	10	14	USA	NE	Falls City

playerID is the foreign key in this table

playerID	yearID	teamID	g	ab	r	h	rbi
aardsda01	2004	SFN	11	0	0	0	0
aardsda01	2006	CHN	45	2	0	0	0
aardsda01	2007	CHA	25	0	0	0	0
aardsda01	2008	BOS	47	1	0	0	0
aardsda01	2009	SEA	73	0	0	0	0
aardsda01	2010	SEA	53	0	0	0	0
aardsda01	2012	NYA	1	0	0	0	0
aardsda01	2013	NYN	43	0	0	0	0
aardsda01	2015	ATL	33	1	0	0	0
aaronha01	1954	ML1	122	468	58	131	69
aaronha01	1955	ML1	153	602	105	189	106

Domain integrity

To ensure that data values follow defined rules for formatting, range, and value using check and default constraints, you use **domain integrity**.

The check constraint is used to ensure that all values in a column are within a range of values. This type of key can be applied to any data type and is used to ensure that values aren't invalid. A check constraint is enforced with user-defined conditions and evaluates as either true or false. You can define a check constraint on a single column or a combination of columns in a table.

Since null doesn't evaluate as false, it can be inserted or updated into a field with a check constraint. So, because null evaluates to unknown, it can bypass a check constraint. If you want the column with a check constraint to not allow null, you need to also set a *not null* constraint on the column.

The following screenshot shows an example of a table where a check constraint would make sense on the inducted column. A player can either be inducted into the hall of fame or not. In this case, you could create a check constraint that only allows Y or N in that field. If the value isn't Y or N, then the row can't be updated or inserted:

playerID	yearID	ballots	needed	votes	inducted
aaronha01	1982	415	312	406	Y
abbotji01	2005	516	387	13	N
adamsba01	1937	201	151	8	N
adamsba01	1938	262	197	11	N
adamsba01	1939	274	206	11	N
adamsba01	1942	233	175	11	N

The following screenshot shows an example of a table where a check constraint can be applied to multiple columns. For instance, you wouldn't want deathYear to be a year before the birthYear, so you can set a check constraint that will only allow you to add or update a birthYear or deathYear that follows a check constraint like birthYear < deathYear:

playerID	birthYear	deathYear
aardsda01	1981	NULL
aaronha01	1934	NULL
aaronto01	1939	1984
aasedo01	1954	NULL
abadan01	1972	NULL
abadfe01	1985	NULL
abadijo01	1850	1905
abbated01	1877	1957

To ensure that all rows in a column have a value, you use a default constraint. This type of key can be applied to any data type. A default constraint assigns a default value to a field. This is used to avoid having a null value for a field if a user doesn't specify a value.

The following screenshot shows an example of a table where a default constraint could make sense on the `ab` column:

playerID	yearID	teamID	g	ab
aardsda01	2004	SFN	11	0
aardsda01	2006	CHN	45	2
aardsda01	2007	CHA	25	0
aardsda01	2008	BOS	47	1
aardsda01	2009	SEA	73	0
aardsda01	2010	SEA	53	0
aardsda01	2012	NYA	1	0
aardsda01	2013	NYN	43	0
aardsda01	2015	ATL	33	1
aaronha01	1954	ML1	122	468
aaronha01	1955	ML1	153	602

A player can be in a game without having any at-bats. In this case, you could create a default constraint that sets the `ab` column to `0` if the user provides no value.

Database normalization

Database normalization is the process of putting your raw data into tables using rules to avoid redundant data, optimize database performance, and ensure data integrity.

Without proper normalization, not only can you have data redundancy, which uses additional storage space, but it can be more difficult to update and maintain the database without data loss.

Normalization requires forms. Forms are sets of rules to follow to normalize your data into database tables. There are three forms that we will discuss: the first normal form, the second normal form, and the third normal form. Each of these forms has a set of rules to ensure that your database complies with the form. Each of the forms builds on the previous forms.

The first normal form

The **first normal form** (**1NF**) is the first level of database normalization. You will need to complete this step before proceeding to other database normalization forms. The primary reason to implement 1NF is to eliminate repeating groups. This ensures that you can use simple SQL statements to query the data. It also ensures that you aren't duplicating data, which uses additional storage and computing time. This step will ensure that you are doing the following:

- Defining data, columns, and data types and putting related data into columns
- Eliminating repeating groups of data:
    - This means that you will not have repeating columns, such as `Year1`, `Year2`, `Year3`, but instead will have a column that is named `Year`, and each row in the table will be a different year.
    - Another example of this is not having multiple values in the same field, such as `1985`, `1987`, `1989`, but instead placing each year in a row.
    - This means that there are no exact duplicate rows. The example following this bullet list will explain this concept in more depth.
- Creating a primary key for each table

In the following example, you could make the first column the primary key in the people table and the foreign key in the salaries table. In the salaries table, you could create a new primary key or create a composite key that is an amalgamation of multiple fields.

Here is a denormalized sample table:

Name	birthYear	Salary	SalaryYear
Jim Jones	1981	2750000, 4500000	2010, 2011
Joe Smith	1974	10600000	2014

There is a right way and wrong way to normalize this table. Let's go over the wrong way first:

Name	birthYear	Salary1	Salary2	SalaryYear1	SalaryYear2
Jim Jones	1981	2750000	4500000	2010	2011
Joe Smith	1974	10600000		2014	

The preceding design has introduced new problems. Even though it doesn't have groups of repeating data in one column, the salary is limited to two values. What if a player has more than two salaries? You don't have anywhere to put another salary without adding a third column. This also wastes space for those players that only have one salary, and searching through this table for a player with a specific salary becomes difficult. The same goes for the SalaryYear columns.

The right way to normalize the denormalized table to the first normal form is to ensure that there aren't repeating groups, as shown in the following table. The people table with player information would look like the following:

playerID	nameFirst	nameLast	birthYear
jjones01	Jim	Jones	1981
jsmith01	Joe	Smith	1974

The Salary value has been removed and placed in another table with the playerID field linking them to each other; therefore, the salaries table will look like the following:

salaryID	playerID	salary	year
1	jjones01	2750000	2010
2	jjones01	4500000	2011
3	jsmith01	10600000	2014

Let's go through a denormalization example by looking at the following table:

playerID	namefirst	namelast	birthYear	franchID	franchname	teamID	RBI	rank	yearID
abbotpa01	Paul	Abbott	1967	PHI	Philadelphia Phillies	PHI	2	2	2004
abreubo01	Bobby	Abreu	1974	PHI	Philadelphia Phillies	PHI	79	1	2000
abreubo01	Bobby	Abreu	1974	PHI	Philadelphia Phillies	PHI	110	3	2001
alcanar01	Arismendy	Alcantara	1991	CHI	Chicago Cubs	CHI	1	8	2015
almoral01	Albert	Almora	1994	CHI	Chicago Cubs	CHI	14	8	2016
almoral01	Albert	Almora	1994	CHI	Chicago Cubs	CHI	46	6	2017
alvarpe01	Pedro	Alvarez	1987	PIT	Pittsburg Pirates	PIT	77	17	2015
alvarto01	Tony	Alvarez	1979	PIT	Pittsburg Pirates	PIT	2	9	2002
alvarto01	Tony	Alvarez	1979	PIT	Pittsburg Pirates	PIT	8	1	2004

To meet the requirements of 1NF, you would need to split this table into multiple tables. Depending on the table you are trying to normalize, you might not need to split it if it's already following the rules of 1NF.

This table only contains the information about the player and has a primary key of `playerID`:

playerID	namefirst	namelast	birthYear
abbotpa01	Paul	Abbott	1967
abreubo01	Bobby	Abreu	1974
alcanar01	Arismendy	Alcantara	1991
almoral01	Albert	Almora	1994
alvarpe01	Pedro	Alvarez	1987
alvarto01	Tony	Alvarez	1979

The other table would contain the rest of the fields from the denormalized table. The following table has a foreign key relationship to the preceding table regarding `playerID`:

playerID	franchID	franchname	teamID	RBI	rank	yearID
abbotpa01	PHI	Philadelphia Phillies	PHI	2	2	2004
abreubo01	PHI	Philadelphia Phillies	PHI	79	1	2000
abreubo01	PHI	Philadelphia Phillies	PHI	110	3	2001
alcanar01	CHI	Chicago Cubs	CHI	1	8	2015
almoral01	CHI	Chicago Cubs	CHI	14	8	2016
almoral01	CHI	Chicago Cubs	CHI	46	6	2017
alvarpe01	PIT	Pittsburg Pirates	PIT	77	17	2015
alvarto01	PIT	Pittsburg Pirates	PIT	2	9	2002
alvarto01	PIT	Pittsburg Pirates	PIT	8	1	2004

The second normal form

The second normal form (2NF) is the second level of database normalization. You will need to complete 1NF before beginning this step. The primary reason to implement 2NF is to narrow tables down to a single purpose, which makes it easier to use and design tables. This step will ensure that you do the following:

- **Meet the requirements of 1NF**: You will need to implement 1NF before you can use 2NF.
- **Remove partial dependencies**: This will entail narrowing tables down to a single purpose where possible.

Starting with the tables from our 1NF example, you can break these down further into additional tables. You will still have the same player table from 1NF since it serves a single purpose of giving us player information. The franchise table has multiple purposes with RBI and rank, so since RBI isn't related to the franchise, you will split the franchise table into two.

The franchise table has all the franchise and team information in it now, and the RBI columns and related columns can be split out into a batting table. The franchise table still has a primary key of `franchID` and `playerID` with a foreign key referring back to the player table on `playerID`:

playerID	franchID	franchname	teamID	rank	yearID
abbotpa01	PHI	Philadelphia Phillies	PHI	2	2004
abreubo01	PHI	Philadelphia Phillies	PHI	1	2000
abreubo01	PHI	Philadelphia Phillies	PHI	3	2001
alcanar01	CHI	Chicago Cubs	CHI	8	2015
almoral01	CHI	Chicago Cubs	CHI	8	2016
almoral01	CHI	Chicago Cubs	CHI	6	2017
alvarpe01	PIT	Pittsburg Pirates	PIT	17	2015
alvarto01	PIT	Pittsburg Pirates	PIT	9	2002
alvarto01	PIT	Pittsburg Pirates	PIT	1	2004

The batting table has a primary key of `playerID` and `teamID` and has a foreign key of `playerID` to the player table and a foreign key of `teamID` to the franchise table:

playerID	teamID	RBI	yearID
abbotpa01	PHI	2	2004
abreubo01	PHI	79	2000
abreubo01	PHI	110	2001
alcanar01	CHI	1	2015
almoral01	CHI	14	2016
almoral01	CHI	46	2017
alvarpe01	PIT	77	2015
alvarto01	PIT	2	2002
alvarto01	PIT	8	2004

Since you split the franchise table into two tables—one table with franchise information and one table with batting information—these tables now comply with 2NF because each table is serving a single purpose.

The third normal form

The third normal form (3NF) is the second level of database normalization. You will need to complete 2NF before beginning this step. The primary reason to implement 3NF is to ensure that your tables aren't created so that dependencies between columns may cause inconsistency. Generally, if a database is described as normalized, then it's normalized according to the third normal form. This step will ensure that you are doing the following:

- **Meeting the requirements of 2NF**: You will need to make sure that your tables comply with 2NF before proceeding with 3NF.
- **No attributes depend on other non-key attributes**: This means that you will need to look at your tables and see whether more fields can be split into other tables since they aren't dependent on a key.

Working from our 2NF example, you can further split the franchise table into a franchise table and a team table. The rank of the team isn't dependent on the primary key of the franchise table.

In 3NF, our franchise table becomes the following two tables.

`franchID` becomes the primary key in the franchise table:

franchID	franchname
PHI	Philadelphia Phillies
CHI	Chicago Cubs
PIT	Pittsburg Pirates

The team table has a primary key of `teamID` and a foreign key of `franchID` referring to the franchise table:

franchID	teamID	rank	yearID
PHI	PHI	2	2004
PHI	PHI	1	2000
PHI	PHI	3	2001
CHI	CHI	8	2015
CHI	CHI	8	2016
CHI	CHI	6	2017
PIT	PIT	17	2015
PIT	PIT	9	2002
PIT	PIT	1	2004

To summarize the process of taking data from denormalized to the third normal, here's a diagram of the changes that are made:

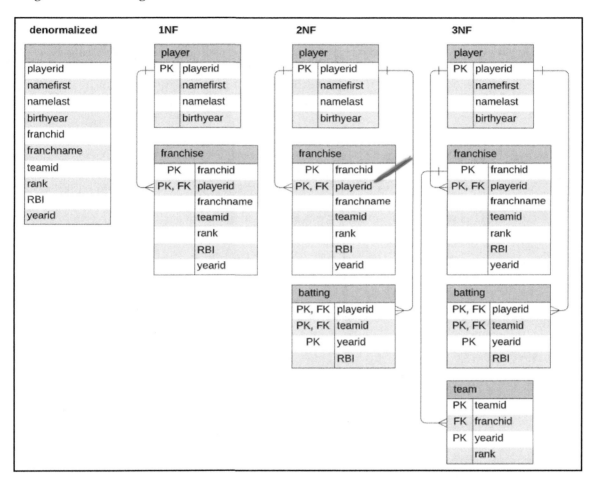

The preceding diagram shows how you went from denormalized to 3NF. Following the rules of the normal forms, you took a single table and turned it into four tables. To begin with, you split up one denormalized table into two tables as part of 1NF. 1NF ensured that you didn't have duplicate data and repeating groups. This resulted in a player and franchise table. Next, you split the tables out into three tables as part of 2NF. 2NF resolved the issue of not giving each table a specific purpose, resulting in a player, franchise, and batting table. For the final step, you split the tables into four tables as part of 3NF. 3NF ensured that you didn't have any fields in a table that weren't dependent on the primary key, resulting in a player, franchise, batting, and team table.

By going from a denormalized table to 3NF, you accomplished several things, including ensuring that you don't have duplicate data, that you have keys linking data to each other in the tables, that you have a single purpose for each table, and that you have minimized the storage and compute costs for your queries.

Even adhering to the third normal form can be taken to extremes, so while the third normal form is desirable, it's not always required. For instance, with zip codes, you could create a table with just zip codes since they may be duplicated in a table with users' addresses, but this may degrade performance instead of helping performance.

Types of RDMS

An RDMS is a database that stores data in tables using rows and columns. The values in the tables are related to one other, and the tables may also be related to one another, hence the term *relational*. This relationship makes it possible to access data across multiple tables with a single query.

In this section, we will review the top four relational database management systems. The top four are Oracle, MySQL, SQL Server, and PostgreSQL.

According to the DB-Engines Ranking, here are the scores for the top RDMSes at the time of writing this book:

Rank			DBMS	Database Model	Score		
Sep 2019	Aug 2019	Sep 2018			Sep 2019	Aug 2019	Sep 2018
1.	1.	1.	Oracle ➕	Relational, Multi-model ℹ	1346.66	+7.18	+37.54
2.	2.	2.	MySQL ➕	Relational, Multi-model ℹ	1279.07	+25.39	+98.60
3.	3.	3.	Microsoft SQL Server ➕	Relational, Multi-model ℹ	1085.06	-8.12	+33.78
4.	4.	4.	PostgreSQL ➕	Relational, Multi-model ℹ	482.25	+0.91	+75.82

The preceding screenshot can be found at `https://db-engines.com/en/ranking`.

Oracle

Oracle was first released in 1979. Oracle was the first commercially available SQL-based RDMS. It does have one free version, Oracle Database XE, which has some limitations compared to its licensed versions. Oracle runs best on Linux, but can be installed on Windows. Oracle is a great choice for organizations that need an RDMS and can handle very large databases and a variety of features.

The advantages of Oracle are that it offers a lot of functionality for system and database administrators, it's fast and stable, and it has lots of support and documentation.

The disadvantages of Oracle are that licensing is expensive and it may require significant database administrator resources to maintain it after installation.

MySQL

MySQL is a free, open source SQL database that started in 1995. It also has proprietary licensing available, which includes support and maintenance. Sun Microsystems bought MySQL in 2008, which was then acquired by Oracle in 2010. MySQL is commonly used in conjunction with PHP web applications. MySQL is a great choice for organizations that need a good RDMS but have a tight budget.

The advantages of MySQL are that it's available for free, it offers a lot of functionality for system and database administrators, it's easy to use and implement, and it's fast and stable.

The disadvantages of MySQL are that while support is available, it's not free. Also, since it's under Oracle, not all features are free, including paid-for options, such as enterprise monitoring, backup, high availability, scalability, and security.

SQL Server

Initially released in 1989, **SQL Server** is available with a commercial license. It does have one free version, SQL Server Express, with a limitation of 10 GB per database, along with other resource limitations. SQL Server is usually installed on Windows, but can also be installed on Linux. SQL Server is a great choice for organizations that need a good RDMS, and use a lot of other Microsoft products.

The advantages of SQL Server are that it offers a lot of functionality, including replication, and high availability and partitioning works very well with other Microsoft products, such as .NET Framework and Visual Studio. It is also fast and stable.

The disadvantages of SQL Server are that licensing is expensive, especially for the Enterprise edition, and not all features are included in all editions, such as some high-availability options and partitioning.

PostgreSQL

The first release of **PostgreSQL** was in 1989. This indefinitely and doesn't enforce any limits at all. PostgreSQL is usually installed on Linux machines and can be used to store structured and unstructured data. PostgreSQL is a great choice for organizations that need a good RDMS, already use Linux, and don't want to spend a lot of money on licensing.

The advantages of PostgreSQL are that it offers a lot of functionality, such as high availability and partitioning, it's scalable and can handle terabytes of data, and it's fast and stable.

The disadvantages of PostgreSQL are that documentation may be harder to come by and configuration can be confusing. It also runs on Linux, and you need to know how to run commands from Command Prompt.

RDMS SQL differences

Even though there is an ANSI/ISO standard, there are different versions of SQL. Still, to be compliant, they all similarly support the major commands, so SELECT, WHERE, INSERT, UPDATE, and DELETE would all have a syntax that matches.

Each subsequent chapter of this book will also note differences in the language or functionality of SQL where there are differences between MySQL and SQL Server, PostgresSQL, and Oracle.

Summary

This chapter introduced the concepts required to understand the basics of relational database management systems. It introduced you to foundational topics such as understanding SQL, what SQL can do, and its basic components. You learned that there are three subdivisions of SQL called DML, DDL, and DCL, and that the SQL language is comprised of several elements that make up a statement. We walked through a description of the relational model, what a database is, and what is in a database, including what a table, row, column, and field are.

We followed with an explanation of data integrity, including the different types of data integrity, such as entity, referential, and domain integrity, and looked at how to use keys and constraints. This understanding of data integrity helped you understand database normalization, including the different forms of normalization, 1NF, 2NF, and 3NF.

Lastly, you learned about the types of relational database management systems, including Oracle, MySQL, SQL Server, and PostgreSQL, and their advantages and disadvantages. You also learned what makes these RDMS different from each other in terms of SQL syntax.

In the next chapter, we will look at how to install MySQL Workbench on Windows and Mac, and go through step-by-step instructions to help you walk through each part of the installation process. The instructions will also include the configuration of MySQL Workbench on both Windows and Mac. We will walk through some examples of how to connect to your local MySQL and set up connections to other MySQL servers. We'll conclude with a step-by-step explanation of how to restore a database to MySQL.

Questions

1. What is SQL?
2. What are the different subdivisions of SQL?
3. What are the elements of a SQL statement?
4. What are the reasons to normalize a database?
5. What are the levels of database normalization?
6. What is data integrity?
7. What are the different ways you can enforce data integrity?
8. What types of RDMS exist?
9. What is the main advantage of MySQL?
10. What is the main disadvantage of Oracle and SQL Server?

2
Installing and Using MySQL Workbench

In this chapter, we will discuss how to install MySQL Workbench on Windows and Mac, including step-by-step instructions to help you walk through each part of the installation process. The instructions will also show you how to configure MySQL Workbench on both Windows and Mac. We will walk through some examples of connecting to your local MySQL server and also setting up connections to other MySQL servers. We'll conclude with a step-by-step explanation of how to restore a database to MySQL.

In this chapter, we will cover the following topics:

- Installing MySQL Workbench
- Using MySQL Workbench
- Restoring a database

Technical requirements

Installing MySQL on any platform will require that you have elevated privileges on your system. For Windows, you will need either Administrator or Power User privileges. For Mac, you will need Administrator privileges. The code files of this chapter can be found at `https://github.com/sqlkitty/Learn-SQL-Database-Programming/tree/master/baseball-database`.

Installing MySQL Workbench

MySQL Workbench can be installed on various operating systems. In this section, we will cover the installation steps for the Windows and Mac operating systems.

Installing on Windows

The installer process involves several steps, some of which are repeating and non-repeating. The following diagram shows the steps that are repeating and non-repeating during the MySQL installation process:

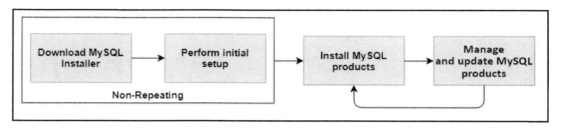

Installing MySQL on Windows

This section provides step-by-step instructions on how to install MySQL Server on Windows. To begin, go to `https://dev.mysql.com/downloads/windows/installer/`:

1. Click **Download** on the installer of your choice. You can choose either the web community or community version, as shown in the following screenshot. The final setup procedures will be the same. The web community download will download all the files from online while the installer runs. The community download includes all the files needed to install MySQL, including MySQL Workbench. It's just a decision as to whether you want to be online during installation (web community install) or offline during installation (community install). I prefer to download the larger community file to ensure that if my internet connection fails midway through, I don't have to worry about the installation failing, but it's up to you:

2. If you aren't interested in logging in or signing up, choose **No thanks, just start my download**:

3. Install the file you just downloaded by clicking on it from your browser downloads or by double-clicking on the file in Windows Explorer.

4. You may or may not have products to upgrade. If you aren't prompted to upgrade, you may be able to skip to the section where you can configure MySQL, as shown in the following screenshot:

5. Click **Next**.

6. Leave everything checked and click **Next**. Note that your list of products to upgrade may look different than the ones shown in the following screenshot:

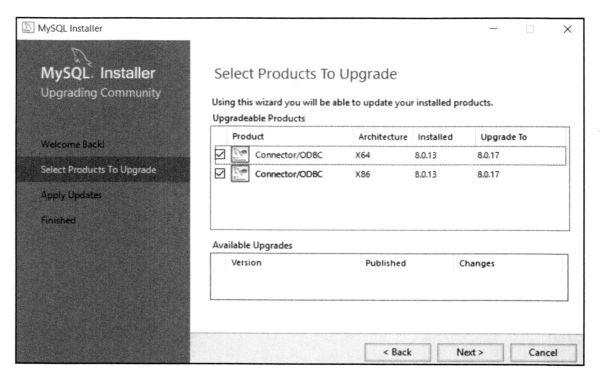

7. Review the list to make sure everything was successful and click **Next**.

8. Click **Finish**. This will bring you to the **MySQL Installer** page. It will list the products you have installed and allows you to **Add**, **Modify**, **Upgrade**, or **Remove** products. You will see the products that you were just required to upgrade listed here:

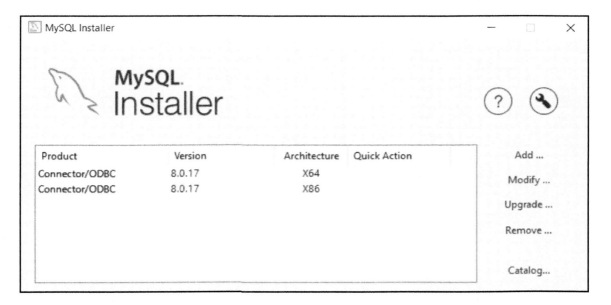

9. Click **Add**.

10. On the **License Agreement** page, accept the license terms and click **Next**:

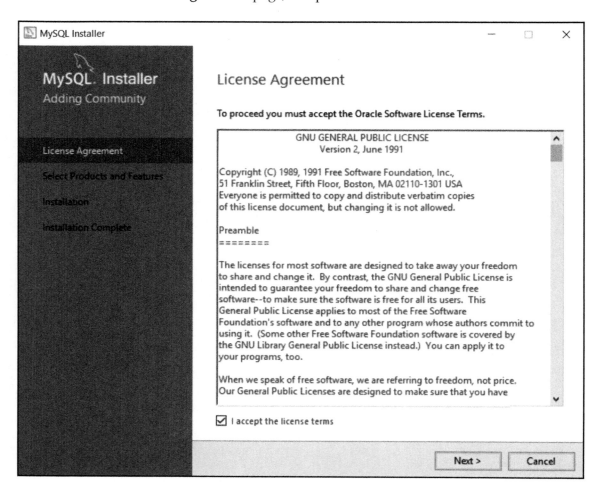

11. This will bring you to a page called **Select Products and Features**. If you already have a MySQL database server to connect to, you can just install MySQL Workbench. If you don't have a MySQL database server, MySQL Server install will allow you to connect to a database server to create and work with a MySQL database. This will be very beneficial to you if you plan to restore the database later in this chapter as this will help you walk through the exercises throughout this book.

The following screenshot shows the options for installing both **MySQL Server** and **MySQL Workbench**, so this way, you can have a local instance of MySQL to work on for the examples throughout this book:

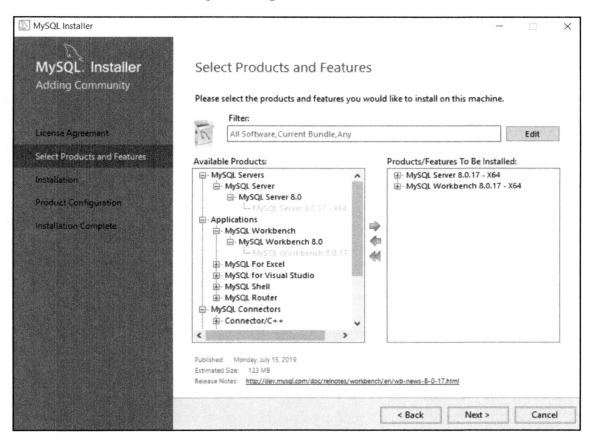

12. Click **Next**.

13. When the installer has completed successfully, click **Next**:

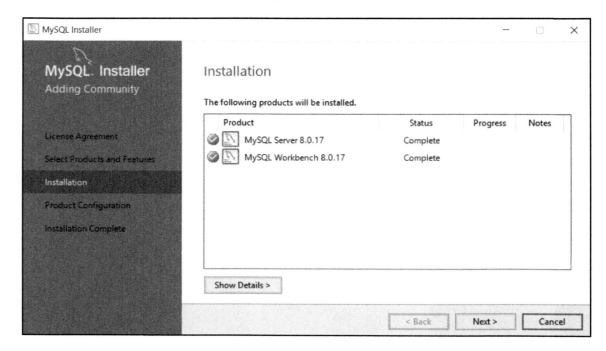

This will bring you to the configuration section of the installer, which we will cover in the next section.

Configuring MySQL on Windows

This section provides information on how to configure MySQL on Windows. Your installation may or may not need product upgrades, so your installation may start at this point. Let's get started:

1. On the **Product Configuration** page, click **Next**:

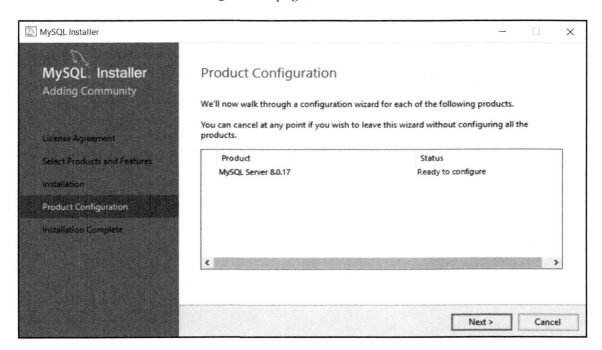

 The **Product Configuration** page will only display if you chose to install **MySQL Server** in addition to **MySQL Workbench**.

2. Choose **Standalone MySQL Server / Classic MySQL Replication** and click **Next**:

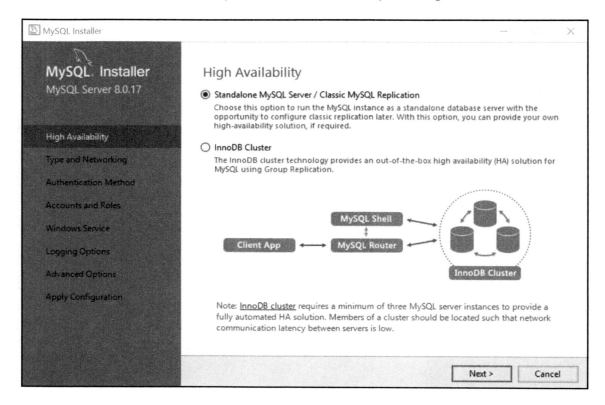

3. Leave all the defaults as is for **Type and Networking** and click **Next**:

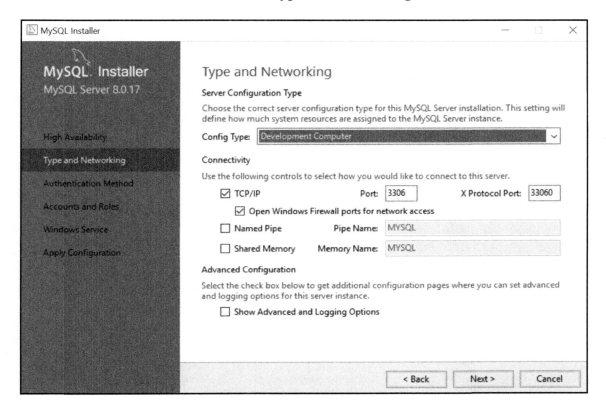

4. Choose **Use Strong Password Encryption for Authentication (RECOMMENDED)** and click **Next**:

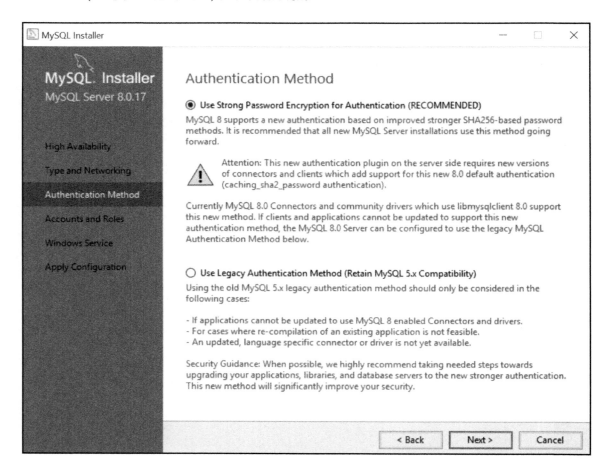

5. Enter a strong password on the **Accounts and Roles** page:

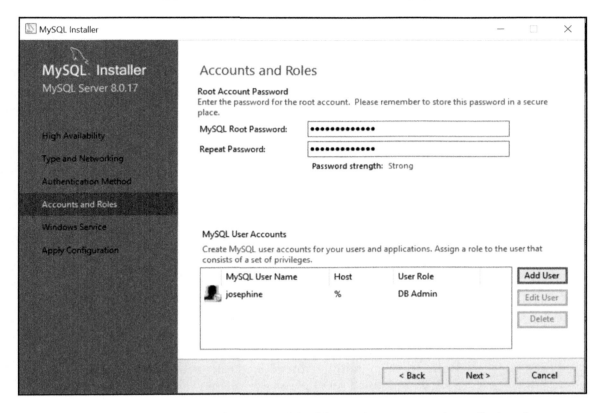

At this point, you can choose to add additional users or wait until after the installation is complete. You can add a user by clicking the **Add User** button.

6. You can then add a user by filling out the fields:

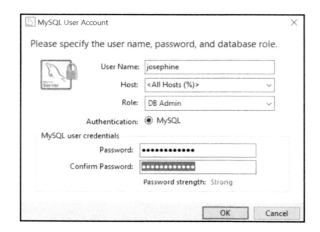

The following fields have to be filled:

- **User Name**: This can be up to 32 characters long.
- **Password**: The strength of the password is assessed as you type.
- **Host**: You can use `localhost` if only local connections will be made, or you can choose `<All Hosts (%)>` if remote connections will be made. I recommend selecting `<All Hosts (%)>` if you aren't sure.
- **Role**: There are multiple predefined roles available. Each role is set up with a predefined set of permissions. They are described when you click the dropdown:

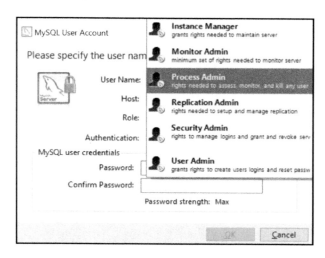

7. Then, click **OK**.
8. Click **Next**.
9. On the **Windows Service** page, leave the defaults as they are and click **Next**:

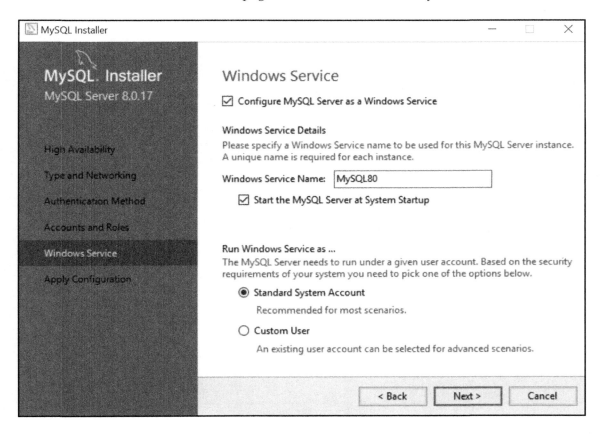

10. On the **Apply Configuration** page, click **Execute**:

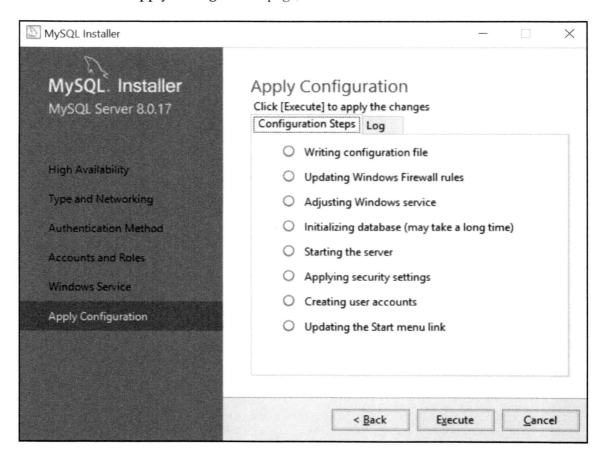

11. When the configuration operation has finished, click **Finish**:

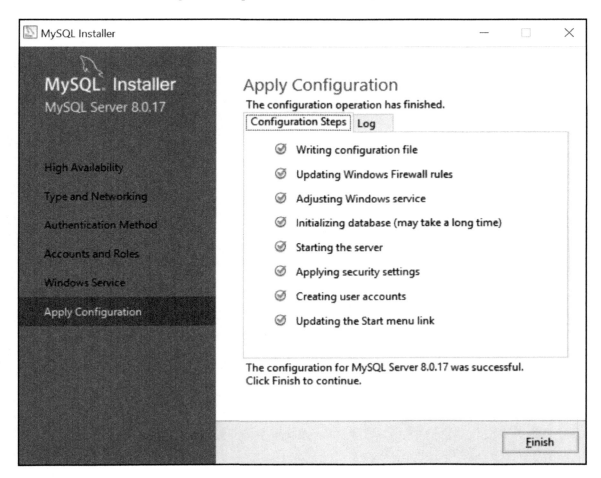

12. Click **Next** on the page that shows that the configuration is complete:

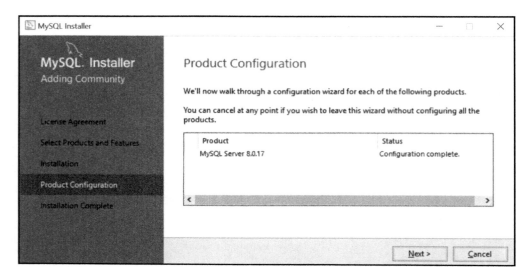

13. On the **Installation Complete** page, make sure **Start MySQL Workbench after Setup** is checked and click **Finish**:

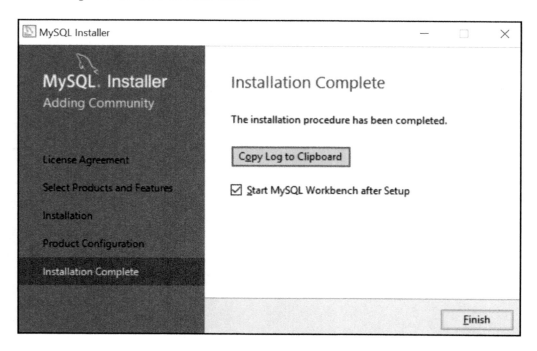

14. This brings you to a page that shows the MySQL products you have installed. You can **Add**, **Modify**, **Upgrade**, or **Remove** products from this page. In the following screenshot, you can see the products you've upgraded and installed:

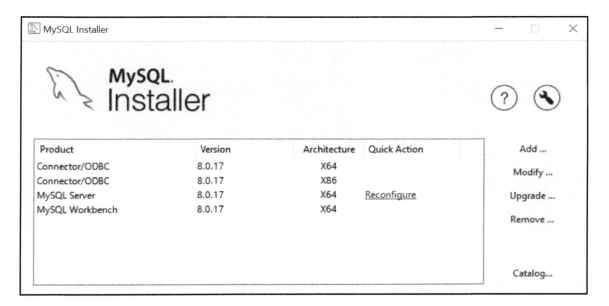

Installing on Mac

The installer process for Mac is slightly different than it is for Windows. There are separate installers for MySQL Server and MySQL Workbench. There are various ways to configure MySQL, all of which we will cover in this chapter.

Installing MySQL Server on Mac

If you already have a MySQL database server to connect to, you can skip to the instructions later in this chapter regarding how to install MySQL Workbench.

If you don't have a MySQL database server, the MySQL Server installation will allow you to connect to your database server to create and work with a MySQL database. This will be very beneficial to you if you plan to restore the database later in this chapter so that you can walk through the exercises throughout this book with ease.

To install MySQL Server on Mac, go to `https://dev.mysql.com/downloads/mysql/` and follow these steps:

1. Click **Download** on the DMG archive.
2. If you are not interested in logging in or signing up, choose **No thanks, just start my download**.
3. Choose **Save File**:

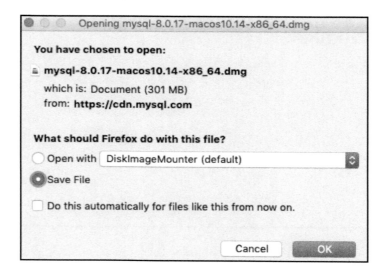

4. Install the file you just downloaded by double-clicking on it from your **Download** folder.
5. Double-click on the `.pkg` file:

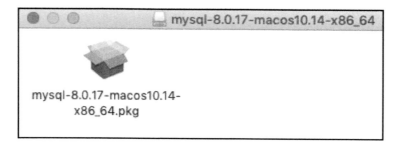

6. Click **Continue** on the **This package will run a program to determine if the software can be installed** popup:

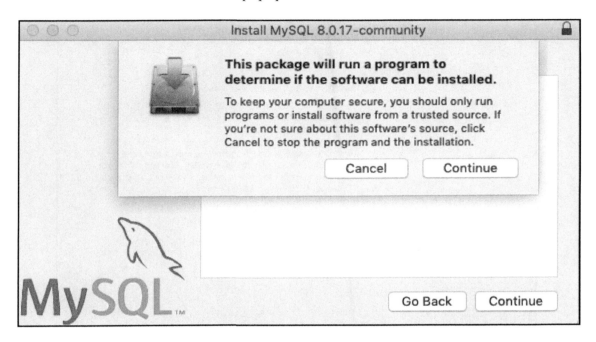

7. Click **Continue** on the **Welcome to the MySQL 8.0.17-community installer** page.
8. Click **Continue** on the **Software License Agreement** page.
9. Click **Agree** on the agree to the terms popup.
10. Click **Install** on the **Standard Install** page.
11. Enter your username and password on the popup window and click **Install Software**.

12. Choose **Use Strong Password Encryption** on the **Configure MySQL Server** page and click **Next**:

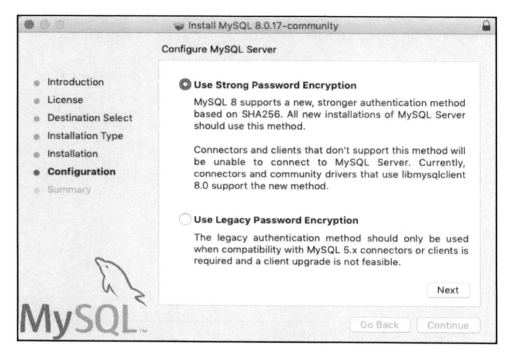

13. Enter a password for the "**root**" user on the **Configure MySQL Server** page and make sure **Start MySQL Server once the installation is complete** is checked. Then, click **Finish**:

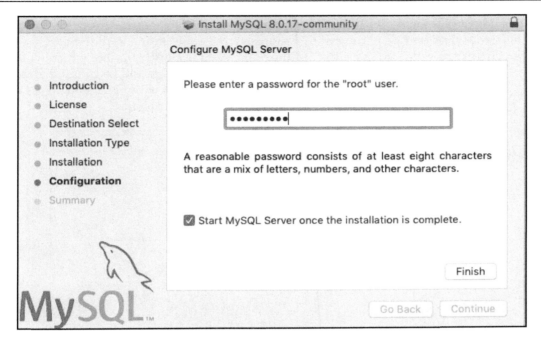

14. Enter your username and password on the popup window and click **OK**.
15. Click **Close** on the **The installation was completed successfully** page.
16. Click **Move to Trash** on the **Do you want to move the installer to the trash?** popup.

Checking the status of MySQL Server on Mac

This section provides information on how to check the status of MySQL Server. This is not a required step in the installation process, but this section provides you with details in case you need to troubleshoot your MySQL Server:

1. Open **System Preferences**.
2. Click **MySQL**. By doing this, you can view the status and configuration options available to you.

The following screenshot shows the status of MySQL Server. It indicates that MySQL Server is running. If this showed a message stating that MySQL Server wasn't running, you would click the **Start MySQL Server** button, which would be in place instead of the **Stop MySQL Server** button. It should be running after the installation process, and you shouldn't have to start it. This gives you an idea of where to go if you have to troubleshoot connection problems:

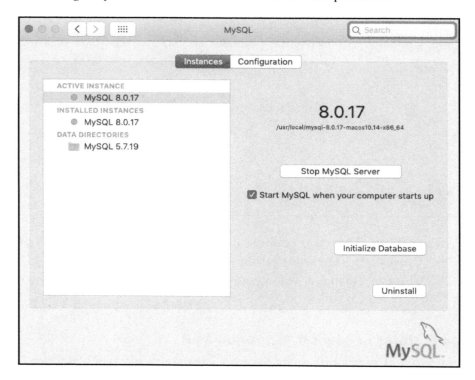

Installing MySQL Workbench on Mac

This section provides step-by-step instructions on how to install MySQL Workbench on Mac. To begin, go to `https://dev.mysql.com/downloads/workbench/`. Then, follow these steps:

1. Click **Download** on the DMG archive.
2. If you are not interested in logging in or signing up, choose **No thanks, just start my download**.
3. Choose **Save File**.

4. Install the file you just downloaded by double-clicking it in your `Download` folder.
5. Drag **MySQLWorkbench** to **Applications**, as shown in the following screenshot. This step will copy the MySQL Workbench application to the `Applications` folder:

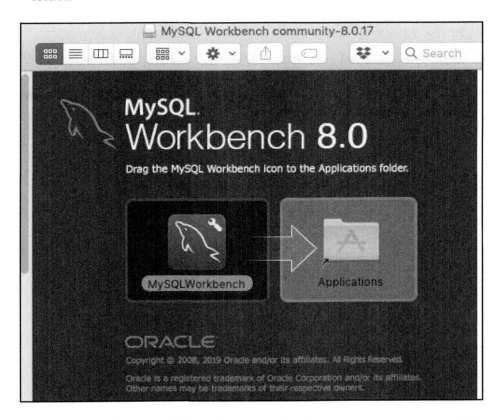

With that, MySQL Workbench will have been installed in your `Applications` folder. In the next section, we will cover how to use MySQL Workbench.

Using MySQL Workbench

This section will show you how to use MySQL Workbench on both Windows and Mac. These steps include connecting to your local instance and creating a connection to a different MySQL server than the one installed on your local computer.

Let's begin by launching MySQL Workbench.

To launch MySQL Workbench on Windows, do the following:

1. Select **Start** and begin typing `MySQLWorkbench`.
2. Click on **MySQL Workbench** to open it.

To launch MySQL Workbench on Mac, do the following:

1. Navigate to the `Applications` folder.
2. Double-click on **MySQL Workbench**.
3. If prompted, click **Open** on the **"MySQLWorkbench" is an app downloaded from the Internet. Are you sure you want to open it?** popup:

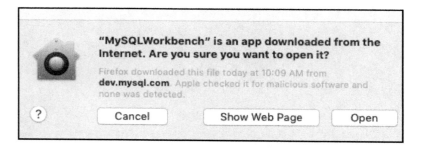

Next, we will cover connecting to your local instance.

Connecting to your local instance

In MySQL Workbench, click on your local instance of MySQL to connect to it. Yours may be named differently than mine, but it will have a connection to the localhost configured in it:

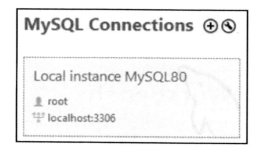

Enter your password and choose **Save password in vault**.

If you have no local connection set up, then don't worry – instructions on how to create new MySQL connections have been included in the next section.

Connecting to another instance or setting up your local instance

If you want to connect to a different MySQL instance other than the one we just installed together, then you can click the + sign next to **MySQL Connections** in MySQL Workbench:

Then, fill in your connection information, including **Connection Name**, **Hostname**, **Port** (3306 by default in MySQL), **Username**, and **Password**. Afterward, click **Test Connection** to make sure it will connect successfully before clicking **OK**.

To set up the local instance, use the settings shown in the following screenshot:

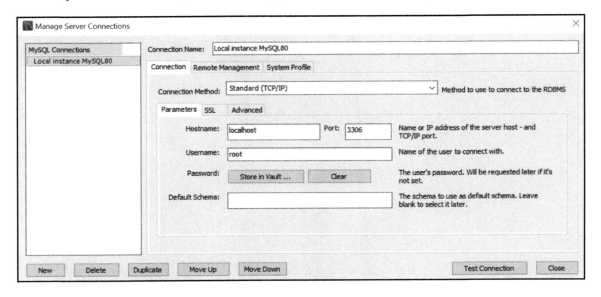

MySQL Workbench should look something like the following when you open it for the first time:

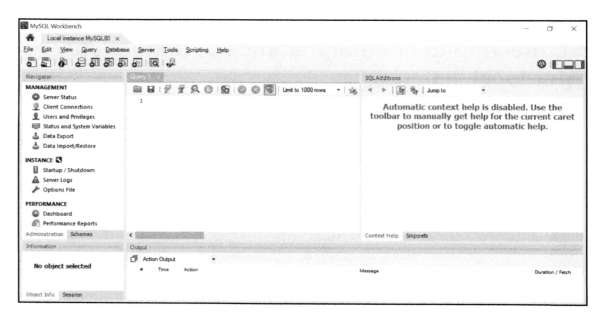

You can change the layout of MySQL Workbench by using the **View** menu, as shown in the following screenshot:

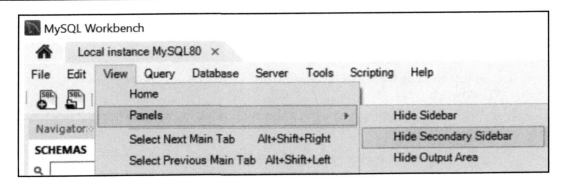

You can choose to hide the navigator (the **Hide Sidebar** option), hide the SQL additions (the **Hide Secondary Sidebar** option), and hide the output (the **Hide Output Area** option).

Restoring a database

In this section, we will walk through how to restore a database to a MySQL Server instance. Restoring is the process of taking a backup (or copy) of a database and turning it back into a database on the same database server with a different database name or on a separate database server with the same database name as the original database. You can also restore over a database on a server – in other words, replacing the current database with a backup of the database – but be cautious with this because you will lose data if the database has changed since the last backup. When you back up a MySQL database, the backup process creates SQL files of the entire structure and data of the database. When you restore a database backup, MySQL runs these scripts to recreate the database so that you have an exact copy of the database you backed up. Restoring the database outlined in this section will allow you to use the examples provided throughout this book.

To begin with, download the baseball database from GitHub, which can be found at `https://github.com/sqlkitty/Learn-SQL-Database-Programming/tree/master/baseball-database`. Now, follow these steps:

1. Connect to your local instance or the instance of your choosing in MySQL Workbench.
2. In the **Navigator** panel, from the **Administration/Management** tab, click **Data Import/Restore**:

3. Choose **Import from Dump Project Folder** and navigate to the folder where the files you downloaded from GitHub live.

4. Click **Load Folder Contents**.
5. Select **Database Objects to Import**.
6. This will display a list of schema objects to import. Leave them all checked.
7. Click **Start Import**:

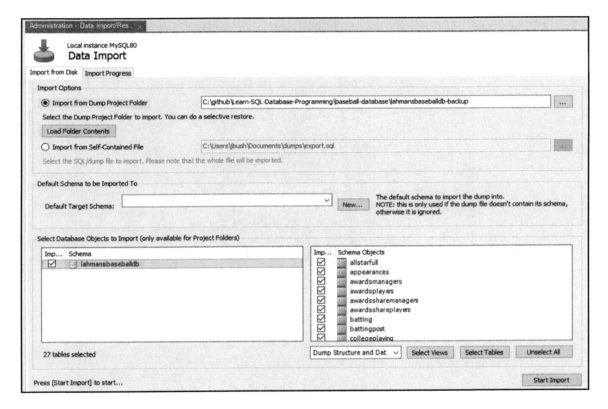

8. Progress is updated in the **Import Progress** tab.

9. Click on the **SCHEMAS** tab and the refresh icon at the top of the **SCHEMAS** tab area:

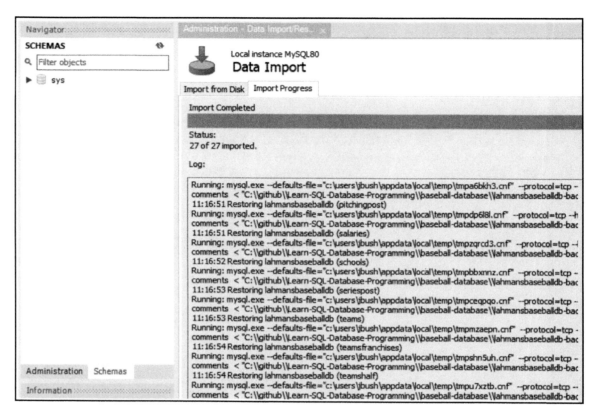

10. You will now see the database you imported:

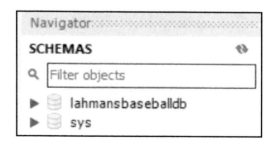

To run a query against **lahmansbaseballdb**, you will need to do the following:

1. Click the down arrow next to **lahmansbaseballdb**.
2. Click the down arrow next to **Tables**.
3. In Windows, right-click **appearances** and choose **Select Rows – Limit 1000**:

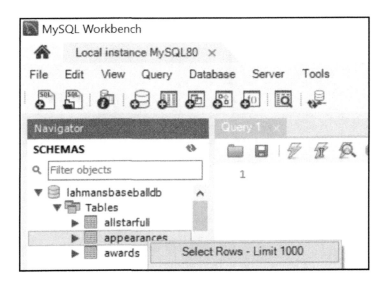

4. In Mac, right-click **appearances** and choose **Select Rows**. You will learn how to limit query results in Chapter 6, *Querying a Single Table*:

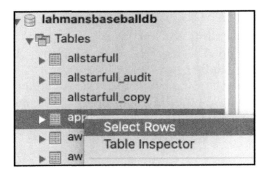

This will query the table and return 1,000 rows. The following screenshot shows you the results and outputs of the query we just ran:

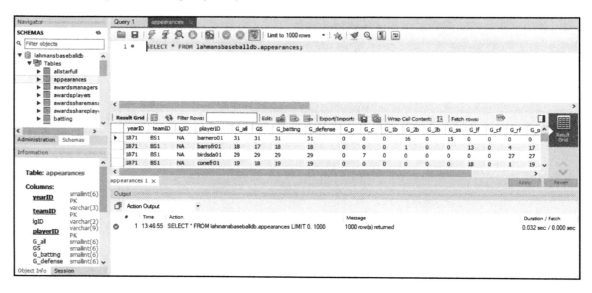

It will display the results, information about the table, and information about the output, such as the time the action started, the action statement, messages about the output, and the duration of the query.

Summary

In this chapter, we covered installing MySQL Workbench on Windows and Mac. This included step-by-step instructions to help you walk through each part of the installation process. The guidelines also included how to configure MySQL Workbench on both Windows and Mac. We walked through some examples of connecting to your local MySQL and also setting up connections to other MySQL servers. We concluded with a step-by-step explanation of how to restore a database to MySQL.

In the next chapter, we will cover what data types are and how to use them. We will learn about specific data types and what data can be stored in each. Data types include string, numeric, and date and time, as well as other types such as JSON. String data types include `char` and `varchar`, `binary` and `varbinary`, `blob`, `enum`, and `text`. Numeric data types include `bit`, `int`, `float`, `double`, and `decimal`. Date and time data types include `date`, `time`, `datetime`, `timestamp`, and `year`. We will be learning about these from the perspective of MySQL data types, but where there are differences versus Oracle, PostgreSQL, and SQL Server, we will take note of them.

Questions

1. What operating systems can you install MySQL Workbench on?
2. How do you check the status of the MySQL service on Mac?
3. How do you connect to your or another instance of MySQL in MySQL Workbench?
4. How do you restore a database in MySQL Workbench?
5. How can you view the duration/fetch time for a query?
6. How can you view the column names and types for a table in MySQL Workbench?
7. How do you hide the secondary sidebar in MySQL Workbench?
8. Where can you find a history of the queries you've executed in MySQL Workbench?
9. How can you see how many rows a query returned in MySQL Workbench?
10. How do you select 1,000 rows from a table in MySQL Workbench?

3
Understanding Data Types

In this chapter, we will learn what data types and their usage. We will go through the specific data types and understand what data can be stored in each of them. The data types include `string`, `numeric`, `date` and `time`, and other data types. `String` data types include `char` and `varchar`, `binary` and `varbinary`, `blob`, `enum`, `set`, and `text`. Numeric data types include `bit`, `int`, `float`, `double`, and `decimal`. Date and time data types include `date`, `time`, `datetime`, `timestamp`, and `year`.

We will learn from the perspective of MySQL data types, and will keep noting the differences between Oracle, PostgreSQL, and SQL Server wherever needed. We will also go through some examples of types and values of data to see how to assign them correctly to data types, including an explanation of why you need to be careful when selecting a data type and how it can impact database performance.

In this chapter, we will cover the following topics:

- Understanding `string` data types
- Understanding `numeric` data types
- Understanding `date` and `time` data types
- Understanding other data types
- Choosing the right data type

Understanding string data types

String data types can hold plain text and binary data. This section walks you through the different string data types in MySQL. This section also shows you the differences between Oracle, PostgreSQL, and SQL Server string data types.

String data types in MySQL

Let's discuss the string data types in MySQL:

- CHAR: It is a fixed-length string, which can contain letters, numbers, and special characters. This type is blank-padded and contains trailing blanks in the field. This field can range from 0 to 255, and the default (if nothing is specified, that is, just using CHAR instead of CHAR(10)) is 1. The size in parenthesis denotes the maximum length of the char specified by the user when creating the data field with this type. The storage requirement for CHAR is size * *n*, where *n* <= *size* <= 255, where *n* is the number of bytes required for the max length character.
- VARCHAR: It is a variable-length string, which can contain letters, numbers, and special characters. This field can range from 0 to 65535.

 When deciding whether to use CHAR or VARCHAR, CHAR is an excellent choice for storing strings that are always, or very close to, the same length. This is because it will take less storage and be slightly faster upon querying versus VARCHAR. VARCHAR is better when the length of the field will vary significantly, like in first names.

The following table shows the difference in how values are stored between CHAR and VARCHAR:

Example text	CHAR(5)	Field Size	VARCHAR(5)	Field Size
' '	' '	5 bytes	' '	1 byte
'as'	'as '	5 bytes	'as'	3 bytes
'asdf'	'asdf '	5 bytes	'asdf'	5 bytes
'asdfghj'	'asdfg'	5 bytes	'asdfg'	7 bytes

- BINARY: BINARY is like CHAR, but stores byte strings instead of character strings. This field can range from 0 to 255, and the default size is 1. For example, 'b' in a BINARY column becomes 'b\0' when inserted.
- VARBINARY: VARBINARY is like VARCHAR, but stores binary byte data instead of character data. This field can range from 0 to 65535.
- BLOB: BLOB stands for binary large objects, and treats values like they are binary strings. They can hold a variable amount of data. There are four types of BLOB values: TINYBLOB, BLOB, MEDIUMBLOB, and LONGBLOB. The only difference between them is the amount of data they can hold.

The BLOB type can have a size specified up to 65,535 bytes. BLOB doesn't have a default value, so a value must be specified. TINYBLOB can store up to 255 bytes, MEDIUMBLOB can store up to 16,777,215 bytes, and LONGBLOB can store up to 4,294,967,295 bytes.

Avoid BLOB data types since they make your database much larger and hurt database query performance. Instead, store BLOB information in a file on disk, then store a path in the database to the file on disk.

- TEXT: TEXT values are stored in a text field and treated as character strings instead of binary strings. They can hold a variable amount of data. There are four types of TEXT values: TINYTEXT, TEXT, MEDIUMTEXT, and LONGTEXT. The only difference between them is the amount of data they can hold.

The TEXT type can have a size specified up to 65,535 bytes. TEXT doesn't have a default value, so a value must be specified. TINYTEXT can store up to 255 bytes, MEDIUMTEXT can store up to 16,777,215 bytes, and LONGTEXT can store up to 4,294,967,295 bytes.

- ENUM: ENUM stands for an enumerated list. With ENUM(val1, val2, val3, ...), you put your values in place of val1, val2, val3, and so on with values separated by commas. When inserting a value into this data type, you are allowed to insert one value from the list of enumerated values. You can have up to 65,535 values in an ENUM list. For example, if the ENUM list includes red, green, blue, then you can insert one of those values into the field, and not multiple values in one field. If you insert a value that isn't in the list, then you will receive an error. The following screenshot shows you a table with an enumerated column:

id	emumerated_col
1	red
2	green
3	blue
4	red
5	red

- SET: As with ENUM, SET(val1, val2, val3, ...) allows you to put your values in place of val1, val2, val3, and so on. However, this string object can have zero or more values chosen from a list of specified values. You can have up to 64 values in a SET list. For example, if the SET list includes red, green, blue, then you can insert one or more of those values into the field, which allows you to have multiple values in a field. If you insert a value that isn't in the list, then a blank value will be inserted. The following screenshot shows you a table with a set column:

id	set_col
1	red,green
2	red
3	red,green,blue
4	green
5	green,blue

The SET data type generally isn't used because it doesn't follow proper data normalization.

MySQL string data type table summary

The following table lists the string data types available in MySQL. When the syntax shown in the following table includes square brackets ([ ]), this indicates an optional part of the syntax. For example, in CHAR[(size)], the square brackets indicate that the size is optional:

Data Type	Description	Storage Used
CHAR[(size)]	Fixed-length string with size from 0-255 allowed; default of 1 if size not specified	Size in bytes
VARCHAR(size)	Variable-length string with size from 0-65535 allowed	Length of string + 1 byte if less than 255 bytes + 2 bytes if greater than 255 bytes
BINARY[(size)]	Binary fixed-length string with size from 0-255 allowed; default of 1 if size not specified	Size in bytes
VARBINARY(size)	Binary variable-length string with size from 0-65535 allowed	Size in bytes + 1 byte if less than 255 bytes + 2 bytes if greater than 255 bytes
BLOB(size)	Binary large objects with up to 65,535 bytes	Size in bytes + 2 bytes

TINYBLOB	Binary large objects up to 255 in size	Size in bytes + 1 bytes
MEDIUMBLOB	Binary large objects up to 16,177,215 in size	Size in bytes + 3 bytes
LONGBLOB	Binary large object up to 4,294,967,295 in size	Size in bytes + 4 bytes
TEXT(size)	Character strings with up to 65,535 bytes	Size of string + 2 bytes
TINYTEXT	Character strings up to 255 in size	Size of string + 1 bytes
MEDIUMTEXT	Character strings up to 16,177,215 in size	Size of string + 3 bytes
LONGTEXT	Character strings up to 4,294,967,295 in size	Size of string + 4 bytes
ENUM(val1, val2,val3, ...)	String object that allows one value from a chosen list. The chosen list can be up to 65,535 values.	1 or 2 bytes depending on the number of enumerated values
SET(val1, val2,val3, ...)	String object that allows zero or more values from a chosen list. The chosen list can be up to 64 values.	1,2,3,4, or 8 bytes depending on number of set members

The preceding table lists the string data types available in MySQL. It's important to note the storage used because the less storage you use, the better it is for performance. The *Choosing the Right Data Type* section covers the reasons behind this.

String data types in other RDMS

MySQL doesn't have all the same data types as other popular RDBMSes. This section will outline some of the string data types that exist in others, but not in MySQL. It also outlines the differences where they exist.

Oracle

The additional string data types in Oracle include the following:

- NCHAR: Oracle supports Unicode data types, including NCHAR and NVARCHAR2. You can store different languages in Unicode data types.
- VARCHAR2: Oracle has an additional VARCHAR type called VARCHAR2, which doesn't distinguish between a null and empty string value.

PostgreSQL

There are no additional string data types in PostgreSQL compared with MySQL.

SQL Server

SQL Server uses VARBINARY(MAX) instead of a BLOB to store BLOB data.

The additional string data types in SQL Server include the following:

- VARCHAR(MAX): Like VARCHAR in MySQL, this is a variable-length string, which can contain letters, numbers, and special characters. The size in parenthesis denotes the maximum length of the varchar specified by the user when creating the data field with this type. This field can range from 0 to 8,000 characters. The main difference in SQL Server is a MAX option used like this: VARCHAR(MAX). The MAX option allows up to 1,073,741,824 characters.
- VARBINARY(MAX): SQL Server supports an IMAGE type field to hold binary data. Future releases will not include IMAGE, so use VARBINARY(MAX) instead.
- Unicode data types: SQL Server supports Unicode data types, including NVARCHAR, NVARCHAR(max), NCHAR, and NTEXT. You can store different languages in Unicode data types.

String data types RDMS table comparison

The following table lists the string data types available in MySQL and shows whether or not they are available in Oracle, PostgreSQL, and SQL Server:

 NOTE: The size allowances on SQL Server, PostgreSQL, and Oracle may be different even if the data type name is the same.

String data types in MySQL	Also available in		
Data Type	SQL Server	PostgreSQL	Oracle
CHAR	Yes	Yes	Yes
VARCHAR	Yes	Yes	Yes

BINARY	Yes	No	No
VARBINARY	Yes	No	No
BLOB	No	No	No
TINYBLOB	No	No	No
MEDIUMBLOB	No	No	No
LONGBLOB	No	No	No
TEXT	Yes	Yes	No
TINYTEXT	No	No	No
MEDIUMTEXT	No	No	No
LONGTEXT	No	No	No
ENUM	No	No	No
SET	No	No	No

Understanding numeric data types

Numeric data types can hold integers, which include positive and negative whole numbers. Numeric data types can also contain fixed-point and floating-point numbers, which store fractions of whole numbers. This section walks you through the different numeric data types in MySQL. This section also shows you where Oracle, PostgreSQL, and SQL Server numeric data types are different.

Numeric data types in MySQL

The numeric data types in MySQL include the following:

- INT: An INT value can range from -2147483648 to 2147483647. An INT can only store whole numbers. It can't store numbers with decimal places. Any value you try to place with decimal places will be rounded up or down depending on the decimal value. If you try to store a number outside the range, the number won't be stored, and you will receive an error.

Value to insert	INT value
12.34	12
12.76	13

INT values can be signed or unsigned. Unsigned only stores positive numbers and signed ones can store both positive and negative numbers.

 Unsigned doesn't affect the size of the column, but just shifts the range to only positive numbers. Use unsigned when you are concerned about the upper bounds of the range on your INT value.

With INT, there are different varieties from which to choose. They are BIGINT, SMALLINT, MEDIUMINT, INT, and TINYINT. The following table outlines the range of values that each can store:

Types	Signed Range	Unsigned Range
TINYINT	-128 to 127	0 to 255
SMALLINT	-32768 to 32767	0 to 65535
MEDIUMINT	-8388608 to 8388607	0 to 16777215
INT	-2147483648 to 2147483647	0 to 4294967295
BIGINT	-9223372036854775808 to 9223372036854775807	0 to 18446744073709551615

When choosing an INT data type, it's vital to select the smallest size INT value that will accommodate your data to reduce storage space:

- FLOAT: FLOAT is a floating-point number. A floating-point number means that there isn't a fixed number of digits before and after the decimal place so that the decimal point can float. To use the FLOAT data type, you use FLOAT(size, p), where size is the total number of digits, and p is the number of digits after the decimal place. The maximum size is 24. If your value's size is above 24, use DOUBLE (see below) instead. FLOAT is accurate up to approximately 7 decimal places.

  To store a number like 1234.5678, you would create the data type as FLOAT(8,4). FLOAT is useful for scientific kinds of calculations where extra decimal places are helpful. Don't use FLOAT for financial data since FLOAT isn't as accurate as DECIMAL.

- DOUBLE: DOUBLE is a floating-point number. To use the DOUBLE data type, you use DOUBLE(size, d), where size is the total number of digits, and d is the number of digits after the decimal place.

  DOUBLE is accurate up to approximately 14 decimal places. To store a number like 123456789012345678901234.1234567, you would create the data type as DOUBLE(33,7). DOUBLE is useful for scientific kinds of calculations where extra decimal places are helpful. Don't use DOUBLE for financial data since FLOAT isn't as accurate as DECIMAL.

- DECIMAL: DECIMAL is an exact fixed-point number. To use the DECIMAL data type, you use DECIMAL(size, d), where size is the total number of digits, and d is the number of digits after the decimal place. The maximum size is 65, and the maximum d is 30. If size and d aren't specified, the default size is 10, and the default d is 0.

  To store a number like 1234567.89, you would create the data type as DECIMAL(9,2). DECIMAL is suitable for financial data because it more accurately represents all numbers, whereas FLOAT and DOUBLE aren't as accurate. The storage usage of a DECIMAL data type varies based on the size of the value stored.

- BIT: The BIT data type stores binary values. The syntax is BIT(size), where size is the number in bits a value can have. The value range is 1 to 64. If you leave off the size on BIT, the default size will be 1. Generally, BIT stores 0 and 1 boolean values, where 0 is false, and 1 is true. There are other edge use cases, such as storing values as binary, such as months that have 30 days in them, like so: 000101001010. The 1's in this BIT represent the months that have 30 days, and the 0's represent the months that don't. The following table shows you what the 0's and 1's correspond to in the bit value 000101001010:

Month	Number of days	Bit stored
January	31 days	0
February	28 or 29 days	0
March	31 days	0
April	30 days	1
May	31 days	0
June	30 days	1
July	31 days	0
August	31 days	0
September	30 days	1
October	31 days	0
November	30 days	1
December	31 days	0

MySQL numeric data type table summary

The following table lists the numeric data types available in MySQL. When the syntax shown in the following table includes square brackets ([]), this indicates an optional part of the syntax. For example, in BIT[(size)], the square brackets indicate that the size is optional:

Data Type	Description	Storage Used
INT(size)	Stores whole numbers. Ranges from −2147483648 to 147483647 for signed and 0 to 4294967295 for unsigned.	4 bytes
INYINT(size)	Stores whole numbers. Ranges from −128 to 127 for signed and 0 to 255 for unsigned.	1 byte

SMALLINT(size)	Stores whole numbers. Ranges from −32768 to 32767 for signed and 0 to 65535 for unsigned.	2 bytes
MEDIUMINT(size)	Stores whole numbers. Ranges from −8388608 to 8388607 for signed and 0 to 16777215 for unsigned.	3 bytes
BIGINT(size)	Stores whole numbers. Ranges from −9223372036854775808 to 9223372036854775807 for signed or 0 to 8446744073709551615 for unsigned.	8 bytes
FLOAT(size, d)	Floating-point number. Where size is the digits in total, and d is the digits after the decimal place. The size ranges from 0 to 23. FLOAT(8,4) would display as 1234.5678	4 bytes
DOUBLE(size, d)	Floating point number. Where size is the digits in total, and d is the digits after the decimal place. The size ranges from 24 to 53. FLOAT(24,3) would display as 12345678901234567890.123	8 bytes
DECIMAL(size, d)	Exact fixed-point number. Maximum size is 65, and maximum d is 30. The default size is (10,0).	Variable
BIT[(size)]	The range is 1 to 64. The default size is 1.	(Size+7)/8 bytes

 For more information on DECIMAL storage requirements, visit https://dev.mysql.com/doc/refman/8.0/en/storage-requirements.html.

The preceding table lists the numeric data types available in MySQL. It's important to note the storage used because the less storage you use, the better it is for performance. The *Choosing the right data type* section covers the reasons behind this.

Numeric data types in other RDMSes

MySQL doesn't have all the same data types as other popular RDMSes. This section will outline some of the numeric data types that exist in others, but not in MySQL. This section will also outline any differences between other RDMSes and MySQL.

SQL Server

There aren't unsigned versions of INT in SQL Server. BIT exists in SQL Server, but you can only store 0, 1, or null.

Additionally, SQL Server has the data types MONEY and SMALLMONEY. These two data types represent monetary values. MONEY holds monetary values that are accurate to ten-thousandths. SMALLMONEY has a smaller range than MONEY. In MySQL, you can use DECIMAL for money values.

Oracle

Oracle has the NUMBER data type and it's used like the INT, FLOAT, DOUBLE, or DECIMAL data types in MySQL. Instead of having a lot of different numeric types, like in MySQL, Oracle handles all numeric types in one data type. Depending on the value you are storing, you would use INT, FLOAT, DOUBLE, or DECIMAL in MySQL for the NUMBER data type in Oracle. There aren't unsigned versions of NUMBER in Oracle.

PostgreSQL

PostgreSQL uses INTEGER in place of INT. It works the same as INT in MySQL, except there is no unsigned version in PostgreSQL.

PostgreSQL uses DOUBLE PRECISION instead of the DOUBLE data type.

PostgreSQL uses REAL instead of the FLOAT data type.

Additionally, PostgreSQL has a data type called BOOLEAN. It can have a value of true, false, or null. A true value includes true, yes, on, or 1. A false value includes false, on, off, or 0. In MySQL, there isn't a BOOLEAN type. Use TINYINT(1) instead. MySQL Workbench will provide you with a type listed as Boolean, but it immediately converts it to TINYINTX. You can also store Boolean values in a BIT field.

Numeric data types table comparison

The following table lists the numeric data types available in MySQL and shows whether or not they are available in Oracle, PostgreSQL, and SQL Server.

 The size allowances on Oracle, PostgreSQL, and SQL Server may be different even if the data type name is the same.

Numeric data types in MySQL	Also available in		
Data Type	SQL Server	PostgreSQL	Oracle
INT	Yes	Use INTEGER instead	Use NUMBER instead
TINYINT	Yes	No	No
SMALLINT	Yes	Yes	No
MEDIUMINT	No	No	No
BIGINT	Yes	Yes	No
FLOAT	Yes	No	Use NUMBER instead
DOUBLE	Use FLOAT instead	Use DOUBLE PRECISION instead	Use NUMBER instead
DECIMAL	Yes	Yes	Use NUMBER instead
BIT	Yes	No	No

The preceding table lists the numeric data types available in MySQL and shows whether or not they are available in Oracle, PostgreSQL, and SQL Server.

Understanding date and time data types

Date and time data types can hold dates, times, and combinations of dates and time, timestamps, and years. This section walks you through the different date and time data types in MySQL. This section also shows you where Oracle, PostgreSQL, and SQL Server date and time data types are different.

Date and time data types in MySQL

The date and time data types in MySQL include:

- DATE: This data type can hold a date in the format of YYYY-MM-DD. The range is from '1000-01-01' to '9999-12-31'. For example, December 15, 1997, would be stored as 1997-12-15.
- TIME: This data type holds time values in the format of hh:mm:ss. The range is from '-838:59:59' to '838:59:59'.
- DATETIME: This data type can hold a combination of date and time in the format of YYYY-MM-DD hh:mm:ss. The range is from '1000-01-01 00:00:00' to '9999-12-31 23:59:59'. For example, January 19, 2003, at 3:30 p.m. would be stored as 2003-01-19 15:30:00.
- TIMESTAMP: This data type can hold values that contain both date and time parts. This has a range of '1970-01-01 00:00:00' UTC to '2038-01-19 03:14:07' UTC (Coordinated Universal Time; formerly Greenwich Mean Time). The value is stored in the number of seconds since '1970-01-01 00:00:00'.

 The significant difference between DATETIME and TIMESTAMP is that TIMESTAMP values are stored in UTC and converted to the current timezone when a query returns the values. In contrast, DATETIME data type values are stored in the current time zone.

- YEAR: This data type can hold the values of a year in four-digit format. The range is 1901 to 2155, and 0000.

MySQL date and time data type table summary

The following table lists the date and time data types available in MySQL:

Data Type	Description	Storage Used
DATE	Stores dates in the format 'YYYY-MM-DD' Ranges from '1000-01-01' to '9999-12-31'	3 bytes
TIME	Stores time in format: hh:mm:ss Ranges from '-838:59:59' to '838:59:59'	3 bytes
DATETIME	Stores date and time combination in format YYYY-MM-DD hh:mm:ss Ranges from '1000-01-01 00:00:00' to '9999-12-31 23:59:59'	8 bytes

TIMESTAMP	Stores time in number of seconds since '1970-01-01 00:00:00' UTC Ranges from '1970-01-01 00:00:01' UTC to '2038-01-09 03:14:07' UTC	4 bytes
YEAR	Stores year in four-digit format Ranges from 1901 to 2155, and includes 0000	1 byte

The preceding table lists the date and time data types available in MySQL. It's important to note the storage used because the less storage you use, the better it is for performance. The *Choosing the right data type* section covers the reasons behind this.

Date and time data types in other RDMSes

MySQL doesn't have all the same data types as other popular RDMSes. This section will outline some of the date and time data types that exist in others, but not in MySQL.

Oracle

Listed here are the additional date and time data types for Oracle:

- TIMESTAMP WITH TIME ZONE: This data type in Oracle is a variation on TIMESTAMP and includes the time zone and time zone offset. The time zone offset shows the difference from UTC to the local time zone in hours and minutes. MySQL doesn't allow for time zone awareness with data types, so you will need to store the date in the DATETIME field without time zone information.
- TIMESTAMP WITH LOCAL TIME ZONE: This data type in Oracle is a variation on TIMESTAMP, but doesn't include the time zone and time zone offset. The time zone offset shows the difference from UTC to the local time zone in hours and minutes. In this data type, the data is stored in the database time zone. When the data is returned to a user, it is returned in the user's local session time zone. MySQL doesn't allow time zone awareness with data types, so you will need to store the date in the DATETIME field without time zone information.
- INTERVAL YEAR TO MONTH: This Oracle data type stores a time period using the YEAR and MONTH datetime fields. This data type is useful for showing differences between two datetime values when only using Year and Month. MySQL doesn't allow storing intervals, so there is no equivalent for this, for example:
  - INTERVAL '100' YEAR(3) is an interval of 100 years and 0 months.
  - INTERVAL '50' MONTH is an interval of 50 months. This is the same as INTERVAL '4-2' YEAR TO MONTH.

- INTERVAL DAY TO SECOND: This Oracle data type stores a time period using days, hours, minutes, and seconds. This data type is useful for showing the differences between two datetime values to the second. MySQL doesn't allow storing intervals, so there is no equivalent for this:
  - INTERVAL '200 20' DAY(3) TO HOUR is an interval of 200 days and 20 hours.
  - INTERVAL '555' DAY(3) is an interval of 555 days.
  - INTERVAL '10 09:08:07.456' DAY to SECOND(3) is the interval 10 days, 9 hours, 8 minutes, 7 seconds, and 456 thousands of a second.

PostgreSQL

Listed here are the additional date and time data types available in PostgreSQL:

- TIMESTAMP WITH TIME ZONE: This PostgreSQL data type shows both the date and time of day with the time zone. MySQL doesn't allow time zone awareness with data types, so you will need to store the date in the DATETIME field without time zone information.
- INTERVAL: This PostgreSQL data type sets a time interval. It allows you to store and manipulate a time period in years, months, days, hours, and seconds. MySQL doesn't allow storing intervals, so there is no equivalent for this.

SQL Server

Listed here are the additional SQL Server date and time data types:

- DATETIME2: This data type in SQL Server is very similar to DATETIME, in that it holds a date with a time of day based on the 24-hour clock, but DATETIME2 allows a larger date range and larger default fractional precision for seconds. The date range for this type is 0001-01-01 through 9999-12-31, and the time range is 00:00:00 through 23:59:59.9999999. In MySQL, use DATETIME for this data type.

- SMALLDATETIME: This data type in SQL Server is similar to DATETIME, in that it holds a date with a time of day based on the 24-hour clock, but SMALLDATETIME doesn't allow fractional seconds. The date range for this type is 1900-01-01 through 2079-06-06, and the time range is 00:00:00 through 23:59:59. If you don't need fractional seconds stored, then you can save storage space when using this data type versus DATETIME or DATETIME2. In MySQL, use DATETIME for this data type.

- DATETIMEOFFSET: This data type in SQL Server is similar to DATETIME, in that it holds a date with a time of day based on the 24-hour clock, but DATETIME2 has time zone awareness, allowing you to store data that preserves the local time zone time. The time zone offset allows you to specify how much the date/time differs from UTC. The date range for this type is 0001-01-01 through 9999-12-31, and the time range is 00:00:00 through 23:59:59.9999999, with a time zone offset range of -14:00 through +14:00. MySQL doesn't allow time zone awareness with data types, so you will need to store the date in the DATETIME field without time zone information.

Date and time data types table comparison

The following table lists the date and time data types available in MySQL and shows whether or not they are available in Oracle, PostgreSQL, and SQL Server:

 NOTE: The size allowances on Oracle, PostgreSQL, and SQL Server may be different even if the data type name is the same.

Date and time data types in MySQL	Also available in		
Data Type	SQL Server	PostgreSQL	Oracle
DATE	Yes	Yes	Yes
TIME	Yes	Yes	No
DATETIME	No	No	No
TIMESTAMP	Yes	Yes	Yes
YEAR	No	No	No

The preceding table lists the date and time data types available in MySQL and shows whether or not they are available in Oracle, PostgreSQL, and SQL Server.

Understanding other data types

MySQL supports some other types of data beyond string, numeric, and date and time data types. The following sections cover these data types in more detail, including JSON and spatial data types.

Other data types in MySQL

We will briefly cover some other data types in MySQL. These will be high-level explanations since we won't be using these types throughout the book, but this will show you that other types do exist and may be in use in databases you are using:

- **JSON**: This data type holds values in the native **JSON (JavaScript Object Notation)** language. Use curly braces to surround JSON key/value pairs. Here is an example of JSON syntax:

  ```
  {"Author":"Josephine Bush", "book": "Learn SQL Programming"}
  ```

  MySQL provides automatic validation of a JSON document and the optimal storage format. Storing JSON in a field with a type of JSON ensures you have well-formed JSON data. This is opposed to storing it in a character field, which offers no guarantee that your JSON is well-formed.

   For more information on JSON data, visit https://dev.mysql.com/doc/refman/8.0/en/json.html

- **Spatial data types**: These data types hold data that represents two-dimensional spatial objects. The GEOMETRY data type can store geometry values of any type. There are a few geometry data types that require specific values relating to particular geometry types, such as POINT, LINESTRING, and POLYGON. The POINT data type allows you to store the data for one point, like POINT (10 15). LINESTRING allows you to store points related to a line like LINESTRING (1 2, 3 4, 8 6) where each of the value pairs correspond to a point on the line. The POLYGON data type allows you to store points related to a polygon like POLYGON ((1 2, 3 4, 7 6, 9 8, 4 3, 1 2)) where each value pair corresponds to a point on the polygon.

For more information on MySQL spatial types, visit `https://dev.mysql.com/doc/refman/5.7/en/spatial-type-overview.html`

MySQL comes with over 5,000 different supportable coordinate systems to help support spatial data in the geometric data types referenced in the previous paragraph, such as NAD 1927 and NAD 1983.

For more information on coordinate systems, visit `https://desktop.arcgis.com/en/arcmap/latest/map/projections/about-projected-coordinate-systems.htm`

Other data types in other RDMSes

MySQL doesn't have all the same data types as other popular RDMSes. This section will outline some of the other data types that exist in other RDMSes, but not in MySQL. The differences are also outlined, if they exist.

Oracle

In Oracle, we use `VARCHAR2` for JSON. PostgreSQL also supports the JSON data type. For more information about how to use JSON in PostgreSQL, visit `https://www.postgresql.org/docs/11/functions-json.html`.

Oracle can support geometric data via the `SDO_GEOMETRY` data type. This type allows you to define points, lines, and polygons but works a bit differently than MySQL. For more details, visit `https://docs.oracle.com/en/database/oracle/oracle-database/18/sqlrf/Data-Types.html#GUID-022A5008-1E15-4AA4-938E-7FD75C594087`.

XML: Oracle supports XML data type using `XMLTYPE`. `XMLTYPE` implicitly stores the data in a `CLOB` data type column. A `CLOB` data type stores large character data up to 2 GB in size.

PostgreSQL

XML: PostgreSQL supports the XML data type and checks whether it is well-formed upon insertion. For more information on the PostgreSQL XML data type, visit `https://www.postgresql.org/docs/11/datatype-xml.html`.

Network Address Types: PostgreSQL offers some data types to hold IP and MAC addresses. The following table shows examples of what values can be placed in each of these data types:

CIDR	INET	MACADDR	MACADDR8
`192.168.0.7`	`192.168.0.7/24`	`'07:01:3b:02:05:01'`	`'07:01:3b:02:05:01:07:08'`

These data types are not available in SQL Server or Oracle either. You would need to store these types of values in a `VARCHAR`, `BINARY`, or `INT` data type instead.

SQL Server

SQL Server supports JSON through the data type `NVARCHAR(MAX)`.

XML: SQL Server supports the **XML (Extensible Markup Language)** data type. This data type allows you to store XML in a table column. XML documents contain one root that is the parent of all elements. The following is an example of XML syntax:

```
<books>
 <book>
 <name>Learn SQL Programming</name>
 <author>Josephine Bush</author>
 </book>
</books>
```

 For more information about the SQL Server XML data type, visit `https://docs.microsoft.com/en-us/sql/relational-databases/xml/xml-data-type-and-columns-sql-server?view=sql-server-ver15`.

XML doesn't exist in MySQL; use the `BLOB` data type instead. See the *String Data Types* section for more information on the `BLOB` data type.

Choosing the right data type

It's essential to understand how storage usage affects your database. Most databases are stored on disk (with some exceptions that allow data to be stored in memory). When the database needs to fetch data for you, it needs to read from the disk and return results to you. This is where disk I/O comes into play. I/O stands for input/output, and it's the communication between a system or computer and a person or another system/computer. Disk I/O is the reads and writes that are happening against a disk, and its rate is dependent on the speed at which the data can be transferred from disk to memory. This is the time it will take to return the data for your query. The more data you request, the longer it's going to take, and if you have a lot of people requesting a lot of data, then it may take much longer than is acceptable. This is why it's vital to choose the right data type for your data.

Here are some reasons why you need to choose wisely:

- If you choose a data type that is too large for the data it will hold, it will cause extra stress for your database because you will be using additional storage. The less storage you use, the more data you can have in memory (RAM). This will increase your database performance.
- If you choose a data type that is too small for the data, this will cause your data to be truncated upon insert, or to have failures upon insertion because the data type won't allow those sizes of data to be inserted.

Examples of choosing a data type

The following table takes you through some examples of how to choose data types. It also helps you understand the reasoning behind why you would choose the recommended data type.

Value(s) or type of data	Type in MySQL
State abbreviations that are always two letters, such as CA, CO – we would use CHAR here instead of VARCHAR because these values will always be the same length.	CHAR(2)
States names like California or Colorado – we would use VARCHAR here because there is a variable length, and we would set the VARCHAR value to the longest length string, which in this case would be South or North Carolina.	VARCHAR(14)

Large amounts of text – consider putting TEXT columns in a separate table to optimize table performance. Database and table design will be covered more in Chapter 4, *Designing and Creating a Database*.	TEXT
Storing files including images – for the most part, you should use the filesystem for what it was intended, storing files, and don't store them in the database.	BLOB
Enumerated and set values – you should avoid these data types because if you ever decide you want to add something else to the ENUM or SET declaration, MySQL has to rebuild the table, and if you have a lot of rows, this could be very time-consuming. Plus, developers can use logic on the application side to handle this much better than a MySQL table can.	ENUM or SET
Storing 0 and 1 values, such as whether a value is true or false.	BIT
Storing zip codes (11155)	TINYINT
Storing money values ($115.25)	DECIMAL
Social security numbers (123-45-6789) – these are numbers, but you won't be doing calculations on them, and you may want to store the hyphens for proper formatting.	VARCHAR
Dates with time – don't use string types to store dates.	DATETIME
Scientific data or data where you don't need exact precision.	FLOAT or DOUBLE

The preceding table took you through some examples of how to choose data types. It also helped you understand the reason for choosing the recommended data type.

Summary

In this chapter, we covered what data types are and how they are used. We learned about specific data types and what data can be stored in each. Data types include string, numeric, date and time, and other types such as JSON and spatial types. String data types include char and varchar, binary and varbinary, blob, enum, set, and text. Numeric data types include bit, int, float, double, and decimal. Date and time data types include date, time, datetime, timestamp, and year. We learned from the perspective of MySQL data types, but where there were differences versus Oracle, PostgreSQL, and SQL Server, those differences were noted.

We also went through some examples of types and values of data to see examples of how to assign them correctly to data types. This section included an explanation of why you need to be careful when selecting a data type and how it can impact database performance.

In the next chapter, we will cover designing and creating a database. The chapter will discuss indexing, what it is, how to use it, and what it means for database performance. The chapter will also explain how to create a database and table. This includes guidelines for naming conventions, understanding SQL code errors, formatting SQL code for readability, and how to apply data types and integrity to your tables.

Questions

1. Which data types are available for you to use when dealing with string data types?
2. Why would you not want to use blob or text data types?
3. What types of data types are available for you to use when dealing with numeric data types?
4. Why would you want to use an unsigned versus a signed `int`?
5. What types of data types are available for you to use when dealing with date and time data types?
6. What types of RDMS support time zone awareness when storing datetime values?
7. What types of other data types are available in MySQL?
8. Why do you need to be careful when choosing data types?
9. What data type would you use to store zip codes?
10. What data type can you use to store social security numbers?

4
Designing and Creating a Database

This chapter introduces you to the process of designing and creating a database. We'll walk through the guidelines for the naming conventions and learn about the SQL code errors. You will learn how to format SQL code for readability, apply data types, and apply data integrity in your tables. You will also learn about the different types of table relationships and how to build entity-relationship diagrams. You will also learn how to create a database and a table in a database. Going further, we will discuss the concept and usage of indexing. Then, you will gain an understanding of how indexing helps database performance.

In this chapter, we will cover the following topics:

- Creating a database
- Understanding table relationships
- Creating a table in the database
- Understanding indexes

Technical requirements

The code files of this chapter can be found at `https://github.com/PacktPublishing/learn-sql-database-programming/tree/master/chapter-4`.

Creating a database

In `Chapter 1`, *Introduction to Relational Database Management Systems*, we learned what a database is and its essential parts, such as tables, columns, rows, and fields. In this section, we will learn how to create a database. We'll also go through the guidelines for naming conventions and discuss SQL code errors.

Guidelines for naming conventions

Naming conventions are essential for multiple reasons. You must ensure that you name things accurately and descriptively, but, at the same time, avoid keywords that will create confusion. You should avoid spaces, choose the proper case, and stick to one convention. You should make sure that you use only permitted characters when naming a database object. Each of these guidelines will be covered in more detail throughout this section.

Avoiding keywords

A **keyword** in MySQL is a word that has a special meaning and is reserved for specific uses, such as SELECT, which is covered more in Chapter 6, *Querying a Single Table*. There are lots of keywords or reserved words in MySQL. You should avoid naming your database and database objects with keywords.

 For the entire list of keywords in MySQL, visit https://dev.mysql.com/doc/refman/8.0/en/keywords.html.

For instance, you wouldn't want to name your table DATETIME because this is a keyword reserved for the DATETIME data type. If you inadvertently did name a table with a keyword, you would need to use backticks or double quotes around it every time you query it or you would receive an error. As another example, if you named a column in a table select, then you would need to use backticks or double quotes around it each time you queried it.

The following code block would return Error Code: 1064. You have an error in your SQL syntax; check the manual that corresponds to your MySQL server version for the right syntax to use near '[select] FROM databasename.tablename' at line 1:

```
SELECT select FROM databasename.tablename;
```

The queries would run successfully with the corrections in the following sample syntax. This is just an example code to show you what you can do in this scenario:

```
SELECT `select` FROM databasename.tablename;
SELECT "select" FROM databasename.tablename;
```

In Oracle, PostgreSQL, and SQL Server, you can enclose objects, such as tables, with spaces in double quotes, as in SELECT "select" FROM databasename.tablename;.

Avoiding spaces

If you use spaces in a database name or database object, then you will always need to use backticks around that name when querying.

The following code block would return Error Code: 1146. Table 'databasename.table' doesn't exist:

```
SELECT column1 FROM databasename.table name;
```

The queries would run successfully with the corrections in the following sample syntax:

```
SELECT column1 FROM databasename.`table name`;
```

In Oracle, PostgreSQL, and SQL Server, you can enclose objects with spaces in double quotes, as in SELECT column1 FROM databasename."table name";.

In SQL Server, you can also use square brackets around an object name that has spaces, as in SELECT column1 FROM databasename.[table name];.

Descriptive and accurate naming

Since abbreviations can be misunderstood, try to use full words as much as possible. Name a table as accurately as possible, and describe its purpose as much as you can so that it's easy to understand what's in the table just by looking at its name.

For example, the table name tblName may make it hard to understand what's inside it. It uses the abbreviation tbl for table and Name, which doesn't help you know what's inside it. If the table contains cat breeds, then you could name the table CatBreeds, and that will make it clear what is contained in the table.

Something important to bear in mind when naming database objects is whether you should name them so that you know whether it is a table, view, or stored procedure (more on these types of objects in `Chapter 12`, *Programmable Objects*). You could name a table with `tblCatBreeds`, but I don't recommend using the `tbl` part. You may want to change the table to another type of database object later and would not want the name to imply that it's a table. Instead, you could name the table `CatBreeds`.

Case and separating words

There are different ideas behind how to use case and how to separate words in database object names. You shouldn't use spaces to separate words, but you can use cases or underscores.

Depending on the configuration of the MySQL server, it may not be possible to use anything but lowercase naming, so the following information is more generalized to apply to all RDMS.

The different types of case naming are as follows:

- **lowercase naming**: This means that the entire object name is lowercase. For example, `catbreeds` and `dogbreeds` are table names with a lowercase naming convention.
- **UPPERCASE naming**: This means that the entire object name is uppercase. For example, `CATBREEDS` or `DOGBREEDS` are table names with an uppercase naming convention.
- **camelCase naming**: This means that the name starts with lowercase, and each new word starts with an uppercase letter. For example, `catBreeds` and `dogBreeds` are table names with a camelCase naming convention.
- **PascalCase naming**: This means that the first letter in each word is capitalized. For example, `CatBreeds` and `DogBreeds` are table names with a PascalCase naming convention.

By default, MySQL doesn't support anything but lowercase naming, so I would recommend using underscores (_) between words in a database object's name if the name is long to avoid confusion with all lowercase naming.

The different ways to separate words in database objects are as follows:

- **Separating by case as outlined previously**: With lowercase, UPPERCASE, camelCase, or PascalCase.
- **Separating the words with an underscore**: Like `cat_breeds` or `dog_breeds`.
- **Separating the words with spaces**: Don't use this method since it creates issues with errors and SQL querying syntax.

There are many opinions on whether to name a table as singular or plural (for example, `CatBreed` or `CatBreeds`) and plenty of opinions around case and separation. Ultimately, it's good to stick with the same convention throughout, especially a convention that makes it easy to read the name. For instance, if you had a long table name such as `citiesinamerica`, it would be kind of hard to read in all lowercase or uppercase, so you might want to pick camelCase or PascalCase since it would be easier to read names such as `CitiesInAmerica`. You could also insert underscores to make it more readable if you prefer, and with underscore spacing, you can use any of the case choices. I like camelCase or PascalCase because they are the easiest to read, and I prefer not to use underscores in naming database objects:

lowercase	UPPERCASE	camelCase	PascalCase	underscore spacing
catbreeds	CATBREEDS	catBreeds	CatBreeds	cat_breeds

The most important thing is to pick a convention for the case and separation of database object naming and stick with it.

Allowed characters when naming database objects

When creating a database object, you can't use any character. You need to use the permitted characters, which include numbers (0–9), lowercase letters (a–z), uppercase letters (A–Z), the dollar sign ($), and underscore (_).

You can use characters other than these permitted ones, but then you will find yourself with the same problem regarding what happens when you put a space in a name. You have to use backticks (`) in MySQL when creating it or using the object if you use non-permitted characters. It's best to steer away from non-permitted characters.

To summarize this section, you want to ensure that you avoid keywords and spaces, and make sure that you use descriptive and accurate naming. You also want to choose your case and method for separating words and stick to one convention, and make sure that you use only permitted characters when naming a database object.

Learning how to create a database

We'll go through a couple of different ways to create a database in this section. The first way is with the MySQL Workbench interface, and the second way is with SQL scripts only.

Creating a database via the MySQL Workbench interface

Creating a database using MySQL Workbench is fairly straightforward. Simply go through the following steps:

1. Open **MySQL Workbench**.
2. Connect to your local instance or a `dev/test` instance. *Don't perform any of these steps on a live production server.* Connecting to a MySQL instance is covered in more detail in `Chapter 2`, *Installing and Using MySQL Workbench*.
3. Click the button for creating a new schema, which is highlighted in the following screenshot. The word *schema* is synonymous with *database* in MySQL:

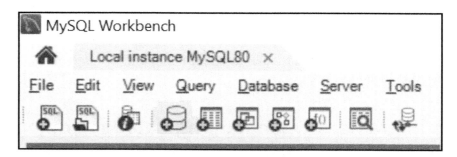

In Oracle, PostgreSQL, and SQL Server, 'schema' is not synonymous with 'database', and these two things are distinctly different. In these other RDMSes, a schema is contained within a database.

4. Type in the database (schema) name, as shown in the following screenshot, remembering to follow the naming conventions outlined in the previous section:

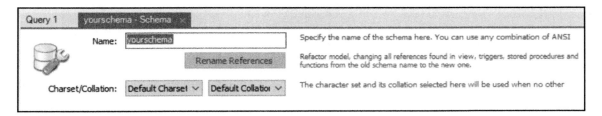

5. Click on **Apply**.
6. If your MySQL is configured only to use lowercase table names, you will get the following error message if you name it with more than lowercase letters. The lowercase letters setting is unchangeable after the MySQL server is initialized:

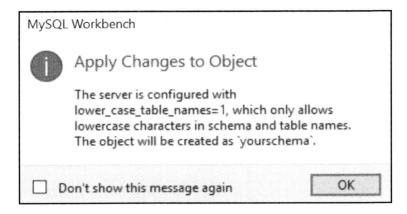

7. Click on **OK**.

8. The following screenshot shows you what script MySQL Workbench will run for you to create the new database:

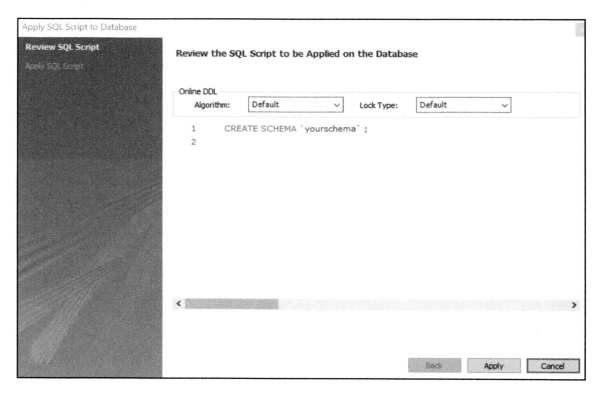

9. Click on **Apply**.
10. On the next screen, click on **Finish** if the script was successfully applied. If it was not successfully applied, you can click **Back** to fix any issues or **Show Logs** to see additional error information:

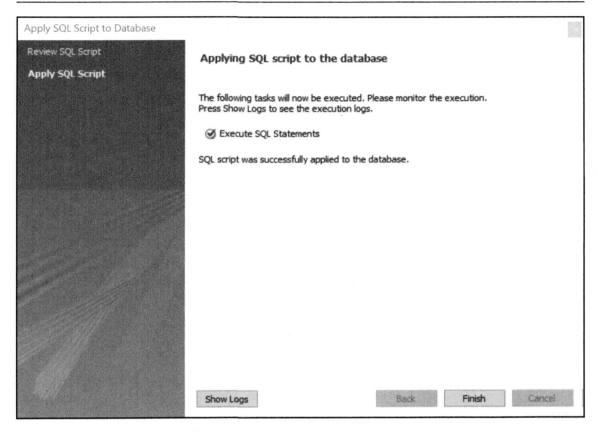

11. You will see your database listed in the **SCHEMAS** panel in MySQL Workbench, as shown in the following screenshot:

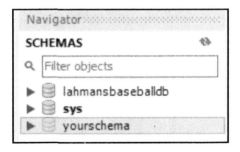

Now, you will be able to add database objects, such as tables, to your new database. We will do a walkthrough of this in the *Creating a database table* section later in this chapter.

Creating a database via MySQL Workbench with a SQL script

Creating a database using MySQL Workbench with a SQL script is relatively straightforward. Simply go through the following steps:

1. Open **MySQL Workbench**.
2. Connect to your local instance or a dev/test instance. *Don't perform any of these steps on a live production server.*
3. Click the new SQL script button, which is highlighted in the following screenshot:

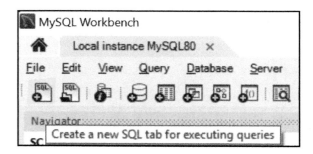

4. Copy or type the following script into the script window in MySQL Workbench:

```
CREATE DATABASE yourschema;
```

5. Click the execute script button, highlighted in the following screenshot:

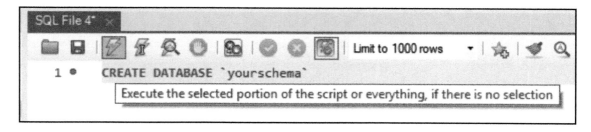

6. Once the script is done executing, the **Output** panel will show that it is successful:

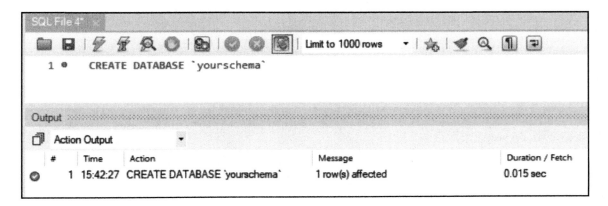

> You don't need the backticks (`) around `yourschema` in the preceding script, but MySQL puts them there by default whenever you script an object. We will walk through how to script objects later in this chapter.

7. Once you click the refresh button on your **SCHEMAS** panel, you will see your new database, as shown in the following screenshot:

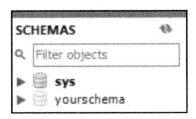

Now, you will be able to add database objects, such as tables, to your new database. We will do a walkthrough of this in the *Creating a table in the database table* section later in this chapter.

Understanding SQL code errors

When MySQL encounters errors with your script or actions in MySQL Workbench, it puts a message for you in the **Output** panel.

By default, the **Output** panel is at the bottom of the MySQL Workbench application. You can resize it by clicking on the divider between the script file area and the **Output** panel.

I changed the script that we ran in the previous section so that there is a space in the schema name that isn't allowed unless you have backticks around it (because it is a MySQL keyword). MySQL will show an error in the **Output** panel when I run it, as shown in the following screenshot:

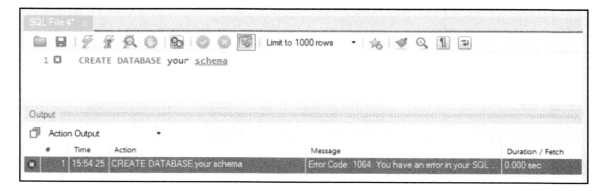

The **Output** window will show you the time, the action, the message, and the duration/fetch:

- The **Time** column tells you the time of the day that you ran the query.
- The **Action** column shows you what query was executed.
- The **Message** column shows you whether the action was successful and also tells you the number of rows that a query returned, if any.
- The **Duration/Fetch** column shows you how long the action took to complete.

To see the entire error message, right-click it, and select **Copy Response**, as shown in the following screenshot:

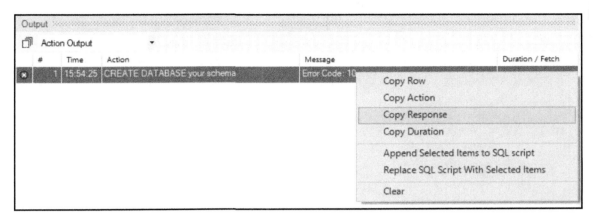

You can then paste this response information into a query window or a text editor of your choosing. The important thing is to see the entire message. The whole message is **Error Code: 1064. You have an error in your SQL syntax; check the manual that corresponds to your MySQL server version for the right syntax to use near 'schema' at line 1**.

The error message will show any information it can tell you about the error you and the line in which you have the problem. Sometimes the errors are cryptic, but you can usually tell where the problem is on the line because MySQL Workbench will put red squiggly lines under the problem area. In the preceding screenshot with the script in it, you can see that MySQL Workbench has a red squiggly line under the schema. We know that we can't have spaces in a schema name (without using backticks), so MySQL Workbench is warning us that this won't work, and sure enough, when we run the script, it gives us an error. You will either need to make your schema one word in the script or put your schema in backticks—for example, `your schema`. I highly advise against using spaces in a database (schema) name.

The **Output** panel will show you any errors that you have, and they will accumulate there over time. If you want to clear out the errors, then you can right-click in the **Output** panel and select **Clear**, as shown in the following screenshot. This will clear all your messages from the **Output** window, so only use this if you want to clear everything out:

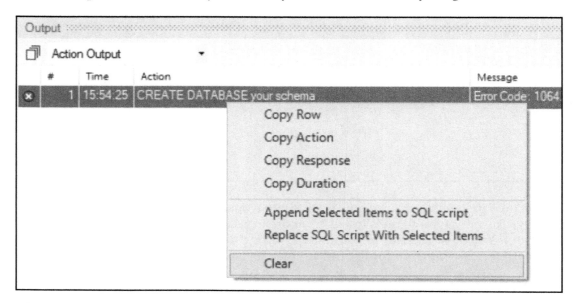

The **Output** window is a useful panel. As described in Chapter 2, *Installing and Using MySQL Workbench*, the **Output** window also shows you successful queries, and it's where you can go to look for success and failure messages.

Understanding table relationships

As we covered in Chapter 1, *Introduction to Relational Database Management Systems*, relational databases contain tables that are related to one another. Once you need to query more than one table, you can rely on these relationships to join the tables together. There are three types of table relationships: one-to-one, one-to-many, and many-to-many. First, let's go over how to display these relationships in a diagram.

Understanding entity-relationship diagrams

You can use entity-relationship diagrams to visualize table relationships. This is sometimes referred to as an E-R diagram, or an ERD. In MySQL Workbench, the entity-relationship diagram, is referred to as an enhanced entity-relationship diagram or EER diagram. This just means that it's an entity-relationship diagram with enhanced features, such as being able to see object properties and constraints more easily. The lines that connect the tables to each other help you to determine what kind of relationships exists between the tables. The following table shows the connector lines and a description of what they mean:

Connector	Description
———O+	Zero or one row matches between tables
———++	One, and only one, row matches between tables
———O<	Zero to many rows match between tables
———K<	One to many rows match between tables
———<	Many rows match between tables

You can mix the line connectors to make both ends show the relationship between the tables. Let's now look at some examples of table relationships and their associated connectors.

Understanding one-to-one table relationships

In a one-to-one relationship, one table has just one corresponding row in another table. An example of this could be two tables, one with employees and one with computers. Each employee has one computer. A one-to-one relationship is not a common table relationship. You might separate a table's data into multiple tables for security purposes—for example, you could have a table of employees, but want the pay in a separate table so that only certain people can access the employee pay information.

The following screenshot shows an example of a one-to-one relationship:

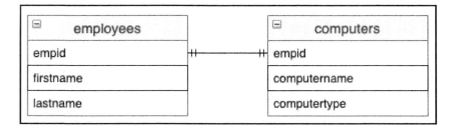

Understanding one-to-many table relationships

In a one-to-many relationship, one table has none, one, or many corresponding rows in another table. An example of this could be two tables, one with adults and one with children. An adult table row may have none, one, or many rows in the child table. One-to-many is a common table relationship. In the case of the baseball database, an example of a one-to-many relationship is the people table to the appearance table. There is one playerid per row in the people table and there are many appearances for each of those playerids in the appearances table. In addition, a one-to-many relationship can be viewed as a many-to-one relationship depending on the direction from which you are looking at it. The following screenshot shows an example of a one-to-many relationship:

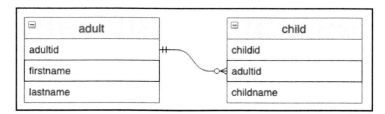

Understanding many-to-many table relationships

In a many-to-many relationship, one table corresponds to many rows in another table. In addition, one item from one table can correspond to multiple rows in the other. An example of this could be tables of customers and products. Customers could purchase many products, and many products can be purchased by many customers. In the case of the baseball database, an example of a one-to-many relationship is the appearances table's relationship to the batting table. There are many rows per playerid in the appearances table and there are many rows for each of those playerids in the batting table.

The following screenshot shows an example of a many-to-many relationship:

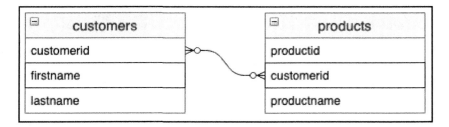

The following screenshot shows you an example of an entire ERD:

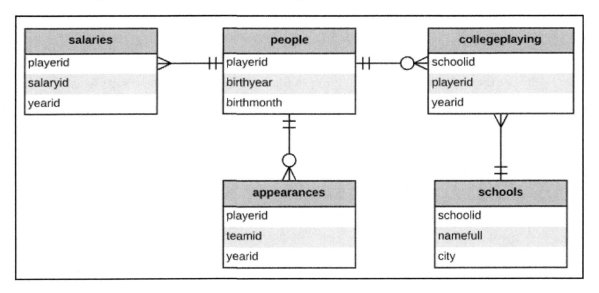

In the preceding screenshot, the people table has a one-to-many relationship with the salaries table, a one-to-zero or many relationship with the collegeplaying table, and a one-to-zero or many relationship with the appearances table. In addition, the collegeplaying table has a many-to-one relationship with the schools table.

You can reverse engineer an entity-relationship diagram in MySQL Workbench. It works best if all the tables have foreign key references, but if they don't, then you can add them via the diagram.

To reverse engineer a diagram in MySQL Workbench, you can go through the following steps:

1. Select **Database** in the menu, and then select **Reverse Engineer**:

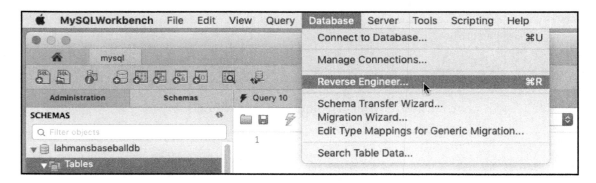

2. Set the parameters for connecting to the DBMS—in this case, it's my local instance—and then click **Continue**:

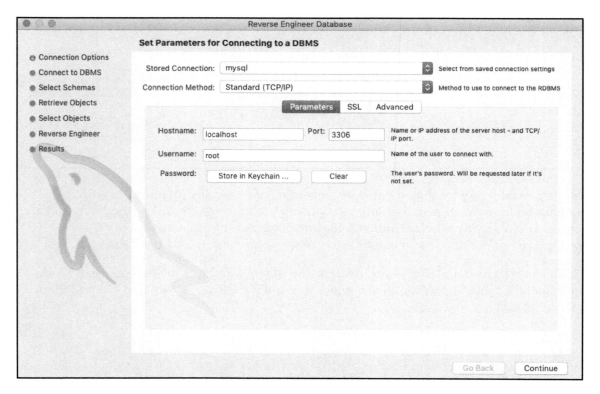

3. Click on **Continue** on the **Connect to DBMS and Fetch Information** page after it shows **Execution Completed Successfully** and **Fetch finished**:

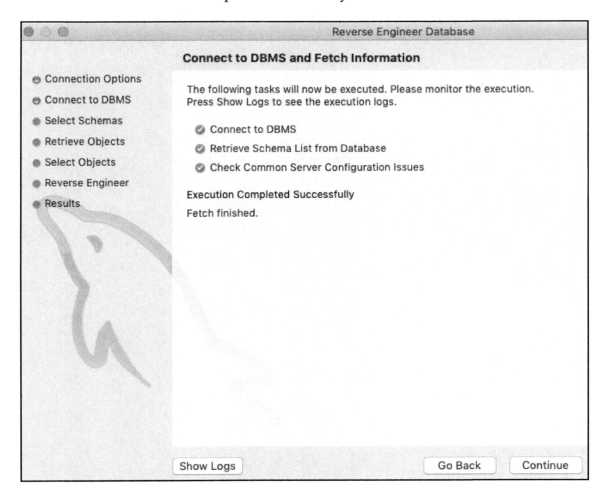

4. Select a schema and then click on **Continue**. In this case, I'm selecting the schema we created in a previous chapter of this book (yourschema):

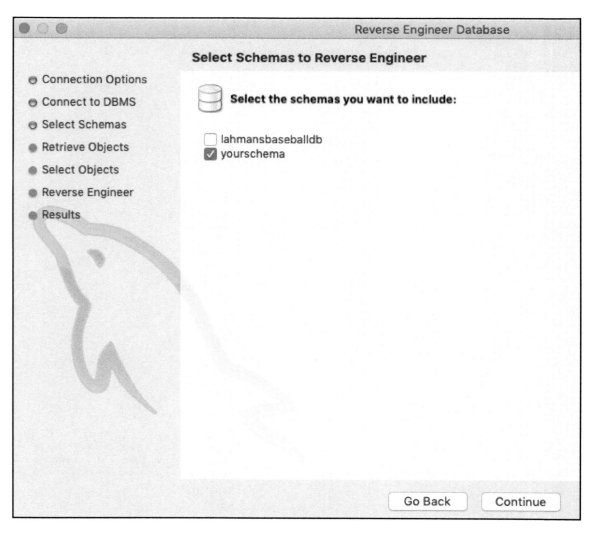

5. Click on **Continue** on the **Retrieve and Reverse Engineer Schema Objects** page after it shows **Execution Completed Successfully** and **Fetch finished**.

6. On the **Select Objects to Reverse Engineer** page, click the **Show Filter** button to see all the objects that it will reverse engineer. You can exclude objects by clicking the arrows between the boxes that show **Objects to Process** and **Excluded Objects**. Click **Execute** when you have included the objects that you want:

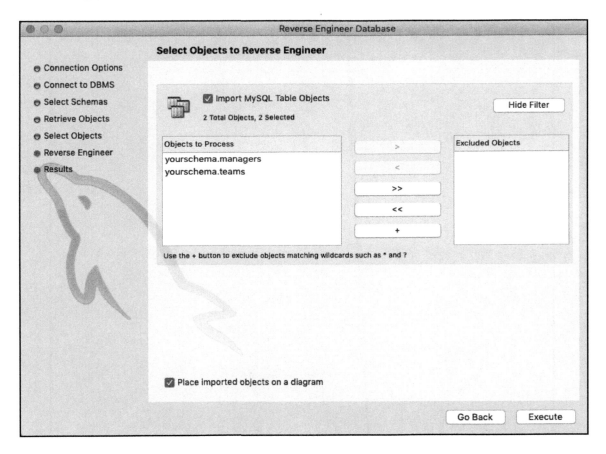

7. Click **Continue** on the **Reverse Engineer Progress** page after it shows **Operation Completed Successfully**.

8. Click **Close** on the **Reverse Engineering Results** page, which shows you the summary of the reverse-engineered objects:

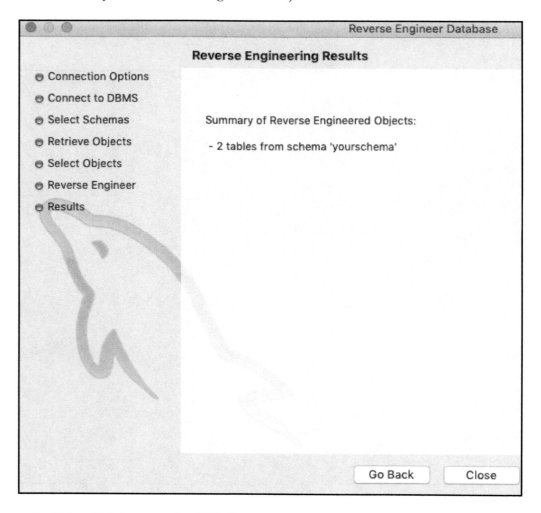

9. This will bring you the EER diagram. As you can see in the following screenshot, there is a one-to-one or many relationship between the **teams** table and the **managers** table:

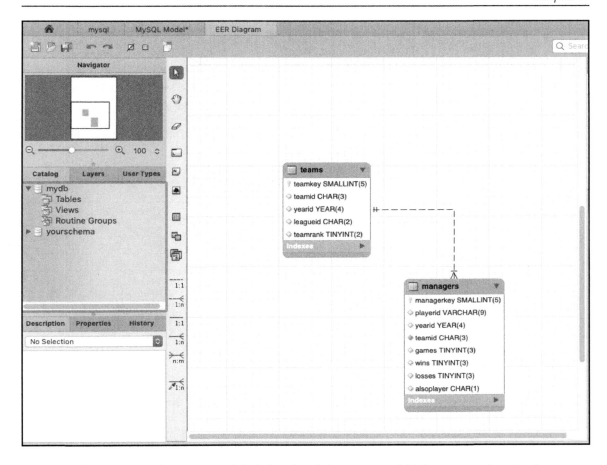

The EER diagram can be very useful right after it is generated if the proper foreign key constraints have been set up. If your database doesn't have these, you will have to manually map table relationships inside the EER diagram.

Creating a table in the database

Now that we've created a database, we can walk through how to create a table in the database. We need to remember what we learned in Chapter 3, *Understanding Data Types*, regarding how to correctly apply data types. We also need to remember what we covered in Chapter 1, *Introduction to Relational Database Management Systems*, about data integrity. This information will form a vital part of our method when we properly create a table.

Understanding how to apply data types and data integrity to your table

Let's briefly review what we covered about data integrity in `Chapter 1`, *Introduction to Relational Database Management Systems*.

Database integrity refers to the consistency and accuracy of data. It is typically enforced by the procedures and guidelines in the database design phase. In RDMS, data integrity is enforced by using keys. A key forces values in a table to conform to a specified standard. There are many types of key to ensure data integrity and enforce table relationships:

Entity integrity	Referential integrity	Domain integrity
Unique constraint	Foreign key	Check constraint
Not null constraint		Default constraint
Primary key		

You need to remember to use these keys and constraints while designing and creating your database tables.

Learning to create a database table

We'll go through a couple of different ways to create a database table in this section. We will use MySQL Workbench for both methods, but one method will not require scriptwriting and the other one will.

First, let's download and analyze the data that will be used for creating the tables:

1. Download the CSV files from `https://github.com/PacktPublishing/learn-sql-database-programming/tree/master/baseballdatabank-csv/csv-files`. The files we will be using in this section are in the `baseballdatabank-csv/csv-files` folder. You will set up just a couple of small tables from this data so that you can have an idea of how the data integrity and keys will work on tables.

2. Working with the `Managers.csv` file, the columns we will be using in `Managers.csv` are `playerID`, `yearID`, `teamID`, `G`, `W`, `L`, and `plyrMgr`. The following screenshot shows some of the data in this file:

playerID	yearID	teamID	lgID	inseason	G	W	L	rank	plyrMgr
wrighha01	1871	BS1	NA	1	31	20	10	3	Y
woodji01	1871	CH1	NA	1	28	19	9	2	Y
paborch01	1871	CL1	NA	1	29	10	19	8	Y
lennobi01	1871	FW1	NA	1	14	5	9	8	Y
deaneha01	1871	FW1	NA	2	5	2	3	8	Y
fergubo01	1871	NY2	NA	1	33	16	17	5	Y
mcbridi01	1871	PH1	NA	1	28	21	7	1	Y
hastisc01	1871	RC1	NA	1	25	4	21	9	Y
pikeli01	1871	TRO	NA	1	4	1	3	6	Y

3. Working with the `Teams.csv` file, we can see that this file has many columns, but we will set up a table with `yearID`, `lgID`, `teamID`, and `rank`. The following is a screenshot of some of the data in this file:

yearID	lgID	teamID	franchID	divID	Rank	G	Ghome	W	L
1871	NA	BS1	BNA		3	31		20	10
1871	NA	CH1	CNA		2	28		19	9
1871	NA	CL1	CFC		8	29		10	19
1871	NA	FW1	KEK		7	19		7	12
1871	NA	NY2	NNA		5	33		16	17
1871	NA	PH1	PNA		1	28		21	7
1871	NA	RC1	ROK		9	25		4	21
1871	NA	TRO	TRO		6	29		13	15
1871	NA	WS3	OLY		4	32		15	15

4. We need to determine how these tables relate to each other and how we can set up data integrity with keys and constraints. One thing that will be very helpful is to see the distinct values in each of the columns that we want to add to our database tables. Using an advanced filter in Excel shows the distinct values in each column. To learn how to use the advanced filter in Excel, visit https://support.office.com/en-us/article/Filter-for-unique-values-or-remove-duplicate-values-ccf664b0-81d6-449b-bbe1-8daaec1e83c2. This will show you the values that you need to account for when choosing data types, remembering that we want to use the smallest data type for the data we will be storing. More details on this were provided in `Chapter 3`, *Understanding Data Types*.

A quick recap of data types will remind you that most databases are stored on disk (with some exceptions that allow data to be stored in memory). When the database needs to fetch data for you, it needs to read from the disk and return results to you. This is where disk I/O comes into play. I/O stands for input/output, and it's the communication between a system or computer and a person or another system or computer. Disk I/O is the reads and writes that are happening against a disk, and its rate is dependent on the speed with which the data can be transferred from disk to memory. This is the time that it will take to return the data for your query. The more data you request, the longer it will take, and if you have a lot of people requesting a lot of data, then it may take much longer than is acceptable. This is why it's imperative to choose the right data type for your data. For more information about data types and choosing the right data type, visit Chapter 3, *Understanding Data Types*.

Let's continue with our analysis of the managers and teams CSV files.

5. By getting the distinct values in each of the columns that we want to add to our table, we can see the following things that are outlined in the following table for the Managers.csv file. In this case, I also got the max length of the **playerID** column to be sure of what the longest value is. It's also good to note how many rows are in each file. In the managers.csv file, there are 3,504 rows, and in the teams.csv file, there are 2,895 rows. This information will be important when we are deciding on an autoincrementing primary key for the tables:

Column	Value range
playerID	All the values are alphanumeric codes with up to 9 characters.
yearID	1871 to 2018.
teamID	All the values are alphanumeric codes with 3 characters.
G	Integers ranging from 1 to 165.
W	Integers ranging from 0 to 116.
L	Integers ranging from 0 to 116.
plyrMgr	Y or N.

6. Also, by getting the distinct values in each of the columns that we want to add to our table, we can see the following things that are outlined in the following table for the `Teams.csv` file:

Column	Value range
yearID	1871 to 2018.
lgID	All the values are alphanumeric codes with 2 characters.
teamID	All the values are alphanumeric codes with 3 characters.
Rank	Numeric ranking from 1 to 12.

7. Now that we know what each of these columns contains, we can decide on the data types for them, choose the keys and constraints, and choose a proper name. For the `Managers.csv` file, the following table shows the naming, data type, and any keys or constraints:

Original column name	Table column name	Data type	Key or constraint
doesn't exist in CSV	managerkey	SMALLINT(5)	Primary key autoincrementing
playerID	playerid	VARCHAR(9)	Part of unique composite key Not null constraint
yearID	yearid	YEAR	Check constraint for range 1871–2155 Part of unique composite key Not null constraint
teamID	teamid	CHAR(3)	Part of unique composite key Foreign key to the teams table on `teamid` Not null constraint
G	games	TINYINT(3)	Check that constraint is between 0 and 165 Not null constraint
W	wins	TINYINT(3)	Check that constraint is between 0 and 165 Not null constraint
L	losses	TINYINT(3)	Check that constraint is between 0 and 165 Not null constraint
plyrMrg	alsoplayer	CHAR(1)	Check that constraint is only Y or N Not null constraint

For the `Teams.csv` file, the following table shows the naming, data type, and any keys or constraints:

Original column name	Table column name	Data type	Key or constraint
doesn't exist in csv	teamkey	SMALLINT(5)	Primary key autoincrementing
yearID	yearid	YEAR	Part of unique composite key Not null constraint
lgID	leagueid	CHAR(2)	Part of unique composite key Not null constraint
teamID	teamid	CHAR(3)	Part of unique composite key Not null constraint
rank	teamrank	TINYINT(2)	Check that constraint is between 0 and 12 Not null constraint

The rationale behind the naming changes was to make it a bit more obvious as to what the columns contain. If you didn't know about baseball, then you might not know that `lgID` is the league ID, or that `G` is games. We want all naming to be descriptively accurate. Also, `'rank'` is a keyword in SQL, so we had to change it to `'teamrank'` to avoid any confusion.

The rationale behind the check constraints is to ensure that there isn't any data that is going into fields that aren't inside the proper range for those fields. We also want to ensure that none of the fields are null so that we can analyze the data in each row properly.

The rationale behind the unique composite keys in each table is that no field column is distinct on its own, so you can create a unique composite key for those combinations of fields that are unique when combined. As for the primary key with autoincrementing, we want to have a column that is the smallest column for uniquely identifying a row of data.

Natural and surrogate primary keys

Now let's talk a little bit more about choosing a primary key. There are two types of primary keys: natural and surrogate. With a natural key, you are using unique columns, and the data in those columns exists outside the database (that is, in the business world). With a surrogate key, you are creating a column to hold a unique value for each row, and that value isn't used anywhere outside the database.

If there was an obvious choice for a primary key (remembering that this is unique and not null), we could use that column. For instance, we could use an obvious primary key if one of these tables contained information about books. Each book has a unique, not null ISBN. This natural key would be an excellent choice for a primary key. When your tables contain multiple columns that are unique and not null to make a composite primary key, it may be better to have one column that uniquely identifies each row. You can then still have a unique, not null composite key on those columns that uniquely identify rows, but you must still always ensure that the easiest way to identify a row with one column is with a surrogate primary key.

Creating a database table via MySQL Workbench

Creating a database table using MySQL Workbench is relatively straightforward. Let's go through the following steps:

1. Open **MySQL Workbench**.
2. Connect to your local instance or a `dev/test` instance by clicking on it in `MySQL Workbench`. *Don't perform any of these steps on a live production server*:

3. Click the down arrow next to the new schema that you created in the previous section:

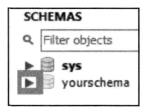

4. Right-click **Tables** and select **Create Table...**:

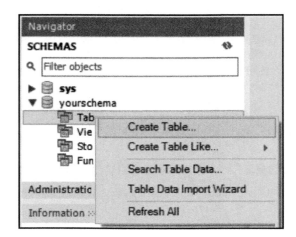

5. This will bring up a tab to allow you to fill in the details of your table; there will be a lot of blank areas for you to fill in and it will have the default table name of `new_table`.

6. We will fill in these details with information from the following table:

Table column name	Data type	Key or constraint
teamkey	SMALLINT(5)	Primary key autoincrementing
yearid	YEAR	Part of unique composite key Not null constraint
leagueid	CHAR(2)	Part of unique composite key Not null constraint
teamid	CHAR(3)	Part of unique composite key Not null constraint
teamrank	TINYINT(2)	Check that constraint is between 0 and 12 Not null constraint

7. First, we fill out the **Columns** tab so that it matches the following screenshot. Before hitting **Apply**, we need to use a couple more tabs; go through the following steps to see the information that we need for these tabs, along with the screenshots showing you the relevant information:

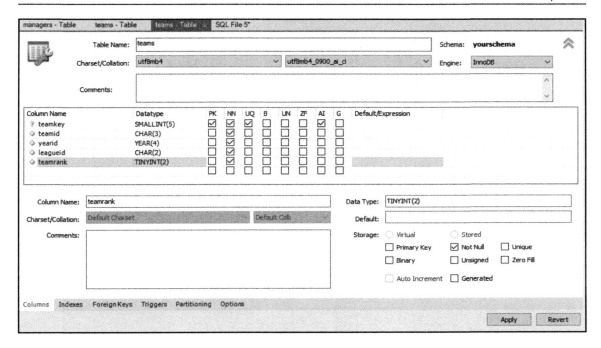

8. Click on the **Indexes** tab so that we can add the **Unique** index on the **teamid**, **leagueid**, and **yearid** columns. Refer to the following screenshot for details:

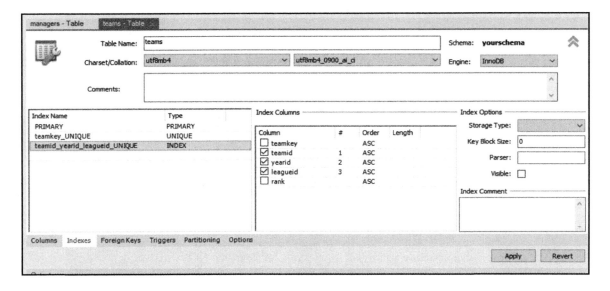

9. Click on **Apply**.
10. Review the script to apply.
11. Click on **Apply**.
12. Click on **Finish**.
13. Click the down arrow on the schema that you created in this chapter and click the down arrow on **Tables**. You should see the **teams** table in the list now:

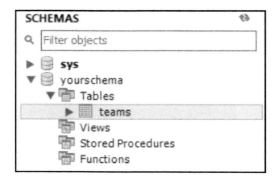

14. Click the New SQL script button:

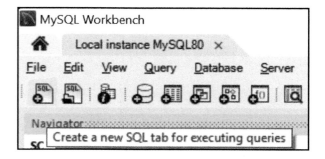

15. Run the following script to add the CHECK constraints:

```
ALTER TABLE yourschema.teams ADD CONSTRAINT check_year CHECK
(yearid >=1871 and yearid <=2155) enforced;
ALTER TABLE yourschema.teams ADD CONSTRAINT check_teamrank CHECK
(teamrank >=0 and teamrank <=12) enforced;
```

16. Click the **New SQL script** button.
17. Right-click on the **teams** table and click on **Send to SQL Editor** and then **Create Statement**:

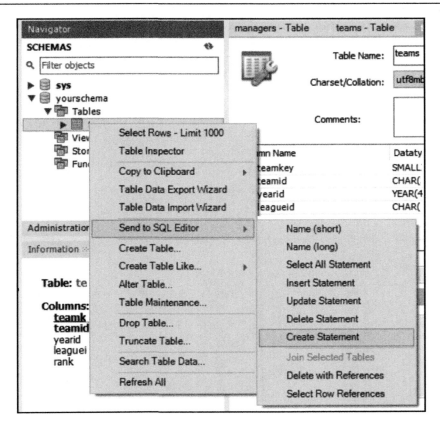

This will show you the following script for your table:

```
CREATE TABLE `teams` (
  `teamkey` smallint(5) NOT NULL AUTO_INCREMENT,
  `teamid` char(3) NOT NULL,
  `yearid` year(4) NOT NULL,
  `leagueid` char(2) NOT NULL,
  `teamrank` tinyint(2) NOT NULL,
  PRIMARY KEY (`teamkey`),
  UNIQUE KEY `teamkey_UNIQUE` (`teamkey`),
  KEY `teamid_yearid_leagueid_UNIQUE` (`teamid`,`yearid`,`leagueid`) /*!80000 INVISIBLE */,
  CONSTRAINT `check_teamrank` CHECK (((`teamrank` >= 0) and (`teamrank` <= 12))),
  CONSTRAINT `check_year` CHECK (((`yearid` >= 1871) and (`yearid` <= 2155)))
) ENGINE=InnoDB DEFAULT CHARSET=utf8mb4 COLLATE=utf8mb4_0900_ai_ci;
```

You can go through some similar steps to create the managers table, or you can proceed to the section on how to run the scripts to create the tables, since this will also include information on how to create the scripts for both tables. The following screenshots show how to set up the `managers` table, including the foreign key association for the `teams` table.

We will set up the `managers` table in much the same way as the `teams` table, but we will add a foreign key reference from the `managers` table to the `teams` table.

The following screenshot shows the setup for the columns in the `managers` table:

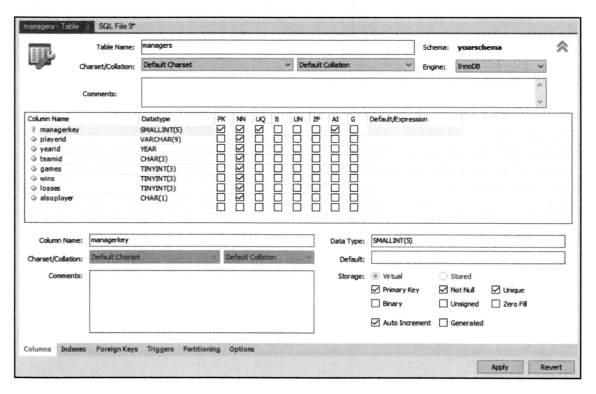

The following screenshot shows the setup for the indexes in the `managers` table:

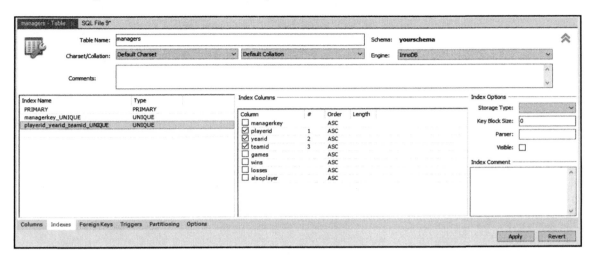

The following screenshot shows the setup for the foreign key reference for the `teamid` from the `managers` table to the `teams` table on `teamid`. Note that under **Foreign Key Options**, we are going to set **On Update** and **On Delete** to **RESTRICT**. This means that you won't be allowed to delete a team from the `teams` table unless you delete or update the corresponding manager record first:

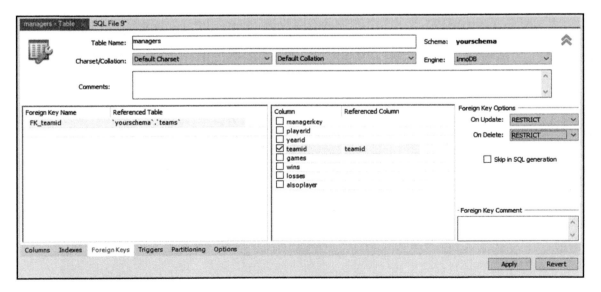

Once the `managers` table is set up, add the check constraints with the following script:

```
ALTER TABLE yourschema.managers
ADD CONSTRAINT check_year CHECK (yearid >=1871 and yearid <=2155) enforced;

ALTER TABLE yourschema.managers
ADD CONSTRAINT check_games CHECK (games >= 0 and games <= 165) enforced;

ALTER TABLE yourschema.managers
ADD CONSTRAINT check_wins CHECK (wins >=0 and wins <=165) enforced;

ALTER TABLE yourschema.managers
ADD CONSTRAINT check_losses CHECK (losses >=0 and losses <=165) enforced;

ALTER TABLE yourschema.managers
ADD CONSTRAINT check_alsoplayer CHECK (alsoplayer = 'N' or alsoplayer =
'Y') enforced;
```

The next section will show you how to run the scripts to create both of the tables.

Creating a database table via MySQL Workbench with SQL scripts

This section will show you how to create the tables that we discussed earlier in the section via scripts:

1. Open **MySQL Workbench**.
2. Connect to your `local` instance or a `dev/test` instance. *Don't perform any of these steps on a live production server.*
3. Click the **New SQL script** button:

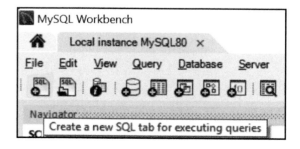

4. Copy or type the following script into the script window and click the **run** button:

```
CREATE TABLE yourschema.`teams3` (
`teamkey` smallint NOT NULL AUTO_INCREMENT,
`teamid` char(3) NOT NULL,
`yearid` year(4) NOT NULL,
`leagueid` char(2) NOT NULL,
`teamrank` tinyint NOT NULL,
PRIMARY KEY (`teamkey`),
UNIQUE KEY `teamkey_UNIQUE` (`teamkey`),
KEY `teamid_yearid_leagueid_UNIQUE` (`teamid`,`yearid`,`leagueid`),
CONSTRAINT `check_teamrank` CHECK (((`teamrank` >= 0) and
(`teamrank` <= 12))),
CONSTRAINT `check_year` CHECK (((`yearid` >= 1871) and (`yearid` <=
2155))));
```

5. Once the `teams` table is successfully created, run the following script to create the `managers` table:

```
CREATE TABLE yourschema.`managers` (
`managerkey` smallint NOT NULL AUTO_INCREMENT,
`playerid` varchar(9) NOT NULL,
`yearid` year(4) NOT NULL,
`teamid` char(3) NOT NULL,
`games` tinyint NOT NULL,
`wins` tinyint NOT NULL,
`losses` tinyint NOT NULL,
`alsoplayer` char(1) NOT NULL,
PRIMARY KEY (`managerkey`),
UNIQUE KEY `managerkey_UNIQUE` (`managerkey`),
UNIQUE KEY `playerid_yearid_teamid_UNIQUE`
(`playerid`,`yearid`,`teamid`),
KEY `FK_teamid_idx` (`teamid`),
CONSTRAINT `FK_teamid` FOREIGN KEY (`teamid`) REFERENCES `teams`
(`teamid`) ON DELETE RESTRICT ON UPDATE RESTRICT,
CONSTRAINT `check_alsoplayer` CHECK ((`alsoplayer` in
(_utf8mb4'Y',_utf8mb4'N'))),
CONSTRAINT `check_games` CHECK (((`games` >= 0) and (`games` <=
165))),
CONSTRAINT `check_losses` CHECK (((`losses` >= 0) and (`losses` <=
165))),
CONSTRAINT `check_manager_year` CHECK (((`yearid` >= 1871) and
(`yearid` <= 2155))),
CONSTRAINT `check_wins` CHECK (((`wins` >= 0) and (`wins` <=
165))));
```

Now, you have the `teams` and the `managers` tables set up as per the specifications outlined in the previous section.

 Creating databases and tables is slightly different in each of the other RDMSes. The interfaces are different in Oracle, PostgreSQL, and SQL Server, and the SQL used to create databases and tables could also be slightly different.

Learning how to format SQL code for readability

Formatting your SQL code for readability is vital so that you and others can quickly understand your SQL code. SQL ignores whitespace, making it easy to format for readability. You can write SQL code all on one line, but it's much easier to read if you place different parts of the SQL on separate lines.

For example, you could write code as shown in the following example, which has all the code on one line and wraps around:

```
CREATE TABLE `managerstest` (`managerkey` smallint NOT NULL, `playerid`
varchar(9) NOT NULL, `yearid` year(4) NOT NULL, `teamid` char(3) NOT NULL);
```

Instead, think about writing it so that it is easier to read, like the following code:

```
CREATE TABLE `managerstest`
(`managerkey` smallint NOT NULL,
`playerid` varchar(9) NOT NULL,
`yearid` year(4) NOT NULL,
`teamid` char(3) NOT NULL);
```

Commenting SQL code

Commenting is essential for writing SQL scripts. You need to use comments so that others can understand why your code works the way it does. If you don't include comments, it will be difficult to use and modify the code later.

Commenting helps you make clear what you are trying to accomplish with each piece of your code. There is an optimal amount of commenting that you should use. For instance, you don't want to not include any comments, but you probably don't want to include comments for every single line. In the preceding CREATE TABLE code sample, you could add a comment at the top that explains why you are creating this table, what it contains, who you are, and when you created it.

To create a single-line comment, use #, and to create a multiline comment, use /* */. The following code sample shows you how to use each of the comments:

```
# this is single line comment

/*
this is a
multi line
comment
*/
```

The following is a code sample without comments:

```
CREATE TABLE `managerstest`
(`managerkey` smallint NOT NULL,
`playerid` varchar(9) NOT NULL,
`yearid` year(4) NOT NULL,
`teamid` char(3) NOT NULL);
```

The following is a code sample with comments:

```
/*
creating managers table for data relating to baseball team manager data
*/
CREATE TABLE `managerstest`
(`managerkey` smallint NOT NULL,
`playerid` varchar(9) NOT NULL,
`yearid` year(4) NOT NULL,
`teamid` char(3) NOT NULL);
```

Commenting will be covered in more detail in Chapter 6, *Querying a Single Table*.

Understanding indexes

This section will take the reader through an explanation of what indexing is, how it relates to data integrity, and how it impacts performance.

Indexing is a method of optimizing database performance to boost the speed of database queries. Indexes are placed on column(s) in a table. Tables can have more than one index, but there tends to be an optimal number of indexes before indexes impair performance instead of helping it. The optimal number can vary depending on the table. This is why index tuning can be an art as well as a science. To properly index a table, you need an understanding of how to streamline the process of query results that are returned to a user.

It's good to plan out the indexing that you will need before adding data, if possible. When you add an index to an empty table, it adds it pretty much instantaneously. It can take quite a while to add an index later—depending on how much data you have in the table—because of the way that indexes may have to sort or add pointers to data.

Understanding how indexing relates to data integrity

Whenever you create a primary key, unique constraint, or foreign key, MySQL stores them as indexes. These indexes will be directly related to data integrity since they are related to keys and constraints that ensure data integrity. Not all indexes relate to data integrity, but the indexes created as part of primary keys, foreign keys, and unique constraints do.

Types of indexes

There are two types of indexes:

- **Clustered**: Clustered indexes store the data in order, so whatever columns you choose in a clustered index, that's the way the data will be sorted in a table. The data is stored physically on disk in the order of the clustered index. A clustered index can be viewed as a tree built on top of a table. The columns (key) that you place in the clustered index determines the order of the rows in the table. The following diagram shows an example of how a clustered index is structured:

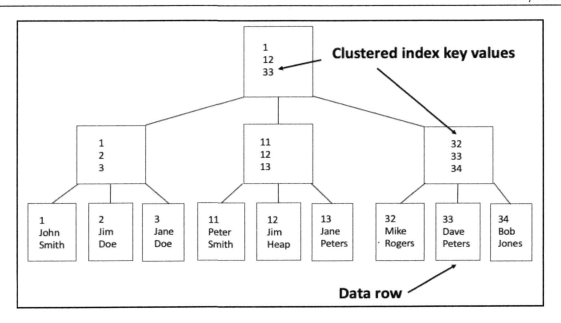

- **Non-clustered**: Nonclustered indexes don't sort the data. They instead use pointers to the physical data to quickly locate the data when the index is used to query data. You can have multiple nonclustered indexes on a table, but you need to be careful not to create too few or too many because your queries can be slowed down either way. The following diagram shows an example of how a nonclustered index is structured:

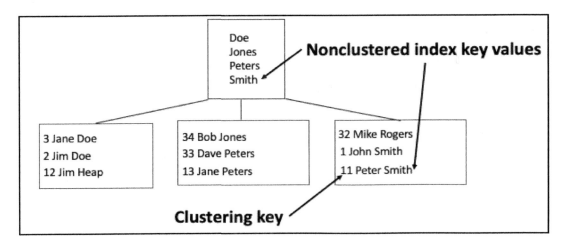

Looking back at the two tables that we created in the previous section, we can see that the primary key, foreign key, and unique constraints all have indexes associated with them, as shown in the following screenshot:

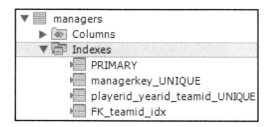

- The primary key (**PRIMARY** and **managerkey_UNIQUE**) will be your clustered index, and it will have the primary key field in ascending order in the table. This will be the **managerkey** for the managers.
- The unique key (**playerid_yearid_teamid_UNIQUE**) will be a nonclustered index. The unique key will enforce the uniqueness of the columns in the key, but it will also allow you to use the nonclustered index that exists as part of the unique key to speed up queries concerning those fields.
- The foreign key (**FK_teamid_idx**) will also be a nonclustered index. This will speed up queries when you query the field that is in the foreign key.

Further details regarding how you should use these fields in a query to speed up query performance can be found in the next section.

Understanding how indexing impacts performance

When you run a query, MySQL has to decide how to get the data from the table(s). If your table has no index, then the query will need to scan through the entire table to find the data in much the same way that you would have to scan through an entire book if it didn't have an index in the back. That would be very time-consuming, depending on how long the book is. The same thing goes for an index on a table. You might not notice any issue with your query running long if the table is small, but once the table is large, scanning the entire table to get the results could take quite a while. Plus, if other people are also running queries on the same table, then the results may never return since queries may block each other or deadlock.

Locking happens when you run a query. Locking isn't bad in and of itself, but it becomes an issue when different queries interfere with each other and cause blocking. Blocking happens when more than one query is trying to read or write the same data. Sometimes blocking happens, and it's just for a short period, so blocking isn't necessarily bad. If two or more queries are requesting the same data, creating locks that won't be resolved, then MySQL will decide which is easiest to kill (usually based on how long it will take to roll back any given query), and this is what is referred to as a deadlock. MySQL will need to roll back a query if it hasn't finished inserting, updating, or deleting data to keep the data in a consistent state. Rolling back, locking, blocking, and deadlocking will be discussed in greater detail in Chapter 11, *Advanced Querying Techniques*.

If you create indexes and use them properly with your queries, then you will have less blocking and deadlocking to deal with because the index will allow you to query data more quickly.

The main way that indexes can speed up a query is by using the columns in the index when joining tables, when filtering results (for example, **yearid** = 2017), and when ordering results (for example, order by year).

If we look back at the mangers table, we can see that we can use the unique index to query the managerid, teamid, and yearid. When I say *use the index*, it doesn't mean that you will specify the index in a query, but that MySQL will use the index when you write a query correctly. For example, if you want to get back the managerid, yearid, games, wins, and losses for the year 2017, you would build a query that searches the table for yearid = 2017. It could use the index that you created as part of the unique key, so instead of having to scan the entire table, it could search for a specific location in the read-only parts of the table.

In SQL Server, there is an additional way in which you can implement indexing using something called filtered indexes. This enables you to create an index that filters results in the index. As an example, if you only wanted to index one year of baseball data, then you could set the index to **yearid** = 2018, and it will then filter the index accordingly.

Here are some important things to note regarding indexing:

- Indexing doesn't speed up everything that happens in a database table. It won't speed up writes (the inserting, updating, and deleting of data). It only speeds up reading (querying data from the database), so you need to be careful that you don't add an index for reads that then slows down writes too much. Indexing slows down writes because the index has to be updated each time data is written.

- The order of the columns in indexes matters. If you wanted to sort your query data only on `yearid`, but your index is ordered by `managerid` and then `yearid`, then your query won't be as performant. If you need to sort using `yearid` most of the time, then you should have an index that has `yearid` as the first column in the index.

- Indexes can take up a lot of storage. A clustered index shouldn't take up space on disk since it's an ordering of the data already sitting on disk, but nonclustered indexes can take up quite a bit of room depending on the size of the table and the number of columns in the index.

- When adding columns, be careful that you don't have too many columns in your index. For instance, adding all of the columns in your table to an index won't make it faster, especially if the table has many columns. If your table only has a few columns, then adding them all to an index may be a correct implementation.

- Indexing columns that contain a lot of non-unique values may not provide much performance improvement. If you have to decide which columns you need to index, choose a column with more variability in its values, such as first names as opposed to state names.

In `Chapter 6`, *Querying a Single Table*, and `Chapter 7`, *Querying Multiple Tables*, we will go over how to see what indexes your query is using and how to change your query to ensure that you are getting the best performance you can have.

Understanding naming conventions for indexes

When naming indexes, much the same as naming other database objects, it's important to name them so that they are descriptive enough that you can easily see what they are indexing.

As we can see from the keys that we created for the `managers` table, they tend to get default names. We changed the ones that needed more descriptive naming. The `PRIMARY` key naming isn't changeable in MySQL.

When adding an index, you should name it so that you can tell what kind of index it is and what columns are in the index. The naming of indexes will be similar to the naming conventions for naming database objects that we looked at earlier in this chapter. The most important thing is to pick a naming convention and stick to it.

The big difference with indexing is that it's good to include a prefix (or suffix) in the name describing what it's for. The following table gives some suggestions for naming indexes:

Sample index name	What it contains
cix_firstname_lastname	Clustered index of first and last names
ix_firstname_lastname	Nonclustered index of first and last names
ncix_firstname_lastname	Nonclustered index of first and last names
idx_firstname_lastname	Nonclustered index of first and last names

By now, you should have developed a good understanding of indexing and its types.

Summary

This chapter covered how to design and create a database. We discussed the guidelines regarding naming conventions, understanding SQL code errors, formatting SQL code for readability, and how to apply data types and integrity to your tables.

You learned about the types of table relationships, including one-to-one, one-to-many, and many-to-many relationships. You also learned about entity relationship diagrams, including how to create them and how to understand table relationships in them.

We also discussed indexing, and learned about what it is, how to use it, and what it means for database performance. We also went through the steps of creating a database and table using MySQL Workbench and SQL scripts.

In the next chapter, you will be introduced to importing and exporting data. There are many ways to import and export data in MySQL. You will learn how to import and export data via MySQL Workbench using Table Data, SQL Data, and Result Data. You will also learn how to import and export data via SQL syntax.

Further reading

For more information:

- For more information on SQL Server, visit `https://docs.microsoft.com/en-us/sql/t-sql/lesson-1-creating-database-objects?view=sql-server-ver15`.
- For more information on Oracle, visit `;https://docs.oracle.com/en/database/oracle/oracle-database/18/cncpt/tables-and-table-clusters.html#GUID-F845B1A7-71E3-4312-B66D-BC16C198ECE5`.
- For more information on PostgreSQL, visit `https://www.postgresql.org/docs/11/ddl-basics.htm`.
- For more information on filtered indexes, visit `https://docs.microsoft.com/en-us/sql/relational-databases/indexes/create-filtered-indexes?view=sql-server-ver15`. In PostgreSQL, this is called a partial index. For more information on this, visit `https://www.postgresql.org/docs/11/indexes-partial.html`.

Questions

1. What things should you avoid when naming database objects?
2. What characters are allowed when naming database objects?
3. What is the SQL syntax to create a new database?
4. Where can you find SQL error codes in MySQL Workbench?
5. What are natural and surrogate primary keys?
6. How do you make a single-line comment?
7. How do you make a multiline comment?
8. What's the difference between a clustered and a nonclustered index?
9. What is deadlocking?
10. Does the order of columns in an index matter?

5
Importing and Exporting Data

This chapter introduces you to importing and exporting data. There are many ways to import and export data in MySQL. You will learn how to import and export data from and to **comma-separated values (CSV)** files using MySQL Workbench via table data. We will also cover importing and exporting via **Structured Query Language (SQL)** data with SQL scripts. An additional way to export data via result data and query results will also be covered. The final topic discussed is using SQL syntax to import and export data.

In this chapter, we will cover the following topics:

- Understanding table data import and export
- Understanding SQL data import and export
- Understanding result data export
- Understanding SQL syntax for importing and exporting data

Technical requirements

The code files of this chapter can be found at the following GitHub link: `https://github.com/PacktPublishing/learn-sql-database-programming/tree/master/chapter-5`.

The CSV files required for this chapter can be found on the following GitHub link: `https://github.com/PacktPublishing/learn-sql-database-programming/tree/master/baseballdatabank-csv/csv-files`.

Understanding table data import and export

In this section, you will learn how to import and export data with the table data import and export processes in MySQL Workbench. Table data import and export allows you to import and export both CSV and **JavaScript Object Notation (JSON)** files via MySQL Workbench. It provides you with many configuration options—for example, column separator types such as a comma or a semicolon—and it allows you to map columns in the file to columns in the table.

Importing CSV files with table data import

Using the database (schema) and the tables you created in the last chapter, we will add data to those tables via table data import. I named that schema `yourschema`, so the directions will reflect that naming convention. Swap out that name for whatever name you called your database. We will be using the GitHub CSV files that are referenced in the *Technical requirements* section of this chapter. Follow these steps:

1. Open **MySQL Workbench**.
2. Connect to your `local` or `dev/test` instance where you created your database in the last chapter.
3. Open the database you created in the previous chapter (`yourschema`, in the following example) by clicking the down arrow.
4. Open **Tables** by clicking the down arrow.
5. Right-click the table you want to import data into and choose the **Table Data Import Wizard** option. In this step, we will be using the **teams** table and the `teams.csv` file since **teams** has a foreign key to managers (in that managers rely on a key in the **teams** table). The following screenshot shows the selection of **Table Data Import Wizard** on the **teams** table:

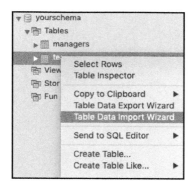

6. As shown in the following screenshot, browse to the path of the `teams.csv` file, then click **Next >**. This file is in the GitHub repository you downloaded in the *Technical requirements* section of this chapter. Use the **Browse...** button to navigate to the file so that the wizard will apply the correct path with slashes or backslashes, depending on your operating system. The following screenshot path shows a Mac path to files:

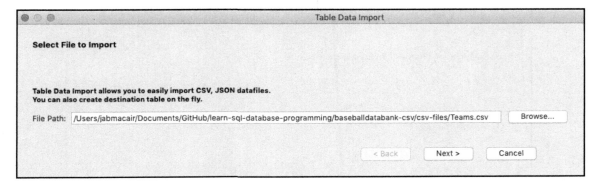

7. On the next screen, leave the default of **Use existing table** selected, then proceed as follows:

   - If the table already exists and you don't want to keep the data that exists in it, choose **Truncate table before import**. Since this table is empty already, we don't need to truncate, as shown in the following screenshot:

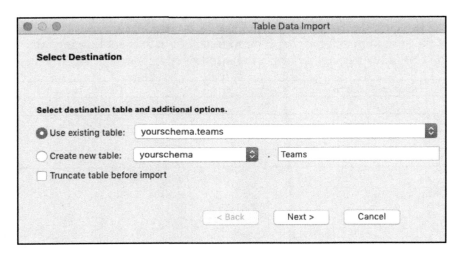

- If the table didn't already exist, you can choose **Create new table**. This will also give you the option to drop the table if it already exists, as shown in the following screenshot:

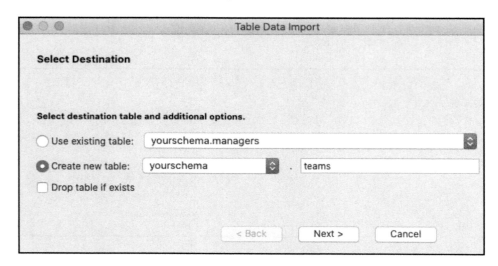

8. After clicking **Next >** in the previous step, you will see a listing of all the columns in the CSV file. Since we don't want to import most of them into the **teams** table, first click the **Source Column** checkbox to unselect all the fields in the CSV file, then select the fields you want to import that have existing columns in the table. If you were creating a table instead of populating an existing table, it would create the columns for you. Also, make sure to map the source columns to the existing columns in the table. The following table shows the **Source Column** (the columns in the CSV file) and the **Dest Column** (the columns in the MySQL table). Make sure to match the mapping to that shown in the following table to ensure the CSV data is correctly imported into the table:

Source Column	Dest Column
yearID	yearid
lgID	leagueid
teamID	teamid
Rank	teamrank

The following screenshot shows you the right configuration for the **Configure Import Settings** setting. Click **Next >**:

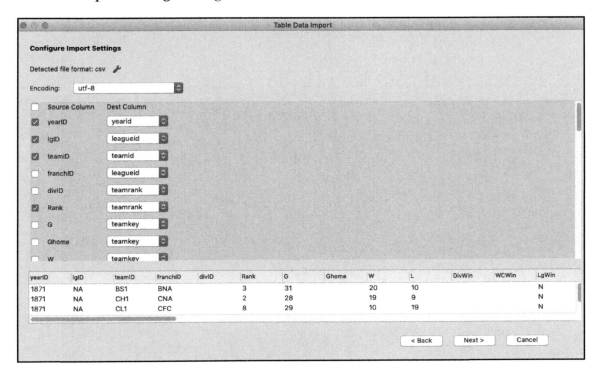

9. If you are creating a table from the CSV file, you will instead need to choose the data types for the columns instead of mapping the CSV columns to the table columns, as shown in the following screenshot (note that you don't get as many choices of data types when importing to a new table, so it's recommended to create the table first with the data types you want, and then import the CSV file to the existing table):

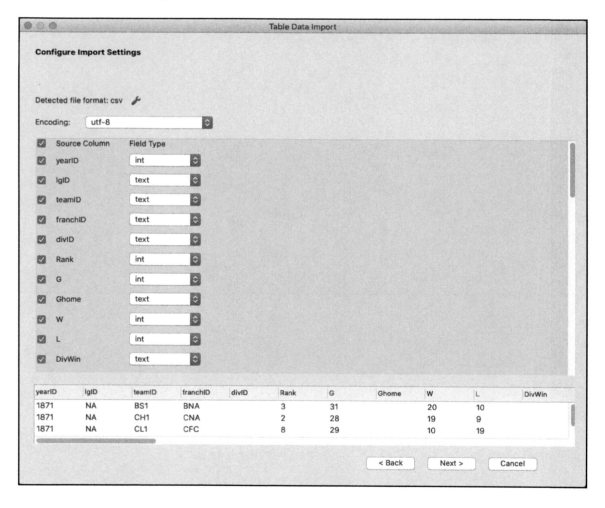

10. On the next screen, review the information and click **Next >**, as illustrated in the following screenshot:

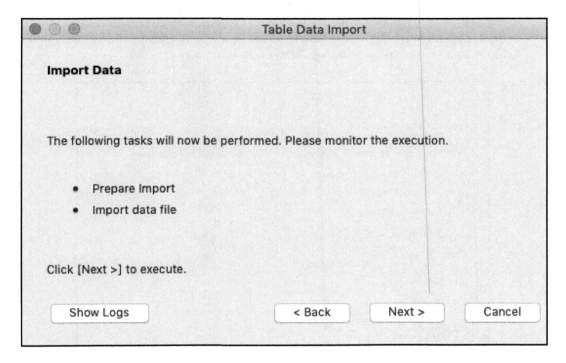

11. When it's finished (it will show progress as it's completing and green check marks next to the task when it's done), click **Next >**. If you want or need to view the logs, click the **Show Logs** button. The logs can help you determine the kind of error that happened if an error occurs. You can also click **Show Logs** (shown in the preceding screenshot) while it's in progress if you want to see the current process as it executes, as shown in the following screenshot:

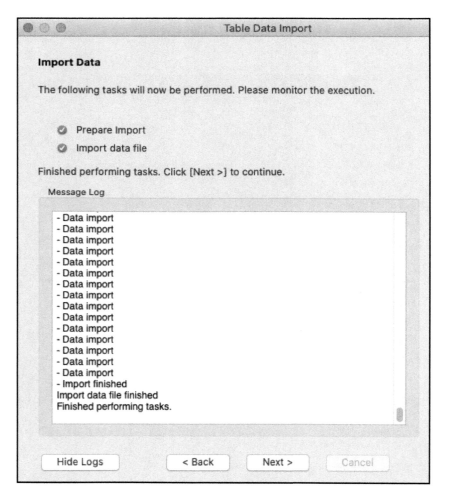

12. Once you are done reviewing the logs or don't need to review the logs, click **Next >**.

13. Click **Finish** to exit the **Table Data Import Wizard** feature.

   If you select from the **teams** table, as shown in the following screenshot, you will see that the data has been imported:

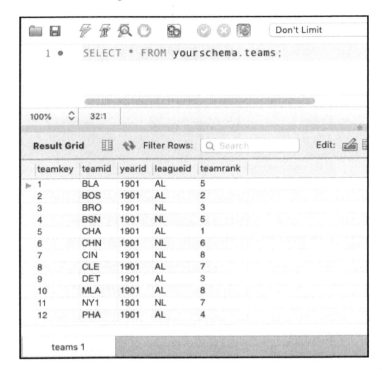

You can follow the same steps to import the **managers** table data from the CSV file.

Exporting to CSV files with table data export

Using the **teams** table that you imported data into in the last section, let's walk through how to export data via the **Table Data Export Wizard** feature, as follows:

1. Open **MySQL Workbench**.
2. Connect to your `local` or `dev/test` instance where you created your database in the last chapter.
3. Open the database that you created in the previous chapter by clicking the down arrow.

4. Open **Tables** by clicking the down arrow.

5. Right-click the **teams** table and choose **Table Data Export Wizard**, as shown in the following screenshot:

6. This will bring you to the **Select data for export** box. This is where you can select which columns to export, how many rows to offset, and the count of the rows exported. If you choose **Row Offset: 500** and **Count: 1000**, as shown in the following screenshot, the results exported will start at row 500 and include 1,000 rows:

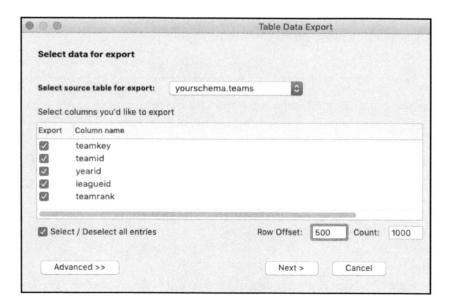

7. If you click **Advanced >>**, you can see the following associated query, or write your own query to export data and click on **Next >**:

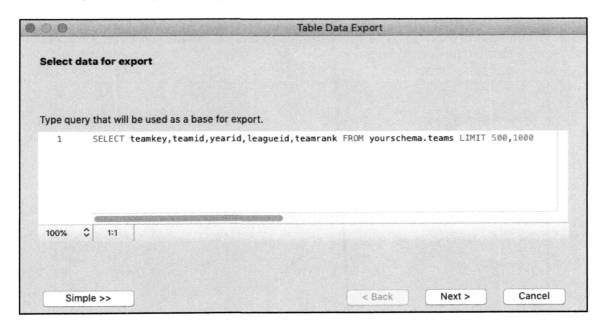

8. The next screen will allow you to select the file location, the file type (**csv** or **json**), a **Line Separator** option, an **Enclose Strings in** option, a **Field Separator** option, and a **null and NULL word as SQL keyword** option. There may also be an option for **Export to local machine**. Choose the file path, and you can leave the rest of the fields with the default values. Click on **Next >**. For the **csv** option, you have this configuration:

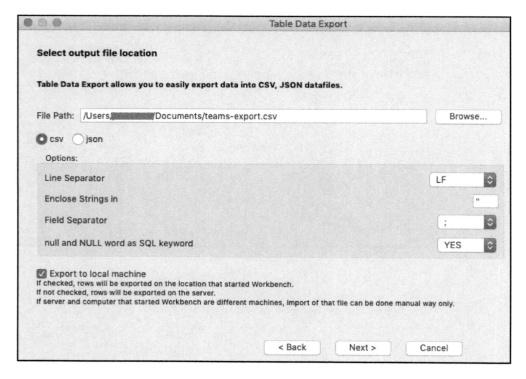

For the **json** option, you have this configuration:

9. On the next screen, review the execution information and click **Next >**.
10. When it's finished (it will show progress as it's completing and green check marks next to the task when it's done), click **Next >**.

10. The next screen will display the results of the export. Click **Finish**.

When you open the CSV file, you can see in the following screenshot that it starts with row 500 and contains 1,000 rows:

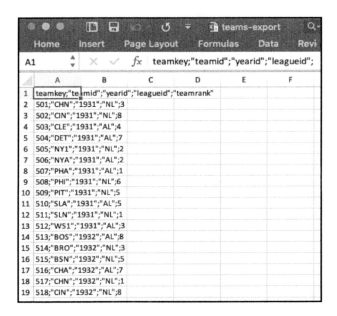

When you open the JSON file, you can see in the following screenshot that it begins with row 500 and contains 1,000 rows:

```
teams.json
[{"teamkey":501, "yearID":1908, "lgID":"NL", "teamID":"CIN", "Rank":5},
 {"teamkey":502, "yearID":1908, "lgID":"AL", "teamID":"CLE", "Rank":2},
 {"teamkey":503, "yearID":1908, "lgID":"AL", "teamID":"DET", "Rank":1},
 {"teamkey":504, "yearID":1908, "lgID":"NL", "teamID":"NY1", "Rank":2},
 {"teamkey":505, "yearID":1908, "lgID":"AL", "teamID":"NYA", "Rank":8},
 {"teamkey":506, "yearID":1908, "lgID":"AL", "teamID":"PHA", "Rank":6},
 {"teamkey":507, "yearID":1908, "lgID":"NL", "teamID":"PHI", "Rank":4},
 {"teamkey":508, "yearID":1908, "lgID":"NL", "teamID":"PIT", "Rank":2},
 {"teamkey":509, "yearID":1908, "lgID":"AL", "teamID":"SLA", "Rank":4},
 {"teamkey":510, "yearID":1908, "lgID":"NL", "teamID":"SLN", "Rank":8},
 {"teamkey":511, "yearID":1908, "lgID":"AL", "teamID":"WS1", "Rank":7},
 {"teamkey":512, "yearID":1909, "lgID":"AL", "teamID":"BOS", "Rank":3},
 {"teamkey":513, "yearID":1909, "lgID":"NL", "teamID":"BRO", "Rank":6},
 {"teamkey":514, "yearID":1909, "lgID":"NL", "teamID":"BSN", "Rank":8},
 {"teamkey":515, "yearID":1909, "lgID":"AL", "teamID":"CHA", "Rank":4},
 {"teamkey":516, "yearID":1909, "lgID":"NL", "teamID":"CHN", "Rank":2},
 {"teamkey":517, "yearID":1909, "lgID":"NL", "teamID":"CIN", "Rank":4},
 {"teamkey":518, "yearID":1909, "lgID":"AL", "teamID":"CLE", "Rank":6},
 {"teamkey":519, "yearID":1909, "lgID":"AL", "teamID":"DET", "Rank":1},
 {"teamkey":520, "yearID":1909, "lgID":"NL", "teamID":"NY1", "Rank":3},
```

You can change the options for how it exports the data. For instance, if you want comma-separated values instead of semicolon-separated values between columns on your CSV file, change the **Field Separator** value when exporting, as in the following screenshot:

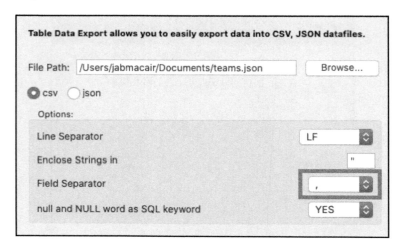

Table Data Export allows you to easily export data into CSV, JSON datafiles.

File Path: `/Users/jabmacair/Documents/teams.json` | Browse...

⦿ csv ◯ json

Options:

Line Separator	LF
Enclose Strings in	"
Field Separator	,
null and NULL word as SQL keyword	YES

You can also enclose the strings in a different character instead of double quotes, as well as change the line separator.

Understanding SQL data import and export

In this section, we will walk through how to import and export data with the SQL data import and export processes in MySQL Workbench.

Importing via data import in MySQL Workbench

Let's walk through how to import data via the **Management** or **Administration** tab in the left navigation area. This is what we did in Chapter 2, *Installing and Using MySQL Workbench*, in the *Learning how to restore a database* section. Importing using data import is the same process as restoring a database in MySQL Workbench. Follow these steps:

1. Open **MySQL Workbench**.
2. Connect to your `local` or `dev/test` instance where you created your database in the last chapter.

3. Click **Administration** or **Management** (depending on whether you are using a Mac or a PC) in the navigation panel on the left side of MySQL Workbench.

4. Click **Data Import/Restore**, shown in the following screenshot. Clicking this will bring up the **Data Import** tab:

5. Navigate to the location that you just exported to in the previous section. This will load the folder's contents into the bottom part of the tab, as illustrated in the following screenshot:

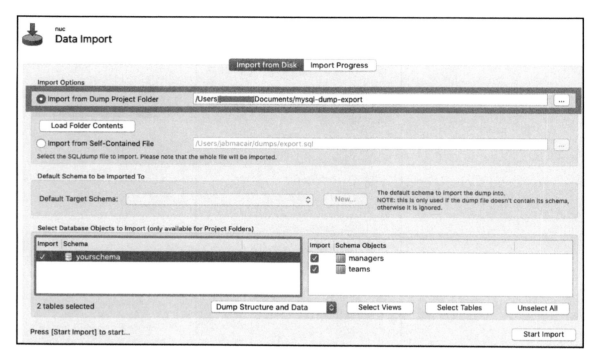

6. Click **New...** under **Default Target Schema:** and name it **newschema**. This will create a new database with the imported schema objects.

7. Click on the schema listed under the **Schema** area. This will then populate the **Schema Objects** panel. There should be two tables checked in this panel.

8. Keep the default option of **Dump Structure and Data**, as shown in the following screenshot, then click **Start Import**:

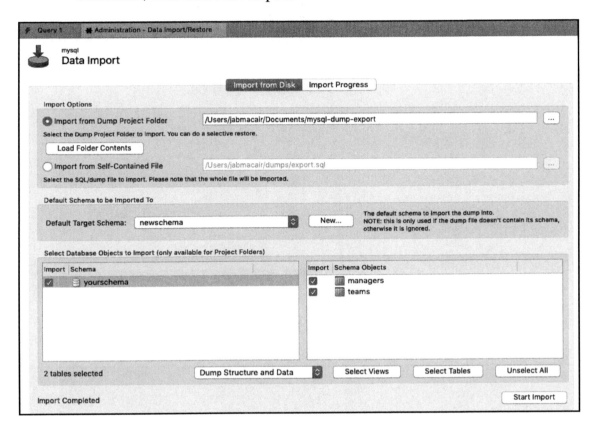

9. The **Import Progress** tab will show you the progress of the import and when it's completed.

Refresh the schema list. You will see that the tables weren't imported into the new schema because the old schema exists, and the old schema is associated with the exported (dump) files. In other words, it imported (or restored) over the existing schema. If the database didn't already exist, it would create a new database and populate it with the objects you selected in the preceding steps.

Additionally, you can just dump the structure of particular objects, as in the following screenshot:

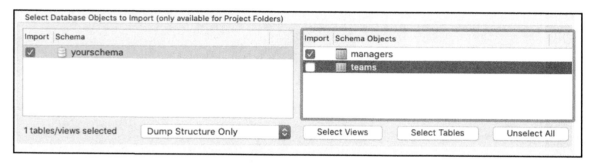

You can also dump only the data of particular objects, as in the following screenshot:

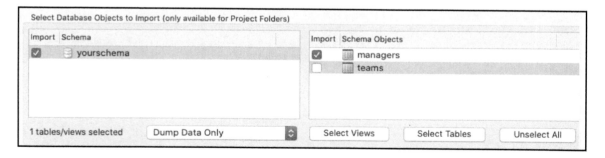

Also, you can import data from a self-contained SQL file. With this option, you can specify which objects you want to be imported. The process will just import everything in the SQL file, as shown in the following screenshot:

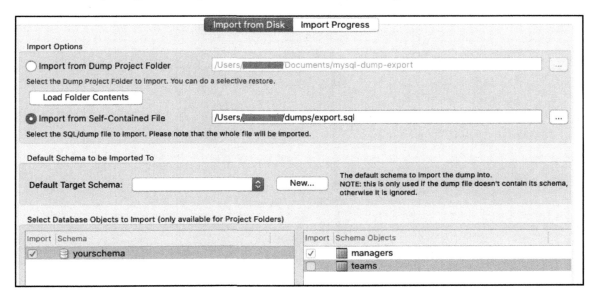

The import process has many options and is quite powerful to use when you need to import data.

Exporting via data export in MySQL Workbench

Let's walk through how to export data via the **Management** or **Administration** tab in the left navigation area, as follows:

1. Open **MySQL Workbench**.
2. Connect to your `local` or `dev/test` instance where you created your database in the last chapter.

3. Click **Administration** or **Management** (depending on whether you are using a Mac or a PC) in the navigation panel on the left side of MySQL Workbench.

4. Click the **Data Export** option highlighted in the following screenshot:

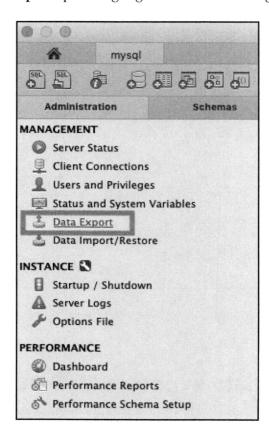

5. This will open a **Data Export** tab, and allows you to export any number of databases and tables in those databases. Also, you can choose to dump (export) the data; the data and the structure; or just the structure of the objects you want to export. You can also choose how the files are created, either into a folder where each object has its own script or as one script that contains all the objects you want to export. For this export, you will choose just the two tables we created together in the last chapter, with their data exported to a folder on your local machine, as shown in the following screenshot:

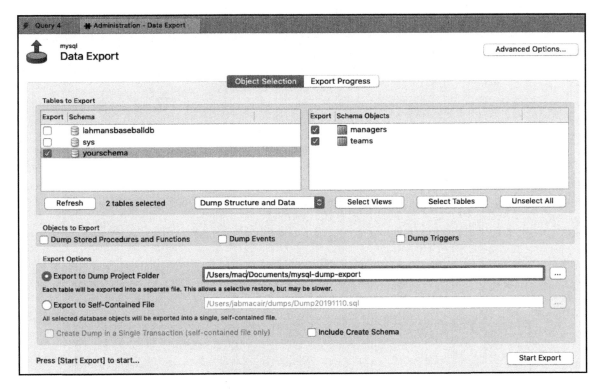

6. Click **Start Export** after choosing the settings for your export.

7. The **Export Progress** screen will show you the progress and let you know when it is complete, as illustrated in the following screenshot:

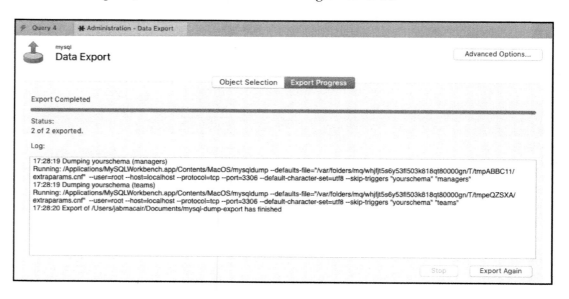

Much the same as the information outlined in the *Importing via data import in MySQL Workbench* section, you can choose to export only data, structure, or both for one or more objects. You can also export to a self-contained file instead of a dump folder.

In the following screenshot, you will now see files in the folder to which you exported. MySQL Workbench will export them as .sql files. You should have one for each table we selected when following the preceding steps:

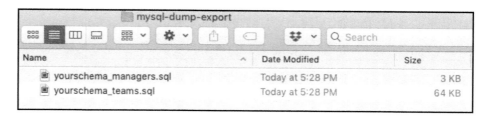

The .sql files will have the script to recreate the tables and insert data if the table contained any data.

Understanding result data export

In this section, we will walk through how to export data with the result data export process in MySQL Workbench. It's best to use the two previous sections to import data, table data, and SQL data, because importing isn't available via a result set in MySQL Workbench.

Exporting data directly from a result set

Let's walk through how to export data directly from a result set, as follows:

1. Open **MySQL Workbench**.
2. Connect to your `local` or `dev/test` instance where you created your database in the last chapter.
3. Expand the `yourschema` database with the down arrow and expand the tables with the down arrow, as illustrated in the following screenshot:

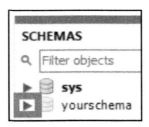

4. Right-click the **teams** table and choose the **Select Rows** option, as illustrated in the following screenshot:

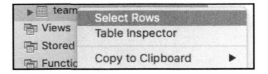

5. On the results of the query shown as follows, click the **Export recordset to an external file** button:

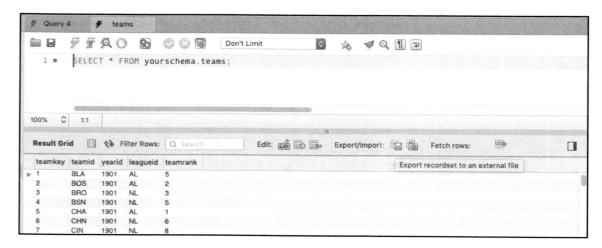

6. Choose a location to save the CSV file. You can also choose other file types from the **Format:** drop-down field shown in the following screenshot if you want to save it in another file format. Then, click on **Save**:

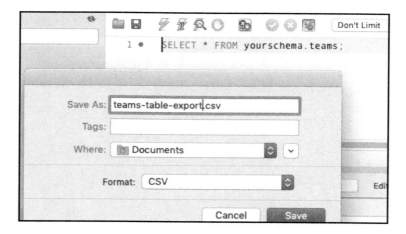

This will save the CSV file to disk with whatever data was returned from the query you executed.

Understanding SQL syntax for importing and exporting data

To import and export data via SQL scripts, the `--secure_file_priv` option must be properly configured. The `secure_file_priv` option may be disabled by default, or it may require you to place your file in a specific folder. You may be able to change this setting on your local instance, but you most likely won't have this level of permissions on a server, especially in a production environment.

Be VERY careful if you decide to change the `ini` **file on your local instance of MySQL.** The `ini` file contains essential configuration information required to run MySQL Server. You can damage the MySQL installation, for which the only solution may be to uninstall and reinstall MySQL. **Do not make any** `ini` **file changes on a server** without consulting a system or database administrator.

To check the `secure_file_priv` configuration, execute the following script:

```
select @@secure_file_priv
```

Depending on the results you receive with the previous query, you may need to reconfigure the `secure-file-priv` option to run the scripts in the following sections. For more information on `secure-file-priv`, visit the *Further reading* section.

Importing with a SQL script

To import with a SQL script, you can run this code:

```
LOAD DATA INFILE '/pathtoyourfiles/baseballdatabank-csv/csv-
files/Teams.csv'
INTO TABLE yourschema.teams
FIELDS TERMINATED BY ',';
```

Once the import is done, you can select the rows from the **teams** table to see the rows, as shown in the following screenshot:

teamkey	teamid	yearid	leagueid	teamrank
1	BLA	1901	AL	5
2	BOS	1901	AL	2
3	BRO	1901	NL	3
4	BSN	1901	NL	5
5	CHA	1901	AL	1
6	CHN	1901	NL	6
7	CIN	1901	NL	8
8	CLE	1901	AL	7
9	DET	1901	AL	3
10	MLA	1901	AL	8
11	NY1	1901	NL	7
12	PHA	1901	AL	4
13	PHI	1901	NL	2

As long as your `secure-file-priv` option is not disabled, your script will import data into the **managers** table.

If you want more details on LOAD DATA, visit the *Further reading* section.

Exporting with a SQL script

To import with a SQL script, you can run this code:

```
SELECT * INTO OUTFILE 'teams-export.csv'
  FIELDS TERMINATED BY ';' OPTIONALLY ENCLOSED BY '"'
  LINES TERMINATED BY '\n'
  FROM yourschema.teams;
```

When your export is done, you will have a CSV file on disk that will look like the following screenshot when it's opened:

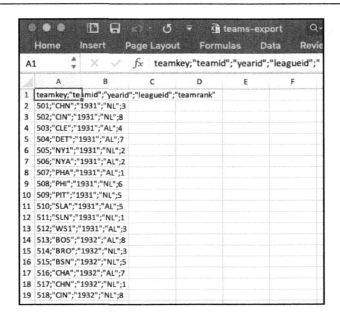

As long as your `secure-file-priv` option is not disabled, your script will appear in the folder configured in `secure-file-priv`.

Summary

In this chapter, you were introduced to importing and exporting data. You learned how to import and export data with the table data import and export functionality in MySQL Workbench. You also learned how to import and export data with the SQL data import and export functionality in MySQL Workbench. In the *Understanding result data export* section, you learned how to export data directly from MySQL Workbench. Finally, you learned how to use SQL syntax to import data with LOAD DATA INFILE, and how to export data with SELECT INTO OUTFILE.

In the next chapter, you will learn how to query a single table. This includes learning how to use the SQL SELECT statement, and FROM, WHERE, and ORDER BY clauses. This will also include how to tell which index your query is using and if you may need additional indexes.

Further reading

For more information, see the following list:

- Refer to this link for more information on the `secure-file-priv` option: `https://dev.mysql.com/doc/refman/8.0/en/server-system-variables.html#sysvar_secure_file_priv`
- Refer to this link for more details on `LOAD DATA` syntax: `https://dev.mysql.com/doc/refman/5.7/en/load-data.html`
- Refer to this link to learn more about importing and exporting in SQL Server: `https://docs.microsoft.com/en-us/sql/integration-services/import-export-data/start-the-sql-server-import-and-export-wizard?view=sql-server-ver15`
- Refer to this link to learn more about importing and exporting in PostgreSQL: `https://www.postgresql.org/docs/11/sql-copy.html`
- Refer to this link to learn more about importing and exporting in Oracle: `https://docs.oracle.com/en/cloud/saas/applications-common/19c/oafsm/manage-setup-using-csv-file-packages.html#OAFSM3573446`

Questions

1. What are the different ways that you can import and export data in MySQL Workbench?
2. How do you import data with the **Table Data Import Wizard** feature?
3. How do you ensure you accurately map columns with the **Table Data Import Wizard** feature?
4. How do you export data with the **Table Data Import Wizard** feature?
5. How do you import data with the **SQL data import wizard** feature?
6. How do you export data with the **SQL Data Import Wizard** feature?
7. How do you export data with result data export?
8. What SQL syntax do you use to import data?
9. What SQL syntax do you use to export data?
10. What MySQL `ini` file setting will prevent you from being able to use SQL scripts to import and export data?

Section 2: Basic SQL Querying 2

Now that you have learned how to create a database and its tables, imported some data, and restored a database, you will learn how to query a single table, query multiple tables, and modify the data in them.

This section comprises the following chapters:

- Chapter 6, *Querying a Single Table*
- Chapter 7, *Querying Multiple Tables*
- Chapter 8, *Modifying Data and Table Structures*

6
Querying a Single Table

In this chapter, you will learn how to query a single table. This includes learning how to use the SQL SELECT statement and the FROM, WHERE, and ORDER BY clauses. You will also learn how to tell which index your query is using and if you may need additional indexes. By the end of this chapter, you will be able to understand how to query data using the SELECT statement and the FROM clause. You will also learn how to limit the results with a WHERE clause, how to use an ORDER BY clause to return results in a specified order, and how to see information about what indexes are being used or may be needed.

In this chapter, we will cover the following topics:

- Using the SELECT statement and FROM clause
- Using the WHERE clause
- Using the ORDER BY clause
- Using indexes with your queries

Let's get started!

Technical requirements

The code files for this chapter can be found at the following GitHub link: https://github.com/PacktPublishing/learn-sql-database-programming/tree/master/chapter-6.

Using the SELECT statement and FROM clause

To extract data from a table, you need to use a SQL SELECT query. The SELECT query allows you to specify what data you want from a table using a simple query structure.

Understanding the SELECT statement and the FROM clause

At a minimum, every SELECT statement on a table needs the SELECT and FROM keywords. If you want to select all the rows and columns from the appearances table in lahmansbaseballdb, you should execute the following query:

```
SELECT * FROM lahmansbaseballdb.appearances;
```

 Make sure to add a semicolon (;) to the end of your SQL statements. The semicolon marks the end of a query. The query may execute without it, but it is good practice to ensure that the SQL code will execute properly.

This query will give you the results shown in the following screenshot:

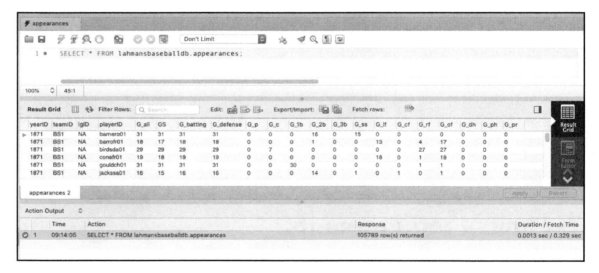

What we are telling MySQL when we execute the preceding query is to select everything from the appearances table.

 When writing SQL statements, keywords such as SELECT and FROM (and any other keywords) don't have to be capitalized, but it can make it easier to read the SQL statements if they are. For example, SELECT * FROM lahmansbaseballdb.appearances is the same as select * from lahmansbaseballdb.appearances.

Learning the correct order of other clauses you can use with SELECT

When writing a SELECT statement, you need to place the keywords in the correct order for the query to work right. For instance, you can't place the FROM keyword in front of the SELECT statement and get results:

```
FROM SELECT * lahmansbaseballdb.allstarfull;
```

If you execute the previous query, you will get an error such as Error Code: 1064. You have an error in your SQL syntax; check the manual that corresponds to your MySQL server version for the right syntax to use near FROM SELECT * lahmansbaseballdb.allstarfull at line 1.

Understanding the different ways to query with a SELECT statement

Generally, you should select the minimum amount of data that you need from a table. When selecting data from a table, you can retrieve a single column, multiple columns, or all columns.

Avoid using SELECT * in a query. Since this selects all columns in a table, it is considered more expensive than if you specify the columns you need. Expensive means that it takes more server resources to return your query results, and when you have many queries executing on a server, you want them to use the minimum resources required.

To retrieve data from just one column, execute the following query:

```
SELECT playerid FROM lahmansbaseballdb.appearances;
```

The preceding query will give the results displayed in the following screenshot. As you can see, only the playerid column is in the results, and the results still include the total number of rows in the table, just like when we use SELECT *:

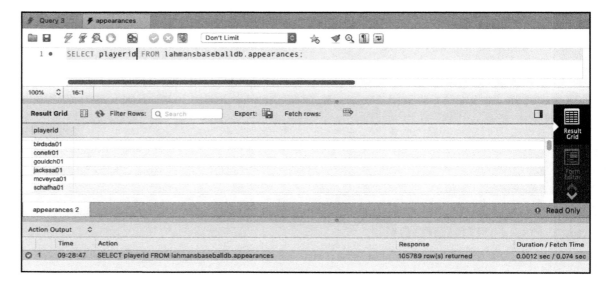

If you want to return multiple columns of all the rows in a table, you should execute this query:

```
SELECT playerid, g_all, g_batting, g_defense FROM
lahmansbaseballdb.appearances;
```

The preceding query will give the results displayed in the following screenshot. As you can see, the playerid, g_11, g_batting, and g_defense columns are in the results, and the results still include the total number of rows in the table, just like when we use SELECT *:

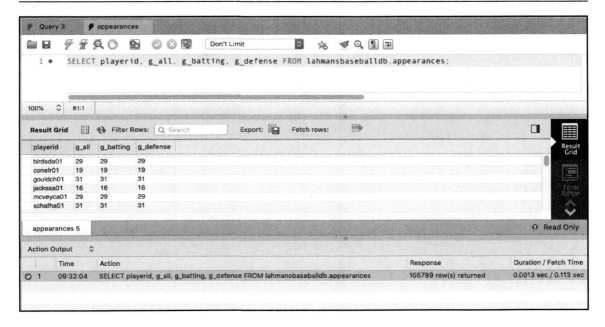

When writing SQL statements, you can place different statements on different lines and give them different spacing, and it won't affect the execution of the script. Just don't put spaces or line breaks in SQL keywords.

For example, this script executes the same as the following script:

```
SELECT playerid FROM lahmansbaseballdb. appearances;
```

The following script executes the same as the previous script:

```
SELECT playerid
FROM lahmansbaseballdb.appearances;
```

However, the following script produces an error because there is a break in the SQL keyword:

```
SEL
ECT playerid FROM lahmansbaseballdb.appearances;
```

Formatting SQL code for readability is essential when you are writing a longer script, if you need to reuse the script, or if you need to share the script with others. With this simple script, it may not seem important, but it is always good to maintain an easily readable SQL format.

You don't have to capitalize SQL keywords such as SELECT and FROM, but it helps the readability of the code. For example, SELECT playerid FROM lahmansbaseballdb. appearances produces the same query results as select playerid from lahmansbaseballdb. appearances. I tend to write in all lowercase because it's faster, but it's important to put in the proper whitespace characters so that the code is still readable, as shown in the following example:

```
select playerid
from lahmansbaseballdb. appearances
```

Learning how to use column aliases

Column aliases allow you to assign a different name to a column in your query. You might be able to see that the columns haven't been named descriptively enough in the original table, or maybe you just want to name them differently in your query results. For example, the g_defense and H columns in the batting table may not be descriptive enough for you to understand what they mean in your results if you aren't familiar with baseball. We can make an alias for these column's names to make them more descriptive, as shown in the following query:

```
SELECT playerid,
       G_defense AS GamesPlayingDefense
FROM lahmansbaseballdb.appearances;
```

In the previous query, we added an alias to one of the columns, as shown in the following code snippet:

```
G_defense AS GamesPlayingDefense
```

The AS clause is optional, and the following code snippet will run the same as the previous code snippet:

```
G_defense GamesPlayingDefense
```

The previous query will give the results shown in the following screenshot:

playerid	GamesPlayingDefense
aardsda01	1
aardsda01	11
aardsda01	25
aardsda01	33
aardsda01	43
aardsda01	45
aardsda01	47
aardsda01	53
aardsda01	73
aaronha01	1
aaronha01	89

You can see that the column headings in the query results match the aliases used in the query instead of the table column name, so `GamesPlayingDefense` shows instead of `G_defense`.

You can use a space in an alias name as long as you use quotes around the alias name. This allows you to place spaces in the alias names, as shown in the following code snippet:

```
G_defense 'Games Playing Defense'
```

This will produce the results shown in the following screenshot:

playerid	Games Playing Defense
aardsda01	1
aardsda01	11
aardsda01	25
aardsda01	33
aardsda01	43
aardsda01	45
aardsda01	47
aardsda01	53
aardsda01	73
aaronha01	1
aaronha01	89

The clauses where you can also use the column aliases are in the ORDER BY, GROUP BY, and HAVING clauses. You can't use column aliases in the WHERE clause. The WHERE and ORDER BY clauses will be covered in more detail later in this chapter. The GROUP BY and HAVING clauses will be covered in more detail in Chapter 10, *Grouping and Summarizing Data*.

Using the USE statement

Note that in the preceding queries, we are referencing the database in front of the table name, like so:

```
lahmansbaseballdb.appearances
```

Another way you can set the database name is by using a USE statement instead. This means that you wouldn't have to prefix the table name with the database name, but instead have a USE statement that sets the database at the top of the query, as shown in the following query:

```
USE lahmansbaseballdb;
SELECT playerid, g_all, g_batting, g_defense FROM appearances;
```

The preceding query will give you the same results as the following query:

```
SELECT playerid, g_all, g_batting, g_defense FROM
lahmansbaseballdb.appearances;
```

The USE statement will set the database name for all subsequent queries, or until another USE statement is used.

Learning how to use the DISTINCT clause

DISTINCT is a keyword that, when added to a SELECT statement, will return only distinct (or different) values within a column. Sometimes, you may want to see what values are contained in a column, and getting the distinct values will help you see this. For example, if you want to see the distinct player IDs in the appearances table, you should execute the following query:

```
USE lahmansbaseballdb;
SELECT DISTINCT playerid FROM appearances;
```

The following screenshot shows the results of the preceding query. Note that the rows returned are far fewer than in the previous section. This list only shows the distinct player IDs, and there are 19,429 of them:

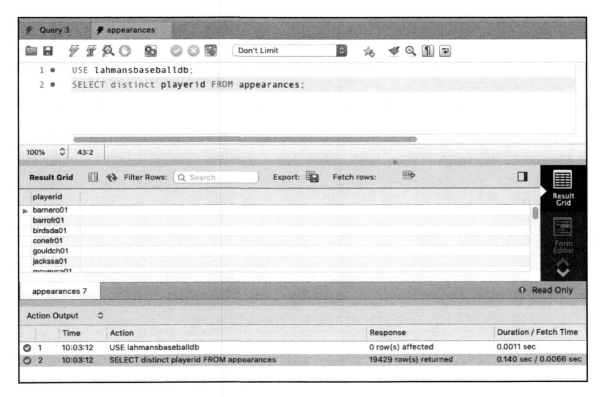

You can also select multiple columns in DISTINCT. For instance, if you want to select distinct teams and players on those teams, you can execute the following query:

```
USE lahmansbaseballdb;
SELECT DISTINCT teamid, playerid FROM appearances;
```

The previous query will give you the results shown in the following screenshot:

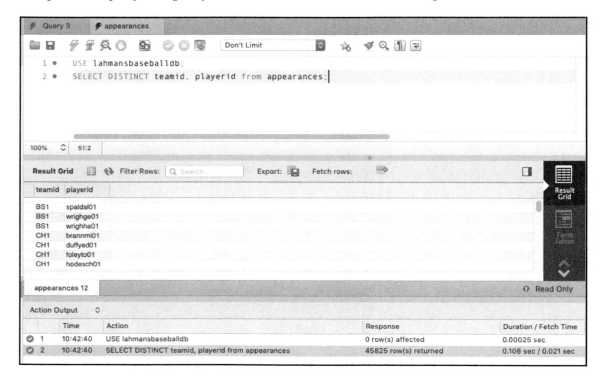

The previous screenshot shows that you are getting distinct teams and players on those teams and that 45,825 rows have been returned.

Learning how to use the LIMIT clause

LIMIT is a keyword that, when added to a SELECT statement, will return only a specified number of rows. Sometimes, you may want to see a cross-section of data, so the LIMIT clause, along with OFFSET, will help you accomplish this. For example, if you want to only see the first 500 rows in the appearances tables, you can execute this query:

```
USE lahmansbaseballdb;
SELECT playerid, g_all, g_batting, g_defense FROM appearances
LIMIT 500;
```

This query will return the first 500 rows with the specified columns in the `appearances` table, as shown in the following screenshot:

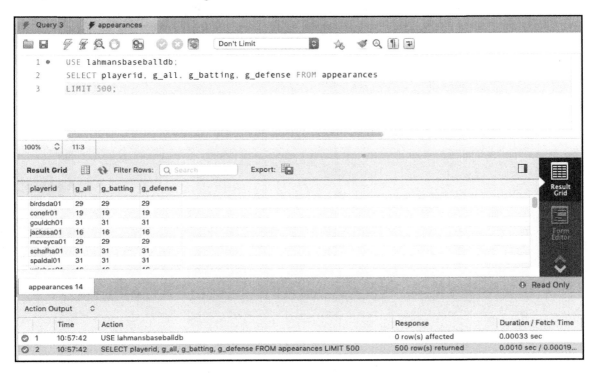

If you want to display the rows starting at a specific row and limit the count of rows returned from there, you can add the `OFFSET` clause to the query, as shown in the following example, which will retrieve 500 rows, starting at row 1,000:

```
USE lahmansbaseballdb;
SELECT playerid, g_all, g_batting, g_defense FROM appearances
LIMIT 500 OFFSET 1000;
```

In the following screenshot, you can see the results of the previous query. It returns 500 rows, but they show different results than the last query because we used the OFFSET clause:

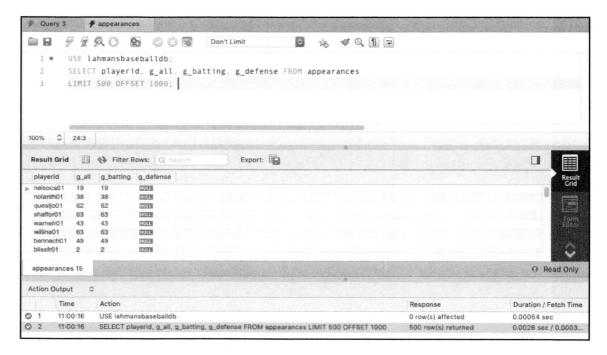

You aren't able to use OFFSET without the LIMIT clause.

Limiting results on other Relational Database Management Systems (RDMSes)

For **Oracle**, you can do the following:

You can limit rows as follows:

```
SELECT playerid, g_all, g_batting, g_defense FROM appearances
OFFSET 0 ROWS
FETCH NEXT 500 ROWS ONLY;
```

If you would also like to offset rows, you can execute the following query:

```
SELECT playerid, g_all, g_batting, g_defense FROM appearances
OFFSET 500 ROWS
FETCH NEXT 1000 ROWS ONLY;
```

There are a couple of ways you can limit rows returned in SQL Server. You can use TOP, as shown in the following query:

```
SELECT TOP 500 playerid, g_all, g_batting, g_defense
FROM appearances;
```

You can also limit rows like so:

```
SELECT playerid, g_all, g_batting, g_defense FROM appearances
ORDER BY playerid
OFFSET 0 ROWS
FETCH NEXT 500 ROWS ONLY;
```

If you would also like to offset rows, you can execute the following query:

```
SELECT playerid, g_all, g_batting, g_defense FROM appearances
ORDER BY playerid
OFFSET 500 ROWS
FETCH NEXT 1000 ROWS ONLY;
```

PostgreSQL works the same way as MySQL for limiting rows.

Learning how to save a SQL query to a file

In this section, we will learn how to save a SQL query to a file. The following steps will help you save a file:

1. To save a SQL query to a file, click the save button in MySQL Workbench. The following screenshot shows the save button:

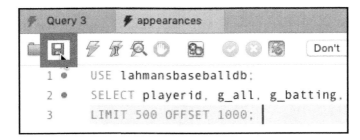

2. Once you've clicked the save button, you will be prompted to save it to a location on disk. Name the file and choose a location for the file and click **Save**, as shown in the following screenshot:

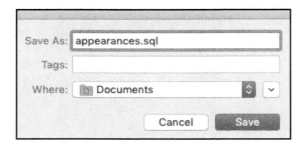

When you have multiple SQL queries in one SQL file, and you want to execute just one of the queries, you can highlight that query and then click the run (lightning bolt) button to run just that one query:

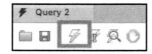

To stop a query when it's running, click the stop button:

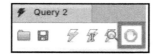

Learning how to open a SQL file

Follow these steps to learn how to open a SQL file:

1. To open a SQL query from a file, click the open button in MySQL Workbench. The following screenshot shows the open button with a red box around it:

2. After clicking the open button, you will be shown a dialog box so that you can navigate to the file you want to open.

You can also open a SQL file from a SQL file tab that is already open. To do so, click the folder icon, as shown in the following screenshot, and choose the file to open:

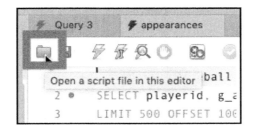

Either way will allow you to open a SQL file.

Learning how to add comments to your SQL code

It's important to add comments to your SQL code to ensure it's clear to you and others what is in the script. You may want to save this script for later or share it with others, and it will make a lot of difference if you comment your code with explanations. For straightforward scripts like we've been running in this chapter, it might not make much difference, but for larger and more complex queries, it will be beneficial.

When creating comments, it's important to note a few things, such as who created the code, when the code was created, who last modified the code, the date of the modification, and an explanation of why it was created or modified.

We briefly covered commenting on your code in Chapter 4, *Designing and Creating a Database*. To create a single-line comment, use #. To create a multi-line comment, place your comment between /* and */. The following code sample shows you how to use each of these comments:

```
# this is single line comment

/*
this is a multi line comment
*/
```

To comment properly in a SQL script, you should put something like this at the top of your script:

```
/*
Created by:   Josephine Bush
Created on:   November 15, 2019
Purpose:      Selecting distinct rows in appearances table to provide in a
report

Modified by   Modified on    Modification notes
JBush         11/16/19       Changed distinct to include teams and
playerids
*/
```

You can set whatever format you want in the comments at the top of the file. The previous code example is just that, an example, but it's good to be as thorough as possible for future reference.

It's also good to make other comments along the way with either single- or multi-line comments, especially if your script file contains a lot of SQL statements.

You can place comments anywhere in your code, as long as it won't cause the code to fail or cause an error. For example, if you want to comment out a section of the SELECT clause, you can do that like this:

```
USE lahmansbaseballdb;
SELECT playerid, g_all, g_batting, /*g_defense*/ FROM appearances
LIMIT 500 OFFSET 1000;
```

In the previous query, g_defense was commented out. The g_defense column will no longer be returned in the results of the query. However, there's a problem here – I didn't comment out the comma before the field I commented out. This syntax will cause an error such as Error Code: 1064. You have an error in your SQL syntax; check the manual that corresponds to your MySQL server version for the right syntax to use near 'FROM appearances LIMIT 500 OFFSET 1000' at line 1. We can fix this like so:

```
USE lahmansbaseballdb;
SELECT playerid, g_all, g_batting/*, g_defense*/ FROM appearances
LIMIT 500 OFFSET 1000;
```

By making this fix, the script will run correctly. It won't include the g_defense column in the results.

Commenting code on other RDMSes

The other RDMSes allow commenting as well, but they may have slightly different syntax for accomplishing this. In Oracle, PostgreSQL, and SQL Server, a multi-line comment is the same as in MySQL, but the single-line comment is different. A single-line comment should look as follows in Oracle, PostgreSQL, and SQL Server:

```
-- this is a single line comment
```

To make a single-line comment in Oracle, PostgreSQL, and SQL Server, you start the comment with two dashes (--).

Using the WHERE clause

The WHERE clause helps limit the results of your queries. For example, if you only wanted to see players with more than 40 appearances in games, you can create a WHERE clause to include only those players that meet the criteria.

Understanding how and when to use the WHERE clause to limit query results

The WHERE clause is placed after the FROM clause in a SELECT query. Using the example of players with more than 40 appearances in games, you can execute the following query:

```
USE lahmansbaseballdb;
SELECT playerid, g_all, g_batting, g_defense FROM appearances
WHERE g_all > 40;
```

The criterion we are setting in the WHERE clause (for example, g_all > 40) is called an **expression**. There are different expression operators you can use.

The following are the comparison operators:

Symbol	Description	Examples
=	Equal to	column = 'text' column = 1
>=	Greater than or equal to	column >= 1
>	Greater than	column > 1
<=	Less than or equal to	column <= 1
<	Less than	column < 1

<>	Does not equal	column <> 'text' column <> 1
!=	Does not equal	column != 'text' column != 1

Expressions will be covered in more detail in Chapter 9, *Working with Expressions*.

Learning how to use the AND and OR operators

Some additional expression operators that you can use in MySQL include AND and OR. These are considered logical operators.

You can add additional WHERE clauses as needed using the AND clause. If you want to see all records where g_all is greater than 40 and g_all didn't equal g_batting, you can execute the following query:

```
USE lahmansbaseballdb;
SELECT playerid, g_all, g_batting, g_defense FROM appearances
WHERE g_all > 40
AND g_all <> g_batting;
```

You can also add additional WHERE clauses as needed using the OR clause. If you want to see all records where g_all is greater than 40 OR g_defense is greater than 30, you can execute the following query:

```
USE lahmansbaseballdb;
SELECT playerid, g_all, g_batting, g_defense FROM appearances
WHERE g_all > 40
OR g_defense > 30;
```

Using parenthesis may become important when filtering results with the WHERE clause. You may only want to see something where both things are true, and something else is false. For example, in the following query, you will get results that are either g_all greater than 60 or the combination of g_all greater than 40 and g_batting less than 30:

```
USE lahmansbaseballdb;
SELECT playerid, g_all, g_batting, g_defense FROM appearances
WHERE (g_all > 40 AND g_defense < 30)
OR g_all > 60;
```

The previous query may give you unexpected results since that combination of data may or may not be useful to what you are trying to query. Still, it gives you an example of how to use parenthesis.

Learning how to use the NOT, IN, and BETWEEN operators

Some additional logical operators are NOT, IN, and BETWEEN:

- IN allows you to list the values that you want to return in your query results. For instance, if you want to return any values in g_all (all games played) that are in 40, 50, or 60, you could run the following query:

```
USE lahmansbaseballdb;
SELECT playerid, g_all, g_batting, g_defense FROM appearances
WHERE g_all IN (40, 50, 60);
```

- BETWEEN allows you to list two values, and your query will return all the values between and including those values. For instance, if you want to return any values in g_all that are between 40 and 60, you could run the following query:

```
USE lahmansbaseballdb;
SELECT playerid, g_all, g_batting, g_defense FROM appearances
WHERE g_all BETWEEN 40 and 60;
```

- NOT allows you to exclude values from your query. For instance, if you want to return any values in g_all that are NOT between 40 and 60, you can execute the following query:

```
USE lahmansbaseballdb;
SELECT playerid, g_all, g_batting, g_defense FROM appearances
WHERE g_all NOT BETWEEN 40 and 60;
```

The previous query will give you the results shown in the following screenshot:

playerid	g_all	g_batting	g_defense
barnero01	31	31	31
barrofr01	18	18	18
birdsda01	29	29	29
conefr01	19	19	19
gouldch01	31	31	31
jackssa01	16	16	16
mcveyca01	29	29	29
schafha01	31	31	31
spaldal01	31	31	31
wrighge01	16	16	16
wrighha01	31	31	31
brannmi01	3	3	3

You can also use NOT with IN. For instance, if you want to return any values in g_all that are NOT IN 40, 50, or 60, you can execute the following query:

```
USE lahmansbaseballdb;
SELECT playerid, g_all, g_batting, g_defense FROM appearances
WHERE g_all NOT IN (40, 50, 60);
```

You can also use NOT in multiple clauses of the WHERE clause, as shown in the following query:

```
USE lahmansbaseballdb;
SELECT playerid, g_all, g_batting, g_defense FROM appearances
WHERE g_all NOT IN (40, 50, 60)
OR g_batting NOT BETWEEN 30 and 40;
```

You can also combine it with AND, as shown in the following query:

```
USE lahmansbaseballdb;
SELECT playerid, g_all, g_batting, g_defense FROM appearances
WHERE g_all NOT IN (40, 50, 60)
AND g_batting NOT BETWEEN 30 and 40;
```

As you can see, there are many ways to use IN, BETWEEN, and NOT.

Learning how to use the LIKE operator and wildcards

You may not be able to match on the entire string in a field. To match on partial values, you can use the LIKE operator with wildcards. A wildcard is put in place of one or more characters in a string. It is used along with the LIKE operator.

When you use wildcards in your WHERE clause, the query may not be using the indexes, depending on how you use the wildcard characters. More information on this will be provided in the *Using indexes with your queries* section, later in this chapter. It's essential to use as few wildcards as possible in any queries you write.

The following table shows the types of wildcards that are available in MySQL:

Wildcard character	Character description	How it works
%	Percent sign	Represents zero or more characters
_	Underscore	Represents one character

Using the percent (%) wildcard

There a few ways you can use the % wildcard, which represents zero or more characters. You can use it to find a value at the beginning, end, or middle of a string. For example, the following query will find all player IDs that start with the letter a:

```
USE lahmansbaseballdb;
SELECT playerid, g_all, g_batting, g_defense
FROM appearances
WHERE playerid LIKE 'a%';
```

The previous query will return the rows shown in the following screenshot:

playerid	g_all	g_batting	g_defense
addybo01	25	25	25
ansonca01	25	25	25
abercda01	1	1	1
allisdo01	27	27	27
allisan01	19	19	19
allisbi01	5	5	5
allisdo01	16	16	16
allisar01	19	19	19
allenha01	16	16	16
arnolbi01	2	2	2
ansonca01	46	46	46
allisdo01	23	23	23

If you move the % sign in front of the letter a, you are filtering on anything that ends in a. In this case, it will find no rows since playerid always ends in a number:

```
USE lahmansbaseballdb;
SELECT playerid, g_all, g_batting, g_defense
FROM appearances
WHERE playerid LIKE '%a';
```

The previous query will return no rows, as shown in the following screenshot:

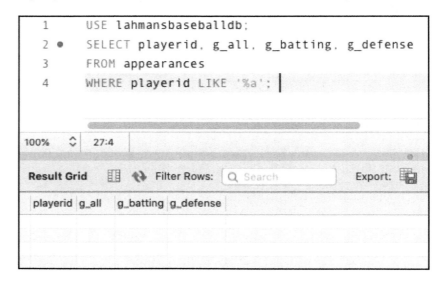

If you add a `%` sign to the end as well, then you will be filtering on any rows that have the letter a somewhere in the `playerid` value, as shown in the following query:

```
USE lahmansbaseballdb;
SELECT playerid, g_all, g_batting, g_defense
FROM appearances
WHERE playerid LIKE '%a%';
```

The results of the previous query will provide the rows shown in the following screenshot:

playerid	g_all	g_batting	g_defense
birdsda01	29	29	29
jackssa01	16	16	16
mcveyca01	29	29	29
schafha01	31	31	31
spaldal01	31	31	31
wrighha01	31	31	31
brannmi01	3	3	3
kingma01	20	20	20
mcatebu01	26	26	26
treacfr01	25	25	25
allisar01	29	29	29
bassjo01	22	22	22

Avoid using wildcards at the beginning of a string, such as '%a' or '%a%'. Wildcards at the beginning of a string slows down the query processing.

You can also place multiple characters before, after, or in-between percent wildcard.

This query will return rows where playerid starts with the letters wr:

```
USE lahmansbaseballdb;
SELECT playerid, g_all, g_batting, g_defense
FROM appearances
WHERE playerid LIKE 'wr%';
```

This query will return rows where playerid contains the letters ds:

```
USE lahmansbaseballdb;
SELECT playerid, g_all, g_batting, g_defense
FROM appearances
WHERE playerid LIKE '%ds%';
```

To summarize, you can use the % wildcard to search for strings at the beginning, middle, or end of strings.

Using the underscore (_) wildcard

There a few ways you can use the underscore (_) wildcard, which represents one character. You can use it to find a value at the beginning, end, or middle of a string. For example, the following query will find all rounds that end with LCS:

```
USE lahmansbaseballdb;
SELECT playerid, yearid, teamid, round, pos
FROM fieldingpost
WHERE round LIKE '_LCS';
```

The previous query will give us the results shown in the following screenshot:

playerid	yearid	teamid	round	pos
aaronha01	1969	ATL	NLCS	RF
aasedo01	1979	CAL	ALCS	P
abbotgl01	1975	OAK	ALCS	P
abbotku01	1997	FLO	NLCS	2B
abbotku01	2000	NYN	NLCS	SS
abbotpa01	2000	SEA	ALCS	P
abbotpa01	2001	SEA	ALCS	P
abreubo01	2009	LAA	ALCS	RF
aceveal01	2009	NYA	ALCS	P

As shown in the preceding results, the underscore wildcard returned all rows that ended in LCS. Now, you can see just those results, instead of the many other values that are in the round column.

Filtering with LIKE is not case-sensitive in MySQL, so LIKE '_LCS' would be considered the same as LIKE '_lcs'.

The following query will find all rounds that begin with W:

```
USE lahmansbaseballdb;
SELECT playerid, yearid, teamid, round, pos
FROM fieldingpost
WHERE round LIKE 'W_';
```

The previous query will give us the results shown in the following screenshot:

playerid	yearid	teamid	round	pos
aaronha01	1957	ML1	WS	CF
aaronha01	1958	ML1	WS	CF
aaronha01	1958	ML1	WS	RF
abbotku01	2000	NYN	WS	SS
abstebi01	1909	PIT	WS	1B
aceveal01	2009	NYA	WS	P
adairje01	1967	BOS	WS	2B
adamsba01	1909	PIT	WS	P
adamsba01	1925	PIT	WS	P
adamsma01	2013	SLN	WS	1B

As shown in the previous results, the underscore wildcard returned all rows that began in W. Now, you can see just those results, instead of the many other values that are in the round column.

The following query will find all rounds that begin with AL and have two characters after AL using two underscores:

```
USE lahmansbaseballdb;
SELECT playerid, yearid, teamid, round, pos
FROM fieldingpost
WHERE round LIKE 'AL__';
```

The previous query will give us the results shown in the following screenshot:

playerid	yearid	teamid	round	pos
aasedo01	1979	CAL	ALCS	P
abadfe01	2014	OAK	ALWC	P
abbotgl01	1975	OAK	ALCS	P
abbotpa01	2000	SEA	ALCS	P
abbotpa01	2001	SEA	ALCS	P
abreubo01	2009	LAA	ALCS	RF
aceveal01	2009	NYA	ALCS	P

As shown in the previous results, the underscore wildcard returned all rows that begin with AL. We placed two underscores after AL so that we only see results that start with AL and have two characters after AL.

The following query will find all rounds that begin with one character, have L, then one character, then S in the middle, and then end with one character:

```
USE lahmansbaseballdb;
SELECT playerid, yearid, teamid, round, pos
FROM fieldingpost
WHERE round LIKE '_L_S_';
```

The previous query will give you the results shown in the following screenshot:

playerid	yearid	teamid	round	pos
abbotje01	2000	CHA	ALDS2	CF
abbotku01	1997	FLO	NLDS1	2B
abbotku01	2000	NYN	NLDS2	SS
abbotpa01	2000	SEA	ALDS2	P
abbotpa01	2001	SEA	ALDS1	P
abreubo01	2006	NYA	ALDS1	RF
abreubo01	2007	NYA	ALDS2	RF
abreubo01	2009	LAA	ALDS2	RF
aceveal01	2009	NYA	ALDS1	P
acunaro01	2018	ATL	NLDS2	LF
adamsma01	2013	SLN	NLDS1	1B

As shown in the previous results, the underscore wildcard returned all rows that begin with one character, have L, then one character, then S in the middle, and then end with one character.

> Avoid using wildcards at the beginning of a string, such as '_a' or
> '_a_'. Wildcards at the beginning of a string slow query processing
> down. If you must use a wildcard at the beginning of a string, then the
> underscore will perform better than the percent sign.
> You can also use NOT LIKE in a similar manner to LIKE by adding NOT. In
> the case of NOT LIKE, you will get results that are NOT LIKE the
> expression you wrote instead of LIKE it.

Escaping wildcard values

If the string you are searching for with your wildcard expression has a wildcard in it, you will need to escape it for the wildcard expression to work as expected. Escaping means to allow a special character in a filter string. For example, if the string you want to filter on has a percent sign or an underscore in the string, you will need to *escape* these characters so that the SQL query doesn't fail or doesn't work as expected.

Let's say your field contains an underscore and you want to filter on those values that have an underscore; you need to escape the underscore to find these values. You can't just use WHERE fieldname LIKE '%_%' in your query because MySQL would think you were filtering on a set of characters (%), then one character (_), then another set of characters (%). Instead, you should use WHERE fieldname LIKE '%_%'. The backslash (\) means that you want the filter to use the underscore as a character instead of a wildcard.

You can also specify a different escape character if you don't want to use the backslash. You should do this with the LIKE clause by using the ESCAPE operator, like this:

```
WHERE fieldname LIKE '%=_%' ESCAPE '='
```

In this case, you can see we've changed the backslash to an equals sign for escaping purposes.

Escape sequences for common characters used in LIKE have been outlined in the following table:

Character	Description	Escape sequence
'	Single quote	\ '
"	Double quote	\ "
\	Backslash	\ \
%	Percent sign	\ %
_	Underscore	_

Differences between LIKE in other RDMSes

The percent (%) and underscore (_) are supported in all RDMSes. It's important to note the case sensitivity of LIKE in the various RDMSes since they are not all alike in their support of it:

- **Oracle** is case-sensitive by default. To search for both lower and uppercase, you will need to use the UPPER function, so you use WHERE UPPER(fieldname) like 'AD%'. This syntax will return the results of anything starting with ad and AD because we've converted all strings in the fieldname column into uppercase. String functions, including UPPER, will be covered more in Chapter 9, *Working with Expressions*.

- **PostgreSQL** is case-sensitive by default. If you need support for searching with LIKE for case-insensitive searching, you need to use ILIKE instead. In other words, if you use LIKE 'ad%' in PostgreSQL, it will return results that begin with ad and not AD. If you wanted to find both ad and AD, you need to use ILIKE 'ad%'.
- **SQL Server** is case-insensitive by default, so when you use LIKE 'ad%', it will return results that begin with ad and AD.

SQL Server supports two additional wildcard operators:

- **Square brackets ([])**: This will match any value in the specified set. If you use [ab], you will get results of any string starting with a and b, which includes A and B. Additionally, you can use a range in square brackets; for example, [a-c], which will return the results of any string that starts with a, b, c, A, B, and C.
- **Caret (^)**: This will match anything that is not in the specified set. This is like adding NOT to the square brackets wildcard operator, so if you used [^a-c], then you are getting results showing everything that doesn't start with a, b, c, A, B, and C

Learning how to filter on NULL values

You can't filter for NULL values the same way you can filter on other values. For instance, you can't use comparison operators, which were covered earlier in this chapter. These include =, >, < , and <>. You need to filter NULL values with IS NULL or IS NOT NULL.

The following query will return the results for NULL values in g_defense:

```
USE lahmansbaseballdb;
SELECT playerid, g_all, g_batting, g_defense
FROM appearances
WHERE g_defense IS NULL;
```

The previous query will return the results shown in the following screenshot. All the g_defense values will be NULL:

playerid	g_all	g_batting	g_defense
barrebi01	1	1	NULL
brainas01	16	16	NULL
careyto01	56	56	NULL
cravebi01	41	41	NULL
cummica01	42	42	NULL
forceda01	49	49	NULL
hallge01	35	35	NULL
hastisc01	30	30	NULL
mcveyca01	38	38	NULL
millsev01	54	54	NULL

The following query will return the results for NOT NULL values in g_defense:

```
USE lahmansbaseballdb;
SELECT playerid, g_all, g_batting, g_defense
FROM appearances
WHERE g_defense IS NOT NULL;
```

The previous query will return the results shown in the following screenshot. All the g_defense values will not be NULL:

playerid	g_all	g_batting	g_defense
barnero01	31	31	31
barrofr01	18	18	18
birdsda01	29	29	29
conefr01	19	19	19
gouldch01	31	31	31
jackssa01	16	16	16
mcveyca01	29	29	29
schafha01	31	31	31
spaldal01	31	31	31
wrighge01	16	16	16

You can use the WHERE clause operators we covered in this chapter together, depending on what query results you may need.

Using the ORDER BY clause

The ORDER BY clause helps you sort your results. You can sort your results in a few different ways, all of which will be covered in the following sections.

Learning how to use the ORDER BY clause to order query results

The ORDER BY clause is placed after FROM, as well as after WHERE, if you have a WHERE clause. You can order columns by ascending or descending order. Ascending is the default sort order, so you don't need to specify ascending explicitly.

 Do not depend on the order of the rows in a result set, unless you have specified an ORDER BY clause. The order in which rows are returned may or may not be the same without an ORDER BY explicitly defined in your query.

To sort the columns in ascending order, use the ASC keyword, and to order them in descending order, use the DESC keyword. To sort a table by g_all in the appearances table, you can execute the following query:

```
USE lahmansbaseballdb;
SELECT playerid, g_all, g_batting, g_defense
FROM appearances
ORDER BY g_all;
```

The previous query will give you the results shown in the following screenshot:

playerid	g_all	g_batting	g_defense
parnebo01	1	1	1
anderbr05	1	1	0
lindbjo01	1	0	1
nerishe01	1	1	1
ambrihe01	1	1	1
bucknbi02	1	1	1
beavabl01	1	0	1
pryorst01	1	0	1
dunnija01	1	1	1

The previous query doesn't have a WHERE clause, but if it required one, then you should place it between the FROM and ORDER BY clauses, as shown in the following query:

```
USE lahmansbaseballdb;
SELECT playerid, g_all, g_batting, g_defense
FROM appearances
WHERE playerid LIKE 'a%'
ORDER BY g_all;
```

To sort in descending order instead, you can add the DESC keyword to your ORDER BY clause, as shown in the following query:

```
USE lahmansbaseballdb;
SELECT playerid, g_all, g_batting, g_defense
FROM appearances
ORDER BY g_all DESC;
```

The previous query will give you the results shown in the following screenshot. You can see that g_all has the highest game total at the top of the results now:

playerid	g_all	g_batting	g_defense
willsma01	165	165	165
paganjo01	164	164	164
santoro01	164	164	164
willibi01	164	164	164
tovarce01	164	164	163
robinbr01	163	163	163
cardele01	163	163	163
wagnele01	163	163	163
bankser01	163	163	162
bufordo01	163	163	162

You can also ORDER BY columns that aren't specified in your SELECT clause. You need to specify them in the ORDER BY clause by the exact column name in the table.

Next, we will learn how to sort by one or more columns.

Learning how to use the ORDER BY clause to sort by one or more columns

Let's say you wanted to sort on more than one column. To do this, you should place the columns you want to order by in the ORDER BY clause in the order in which you want them ordered. For instance, if you wanted to order by playerid, then g_all, you can execute the following query:

```
USE lahmansbaseballdb;
SELECT playerid, g_all, g_batting, g_defense
FROM appearances
ORDER BY playerid, g_all;
```

The previous query will give you the results shown in the following screenshot:

playerid	g_all	g_batting	g_defense
aardsda01	1	0	1
aardsda01	11	11	11
aardsda01	25	2	25
aardsda01	33	30	33
aardsda01	43	41	43
aardsda01	45	43	45
aardsda01	47	5	47
aardsda01	53	4	53
aardsda01	73	3	73
aaronha01	85	85	1
aaronha01	112	112	89
aaronha01	120	120	105

As shown in the previous screenshot, the results are now ordered by ascending `playerid`, then `g_all`.

You can also change the order of either column to descending by adding `DESC` to one or both columns, as shown in the following query:

```
USE lahmansbaseballdb;
SELECT playerid, g_all, g_batting, g_defense
FROM appearances
ORDER BY playerid DESC, g_all DESC;
```

The previous query will give you the results shown in the following screenshot:

playerid	g_all	g_batting	g_defense
zychto01	45	4	45
zychto01	13	0	13
zychto01	12	0	12
zwilldu01	154	154	154
zwilldu01	150	150	149
zwilldu01	35	35	9
zwilldu01	28	28	28
zuverge01	62	62	62
zuverge01	56	56	56
zuverge01	45	45	45
zuverge01	35	35	35

As shown in the previous screenshot, the results are now ordered descending by `playerid`, then `g_all`.

> If you want to, you can order by all the columns in the table, but there will be a performance impact on your query. You need to be careful with choosing which and how many columns to use in your ORDER BY clause. More on this topic will be covered in the *Using indexes with your queries* section, later in this chapter.

Another way to use the order in an ORDER BY clause is to use the column position. In the case of the previous queries, you would use a number to denote the column instead of the column name. This number corresponds to its place in the SELECT clause. For example, in the following query, `playerid` is 1, `g_all` is 2, `g_batting` is 3, and `g_defense` is 4, so we can order the results by their position in the SELECT clause, as shown in the following query:

```
USE lahmansbaseballdb;
SELECT playerid, g_all, g_batting, g_defense
FROM appearances
ORDER BY 1 DESC, 2 DESC;
```

The previous query will give the results shown in the following screenshot, which is the same as the results we got when we used the column names instead:

playerid	g_all	g_batting	g_defense
zychto01	45	4	45
zychto01	13	0	13
zychto01	12	0	12
zwilldu01	154	154	154
zwilldu01	150	150	149
zwilldu01	35	35	9
zwilldu01	28	28	28
zuverge01	62	62	62
zuverge01	56	56	56
zuverge01	45	45	45
zuverge01	35	35	35

I prefer to explicitly specify column names in the ORDER BY clause to avoid confusion. If you change the order of the columns in the SELECT clause, and you've used column position numbers instead of the column names in the ORDER BY clause, you will need to change your ORDER BY clause. Also, it's more confusing to read column position numbers in the ORDER BY clause because you have to correlate them back to the SELECT clause columns. Additionally, you may mistakenly specify the wrong column using the column position number. The last drawback of using column position numbers is that you can't order by a column that isn't specified in your SELECT clause.

Using indexes with your queries

To make sure your queries have been optimized and can run as quickly as they can, you want to ensure they are using the indexes on the table you are querying properly. As you learned in Chapter 4, *Designing and Creating a Database*, locking, blocking, and deadlocking play a role in your queries. If you use indexes properly with your queries, you will have less blocking and deadlocking to deal with because the index will allow you to query data faster.

Learning how to see what indexes your query is using

There is a simple way to see how MySQL will run your query, and that is to append EXPLAIN to the front of your query. For example, you can see EXPLAIN being used in the following query:

```
USE lahmansbaseballdb;
EXPLAIN SELECT playerid, g_all, g_batting, g_defense
FROM appearances;
```

What EXPLAIN will do is give you a table of information about how it's going to run the query. The previous query will give you the results shown in the following screenshot:

id	select_type	table	partitions	type	possible_keys	key	key_len	ref	rows	filtered	Extra
1	SIMPLE	appearances	NULL	ALL	NULL	NULL	NULL	NULL	105113	100.00	NULL

Let's go through what each of these columns means:

- `id`: This is the sequential number of the query this row belongs to. In this case, we have a simple query with only one table, so there is only one row that is associated with the one table we are querying.
- `select_type`: This tells us what kind of query this is. In this case, it's SIMPLE because there is only one table, which is a straightforward query. Many other types may show up here with more complicated queries, such as UNION, SUBQUERY, or DERIVED. These will be covered in more detail in Chapter 7, *Querying Multiple Tables*, and Chapter 11, *Advanced Querying Techniques*.
- `table`: This refers to the table that is being queried.
- `partitions`: This is NULL for nonpartitioned tables, so since our tables are not partitioned, this will be NULL. Partitioning is not covered in this book. If you want to learn more about partitioning, please refer to the *Further reading* section.
- `type`: This refers to the type of join in the query. Joins will be covered in Chapter 7, *Querying Multiple Tables*.
- `possible_keys`: This refers to possible indexes that your query could use. Since this is NULL, there are no relevant indexes that this query can use.
- `key`: This refers to the index that was chosen. Since this is NULL, no index was chosen to run this query.
- `key_len`: This refers to the length of the key that was used. Since the key is NULL, `key_len` is NULL.
- `ref`: This shows what columns or constraints were compared to the key column. Since the key is NULL, this is also NULL.
- `rows`: This shows the estimated number of rows that MySQL thinks it will have to read to return the query results.
- `filtered`: This shows the number of rows unfiltered by the WHERE clause. Since we didn't use a WHERE clause, it's not filtering, so it shows up as 100.00. When the value is less than 100.00, we know that some filtering was done on the query.
- `Extra`: This gives you additional information about the query, such as if a WHERE clause was used, if the query used `filesort`, or if it used temporary tables. Those last two are important for improving performance. If you see using `filesort`, this means that MySQL had to do an extra pass to retrieve rows in sorted order. If you see using `temporary`, this means MySQL had to use a temporary table to store values.

Let's look at an example query that uses some more clauses to see some more information in our EXPLAIN results:

```
USE lahmansbaseballdb;
EXPLAIN SELECT distinct playerid, g_all, g_batting, g_defense
FROM appearances
WHERE playerid LIKE 'a%'
ORDER BY playerid;
```

The previous query gives us the results shown in the following screenshot:

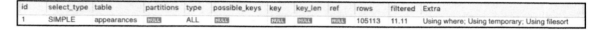

id	select_type	table	partitions	type	possible_keys	key	key_len	ref	rows	filtered	Extra
1	SIMPLE	appearances	NULL	ALL	NULL	NULL	NULL	NULL	105113	11.11	Using where; Using temporary; Using filesort

Here, you can see some more interesting information that we attained with our EXPLAIN results. First, you can see that `filtered` shows that we are only getting approximately 11.11% of the rows returned. It also shows that you are using a WHERE clause, that the query needs a temporary table, and that MySQL had to use an extra pass to sort the records. In this specific case, since it's such a small table, and it won't be growing quickly, you could get away with not changing anything, but if this table were to grow much larger, then you'd need to account for these issues.

Let's say you knew this table would grow much larger shortly. How can you fix the issues you are seeing? Let's take a step back and examine how this query could be changed to use an index. Let's say you execute the following query instead:

```
USE lahmansbaseballdb;
EXPLAIN SELECT distinct playerid
FROM appearances
WHERE playerid LIKE 'a%'
ORDER BY playerid;
```

The following screenshot shows the query results that were obtained from running the previous query:

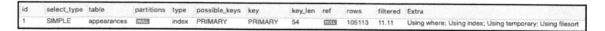

id	select_type	table	partitions	type	possible_keys	key	key_len	ref	rows	filtered	Extra
1	SIMPLE	appearances	NULL	index	PRIMARY	PRIMARY	54	NULL	105113	11.11	Using where; Using index; Using temporary; Using filesort

Since we removed the `g_all`, `g_batting`, and `g_defense` columns from the `SELECT` clause, you can see that the query is now using the `PRIMARY` key (which is the clustered index on this table), so this will make the query faster, but it doesn't have all the columns we may need in our query. This is when you need to think about if you need those columns we've removed, and if so, you may need to add a new index to account for this. This is called adding an index to cover a query, or in other words, adding an index to cover it. This is similar to what we did earlier since this is a small table that isn't going to grow, so it may not be necessary to change anything. Still, if you were going to account for a table growing, and you are planning to run this query frequently, you could add a nonclustered index to cover the additional columns in the query. You also need to keep in mind that when you add indexes, you will affect other queries, possibly making them less efficient, and you will slow down inserts, updates, and deletes. We will talk about inserting, updating, and deleting more in `Chapter 8`, *Modifying Data and Table Structures*.

You can add a nonclustered index in a couple of ways via MySQL Workbench – either with the interface or via a SQL script. First, let's walk through how to alter a table with the MySQL Workbench interface in order to add a nonclustered index:

1. Right-click the `appearances` table.
2. Click **Alter Table...**:

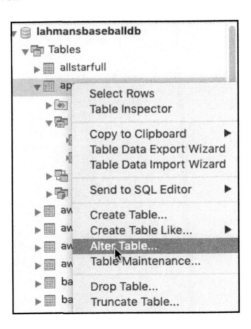

3. Click the **Indexes** tab. You will see that there is the **PRIMARY** index currently:

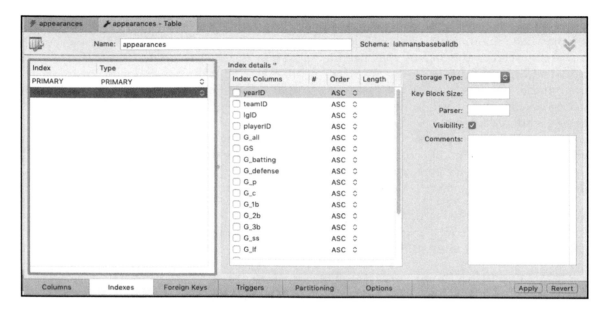

4. Click on **<click to edit>**. This will allow you to enter an index name for the new index we are creating.

5. Name the nonclustered index `NC_playerid_g_cols`, select the `playerid`, `g_all`, `g_batting`, and `g_defense` columns, and then click **Apply**:

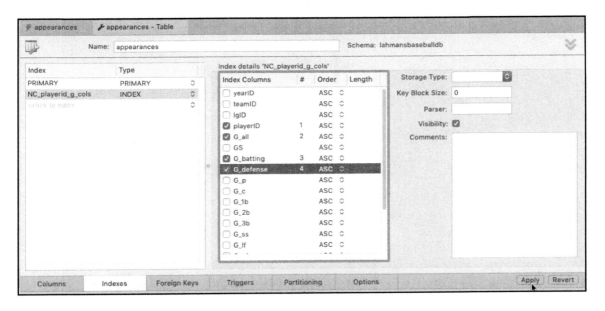

6. This will bring you to a screen where you can review the query that MySQL will run to create the nonclustered index:

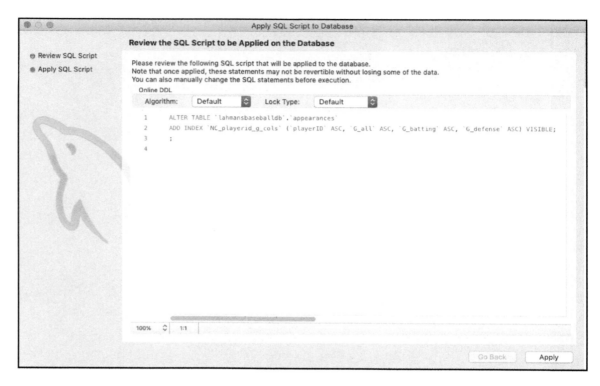

7. Click **Apply**.
8. Click **Close**. With that, the nonclustered index has been added.

If you want to run the script to add the nonclustered index, you can execute the following in a new query window:

```
ALTER TABLE `lahmansbaseballdb`.`appearances`
ADD INDEX `NC_playerid_g_cols` (`playerID` ASC, `G_all` ASC, `G_batting`
ASC, `G_defense` ASC) VISIBLE;
;
```

Let's execute our EXPLAIN for the query again:

```
USE lahmansbaseballdb;
EXPLAIN SELECT distinct playerid, g_all, g_batting, g_defense
FROM appearances
WHERE playerid LIKE 'a%'
ORDER BY playerid;
```

This will give you the results shown in the following screenshot:

id	select_type	table	partitions	type	possible_keys	key	key_len	ref	rows	filtered	Extra
1	SIMPLE	appearances	NULL	range	NC_playerid_g_cols	NC_playerid_g_cols	38	NULL	3282	100.00	Using where; Using index

Here, you can see that the query is using the nonclustered index we just created, and it's no longer using filesort or temporary, thereby making your query much more efficient.

Here are some important things to note about query performance:

- Avoid wildcards at the beginning of the search pattern because they are the slower to process. For example, in the preceding query, you put % at the end of the LIKE filter. If we had put this at the beginning, it could make the query slower. Again, this is a small table, so it's hard to get the feeling for when things are substantially larger, but it will be slower on a much larger table. The same goes for the underscore (_) in the LIKE operator. Try to avoid putting it at the front of the string.
- The underscore will be faster than the percent sign because the parser only has to perform one operation before moving on to the next character. With percent, it has to do more parsing to resolve because it may have to match on more characters.

One last thing to cover is viewing a graphical interface for the query execution plan. To do this, you will need to run your query first:

```
USE lahmansbaseballdb;
SELECT distinct playerid, g_all, g_batting, g_defense
FROM appearances
WHERE playerid LIKE 'a%'
ORDER BY playerid;
```

Now, click **Query** in the MySQL Workbench menu, and then **Explain Current Statement**, as shown in the following screenshot:

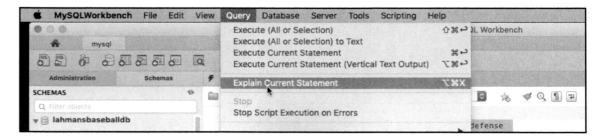

This will bring up a visually explain plan panel below the query window and above the output window, as shown in the following screenshot:

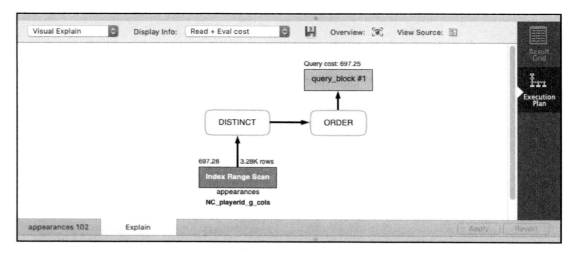

The previous screenshot shows that the query is using the NC_playerid_g_cols index and that it only has to use a range of the index, which is good since it does not have to scan the entire index. This gives you the approximate row count and the time it will take to return the query, which is **3.28K** rows and **697.26** milliseconds, respectively. It also tells you it will be using the appearances table. You can see that it checks for distinct values and orders them, and then returns the query results.

Let's say you didn't have that nonclustered index that you added earlier before looking at the visual explain plan. You can drop the index by running this query:

```
ALTER TABLE `lahmansbaseballdb`.`appearances`
DROP INDEX `NC_playerid_g_cols`;
```

You can rerun the query to see the new visual explain plan, as shown in the following screenshot:

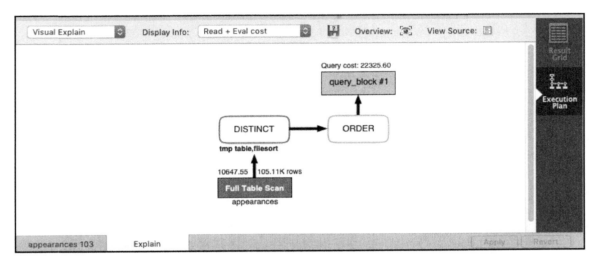

Here, you can see that the entire table has to be scanned when we don't have that nonclustered index. You can see the row count went up from approximately 3,000 rows to over 100,000 rows and that the time went from around 700 milliseconds to over 10,000 milliseconds. Also, note the query cost. In the query that used the nonclustered index, the cost was almost the same as the time to run the query (697.5), but in the query without the nonclustered index, the cost has gone up quite dramatically to over 22,000. Query cost is based on how much CPU and I/O MySQL thinks it will need to use, so these numbers show how beneficial proper indexing is for running queries efficiently.

Differences in other RDMSes for examining what indexes your queries are using: Oracle, PostgreSQL, and SQL Server have different ways of seeing what indexes your queries are using. Please refer to the *Further reading* section to find links that provide more information on this.

Summary

In this chapter, you learned how to query a single table. This included learning how to use the SQL SELECT statement and the FROM, WHERE, and ORDER BY clauses.

With the SELECT and FROM clauses, you learned how to select distinct records with the DISTINCT keyword, how to limit results with the LIMIT keyword, how to save a SQL query to a file, and how to add proper comments to SQL code.

With the WHERE clause, you learned how and when to use the WHERE clause, along with AND, OR, NOT, IN, and BETWEEN, and how to use with the percent sign (%) and underscore (_) wildcards.

With the ORDER BY clause, you learned how to order query results by one or more columns.

Finally, you learned how to tell which index your query is using and if you need additional indexes by using EXPLAIN or the visual explain tool in MySQL Workbench. You also learned how to add an index to make the query more efficient.

In the next chapter, you will learn how to query multiple tables. This includes learning how to use SQL joins. You will learn about INNER, OUTER (LEFT, RIGHT, and FULL), and advanced joins (cross and self joins). Finally, you will learn about set theory, including unioning queries.

Questions

1. What character is required at the end of all SQL statements?
2. What two clauses are required to select data from a single table?
3. Why should you avoid using SELECT * in a query?
4. What does the WHERE clause do to your query results?
5. What two wildcard operators can you use with LIKE?
6. What does an ORDER BY clause do to your query results?
7. What options do you have for sorting results in your ORDER BY clause?
8. What SQL clause can you use to see the explanation of your query, and what indexes will it use?
9. How do you add an index to an existing table?
10. How do you see the explanation of a query plan using MySQL Workbench?

Further reading

For more information:

- **Refer to this link for more information on Oracle execution plans**: https://docs.oracle.com/en/database/oracle/oracle-database/19/tgsql/generating-and-displaying-execution-plans.html#GUID-60E30B1C-342B-4D71-B154-C26623D6A3B1
- **Refer to this link for more information on PostgreSQL execution plans**: https://www.postgresql.org/docs/11/sql-explain.html
- **Refer to this link for more details about SQL Server execution plans**: https://docs.microsoft.com/en-us/sql/relational-databases/performance/display-an-actual-execution-plan?view=sql-server-ver15
- **Refer to this link for more details about MySQL partitioning**: https://dev.mysql.com/doc/refman/8.0/en/partitioning.html

7
Querying Multiple Tables

In this chapter, you will learn how to query multiple tables. You will learn how to use SQL joins to join two or more tables together, including INNER and OUTER (LEFT, RIGHT, and FULL) joins, and advanced joins (cross, natural, and self joins). You will learn about set theory and how to combine queries using UNION and UNION ALL, and how to get the differences and intersections of different queries. Lastly, you will learn how to optimize queries when they contain multiple tables.

In this chapter, we will cover the following topics:

- Understanding joins
- Using INNER JOIN
- Using OUTER JOIN
- Using advanced joins
- Understanding set theory
- Using indexes with your queries

Technical requirements

You can refer to the code files of this chapter at the following GitHub link: https://github.com/PacktPublishing/learn-sql-database-programming/tree/master/chapter-7

Understanding joins

Before we begin a discussion on the types of joins, let's go over what a join is and why you would use one. A join refers to when you connect two or more tables in a query. Joining tables in a query requires you to join them on a related column that is in each table you want to join together. There are a couple of different types of joins, including the following ones:

- **Inner join**: This type of join returns only matching records from each joined table.
- **Outer join**: This type of join has a few types of joins that can be used, including the following:
    - **Left outer join**: This type of join includes all rows from the left table and any matching rows between the left and right tables.
    - **Right outer join**: This type of join includes all rows from the right table and any matching rows between the right and left tables.
    - **Full outer join**: This type of join includes all rows from both the left and right tables. This type of join is not available in MySQL.

Additionally, there are some more advanced joins, including the following ones:

- **Cross join**: This type of join will return a combination of every row from two tables.
- **Natural join**: This type of join will associate columns of the same name in the joined tables with each other. It's similar to an inner join or left outer join, but you don't specify the join columns.
- **Self join**: This type of join is used to join a table to itself.

Understanding results returned with an inner join

The Venn diagram in the following screenshot shows you which records would be returned if you joined **Table A** to **Table B** in an inner join:

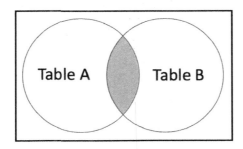

The Venn diagram shows that only records that match in **Table A** and **Table B** would be returned with an inner join.

Understanding results returned with a left outer join

A left outer join includes all rows from the left table and any matching rows between the left and right tables. The following Venn diagram shows in gray the rows that would be returned with two tables:

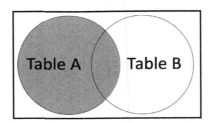

If there are no rows in **Table B** that match **Table A**, only rows from **Table A** will be returned. Rows returned from **Table A** that don't have any matching rows in **Table B** will show null values for the columns in **Table B**.

Additionally, you can use a left excluding join. This would include all rows from the left table that don't match records in the right table, as shown in the Venn diagram depicted in the following image:

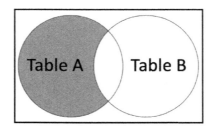

Understanding results returned with a right outer join

A right outer join includes all rows from the right table and any matching rows between the right and left tables. The Venn diagram depicted in the following screenshot shows in gray the rows that would be returned with two tables:

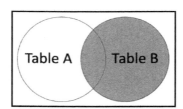

If there are no rows in **Table A** that match **Table B**, only rows from **Table B** will be returned. Rows returned from **Table B** that don't have any matching rows in **Table A** will show null values for the columns in **Table A**.

Additionally, you can do a right excluding join. This would include all rows from the right table that don't match records in the left table, as shown in the Venn diagram depicted in the following image:

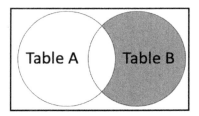

Understanding results returned with a full outer join

A full outer join includes all rows from both the left and right tables. The Venn diagram depicted in the following screenshot shows in gray the rows that would be returned with two tables:

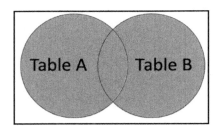

Rows returned from **Table A** that don't have any matching rows in **Table B** will show null values for the columns in **Table B**. Rows returned from **Table B** that don't have any matching rows in **Table A** will show null values for the columns in **Table A**.

Using INNER JOIN

If you want to only return records that have matching rows in each table you join, use an INNER JOIN. The syntax of INNER JOIN and examples will be outlined in this section.

Learning INNER JOIN syntax

To inner join two tables, use the following syntax:

```
SELECT column(s)
FROM table1
INNER JOIN table2
ON table1.column = table2.column
WHERE conditions
ORDER BY column(s);
```

The preceding syntax shows you how to join two tables together with an INNER JOIN. You join a column in table1 that matches a column in table2. The WHERE and ORDER BY clauses are optional. They are there to show you that the INNER JOIN syntax goes between the FROM and WHERE clauses.

The following example will help you to understand how to use the INNER JOIN:

```
SELECT lahmansbaseballdb.people.playerid, birthyear, yearid, teamid
FROM lahmansbaseballdb.appearances
INNER JOIN lahmansbaseballdb.people
ON lahmansbaseballdb.people.playerid =
lahmansbaseballdb.appearances.playerid
WHERE yearid = 2017;
```

In the preceding code example, you will see that you list your columns as usual, but where the column exists in both tables, you will need to specify the table you want the column to be queried from; otherwise, you will get an error. For example, if you didn't preface playerid with lahmansbaseballdb.people, then you would receive this error message:

```
Error Code: 1052. Column 'playerid' in field list is ambiguous
```

In this case, you could preface playerid with either table in the inner join since that field exists and is NOT NULL in either table.

Also, you place a table you want to query FROM the same as in querying a single table. In the case of an INNER JOIN, it doesn't matter which order you place the tables in the INNER JOIN.

Next, you will see the INNER JOIN clause. This clause is where you place the table you want to join to the table in the FROM clause.

Then, you will see the ON clause. This clause tells the query which column you want to join the tables on. In this case, the only column that exists in both is the playerid column, so it's the natural choice for joining.

You will see a WHERE clause to limit the results; otherwise, the query takes a long time to run without the WHERE clause to restrict it.

In the following screenshot, you will see the results returned with the preceding query:

playerid	birthyear	yearid	teamid	G_batting
abadfe01	1985	2017	BOS	4
abreujo02	1987	2017	CHA	156
adamecr01	1991	2017	COL	12
adamsau02	1991	2017	WAS	6
adamsla01	1989	2017	ATL	85
adamsma01	1988	2017	ATL	100
adamsma01	1988	2017	SLN	31
adducji02	1985	2017	DET	29

You can also leave off the INNER on an INNER JOIN. The following query will run the same as the preceding query:

```
SELECT lahmansbaseballdb.people.playerid, birthyear, yearid, teamid
FROM lahmansbaseballdb.appearances
JOIN lahmansbaseballdb.people
ON lahmansbaseballdb.people.playerid =
lahmansbaseballdb.appearances.playerid
WHERE yearid = 2017;
```

For clarity's sake, it's best to use the INNER JOIN syntax, especially if you are joining more tables using other joins besides INNER JOIN.

In MySQL, you can join up to 61 tables in a query. The best practice is to use the fewest joins possible to avoid issues with computer resources. In Oracle, PostgreSQL, and SQL Server, the only limit on table joins is computer resources.

In the following query, you will be joining three tables to each other:

```
SELECT lahmansbaseballdb.people.playerid, birthyear,
       lahmansbaseballdb.appearances.yearid,
          lahmansbaseballdb.appearances.teamid, G_defense, H
FROM lahmansbaseballdb.appearances
INNER JOIN lahmansbaseballdb.people
ON lahmansbaseballdb.people.playerid =
```

```
lahmansbaseballdb.appearances.playerid
INNER JOIN lahmansbaseballdb.batting
ON lahmansbaseballdb.people.playerid = lahmansbaseballdb.batting.playerid
WHERE lahmansbaseballdb.batting.yearid = 2017
      AND H <> 0
ORDER BY lahmansbaseballdb.people.playerid,
         lahmansbaseballdb.appearances.yearid,
         lahmansbaseballdb.appearances.teamid, G_defense, H;
```

In the preceding query, you can see that you are now joining another table, lahmansbaseballdb.batting, to the query. You use the same syntax as joining the lahmansbaseballdb.appearances table. The preceding query will return the rows where the people, batting, and appearances tables have matching rows. The following screenshot shows the results of the previous query:

playerid	birthyear	yearid	teamid	G_defense	H
abreujo02	1987	2014	CHA	109	189
abreujo02	1987	2015	CHA	115	189
abreujo02	1987	2016	CHA	152	189
abreujo02	1987	2017	CHA	139	189
abreujo02	1987	2018	CHA	114	189
adamsla01	1989	2014	KCA	2	30
adamsla01	1989	2017	ATL	41	30
adamsla01	1989	2018	ATL	8	30

The following screenshot shows the Venn diagram of which rows would be returned:

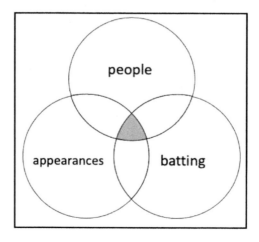

What the query will return is illustrated by the gray area where **people**, **appearances**, and **batting** overlap in the preceding image.

Learning how to use table aliases

Table aliases allow you to assign a different name to a table in your query. As you can see from the queries in the previous section, the naming of columns for joined tables can get long and make your query hard to read. This is where table aliases come in. You can use an alias for your tables in the join and make it easier to read and reference which table your columns belong to. Taking a query from the previous section and putting on aliases, you get the following query:

```
SELECT p.playerid, birthyear,
  a.yearid, a.teamid, G_defense, H
FROM lahmansbaseballdb.appearances AS a
INNER JOIN lahmansbaseballdb.people AS p
ON p.playerid = a.playerid
INNER JOIN lahmansbaseballdb.batting AS b
ON p.playerid = b.playerid
WHERE b.yearid = 2017
AND H <> 0
ORDER BY p.playerid, a.yearid, a.teamid, G_defense, H;
```

The preceding query has an alias on the table names in the FROM and INNER JOIN clauses. For the appearances table, you are using a; for the people table, you are using p; and for the batting table, you are using b. Also, you will see the AS keyword between the table name and the alias, as shown in the following code snippet:

```
lahmansbaseballdb.appearances AS a
```

The AS keyword is optional, so the following code snippet works the same as the preceding one:

```
lahmansbaseballdb.appearances a
```

You can apply this alias naming to the columns in the SELECT, WHERE, and ORDER BY clauses. For example, instead of using lahmansbaseballdb.appearances.yearid, you use a.yearid, thereby making it much cleaner and easier to read. You can also use longer aliases if you choose, such as using batting instead of b for the batting table.

You can't use table aliases with spaces as the `batting` table does. This will cause an error in your code.

Using OUTER JOIN

There are three types of outer joins: LEFT, RIGHT, and FULL joins. Each is described in more detail in the following sections. The LEFT OUTER JOIN includes all rows from the left table and any matching rows between the left and right tables. The RIGHT OUTER JOIN includes all rows from the right table and any matching rows between the right and left tables. The FULL OUTER JOIN includes all rows from both the left and right tables.

Learning LEFT OUTER JOIN syntax

To LEFT OUTER JOIN two tables, use the following syntax:

```
SELECT column(s)
FROM table1
LEFT OUTER JOIN table2
ON table1.column = table2.column
WHERE conditions
ORDER BY column(s);
```

The preceding syntax shows you how to join two tables together with a LEFT OUTER JOIN. You join a column in `table1` that matches a column in `table2`. The WHERE and ORDER BY clauses are optional. They are there to show you that the LEFT OUTER JOIN syntax goes between the FROM and WHERE clauses.

The following example will help you to understand how to use the LEFT OUTER JOIN:

```
SELECT p.playerid, birthyear, schoolid, yearid
FROM lahmansbaseballdb.people p
LEFT OUTER JOIN lahmansbaseballdb.collegeplaying c
ON p.playerid = c.playerid
WHERE birthyear = 1985;
```

You can see in the preceding query that you are joining the `people` table to the `collegeplaying` table with a `LEFT OUTER JOIN`. This will return all rows from the `people` table and only corresponding rows from the `collegeplaying` table when a row in the `people` table has a `birthyear` of `1985`. In the following screenshot, you will see the results of the preceding query:

playerid	birthyear	schoolid	yearid
wootero01	1985	unc	2007
wootero01	1985	unc	2008
worthda01	1985	pepperdi...	2005
worthda01	1985	pepperdi...	2006
worthda01	1985	pepperdi...	2007
zawadla01	1985	sandiegost	2004
zawadla01	1985	sandiegost	2005
zawadla01	1985	sandiegost	2006
abadfe01	1985	NULL	NULL
abreuju01	1985	NULL	NULL
adducji02	1985	NULL	NULL
ascanjo01	1985	NULL	NULL
atilalu01	1985	NULL	NULL
atkinmi01	1985	NULL	NULL

As you can see in the preceding screenshot, the results show NULL for the rows in the `people` table that don't have a corresponding row in the `collegeplaying` table, and the rows that do match between `people` and `collegeplaying` have a complete row of data in the results.

You can also leave off OUTER in the join, and it will run the same as if it were there. For example, the following code snippet will run a `LEFT OUTER JOIN`:

```
LEFT OUTER JOIN lahmansbaseballdb.collegeplaying c
```

This code snippet will work the same way and return the same results as the preceding code snippet:

```
LEFT JOIN lahmansbaseballdb.collegeplaying c
```

You can use either `LEFT JOIN` or `LEFT OUTER JOIN` with the same results.

As with `INNER JOIN`, you can join up to 61 tables in your query. You can `LEFT OUTER JOIN` three tables, as shown in the following SQL query:

```
SELECT p.playerid, birthyear, schoolid, asf.yearid, gameid
FROM lahmansbaseballdb.people p
LEFT OUTER JOIN lahmansbaseballdb.collegeplaying c
ON p.playerid = c.playerid
LEFT OUTER JOIN lahmansbaseballdb.allstarfull asf
ON asf.playerid = p.playerid
WHERE birthyear = 1985;
```

The preceding query will result in rows that have all the `people` table rows, but only the rows matching in the `collegeplaying` table and the `allstarfull` table that match the `people` table rows. The following screenshot shows the results of the previous query:

playerid	birthyear	schoolid	yearid	gameid
cassebo01	1985	NULL	NULL	NULL
castrfa01	1985	NULL	NULL	NULL
cespeyo01	1985	NULL	2014	ALS201407150
cespeyo01	1985	NULL	2016	ALS201607120
chenwe02	1985	NULL	NULL	NULL
ciriape01	1985	NULL	NULL	NULL
clippty01	1985	NULL	2011	NLS201107120
clippty01	1985	NULL	2014	ALS201407150
danksjo01	1985	NULL	NULL	NULL
daviswa01	1985	NULL	2015	NLS201507140
daviswa01	1985	NULL	2016	ALS201607120

Note that in the preceding screenshot, you see `NULL` values in the `yearid` and `gameid` fields for many rows because those `playerids` didn't have a corresponding row in the `allstarfull` table. You will also see some `schoolids` that are `NULL` because those `playerids` didn't have corresponding rows in the `collegeplaying` table.

Additionally, you can use a left excluding join. This would include all rows from the left table that don't match records in the right table.

To use a left excluding join, use the following syntax:

```
SELECT column(s)
FROM table1
LEFT OUTER JOIN table2
ON table1.column = table2.column
WHERE table2.column IS NULL;
```

The previous syntax shows you how to join two tables together with a left excluding join. This is a modified LEFT OUTER JOIN. You join a column in table1 that matches a column in table2.

 The WHERE clause is not optional in this case, and needs to be set to IS NULL for a column in table2.

The following example will help you to understand how to use the left excluding join:

```
SELECT p.playerid, birthyear, schoolid, yearid
FROM lahmansbaseballdb.people p
LEFT OUTER JOIN lahmansbaseballdb.collegeplaying c
ON p.playerid = c.playerid
WHERE birthyear = 1985
AND c.playerid IS NULL;
```

The previous query will return the results in the following screenshot:

playerid	birthyear	schoolid	yearid
abadfe01	1985	NULL	NULL
abreuju01	1985	NULL	NULL
adducji02	1985	NULL	NULL
ascanjo01	1985	NULL	NULL
atilalu01	1985	NULL	NULL
atkinmi01	1985	NULL	NULL
bartoda02	1985	NULL	NULL
bastaan01	1985	NULL	NULL

As you can see in the preceding screenshot, you are only getting rows from the left table (people) where the playerid in the right table (collegeplaying) is NULL. You can combine the results of the LEFT OUTER JOIN and the left excluding join with a set operator, which is covered later in this chapter.

Learning RIGHT OUTER JOIN syntax

To RIGHT OUTER JOIN two tables, use the following syntax:

```
SELECT column(s)
FROM table1
RIGHT OUTER JOIN table2
ON table1.column = table2.column
```

```
WHERE conditions
ORDER BY column(s);
```

The previous syntax shows you how to join two tables together with a RIGHT OUTER join. You join a column in table1 that matches a column in table2. The WHERE and ORDER BY clauses are optional. They are there to show you that the RIGHT OUTER JOIN syntax goes between the FROM and WHERE clauses.

The following example will help you to understand how to use the RIGHT OUTER JOIN:

```
SELECT p.playerid, asf.yearid, gameid, startingpos
FROM lahmansbaseballdb.allstarfull asf
RIGHT OUTER JOIN lahmansbaseballdb.people p
ON p.playerid = asf.playerid;
```

You can see in the preceding query that you are joining the allstarfull table to the people table with a RIGHT OUTER JOIN. This will return all rows from the people table and only corresponding rows from the allstarfull table. In the following screenshot, you will see the results of the previous query:

playerid	yearid	gameid	startingpos
aardsda01	NULL	NULL	NULL
aaronha01	1955	NLS195507120	NULL
aaronha01	1956	ALS195607100	NULL
aaronha01	1957	NLS195707090	9
aaronha01	1958	ALS195807080	9
aaronha01	1959	NLS195907070	9
aaronha01	1959	NLS195908030	9
aaronha01	1960	ALS196007110	9
aaronha01	1960	ALS196007130	9
aaronha01	1961	NLS196107110	NULL
aaronha01	1961	ALS196107310	NULL
aaronha01	1962	ALS196207100	NULL
aaronha01	1962	NLS196207300	NULL
aaronha01	1963	ALS196307090	9

As you can see in the preceding screenshot, the results show NULL for the rows in the people table that don't have a corresponding row in the allstarfull table, and the rows that correspond between people and allstarfull have a complete row of data in the results.

You can also leave off OUTER in the join, and it will run the same as if it were there. For example, the following code snippet will run RIGHT OUTER JOIN:

```
RIGHT OUTER JOIN lahmansbaseballdb.people p
```

This code snippet will work the same way and return the same results as the previous code snippet:

```
RIGHT JOIN lahmansbaseballdb.people p
```

You can use either RIGHT JOIN or RIGHT OUTER JOIN, with the same results.

As with INNER JOIN, you can join up to 61 tables into your query. You will RIGHT OUTER JOIN with three tables, as shown in the following SQL query:

```
SELECT m.playerid, m.yearid, h.votedBy, s.salary
FROM lahmansbaseballdb.managers m
RIGHT OUTER JOIN lahmansbaseballdb.halloffame h
ON m.playerid = h.playerid
RIGHT OUTER JOIN lahmansbaseballdb.salaries s
ON m.playerid = s.playerid;
```

The preceding query will result in rows that have all the salary table rows, but only the rows matching in halloffame and managers that match the salary table rows. The following screenshot shows the results of the previous query:

playerid	yearid	votedBy	salary
NULL	NULL	NULL	240000
NULL	NULL	NULL	483333
NULL	NULL	NULL	779227
NULL	NULL	NULL	1075000
NULL	NULL	NULL	325000
NULL	NULL	NULL	365000
boonebo01	1995	BBWAA	883000
boonebo01	1996	BBWAA	883000
boonebo01	1997	BBWAA	883000
boonebo01	2001	BBWAA	883000
boonebo01	2002	BBWAA	883000
boonebo01	2003	BBWAA	883000
boonebo01	1995	BBWAA	883000
boonebo01	1996	BBWAA	883000

Note that in the preceding screenshot, you see many NULL values in the playerid, yearid, and votedBy rows because those *playerids* didn't have a corresponding row in the salary table.

Additionally, you can do a right excluding join. This join will include all rows from the right table that don't match records in the left table. To execute a right excluding join, use the following syntax:

```
SELECT column(s)
FROM table1
RIGHT OUTER JOIN table2
ON table1.column = table2.column
WHERE table1.column IS NULL;
```

The previous syntax shows you how to join two tables together with a right excluding join. This is a modified RIGHT OUTER JOIN. You join a column in table1 that matches a column in table2.

> The WHERE clause is not optional in this case, and needs to be set to IS NULL for a column in table1.

The following example will help you to understand how to use the right excluding join:

```
SELECT p.playerid, asf.yearid, gameid, startingpos
FROM lahmansbaseballdb.allstarfull asf
RIGHT OUTER JOIN lahmansbaseballdb.people p
ON p.playerid = asf.playerid
WHERE asf.playerid IS NULL;
```

The previous query will return the results in the following screenshot:

playerid	yearid	gameid	startingpos
aardsda01	NULL	NULL	NULL
aaronto01	NULL	NULL	NULL
abadan01	NULL	NULL	NULL
abadfe01	NULL	NULL	NULL
abadijo01	NULL	NULL	NULL
abbated01	NULL	NULL	NULL
abbeybe01	NULL	NULL	NULL
abbeych01	NULL	NULL	NULL

As you can see in the preceding screenshot, you are only getting rows from the right table (people) where the playerid in the left table (allstarfull) is NULL. You could combine the results of the RIGHT OUTER JOIN and right excluding join with a set operator, which is covered later in this chapter.

Exploring differences in other relational data models

In other **relational data models (RDMs)**, you can also use the full outer join. In Oracle, PostgreSQL, and SQL Server, you can use the `FULL OUTER JOIN` syntax to return rows from both tables.

Using FULL OUTER JOIN

To join a table with `FULL OUTER JOIN`, execute the following SQL code:

```
USE lahmansbaseballdb
SELECT p.playerid, asf.yearid, gameid, startingpos
FROM allstarfull asf
FULL OUTER JOIN people p
ON p.playerid = asf.playerid;
```

You can see in the preceding query that you are joining the `allstarfull` table to the `people` table with a `FULL OUTER JOIN`. This query will return all rows from the `people` table and all rows from the `allstarfull` table. Where there isn't a matching row in either table, you will see `NULL` values, as illustrated in the following screenshot:

ᴀʙᴄ playerid	123 yearid	ᴀʙᴄ gameid	123 startingpos
aguaylu01	[NULL]	[NULL]	[NULL]
aguilch01	[NULL]	[NULL]	[NULL]
aguilje01	2,018	NLS201807170	[NULL]
aguilri01	1,991	ALS199107090	[NULL]
aguilri01	1,992	NLS199207140	[NULL]
aguilri01	1,993	ALS199307130	[NULL]
aguirha01	1,962	ALS196207100	[NULL]
aguirha01	1,962	NLS196207300	[NULL]
ahearch01	[NULL]	[NULL]	[NULL]

As you can see in the previous screenshot, the results show `NULL` values for the rows in the `people` table that don't have a corresponding row in the `allstarfull` table, and the rows that correspond between `people` and `allstarfull` have a complete row of data in the results.

You can also leave off the `OUTER` in the join, and it will run the same as if it were there. For example, the following code snippet will execute a `FULL OUTER JOIN`:

```
FULL JOIN lahmansbaseballdb.people p
```

The following code snippet will work the same way and return the same results as the previous code snippet:

```
FULL OUTER JOIN lahmansbaseballdb.people p
```

You can use either FULL JOIN or FULL OUTER JOIN, with the same results.

Using advanced joins

MySQL includes some more advanced joins such as cross, natural, and self joins. These will be discussed in the following sections.

Understanding what a CROSS JOIN is and how to use it

A CROSS JOIN is like an INNER JOIN without the ON clause. It winds up producing results that are like multiplying each table with the other table. This is also referred to as a Cartesian result. A CROSS JOIN will return a combination of every row from two tables. This join will result in a lot of rows returned. It may result in your query never returning results because it's too intensive for the database system to return the results.

To CROSS JOIN two tables, use the following syntax:

```
SELECT column(s)
FROM table1
CROSS JOIN table2
WHERE condition(s);
```

The previous syntax shows you how to join two tables together with a CROSS JOIN. You join a column in table1 that matches a column in table2.

 The WHERE clause is optional but highly recommended to avoid a very long-running query.

The following example will help you to understand how to use CROSS JOIN:

```
SELECT c.playerid, c.schoolid, c.yearid, city, state, country
FROM lahmansbaseballdb.collegeplaying c
```

```
CROSS JOIN lahmansbaseballdb.schools s
WHERE s.schoolid = 'akron';
```

The previous query gives you results of every row in `collegeplaying` that matches every row in `schools`, so it gives you the Cartesian product of those tables, as in the following screenshot:

playerid	schoolid	yearid	schoolid	city	state	country
aardsda01	pennst	2001	akron	Akron	OH	USA
aardsda01	rice	2002	akron	Akron	OH	USA
aardsda01	rice	2003	akron	Akron	OH	USA
abadan01	gamiddl	1992	akron	Akron	OH	USA
abadan01	gamiddl	1993	akron	Akron	OH	USA
abbeybe01	vermont	1889	akron	Akron	OH	USA
abbeybe01	vermont	1890	akron	Akron	OH	USA
abbeybe01	vermont	1891	akron	Akron	OH	USA
abbeybe01	vermont	1892	akron	Akron	OH	USA
abbotje01	kentucky	1991	akron	Akron	OH	USA
abbotje01	kentucky	1992	akron	Akron	OH	USA
abbotje01	kentucky	1994	akron	Akron	OH	USA
abbotji01	michigan	1986	akron	Akron	OH	USA
abbotji01	michigan	1987	akron	Akron	OH	USA
abbotji01	michigan	1988	akron	Akron	OH	USA

As you can see in the preceding screenshot, the `schoolid`, `city`, `state`, and `country` fields from the schools table was placed in every row from the `collegeplaying` table, whereas the `schoolid` from the `school` table was equal to `akron`. Not a useful query in this case, but this is just done to illustrate how the cross joins work. This type of join could be useful for some queries—for example, if you want to know all the colors with sizes of a clothing item.

Also, you can use just the word `JOIN`, and leave off `CROSS`, to return the same results. This following query will return the same results as the query earlier in this section:

```
SELECT c.playerid, c.schoolid, c.yearid, city, state, country
FROM lahmansbaseballdb.collegeplaying c
JOIN lahmansbaseballdb.schools s
WHERE s.schoolid = 'akron';
```

The main thing to keep in mind with cross joins is that they can be very intensive for the database system, and it's best to use the other joins discussed earlier in this chapter if possible, and always use a `WHERE` clause if you are using a `CROSS JOIN`.

Understanding what a NATURAL JOIN is and how to use it

A NATURAL JOIN will associate columns of the same name in the joined tables with each other. It's similar to an INNER JOIN or a LEFT OUTER JOIN.

To NATURAL JOIN two tables, use the following syntax:

```
SELECT column(s)
FROM table1
NATURAL JOIN table2;
```

The previous syntax shows you how to join two tables together with NATURAL JOIN. You explicitly set the columns to be joined.

The following example will help you to understand how to use NATURAL JOIN:

```
SELECT c.playerid, c.schoolid, c.yearid, s.schoolid, city, state, country
FROM lahmansbaseballdb.collegeplaying c
NATURAL JOIN lahmansbaseballdb.schools s;
```

You will receive the results from the previous query, as shown in the following screenshot:

playerid	schoolid	yearid	schoolid	city	state	country
aardsda01	pennst	2001	pennst	State College	PA	USA
aardsda01	rice	2002	rice	Houston	TX	USA
aardsda01	rice	2003	rice	Houston	TX	USA
abadan01	gamiddl	1992	gamiddl	Cochran	GA	USA
abadan01	gamiddl	1993	gamiddl	Cochran	GA	USA
abbeybe01	vermont	1889	vermont	Burlington	VT	USA
abbeybe01	vermont	1890	vermont	Burlington	VT	USA
abbeybe01	vermont	1891	vermont	Burlington	VT	USA
abbeybe01	vermont	1892	vermont	Burlington	VT	USA
abbotje01	kentucky	1991	kentucky	Lexington	KY	USA
abbotje01	kentucky	1992	kentucky	Lexington	KY	USA
abbotje01	kentucky	1994	kentucky	Lexington	KY	USA
abbotji01	michigan	1986	michigan	Ann Arbor	MI	USA

These results will be from NATURAL JOIN finding the common column names in schools and collegeplaying, which in this case will be schoolid. It returns the results where the rows in each table match on schoolid.

Understanding what a SELF JOIN is and how to use it

A SELF JOIN is used to join a table to itself. This join would be useful in the case of a table containing hierarchical data such as employees and managers. Here, we have a table named Employees containing the following columns and rows:

EmployeeID	FirstName	LastName	ManagerID
1	Jane	Smith	NULL
2	Peter	Jones	1
3	Jessica	Lewis	2
4	Donna	Nickols	2
5	Joel	Rogers	3
6	Joseph	Edwards	7
7	Ruth	Chapman	3
8	Theodore	Clark	6
9	Adam	Berry	6
10	Lucy	Slater	5

You can use a query such as this to self-join on the preceding table, as follows:

```
SELECT e.FirstName + ' ' + e.LastName AS EmployeeName,
    m.FirstName + ' ' + m.LastName AS ManagerName
FROM Employees AS e
LEFT OUTER JOIN Employees m
ON e.ManagerID = m.EmployeeID
ORDER BY ManagerName;
```

The previous query will return these results:

EmployeeName	ManagerName
Jane Smith	NULL
Peter Jones	Jane Smith
Joel Rogers	Jessica Lewis
Ruth Chapman	Jessica Lewis
Lucy Slater	Joel Rogers
Theodore Clark	Joseph Edwards
Adam Berry	Joseph Edwards

Jessica Lewis	Peter Jones
Donna Nickols	Peter Jones
Joseph Edwards	Ruth Chapman

If you used an INNER JOIN on the previous query, you wouldn't get the row for Jane Smith because she doesn't report to anyone.

Understanding set theory

Set theory is the underlying concept of SQL. A set is a collection of zero or more objects. Each object in a set is called an **element**. In MySQL, a table corresponds to a set, and a record corresponds with an element. You can get a subset from a set. A subset is a smaller set of elements from the set. In SQL, you can get a subset by using a WHERE clause. A cross product is a set created from two or more sets. In SQL, a cross product is a join. To create different sets of data in SQL, you can use the intersection, difference, and union joins. Each of these is explained in more detail in the following sections.

Understanding what a UNION join is and learning how to use it in a SQL query

UNION allows you to combine two or more result sets into a single result set. There are a few rules that need to be followed to avoid errors, listed as follows:

- The number of columns in the SELECT statements must be the same.
- The order of the columns in the SELECT statements must be the same.
- The data types of the columns must be the same or of a compatible type.
- The ORDERBY clause can only be used on the final SELECT statement.

There are also a couple of things to keep in mind when reviewing your results, as follows:

- The names of the final columns are generated from the column names you use in the first SELECT statement.
- GROUP BY and HAVING clauses can only be used in each query, but can't be used to affect the final results (*Chapter 10*, *Grouping and Summarizing Data*, goes into more detail on GROUP BY and HAVING).

You have two choices when using UNION, as follows:

- UNION: This removes duplicate rows without using DISTINCT in the SELECT statements.
- UNION ALL: This does not remove duplicate rows, and they will remain in the final result. This will perform faster than UNION because it doesn't have to remove duplicates.

The UNION operators both combine results vertically as opposed to a join, which combines results horizontally. The following screenshot shows you the difference between UNION, UNION ALL, and INNER JOIN, and the resulting output from each:

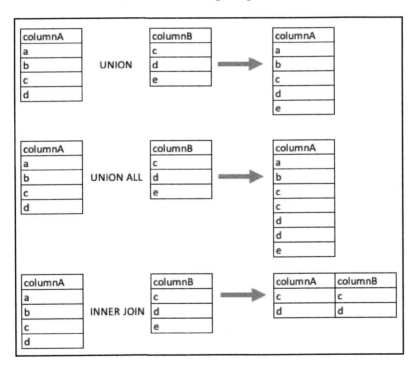

We will walk through how to use UNION and UNION ALL in queries in the next sections.

UNION

To form a union between two tables, use the following syntax:

```
SELECT column(s)
FROM table1
WHERE conditions(s)
UNION
SELECT column(s)
FROM table2
WHERE condition(s)
ORDER BY column(s);
```

The previous syntax shows you how to UNION two queries together. The WHERE clause in each query is optional. The ORDER BY clause is also optional, and can only appear after the last query in the UNION join.

If you want to get all the awards for both managers and players in 1994, execute this query:

```
SELECT am.playerid, namegiven, awardid, yearid FROM
lahmansbaseballdb.awardsmanagers am
INNER JOIN lahmansbaseballdb.people p
ON p.playerid = am.playerid
WHERE yearid = 1994
UNION
SELECT ap.playerid, namegiven, awardid, yearid FROM
lahmansbaseballdb.awardsplayers ap
INNER JOIN lahmansbaseballdb.people p
ON p.playerid = ap.playerid
WHERE yearid = 1994
ORDER BY awardid;
```

The previous query will give you the results shown in the following screenshot:

playerid	namegiven	awardid	yearid
mcgrifr01	Frederick Stanley	All-Star Game MVP	1994
aloufe01	Felipe Rojas	BBWAA Manager of the Year	1994
showabu99	William Nathaniel	BBWAA Manager of the Year	1994
smithoz01	Osborne Earl	Branch Rickey Award	1994
maddugr01	Gregory Alan	Cy Young Award	1994
coneda01	David Brian	Cy Young Award	1994
willima04	Matthew Derrick	Gold Glove	1994
whitede03	Devon Markes	Gold Glove	1994
alomaro01	Roberto	Gold Glove	1994
vizquom01	Omar Enrique	Gold Glove	1994

The previous results are the UNION of the manager awards and the player awards for 1994.

Note that you need to use the WHERE clause on each query, but the ORDER BY clause can only be used on the final query. If you didn't have the same number, order, and type on your columns, it would give you an error. Run the following code on the first SELECT statement:

```
SELECT am.playerid, awardid, yearid FROM lahmansbaseballdb.awardsmanagers
am
```

This results in the following error:

```
Error Code: 1222. The used SELECT statements have a different number of
columns
```

This is because you don't have the same number of columns.

Instead, run the following code on the first SELECT statement:

```
SELECT am.playerid, awardid, yearid, namegiven FROM
lahmansbaseballdb.awardsmanagers am
```

You wouldn't get an error in this case, but instead, MySQL would implicitly convert yearid to the same column type as the namegiven column. There are two types of conversion in MySQL: explicit and implicit. Explicit conversion refers to when you explicitly change a data type. Explicit conversion is covered more in Chapter 9, *Working with Expressions*. Implicit conversion happens when MySQL needs to match data types. In the case of the UNION join, if you use a column with a data type of VARCHAR in the first SELECT statement, and then select a column with a data type of SMALLINT in the second statement, MySQL will implicitly convert the SMALLINT data type to VARCHAR. This conversion happens because the data type of the first SELECT statement is used throughout.

You will get some strange results with an implicit conversion, as shown in the following screenshot:

playerid	awardid	yearid	namegiven
molitpa01	Paul Leo	TSN All-Star	1994
mondera01	Raul Ramon	Rookie of the Year	1994
hamelbo00	Robert James	Rookie of the Year	1994
alomaro01	Roberto	Gold Glove	1994
beckro01	Rodney Roy	Rolaids Relief Man Award	1994
pagnoto01	Thomas Alan	Gold Glove	1994
showabu99	TSN Manager...	1994	William N...
aloufe01	TSN Manager...	1994	Felipe Rojas
boggswa01	Wade Anthony	TSN All-Star	1994
boggswa01	Wade Anthony	Gold Glove	1994
boggswa01	Wade Anthony	Silver Slugger	1994
cordewi01	Wilfredo	Silver Slugger	1994

You can see in the previous results that now, you have `yearid` and `namegiven` mixed in each of the `yearid` and `namegiven` columns. This example impresses on you the importance of the order of the columns specified in the `SELECT` statements. If MySQL couldn't convert the columns to the same type, then it would give you an error. This brings up an important point in general with query writing, which is that just because you don't get an error, this doesn't mean you got what you wanted.

You may want to know whether the `playerid` is associated with a manager or an actual player. To do this, you can add a static column value to your query to note whether the row is a manager or player. You can execute the following query to see how this works:

```
SELECT am.playerid, namegiven, awardid, yearid, "Manager" as playeridType
FROM lahmansbaseballdb.awardsmanagers am
INNER JOIN lahmansbaseballdb.people p
ON p.playerid = am.playerid
WHERE yearid = 1994
UNION
SELECT ap.playerid, namegiven, awardid, yearid, "Player"
FROM lahmansbaseballdb.awardsplayers ap
INNER JOIN lahmansbaseballdb.people p
ON p.playerid = ap.playerid
WHERE yearid = 1994
ORDER BY awardid;
```

The previous query will give the results shown in the following screenshot:

playerid	namegiven	awardid	yearid	playeridType
mcgrifr01	Frederick Stanley	All-Star Game MVP	1994	Player
aloufe01	Felipe Rojas	BBWAA Manager of the Year	1994	Manager
showabu99	William Nathaniel	BBWAA Manager of the Year	1994	Manager
smithoz01	Osborne Earl	Branch Rickey Award	1994	Player
maddugr01	Gregory Alan	Cy Young Award	1994	Player
coneda01	David Brian	Cy Young Award	1994	Player
willima04	Matthew Derrick	Gold Glove	1994	Player
whitede03	Devon Markes	Gold Glove	1994	Player
alomaro01	Roberto	Gold Glove	1994	Player
vizquom01	Omar Enrique	Gold Glove	1994	Player
bagweje01	Jeffrey Robert	Gold Glove	1994	Player

You can see that by adding a static column in each SELECT statement, you wind up with a column that has that static value for each row. For example, on the awardsmanagers table, you added Manager as a playeridType value, and on the awardsplayer table, you added Player. These values show up as a column in the results.

UNION ALL

If you run the same query from the last section on UNION with UNION ALL instead, you will get the same results because there weren't any duplicates to filter out.

You can use the following new query to see how UNION ALL works by removing duplicates:

```
SELECT playerid, yearid, teamid, G AS gamesbatted FROM
lahmansbaseballdb.batting
WHERE yearid = 2005
UNION ALL
SELECT playerid, yearid, teamid, g_batting FROM
lahmansbaseballdb.appearances
WHERE yearid = 2005
ORDER BY yearid, playerid, gamesbatted;
```

The previous query will give us the results shown in the following screenshot:

playerid	yearid	teamid	gamesbatted
acevejo01	2005	COL	36
acevejo01	2005	COL	36
adamsmi03	2005	MIL	12
adamsmi03	2005	MIL	13
adamsru01	2005	TOR	139
adamsru01	2005	TOR	139
adamste01	2005	PHI	14
adamste01	2005	PHI	16
adkinjo01	2005	CHA	0
adkinjo01	2005	CHA	5
affelje01	2005	KCA	3
affelje01	2005	KCA	49

From the preceding screenshot, we can make the following observations:

- In the query results, you see two rows for each `playerid` based on the `yearid`, `teamid`, and `gamesbatted` fields, regardless of whether the `gamesbatted` field has the same value in the `batting` and `appearances` tables.
- If you execute this same query as `UNION`, you would only see one row for each `playerid`, `yearid`, `teamid`, and `gamesbatted` combination.
- The results with `UNION ALL` bring up an interesting question, though. If the `appearances` table has the number of games batted in any given year and the `batting` table also has this value, you would think they would match one another. `UNION ALL` becomes a good way of seeing what discrepancies may lie in different tables in your database.

Understanding what an intersect is and learning how to use it in a SQL query

An intersect allows you to combine two or more results sets that contain the distinct values of each set. The following screenshot shows you what results from an intersect:

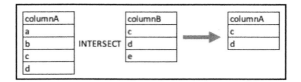

MySQL doesn't support the `INTERSECT` SQL operator, but there is a workaround with a join. This can be done with `DISTINCT` and `INNER JOIN`. The following query shows you how to do this:

```
SELECT DISTINCT a.playerid
FROM lahmansbaseballdb.batting b
INNER JOIN lahmansbaseballdb.appearances a
ON a.playerid = b.playerid
ORDER BY a.playerid;
```

The previous query gives you the results shown in the following screenshot:

playerid
aardsda01
aaronha01
aaronto01
aasedo01
abadan01
abadfe01
abadijo01
abbated01
abbeybe01
abbeych01
abbotda01

The preceding results are the intersection of `batting` and `appearances` under `playerid`. The list of results contains only values that are in both tables. The `DISTINCT` operator removes duplicates, and the `INNER JOIN` returns the rows from both tables.

Looking at intersection in other RDMS

To run queries that intersect in Oracle, PostgreSQL, and SQL Server, you can use the `INTERSECT` operator. The following screenshot shows you the output resulting from `INTERSECT`:

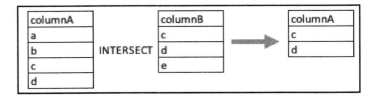

The previous query from MySQL would be rewritten like this for the other RDMS:

```
USE lahmansbaseballdb
SELECT playerid
FROM batting
INTERSECT
SELECT playerid
FROM appearances
ORDER BY playerid;
```

The previous query will return rows where the two tables have overlap.

Understanding what difference is and learning how to use it in a SQL query

To find the difference in MySQL, you can use the right excluding join or left excluding join, since MySQL doesn't support the EXCEPT or MINUS keywords. Please refer to the sections on right outer joins and left outer joins earlier in this chapter, which include information on right excluding joins and left excluding joins in MySQL.

Exploring differences in other RDMS

MINUS and EXCEPT (depending on the RDMS, as outlined here) are the equivalent of right and left excluding joins. The following screenshot shows you the output resulting from a MINUS or EXCEPT join:

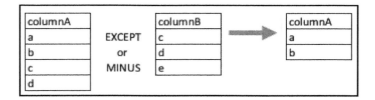

The following is a code example of a right excluding join in MySQL:

```
SELECT p.playerid
FROM lahmansbaseballdb.allstarfull asf
RIGHT OUTER JOIN lahmansbaseballdb.people p
ON p.playerid = asf.playerid
WHERE asf.playerid IS NULL;
```

In the previous query, you are only getting rows from the right table (`people`) where `playerid` in the left table (`allstarfull`) is `NULL`.

EXCEPT

PostgreSQL and SQL Server use the `EXCEPT` operator to accomplish what MySQL does with a right or left excluding join. You can rewrite the code from earlier in this section in PostgreSQL and SQL Server, like this:

```
USE lahmansbaseballdb
SELECT playerid
FROM people
EXCEPT
SELECT playerid
FROM allstarfull;
```

The previous query will return all rows from the `people` table that don't appear in the `allstarfull` table.

MINUS

Oracle uses the `MINUS` operator to accomplish what MySQL does with a right or left excluding join, and what PostgreSQL and SQL Server accomplish with the `EXCEPT` operator. You can rewrite the code from earlier in this section in Oracle, like this:

```
USE lahmansbaseballdb
SELECT playerid
FROM people
MINUS
SELECT playerid
FROM allstarfull;
```

The previous query will return all rows from the `people` table that don't appear in the `allstarfull` table.

Using indexes with your queries

In this section, we will go over how to see which indexes your multiple tables query is using and how to troubleshoot them. Please refer to Chapter 6, *Querying a Single Table*, for an introduction to the `EXPLAIN` syntax you will be using here.

You will begin with a query you used earlier in the chapter and will add EXPLAIN to the query to get information about which indexes your query is using. Execute the following query to get your index explanation information:

```
EXPLAIN SELECT p.playerid, p.birthyear,
  a.yearid, a.teamid, a.G_defense, b.H
FROM lahmansbaseballdb.appearances AS a
INNER JOIN lahmansbaseballdb.people AS p
ON p.playerid = a.playerid
INNER JOIN lahmansbaseballdb.batting AS b
ON p.playerid = b.playerid
WHERE b.yearid = 2017
AND b.H <> 0
ORDER BY p.playerid, a.yearid, a.teamid, a.G_defense, b.H;
```

In the following screenshot, the EXPLAIN results are shown:

id	select_type	table	partitions	type	possible_keys	key	key_len	ref	rows	filtered	Extra
1	SIMPLE	p	NULL	ALL	NULL	NULL	NULL	NULL	19473	100.00	Using where; Using temporary; Using filesort
1	SIMPLE	b	NULL	ref	PRIMARY	PRIMARY	40	lahmansbaseballdb.p.playerID,const	1	90.00	Using where
1	SIMPLE	a	NULL	ALL	NULL	NULL	NULL	NULL	105113	10.00	Using where; Using join buffer (Block Nested Loop)

From the results in the preceding screenshot, you can see the following:

- The tables are in the results as their alias names, such as b for the batting table, p for the people table, and a for the appearances table. If you didn't use aliases, then the actual table name would appear in the table column.
- The batting table is using the primary key to return data. This is good since it will mean that data will most likely be returned faster as the query is using an index. The batting table is filtered to 90.00, using a WHERE clause.
- The people and appearance tables don't have an index used in this query. The people table is using temporary and filesort, which can slow down a query, and the appearances table is using a join buffer (**Block Nested Loop**), which means that data from earlier joins has been placed into a buffer. The data from the appearances table will be joined to this data in the buffer, which also can slow down a query.
- This query (without EXPLAIN) returns 5,520 rows, but you can see that it's looking at quite a few rows in people (19,473 rows) and appearances (105,113 rows). This query (without EXPLAIN) is also taking over 17 seconds to run (the timing may vary on different computers).

- The `type` column shows a couple of different values: `ALL` and `ref`. `type` shows the type of join that was used for the tables. Many different values can be in this table. `ALL` means that a full table scan is happening. This makes sense since you can see that no index is being used for the `people` and the `appearances` table, so the entire table will need to be scanned to find the results. `ref` means that all rows from that table that have a match in the other tables in the query will be read. This makes sense because the `batting` table has an index that can be used, so the query can seek the records it needs instead of having to scan the entire table. For a listing of join types, please refer to the *Further reading* section later in this chapter.

Let's work on getting rid of the `Using temporary` and `Using filesort` clauses on the `people` table, and the `Using join buffer (Block Nested Loop)` clause on the `appearances` table. You can start by looking at your query some more to see whether you can change anything to improve the query without adding or changing indexes. If you change the `WHERE` clause in your preceding query to `WHERE a.yearid = 2017`, then the `WHERE` clause is now using the `appearances` table instead of the `batting` table. With this new `WHERE` clause, you wind up with new `EXPLAIN` results, as shown in the following screenshot:

id	select_type	table	partitions	type	possible_keys	key	key_len	ref	rows	filtered	Extra
1	SIMPLE	a	NULL	ref	PRIMARY	PRIMARY	2	const	1494	100.00	Using temporary; Using filesort
1	SIMPLE	p	NULL	ALL	NULL	NULL	NULL	NULL	19473	10.00	Using where; Using join buffer (Block Nested Loop)
1	SIMPLE	b	NULL	ref	PRIMARY	PRIMARY	38	lahmansbaseballdb.p.playerID	5	90.00	Using where

You can see in the preceding screenshot that the `appearances` table is now using the `PRIMARY` key. It has gone from `105113` rows down to `1494` rows viewed. This is much more efficient and takes only about 5 seconds versus 17 seconds previously. It changes the results of the query, though, and returns `5602` rows instead of `5520` rows. This change may or may not be acceptable to you, depending on what you are trying to achieve with your query results.

You could instead try switching out `a.yearid` and `a.teamid` in both the `SELECT` and `ORDER BY` clauses to `b.yearid` and `b.teamid`, to align with the `b.yearid` you are using in the original `WHERE` clause, but this slows the query down even more.

Another option for this query is to add another `WHERE` clause (`AND a.yearid = 2017`), as in the following code sample:

```
WHERE b.yearid = 2017
AND a.yearid = 2017
AND b.H <> 0
```

This query will filter the results down from 5520 rows to only 956 rows, but the query runs in 1.45 seconds. This also may or may not be acceptable to you, depending on what you wanted the original query to return.

If you go back to the original query and see what you can improve upon by adding an index, you need to look at what indexes are on the people and appearances tables. To see the indexes on appearances, click the down arrow next to the appearances table, and then click the down arrow next to **Indexes**. Any indexes on the table will be listed. You can click the index you want to see the definition of, and it will be displayed in the lower panel, as shown in the following screenshot:

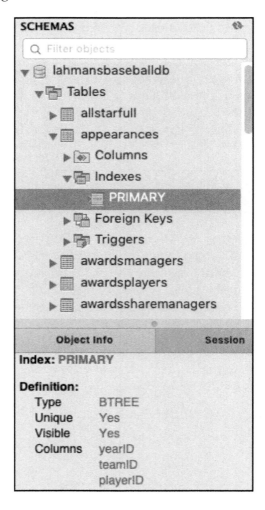

You can see from the previous screenshot that the `appearances` table has one index named `PRIMARY`, and that the index has three columns, which are `yearID`, `teamID`, and `playerID`. If you do the same steps to see the indexes on the `people` table, you can see that it doesn't have any indexes on it.

What you can do to speed up this query is to add a couple of non-clustered indexes, one on the `appearances` table and one on the `people` table. What's important to note at this point is that by adding indexes for this query, you can speed up this query. Note that you will slow down other queries, such as queries inserting, updating, or deleting data, and you could also slow down other queries selecting data, so you need to be careful adding indexes to help one query. You need to analyze all the queries on a MySQL server to understand the impact you may have by adding or removing indexes.

Let's start by adding a non-clustered index on the `people` table by executing the following query:

```
ALTER TABLE lahmansbaseballdb.people
ADD INDEX `NC_playerid_birthyear` (playerID ASC, birthYear ASC) VISIBLE;
```

What you are doing with that previous index creation script is covering the columns you are using in the query. For the `people` table, you are joining on and ordering by `playerid`, and you are filtering on `birthyear`, so you've included those columns in a nonclustered index.

By adding the non-clustered index to the `people` table, your query runs in 1.5 seconds, and produces the `EXPLAIN` results in the following screenshot:

id	select_type	table	partitions	type	possible_keys	key	key_len	ref	rows	filtered	Extra
1	SIMPLE	a	NULL	ALL	NULL	NULL	NULL	NULL	105113	100.00	Using temporary; Using filesort
1	SIMPLE	p	NULL	ref	NC_playerid_birthyear	NC_playerid_birthyear	1023	lahmansbaseballdb.a.playerID	1	100.00	Using where; Using index
1	SIMPLE	b	NULL	ref	PRIMARY	PRIMARY	40	lahmansbaseballdb.p.playerID,const	1	90.00	Using where

You can see in the preceding screenshot that your query is now using the non-clustered index you just created on the `people` table, which is only getting 1 row returned now instead of 19473 rows. Now, let's look at the `appearances` table since it's still getting 105113 rows and not using an index.

Let's add a nonclustered index on the `appearances` table by executing the following query:

```
ALTER TABLE lahmansbaseballdb.appearances
ADD INDEX `NC_playerid_yearid_teamid_G_defense` (playerID ASC, yearID ASC,
teamID ASC, G_defense ASC) VISIBLE;
```

What you are doing with the previous index creation script is covering the columns you are using in the query. For the `appearances` table, you are joining on `playerid` and ordering by `yearID`, `teamID`, and `G_defense`, so you've included those columns in a non-clustered index.

By adding the non-clustered index to the `appearances` table, your query runs in less than 1 second, and produces the `EXPLAIN` results in the following screenshot:

id	select_type	table	partitions	type	possible_keys	key	key_len	ref	rows	filtered	Extra
1	SIMPLE	b	NULL	ALL	PRIMARY	NULL	NULL	NULL	105369	9.00	Using where; Using temporary; Using filesort
1	SIMPLE	p	NULL	ref	NC_playerid_birthyear	NC_playerid_birthyear	1023	lahmansbaseballdb.b.playerID	1	100.00	Using where; Using index
1	SIMPLE	a	NULL	ref	NC_playerid_yearid_teamid_G_defense	NC_playerid_yearid_teamid_G...	38	lahmansbaseballdb.p.playerID	5	100.00	Using where; Using index

You can see from the preceding screenshot that you've eliminated the problem with joining on the `appearances` table, and the query is using the nonclustered index you just created. You can also see that the `batting` table now has **Using temporary** and **Using filesort** in the **Extra** column.

You might be able to remedy this with a nonclustered index on the `batting` table. If you look at the indexes on the `batting` table, you can see that it has one index named `PRIMARY` and it contains three columns: `playerid`, `yearid`, and `stint`. Since you are using `playerid` to join, `yearid` and `H` in the `WHERE` clause, and `H` in the `ORDER BY` clause, create a nonclustered index with those columns, with the following code:

```
ALTER TABLE lahmansbaseballdb.batting
  ADD INDEX `NC_playerid_yearid_H` (playerID ASC, yearID ASC, H ASC)
VISIBLE;
```

After running the previous index creation, the query is slightly faster, but still using `temporary` and `filesort`, as you can see in the following screenshot:

id	select_type	table	partitions	type	possible_keys	key	key_len	ref	rows	filtered	Extra
1	SIMPLE	b	NULL	index	PRIMARY,NC_playerid_yearid_H	NC_playerid_yearid_H	43	NULL	105369	9.00	Using where; Using index; Using temporary; Using filesort
1	SIMPLE	p	NULL	ref	NC_playerid_birthyear	NC_playerid_birthyear	1023	lahmansbaseballdb.b.playerID	1	100.00	Using where; Using index
1	SIMPLE	a	NULL	ref	NC_playerid_yearid_teamid_G_defense	NC_playerid_yearid_teamid_G...	38	lahmansbaseballdb.p.playerID	5	100.00	Using where; Using index

It's probably not worth adding that last non-clustered index since it's not speeding up the query much, and it's not filtering out more rows from the join, so you can drop that index. By adding two non-clustered indexes, you got the original query to run in less than 1 second, where it was previously taking 17 seconds. You can't always get the query to run faster, and it's not always worth adding more indexes to shave off fractions of a second.

You could have stopped after adding the nonclustered index to the `people` table since you got the query down to 1.5 seconds from 17, and it was using an index for both the `batting` table and the `people` table. By adding an index to `appearances`, you just shifted the load but didn't help it a lot. Ultimately, you could drop both the nonclustered indexes you created on the `batting` and `appearances` tables and still have a highly performant query.

Summary

In this chapter, you learned about the types of table joins, including INNER, OUTER, FULL, and advanced joins, such as the cross, natural, and self joins.

Additionally, you learned about set theory and how to combine queries using operators such as UNION and UNION ALL. You also learned about intersection and differences when combining queries.

Lastly, you learned about optimizing your query when it contains multiple tables, using the EXPLAIN operator, and you saw how you could either change your query or add indexes to improve your query.

In the next chapter, you will learn how to modify data in tables. This includes learning how to use INSERT, UPDATE, and DELETE statements. You will also learn about SQL transactions, which help to better control the modification of data. Additionally, you will learn how to modify table structures.

Questions

1. Which types of table joins exist?
2. What does an INNER JOIN do?
3. What is a table alias, and how do you use it?
4. Which types of OUTER JOIN exist in MySQL?
5. What does a right excluding join do?
6. What is a natural join?
7. What is a CROSS JOIN?
8. What is the difference between UNION and UNION ALL?
9. How do you accomplish an intersection query in MySQL?
10. How can you improve multiple table query performance?

Further reading

For a listing of join types in EXPLAIN results, visit `https://dev.mysql.com/doc/refman/8.0/en/explain-output.html#explain-join-types`.

8
Modifying Data and Table Structures

In this chapter, you will learn how to modify data in tables. This includes learning how to use the INSERT, UPDATE, and DELETE statements. You will also learn about SQL transactions, which help to better control the modification of data. Finally, you will learn how to modify table structures.

In this chapter, we will cover the following topics:

- Inserting data into tables
- Deleting data from tables
- Updating data in tables
- Using transactions to save or revert changes
- Modifying the table structure

Technical requirements

You can find the code files used in this chapter at https://github.com/PacktPublishing/learn-sql-database-programming/tree/master/chapter-8.

Inserting data into tables

Inserting data is key to populating your database tables with data. The INSERT statement allows you to insert data into tables in your database. In order to insert data, you need to gather information about your table(s).

Gathering information to insert, update, or delete data

To insert, update, or delete data, you first need to know a few things about the table:

- **The name of each column:** You need to know the exact name of the columns because you will be using them to specify each column in your INSERT, UPDATE, or DELETE statements. These statements are commonly referred to as **data manipulation language (DML)** commands.
- **The order of the columns:** This is especially important when you select data from another table to insert into a table.
- **The data type of each column:** You need to know whether any of the data that you insert will fail because of a data type mismatch.
- **If the column is a part of a key or constraint:** You need to be aware of any NOT NULL, default, unique, or CHECK constraints that are on the table that impact whether your data can be modified. You also need to be aware of any primary or foreign key constraints that prevent inserting, updating, or deleting data from your table.

To get the information in the preceding list, you can execute the following queries to get information about a table:

```
USE yourschema;
describe managers;

SELECT * FROM information_schema.table_constraints
WHERE table_name = 'managers'
AND table_schema = 'yourschema';
```

The first query in the previous code block gives you information about the table, such as column names, column types, whether they allow NULL values, whether they have a key associated with them, whether they have a default value, and any extras they may have, such as auto_increment, as shown:

Field	Type	Null	Key	Default	Extra
managerkey	smallint(5)	NO	PRI	NULL	auto_increment
playerid	varchar(9)	NO	MUL	NULL	
yearid	year(4)	NO		NULL	
games	tinyint(3)	NO		NULL	
wins	tinyint(3)	NO		NULL	
losses	tinyint(3)	NO		NULL	
alsoplayer	char(1)	NO		NULL	

The second query in the previous code block gives you information such as the schema, table and constraint names, what type of constraint there is, and whether a constraint is enforced or not, as shown:

CONSTRAINT_CATALOG	CONSTRAINT_SCHEMA	CONSTRAINT_NAME	TABLE_SCHEMA	TABLE_NAME	CONSTRAINT_TYPE	ENFORCED
def	yourschema	PRIMARY	yourschema	managers	PRIMARY KEY	YES
def	yourschema	managerkey_UNIQUE	yourschema	managers	UNIQUE	YES
def	yourschema	playerid_yearid_teamid_UNIQUE	yourschema	managers	UNIQUE	YES
def	yourschema	check_alsoplayer	yourschema	managers	CHECK	YES
def	yourschema	check_games	yourschema	managers	CHECK	YES
def	yourschema	check_losses	yourschema	managers	CHECK	YES
def	yourschema	check_manager_year	yourschema	managers	CHECK	YES
def	yourschema	check_wins	yourschema	managers	CHECK	YES

If you want to see the definition of the CHECK constraints, you need to script out the definition of your table in MySQL. To view the CHECK constraint information, execute the following query:

```
USE yourschema;
SHOW CREATE TABLE managers;
```

The previous query returns the CREATE statement for the table in the database that you specified in the query. This way, you can examine the table definition to see all the information you need.

 See the *Further reading* section for details on how to get this information in Oracle, PostgreSQL, and SQL Server.

Using the INSERT statement

There are a couple of ways to insert data using the INSERT statement. You can use either a single- or multiple-row insert with specified VALUES.

Single-row inserts

To insert a single row into a table in MySQL, use the following syntax:

```
INSERT INTO lahmansbaseballdb.collegeplaying
 (`playerID`,
 `schoolID`,
 `yearID`)
 VALUES
```

```
(<{playerID: }>,
<{schoolID: }>,
<{yearID: }>);
```

You can get this syntax by taking the following steps:

1. Right-click on **Tables** in MySQL Workbench.
2. Select **Send to SQL Editor**.
3. Choose **Insert Statement**.

This places the INSERT syntax for that table into a SQL query window:

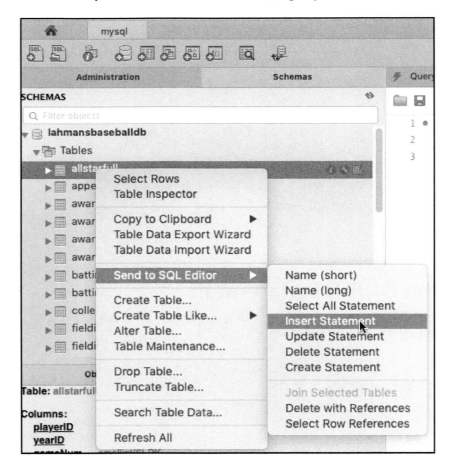

The `INSERT` statement allows you to add values to the `collegeplaying` table. To make the query insert proper values into a row in the `collegeplaying` table, you need to add values to the `VALUES` statement, as in the following query:

```
USE lahmansbaseballdb;
INSERT INTO collegeplaying
 (playerID,
 schoolID,
 yearID)
 VALUES
 ('blaloha01',
'sandiegost',
 1999);
```

You will see the following results from the previous query. It shows that one row is inserted in the `collegeplaying` table. It is seen that the player `blaloha01` attended `sandiegost` State University in the year `1999`:

playerID	schoolID	yearID
blaloha01	sandiegost	1999

To make the query more compact, you can place the columns and values on the same line, as in the following query:

```
USE lahmansbaseballdb;
INSERT INTO collegeplaying
(playerID, schoolID, yearID)
VALUES ('blaloha01','sandiegost',1999);
```

The previous query runs in the same way as the `INSERT` query before it. The previous query is just more compact and takes up less screen space. This is particularly helpful if you have a lot of queries in one SQL file.

You can also insert values into a table without specifying the columns if you make sure to place your values in the correct order. The following query inserts the same values into the table as the previous `INSERT` statements:

```
USE lahmansbaseballdb;
INSERT INTO collegeplaying
VALUES ('blaloha01','sandiegost',1999);
```

If you want to insert values into some fields in the table but not others, you need to specify the columns you want to add them to to ensure the values go into the correct columns.

For instance, if you want to place a `playerID` value into the `collegeplaying` table without a value for `schoolID`, you can execute the following query:

```
USE lahmansbaseballdb;
INSERT INTO collegeplaying
(playerID, yearID)
VALUES ('blaloha01', 1999);
```

The previous query inserts a row into the `collegeplaying` table and the `schoolID` value is NULL, in this case, since we didn't insert a value into it, which gives the results shown in the following screenshot:

playerID	schoolID	yearID
blaloha01	NULL	1999

It doesn't make a lot of sense to have a row in the `collegeplaying` table without a `schoolID` value specified, but this just gives you an example of how it would work.

If you execute the following query, you get an error:

```
USE lahmansbaseballdb;
INSERT INTO collegeplaying
VALUES ('blaloha01', 1999);
```

The error you receive is `Error Code: 1136. Column count doesn't match value count at row 1`. MySQL fails to insert rows if your value count doesn't match the column count in the table. Since you know that the `collegeplaying` table has three columns, the INSERT query fails since you've only specified two values. You need to specify the columns you want those values inserted into.

Let's say you put the values in the wrong order for the columns in the table, as in the following query:

```
USE lahmansbaseballdb;
INSERT INTO collegeplaying
VALUES('blaloha01',1999, 'sandiegost');
```

The previous query gives you an error, `Error Code: 1366. Incorrect integer value: 'sandiegost' for column 'yearID' at row 1`. This error occurs since MySQL can't implicitly convert the `'sandiegost'` value into a `SMALLINT` value, which is what the `yearID` column data type is. Since you placed `'sandiegost'` in the `yearID` column on the `INSERT` line, MySQL assumed you wanted to insert `'sandiegost'` into `yearID`.

Alternatively, if you execute the following query, you won't get an error:

```
USE lahmansbaseballdb;
INSERT INTO collegeplaying
(playerID,schoolID)
VALUES ('blaloha01', 1999);
```

Even though `1999` isn't a `schoolID` value, MySQL doesn't know this and implicitly converts `1999` into a `VARCHAR` value and inserts it into the `collegeplaying` table without showing an error. You will also notice that the `yearID` column is `NULL` since you didn't insert anything into that column. The following screenshot shows you the results of the previous code:

playerID	schoolID	yearID
blaloha01	1999	NULL

If the table you are trying to insert data into defines a default constraint, then you can leave that column out of the listing of columns and not specify a value when inserting.

If you try to insert data into a table with a `CHECK` constraint and the data doesn't conform to the `CHECK` constraint, you will get an error. For example, if you have a `CHECK` constraint on `yearID` in the `collegeplaying` table `((yearID >= 1871) and (yearID <= 2155))` and you try to insert `1870` for `yearID`, the insert action will fail because of the `CHECK` constraint.

If you try to insert a `NULL` value into a column with a `NOT NULL` constraint, then it will fail because you aren't allowed to add `NULL` values to that column.

As for `DEFAULT` constraints, you can place a value into a column with an `INSERT` statement, but if you don't specify a value, the default value will automatically be placed into the column.

If you are inserting a value into a column that is in a primary or foreign key relationship, you must ensure that the value doesn't violate those relationships; otherwise, the `INSERT` statement will fail.

Multiple row inserts

To insert multiple rows into a table in MySQL, use the following query:

```
USE lahmansbaseballdb;
INSERT INTO collegeplaying
(playerID, schoolID, yearID)
VALUES ('blaloha01','sandiegost',2000),
    ('blaloha01','sandiegost',2001),
    ('blaloha01','sandiegost',2002);
```

You will see the following results from the previous query. It shows that your INSERT statement worked by inserting three rows into the collegeplaying table for the playerID blaloha01, it shows that this player attended sandiegost State University in 2000, 2001, and 2002:

playerID	schoolID	yearID
blaloha01	sandiegost	1999
blaloha01	sandiegost	2000
blaloha01	sandiegost	2001
blaloha01	sandiegost	2002

In the previous screenshot, you can see the results from the collegeplaying table for playerID the blaloha01. You can see the yearID 1999 from the last single-row insert and three rows from the multiple-row insert you just did.

Differences in other Relational Database Management Systems

In **Oracle**, you can't use the same syntax for multiple-row inserts. Instead, you need to use an INSERT ALL syntax, as in the following query:

```
INSERT ALL
INTO collegeplaying(playerID, schoolID, yearID)
VALUES('blaloha01','sandiegost',2000)
INTO collegeplaying(playerID, schoolID, yearID)
VALUES('blaloha01','sandiegost',2001)
INTO collegeplaying(playerID, schoolID, yearID)
VALUES('blaloha01','sandiegost',2002)
SELECT * FROM DUAL;
```

PostgreSQL and SQL Server allow the same syntax as MySQL for multiple-row inserts.

Inserting data from one table into another table

When inserting from one table into another table, you have a couple of options:

- You can create a new table and insert data into it from an existing table
- You can insert data into an existing table from another table

If you want to create a new table and insert data into it from an existing table, use the following syntax:

```
CREATE TABLE newtablename
SELECT * FROM existingtablename
```

The previous query creates a new table and inserts the records from the SELECT statement on an existing table into the new table. This gives you a copy of all the data from the original table. The following query creates a new table named managerscopy and places all the data from the existing table, managers, into the new table:

```
USE lahmansbaseballdb;
CREATE TABLE managerscopy
SELECT * FROM managers;
```

You can also filter the results of the original table so that you get a subset of results in the new table, as in the following query:

```
USE lahmansbaseballdb;
CREATE TABLE managers_plyrmgr
SELECT * FROM managers
WHERE plyrMgr = 'Y';
```

The previous query creates a table named managers_plyrmgr and only inserts records from the managers table, where the manager is also plyrMgr.

Additionally, you can create a blank table by executing the following query:

```
USE lahmansbaseballdb;
CREATE TABLE managerscopy
SELECT * FROM managers
WHERE 1=0;
```

In the previous query, WHERE 1=0 can never be true, so it returns no rows and, therefore, places no new rows into the new table. As a result, you wind up with a new, empty table.

A good use case for creating a table and adding records from existing tables is the awardsmanagers and awardsplayers tables. Perhaps you would like to have a combined table with all of the award information—you can execute the following query to accomplish this:

```
USE lahmansbaseballdb;
CREATE TABLE awards
SELECT am.playerID, namegiven, awardid, yearID, "Manager" as playertype
FROM awardsmanagers am
INNER JOIN people p
ON p.playerID = am.playerID
UNION
SELECT ap.playerID, namegiven, awardid, yearID, "Player"
FROM awardsplayers ap
INNER JOIN people p
ON p.playerID = ap.playerID
ORDER BY awardid;
```

The previous query creates the awards table and populates it with the rows from the awardsmanagers and awardsplayers tables.

If you want to insert data into an existing table from another existing table, use the following syntax:

```
INSERT INTO existingtable
SELECT * FROM anotherexistingtable
```

The preceding query populates an existing table with the records from the SELECT statement. To properly illustrate how this works, create a new table in another schema with the following query:

```
USE yourschema;
CREATE TABLE allstarfull (
 playerID varchar(9) NOT NULL,
 yearID smallint(6) NOT NULL,
 gameNum smallint(6) NOT NULL,
 gameID varchar(12) NULL,
 teamID varchar(3) NULL,
 lgID varchar(2) NULL,
 GP smallint(6) NULL,
 startingPos smallint(6) NULL
);
```

Then, insert data into this table from an existing table in another schema using the following query:

```
INSERT INTO yourschema.allstarfull
SELECT * FROM lahmansbaseballdb.allstarfull
WHERE gameid LIKE 'NLS%'
```

The previous query inserted all the data from the `lahmansbaseballdb.allstarfull` table into the `yourschema.allstarfull` table, where `gameid` starts with `NLS`. You can also join tables to insert data into one existing table, as well. Pretty much any of the SQL queries that you've used so far in this book can be used to insert data into an existing table if the columns support the data that is inserted.

Differences to other RDMSes

Oracle, PostgreSQL, and SQL Server all offer the same way of creating a new table and inserting data into it from an existing table; however, they MySQL differs from all of these.

In Oracle, PostgreSQL, and SQL Server, if you want to create a new table and insert data into it, you use the `SELECT...INTO` statement, rather than `CREATE TABLE`, then use the `SELECT` statement, as in MySQL. You can execute the following query to create a new table from an existing table via a `SELECT` statement:

```
SELECT *
INTO managerscopy
FROM managers;
```

You can also specify column names instead of selecting them all, as in the following query:

```
SELECT playerID, yearID, teamID, G
INTO managerscopy
FROM managers;
```

The previous query creates a new table with just the four columns from the existing table specified. You can also use a `WHERE` clause to limit the rows.

Additionally, you can just create the schema of the table by executing the following query:

```
SELECT * INTO managerscopy
FROM managers
WHERE 1 = 0;
```

In the previous query, `WHERE 1=0` will never be true, so the query only creates the table but doesn't populate it with data.

Deleting data from tables

To remove data that you've previously inserted into your database, you need to use the DELETE statement. You can delete all the records from a table, or use a WHERE clause to delete only some of the records from a table.

Using the DELETE statement with a WHERE clause

To avoid deleting everything from your table, you can use the WHERE clause with your DELETE statement. To delete data from a table in MySQL, use the following syntax:

```
DELETE FROM lahmansbaseballdb.collegeplaying
WHERE <{where_expression}>;
```

You can get this syntax by taking the following steps:

1. Right-click on **Tables** in MySQL Workbench.
2. Select **Send to SQL Editor**.
3. Then, select **Delete Statement**.

This places the DELETE syntax for that table into an SQL query window.

Let's analyze what you might want to delete from the collegeplaying table based on some records you inserted in the previous section of this chapter. If you run the following query, you can see what you inserted:

```
USE lahmansbaseballdb;
SELECT * FROM collegeplaying
WHERE playerID = 'blaloha01';
```

The previous query gives you the results shown in the following screenshot:

playerID	schoolID	yearID
blaloha01	sandiegost	1999
blaloha01	NULL	1999
blaloha01	1999	NULL

In the preceding screenshot, you can see some data you may not want to keep, such as the row that has a `schoolID` as `NULL` or the `schoolID` field that has a year in it. You can delete these rows with the following query:

```
USE lahmansbaseballdb;
DELETE FROM collegeplaying
WHERE playerID = 'blaloha01'
AND (schoolID IS NULL OR yearID IS NULL);
```

With the previous query, you may get an `Error Code: 1175. You are using safe update mode, and you tried to update a table without a WHERE that uses a KEY column. To disable safe mode, toggle the option in Preferences -> SQL Editor and reconnect` error.

If you got this error, follow the message and uncheck the **Safe Updates** checkbox, then click **OK**, as in the following screenshot. You will need to restart MySQL Workbench for this to take effect:

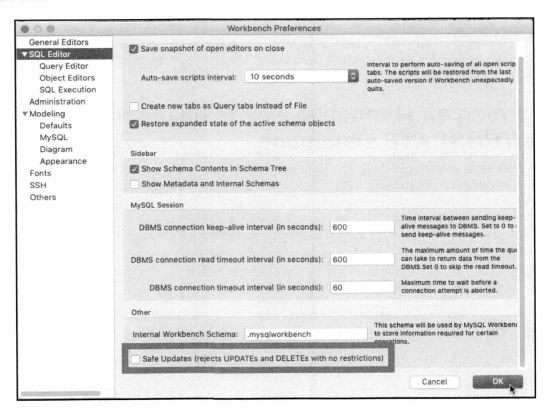

Execute the DELETE query from the preceding code block again. You will see that the rows with the NULL values have been deleted.

Deleting all the data from a table

If you want to delete all the rows from a table, you can use the DELETE clause without the WHERE clause.

> Be very careful with this method since you will be deleting all the rows in a table and once done, *they can't be retrieved.*

You can execute the following code to delete all the rows from the allstarfull table in the yourschema database:

```
USE yourschema;
DELETE FROM allstarfull;
```

The previous code deletes everything from the allstarfull table.

Learning an alternative way to delete data with the TRUNCATE statement

There is a faster way to delete all the rows from a table, called TRUNCATE. Deleting rows is a **data manipulation language(DML)** action, but a truncate is a **data definition language (DDL)** action. Deleting values is a slower process because the database system has to log each delete, but the truncate process doesn't. Another difference between deleting and truncating is that with a TRUNCATE statement, you reclaim the storage that the data used after a truncate; with a DELETE statement, you can't reclaim the storage. If a table has foreign key references, you are unable to truncate and will need to use a DELETE statement to delete the rows from the referenced tables first.

> A TRUNCATE statement is final. *There is no way to roll it back.*

If you are sure you want to delete all the rows in a table, then truncating is the best way to do this. To do so, you can execute the following script:

```
USE yourschema;
TRUNCATE TABLE allstarfull;
```

The previous script deletes all the rows in the `allstarfull` table by performing a truncate against the table.

Updating data in tables

Updating allows you to modify existing rows in a table. You can either update specific rows with a WHERE clause or all the rows in a table with UPDATE without WHERE.

Using the UPDATE statement with a WHERE clause

Let's say you made a mistake when you inserted a record for the college information earlier in this chapter. You can update this information with the UPDATE clause. To update data in a table in MySQL, use the following syntax:

```
UPDATE lahmansbaseballdb.collegeplaying
SET
`playerID` = <{playerID: }>,
`schoolID` = <{schoolID: }>,
`yearID` = <{yearID: }>
WHERE ;
```

You can get this syntax by taking the following steps:

- Right-click on **Tables** in MySQL Workbench.
- Choose **Send to SQL Editor**.
- Choose **Update Statement**.

This places the UPDATE syntax for that table into a SQL query window.

You can execute this UPDATE query to update the record:

```
USE lahmansbaseballdb;
UPDATE collegeplaying
SET schoolID = 'sandiego', yearID = 2000
WHERE playerID = 'blaloha01';
```

The previous query updates the `schoolID` value to `sandiego` and the `yearID` value to `2000`, which is shown in the following screenshot:

playerID	schoolID	yearID
blaloha01	sandiego	2000

You can update one or more columns in an UPDATE statement. If you later discover that you wanted the `yearID` value to be `1999`, you can execute the following query:

```
USE lahmansbaseballdb;
UPDATE collegeplaying
SET yearID = 1999
WHERE playerID = 'blaloha01';
```

The previous query sets the `yearID` value back to `1999`, only for the rows where the `playerID` value is `blaloha01`.

Updating all the data in a table

You can run an UPDATE statement without a WHERE clause. However, *be very careful when doing this since it can be time-consuming on a large table*. If you accidentally update all the rows, it could break the reporting or application functionality that relies on the values as they were before you changed them.

You can update the `managerscopy` table since it is a copy of the `managers` table and it won't do any harm to update a column to all the same values:

```
USE lahmansbaseballdb;
UPDATE managerscopy
SET lgID = '--';
```

The previous query updates all the `lgID` rows to `'--'`, as you can see in the following screenshot:

playerID	yearID	teamID	lgID	inseason	G	W	L	rank	plyrMgr
wrighha01	1871	BS1	--	1	31	20	10	3	Y
woodji01	1871	CH1	--	1	28	19	9	2	Y
paborch01	1871	CL1	--	1	29	10	19	8	Y
lennobi01	1871	FW1	--	1	14	5	9	8	Y

If you need to set this back to the original values, you can carry out an update from an existing table.

Updating table data from another existing table

If you need to update values from an existing table, you can use the following query:

```
USE lahmansbaseballdb;
UPDATE managerscopy mc
INNER JOIN managers m
ON m.playerID = mc.playerID
AND mc.teamID = m.teamID
AND mc.yearID = m.yearID
SET mc.lgID = m.lgID
```

The previous query sets the values back to their original values in the managerscopy table, as in the following screenshot:

playerID	yearID	teamID	lgID	inseason	G	W	L	rank	plyrMgr
wrighha01	1871	BS1	NA	1	31	20	10	3	Y
woodji01	1871	CH1	NA	1	28	19	9	2	Y
paborch01	1871	CL1	NA	1	29	10	19	8	Y
lennobi01	1871	FW1	NA	1	14	5	9	8	Y
deaneha01	1871	FW1	NA	2	5	2	3	8	Y

You can see, in the previous screenshot, that '--' has been replaced in the managerscopy with the original values from the existing managers table.

So far, you've learned how to gather information about your tables in order to insert, delete, or update data in them. You also learned how to insert data via single or multiple-row inserts. Additionally, we covered deleting all or some of the data in a table and how to update all or some of the data in a table. Now, we will cover how to execute SQL statements in transactions. It's important to encapsulate your INSERT, UPDATE, and DELETE statements into transactions; the next section will cover why.

Using transactions to save or revert changes

A SQL transaction is a grouping of one or more changes to the database. Transactions help ensure a consistent state in your database. The common terms in SQL transactions are COMMIT and ROLLBACK. Commit makes the changes permanent and rollback cancels the changes.

There are four properties of transactions to keep in mind:

- **Atomicity**: This ensures all changes in a transaction are completed successfully. If they are successful, the changes are committed. If any change isn't successful, all the changes are rolled back.
- **Consistency**: This ensures any changes can't violate the database's integrity, including constraints. Changes interrupted by errors due to violations of database integrity are rolled back. This includes any changes that don't violate database integrity.
- **Isolation**: All transactions are isolated from each other so that no other transaction can interfere with the other transactions that are running.
- **Durability**: Once a transaction is committed, any interruption to the database's availability, such as a restart or system failure, will not affect the consistency of the data.

These four properties are referred to as ACID. To understand ACID a bit better, let's go through a couple of examples. Let's say you want to transfer money from your checking account into your savings account. For atomicity, the transfer fails unless the balance is updated in the checking account and in the savings account. You don't want the money to go missing because only the checking account is reduced by the amount but the savings account isn't increased by the same amount. For consistency, any error or database integrity violation that happens while the transfer completes causes a rollback to ensure the checking and savings balances are unaffected. For isolation, all banking transactions are isolated from each other, so another person's transfer doesn't affect yours. Lastly, for durability, once the transfer is committed to the database, any interruption in the database's availability doesn't affect your bank balances.

Understanding a SQL transaction

As previously stated, a SQL transaction is a grouping of one or more changes to a database. Let's first discuss some key terms relating to SQL transactions:

- Starting a new transaction involves using the START TRANSACTION or BEGIN keywords. This signifies the beginning of the group of SQL queries that you want to run together. Generally, you can run single queries or statements without using transactions (and if there is an error, it is still rolled back), but it's important to group related queries that update, insert, or delete data into a transaction, as you saw with the bank transfer example.

- Committing your changes involves making the changes permanent and uses the COMMIT keyword at the end of the transaction block.

- Rolling back your changes involves canceling the changes and uses the ROLLBACK keyword at the end of the transaction block.

- Auto-commit is enabled by default in MySQL, but you can disable it for a session with SET autocommit keywords. With auto-commit, you can't roll back changes, but if an error occurs, the changes are automatically rolled back. PostgreSQL and SQL Server have auto-commit enabled by default. With Oracle, you need to enable auto-commit in your SQL client, such as Oracle SQL Developer.

More information on each of these SQL keywords is given later on in this chapter, but this gives you a basis for understanding more about implicit and explicit transactions:

- **Implicit transactions**: You don't specify any transaction commands, as briefly outlined in the preceding point. Implicit transaction causes an auto-commit of the commands you are running. Some things you run force an implicit commit, regardless of whether you use transaction commands, such as DDL changes—including altering or creating tables.

- **Explicit transactions**: You specify the transaction commands. Nothing is committed until you specify the COMMIT keyword. This behavior is overridden if you use a DDL command in your explicit transaction. It reverts to auto-commit if you do this and commits all your changes as if they were implicit.

To understand the states of a transaction, refer to the following diagram:

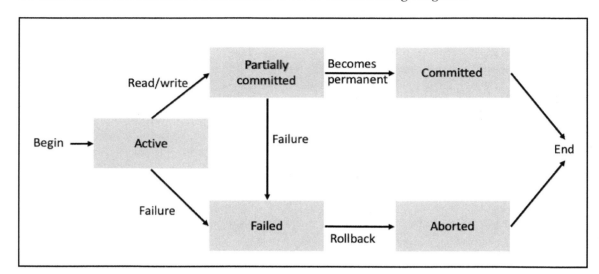

Here is a description of each of the transaction states in the preceding diagram:

- **Active**: When a transaction is executing, it's in an active state.
- **Partially committed**: When a transaction executes its final operation, it's in a partially committed state.
- **Committed**: When a transaction executes all its operations successfully, it's in a committed state and the changes are permanent.
- **Failed**: When a transaction fails checks from the database system and can't proceed any further, it's in a failed state.
- **Aborted**: When a transaction fails, the database system rolls back (undoes) any changes that are in progress.

Learning the SQL syntax for SQL transactions

There are a few keywords in MySQL to ensure your SQL queries are in a transaction. To start a transaction in MySQL, use the START TRANSACTION or BEGIN keywords. To commit the transaction, you can use the COMMIT keyword. To rollback a transaction, use the ROLLBACK keyword.

To see a transaction in action, you can execute a query that we used earlier on in this chapter, but this time in a transaction:

```
USE lahmansbaseballdb;
START TRANSACTION;
UPDATE managerscopy
SET lgID = '--';
```

The previous query updates the managerscopy table and sets all the lgID values to '--', but this time, it's within a transaction, which means if you didn't like the results of the update, you can roll it back. If you are pleased with the results, you can issue a COMMIT command, but if you aren't pleased with them, then you can issue a ROLLBACK command instead. If you don't commit your transaction right away, users in other sessions querying the managerscopy table won't see the changes you've made until you issue the COMMIT command.

You can also issue the COMMIT command along with the original query, as in the following query:

```
USE lahmansbaseballdb;
START TRANSACTION;
UPDATE managerscopy
SET lgID = '--';
COMMIT;
```

The previous query commits the transaction right after it's done so that all users can see the changes you've made right away. When you test your query, it's a good idea to not issue the COMMIT command right away and check the results of your transaction first before issuing the COMMIT command. This way, you can issue a ROLLBACK command instead, if the results of the UPDATE, DELETE, or INSERT commands weren't as you expected.

The following query uses BEGIN instead of START TRANSACTION, but it does the same thing as the previous query:

```
USE lahmansbaseballdb;
BEGIN;
UPDATE managerscopy
SET lgID = '--';
COMMIT;
```

A good use case for using a transaction in the `lahmansbaseballdb` table may be if you want to copy records from one table to another, as in the following query:

```
USE lahmansbaseballdb;
CREATE TABLE awards LIKE awardsmanagers;
START TRANSACTION;
INSERT INTO awards
SELECT * FROM awardsmanagers
WHERE awardid = 'BBWAA Manager of the Year';
DELETE FROM awardsmanagers
WHERE awardid = 'BBWAA Manager of the Year';
```

You check the results of the previous query and realize that you already had the `'BBWAA Manager of the Year'` field in the `awards` table, so you don't want to copy it there but you don't want to delete it out of the other table since you want to keep it in the `awardsmanager` table. This is a good case for issuing a `ROLLBACK` statement, as in the following statement:

```
ROLLBACK;
```

However, let's say that you were happy with the results of the transaction; so, instead, you would execute a `COMMIT` statement, as in the following query:

```
COMMIT;
```

If you want to automate the copying of data, as in the previous transaction, you need to put the `COMMIT` statement in the query so that each time the query runs, it commits automatically, instead of waiting for user intervention to commit, as in the following query:

```
USE lahmansbaseballdb;
START TRANSACTION;
INSERT INTO awards
SELECT * FROM awardsmanagers
WHERE awardid = 'BBWAA Manager of the Year';
DELETE FROM awardsmanagers
WHERE awardid = 'BBWAA Manager of the Year';
COMMIT;
```

The previous query commits once it's completed successfully, but still rolls back if it encounters any errors.

Let's have a look at an example where the transaction auto-commits because you used a DDL statement in your transaction:

```
USE lahmansbaseballdb;
START TRANSACTION;
INSERT INTO awards
SELECT * FROM awardsmanagers
WHERE awardid = 'BBWAA Manager of the Year';
DROP TABLE lahmansbaseballdb.managerscopy;
DELETE FROM awardsmanagers
WHERE awardid = 'BBWAA Manager of the Year';
COMMIT;
```

Everything before the point where you issued DROP TABLE in the transaction is committed, even though you didn't explicitly use the COMMIT statement. Be careful not to place DDL changes in the middle of your transaction because this will cause changes to values that you may not want to auto-commit, and they will commit even if they failed to complete correctly.

MySQL also allows you to turn off auto-commit for your session. You can turn off auto-commit by executing the following script:

```
SET autocommit = OFF;
```

Once you execute the previous script, you will need to execute a COMMIT statement if you want any INSERT, UPDATE, or DELETE queries to become permanent changes to the database.

To turn auto-commit back on, execute the following script:

```
SET autocommit = ON;
```

Remember that MySQL automatically commits changes to the database by default, unless you use a transaction or turn off auto-commit for your session.

MySQL also supports some additional transaction-based keywords. You can utilize savepoints within a transaction to rollback to a specific point in the transaction. You do this by naming the SAVEPOINT and rolling back to it. The following query shows you how to do this:

```
USE lahmansbaseballdb;
START TRANSACTION;
SAVEPOINT firstsavepoint;
INSERT INTO awards
SELECT * FROM awardsmanagers
WHERE awardid = 'BBWAA Manager of the Year';
```

```
SAVEPOINT secondsavepoint;
DELETE FROM awardsmanagers
WHERE awardid = 'BBWAA Manager of the Year';
ROLLBACK TO firstsavepoint;
```

In the previous query, a SAVEPOINT value called firstsavepoint is created after you start the transaction. Then, another SAVEPOINT value is created after you insert data into the awards table. At the end of the query, a ROLLBACK query is issued, which undoes all the changes back to the first SAVEPOINT instance, which in this case is everything in the transaction. You could instead issue a ROLLBACK statement to secondsavepoint. This would only undo the DELETE statement in the transaction. If you issued a ROLLBACK statement without the SAVEPOINT name, the savepoints would no longer be saved and the entire transaction would be rolled back. If you wanted to commit this transaction instead of rolling back, you would issue the COMMIT statement; the whole transaction would be committed and the savepoints removed. The same limitations apply as in a transaction. If you issue a statement such as a drop table in the middle of your transaction or savepoint, all the transactions before that point will be implicitly committed.

Differences in RDMS transaction syntax

Each RDMS has a slightly different syntax for using transactions on your queries:

- **Oracle**: In Oracle, you need to use SET TRANSACTION to start your transactions; there isn't an option to use START TRANSACTION or BEGIN. Another difference is rolling back to a savepoint. You need to use the ROLLBACK TO SAVEPOINT savepointname syntax instead of ROLLBACK TO savepointname.
- **PostgreSQL**: In PostgreSQL, you need to use BEGIN to start your transactions; there isn't an option to use START TRANSACTION. Otherwise, you can use all the same syntaxes as in MySQL.
- **SQL Server**: In SQL Server, you need to use BEGIN TRANSACTION or BEGIN TRAN to start your transactions. There isn't an option to use START TRANSACTION or just BEGIN. Otherwise, you can use all the same syntaxes as in MySQL.

Modifying the table structure

To modify the table structure, you need to use the ALTER TABLE command. This command also allows you to add, delete, and modify the table structure and other objects in the database.

Be careful when making schema changes, such as modifying the table structure. Dropping objects or columns causes data loss.

To use the scripts in this section, you can create a new database and table with the following scripts.

The first script creates a new database:

```
CREATE SCHEMA foraltering;
```

The next script creates a new table:

```
USE foraltering;
CREATE TABLE tableforaltering (
 playerID varchar(9) NOT NULL,
 schoolID varchar(15) NULL,
 yearID smallint NULL
);
```

The last script inserts the following data into the new table that we just created:

```
USE foraltering;
INSERT INTO tableforaltering
VALUES ('aardsda01','pennst',2001),
('aardsda01',NULL,NULL),
('aardsda01','rice',2003),
('abadan01','gamiddl',1992),
('abadan01','gamiddl',1993),
('abbeybe01','vermont',1889),
('abbeybe01','vermont',1890),
('abbeybe01','vermont',1891),
('abbeybe01','vermont',1892),
('abbotje01','kentucky',1991),
('abbotje01','kentucky',1992),
('abbotje01','kentucky',1994);
```

Once you have executed the previous scripts, you will be able to execute the other scripts in this section.

Adding a column

Let's say you wanted to track the number of atbats and hits of a player for each year they were in college. To add a column to an existing table, you need to execute the following scripts:

```
USE foraltering;
ALTER TABLE tableforaltering
ADD COLUMN atbats SMALLINT NULL AFTER yearID;

ALTER TABLE tableforaltering
ADD COLUMN hits SMALLINT NULL AFTER atbats;
```

If you want to add both columns to the same query, you can execute the following query instead:

```
USE foraltering;
ALTER TABLE tableforaltering
ADD COLUMN atbats SMALLINT NULL AFTER yearID,
ADD COLUMN hits SMALLINT NULL AFTER atbats;
```

The following screenshot shows the new columns in the table:

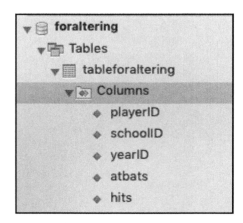

In the next section, you will learn how to drop these columns.

Dropping a column

In a similar way to how you add columns, you can also drop columns. Let's say you changed your mind and don't want to track the number of `atbats` and hits of a player for each year that they were in college. To drop columns from an existing table, you need to execute the following scripts:

```
USE foraltering;
ALTER TABLE tableforaltering
DROP COLUMN atbats;

ALTER TABLE tableforaltering
DROP COLUMN hits;
```

If you want to drop both columns in the same query, you can execute the following query instead:

```
USE foraltering;
ALTER TABLE tableforaltering
DROP COLUMN atbats,
DROP COLUMN hits;
```

The following screenshot shows the new columns are dropped from the table:

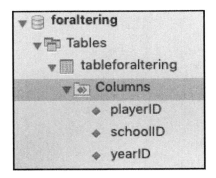

You cannot drop a column or columns that are part of a foreign key relationship; you need to resolve these keys before proceeding. For example, using the `yourschema` database you created in `Chapter 4`, *Designing and Creating a Database*, you could try to drop the column named `teamID` from the `managers` table with the following query:

```
USE yourschema;
ALTER TABLE managers
DROP COLUMN teamID;
```

The previous query gives you an `Error Code: 1828. Cannot drop column 'teamID': needed in a foreign key constraint 'FK_teamID'` error. You need to drop the foreign key first, then drop the column, as in the following query:

```
USE yourschema;
ALTER TABLE managers
DROP FOREIGN KEY FK_teamID;
ALTER TABLE managers
DROP COLUMN teamID;
```

Next, you will learn how to rename a column.

Renaming a column

To change a column's name, re-add the `atbats` column first so that you can change it with the following query:

```
USE foraltering;
ALTER TABLE tableforaltering
ADD COLUMN atbats SMALLINT NULL AFTER yearID;
```

Let's say you wanted to rename this column to `numberofatbats`. You can execute the following script to do that:

```
USE foraltering;
ALTER TABLE tableforaltering
CHANGE COLUMN atbats numberofatbats SMALLINT;
```

You can see, in the previous query, that you put in the current name of the column, then the new column name. You also have to put the column data type in, which in this case stays the same, so you just put the current data type into the query. The following screenshot shows the updated column name:

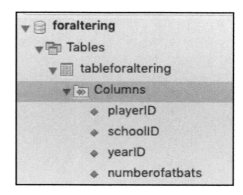

In the next section, you will learn how to change the data type of a column.

Changing the data type of a column

Let's say you discover that you need the schoolID values to be 16 characters long instead of 15 characters long. You can update the length of the field by executing the following query:

```
USE foraltering;
ALTER TABLE tableforaltering
CHANGE COLUMN schoolID schoolID VARCHAR(16);
```

 You will need to specify the same column name twice. This is because you can rename the column at the same time as changing the data type, but since you aren't changing the column name, MySQL requires you to place the column name in the query twice as part of the CHANGE COLUMN statement.

If you realize that you want the schoolID values to be 7 characters long, you can execute the following query to change the length of the field:

```
USE foraltering;
ALTER TABLE tableforaltering
CHANGE COLUMN schoolID schoolID VARCHAR(7);
```

The previous query gives you an Error Code: 1265. Data truncated for column 'schoolID' at row 1 error. This error occurs because the size you want to set the column to is shorter than the data that the column contains. Instead, you can set the schoolID value to VARCHAR(8) to avoid this error. You may come across longer school names in the future, as in the following INSERT query:

```
USE foraltering;
INSERT INTO tableforaltering
VALUES ('blowemi01','washington',1986);
```

The previous query gives you an Error Code: 1406. Data too long for column 'schoolID' at row 1 error. You need to make sure that your column size can accommodate the data that is entered into the column.

Let's say you want to change the `schoolID` column into a numeric type by executing the following query:

```
USE foraltering;
ALTER TABLE tableforaltering
CHANGE COLUMN schoolID schoolID INT;
```

The previous query gives you an `Error Code: 1366. Incorrect integer value: 'pennst' for column 'schoolID' at row 1` error. MySQL isn't able to convert string characters into `INT`, so any numeric data type you try to convert to fails. If you try to convert `yearID` into `VARCHAR`, it succeeds, but you might not want the `yearID` values in `VARCHAR` since year may be the perfect use for the `YEAR` data type. Let's try converting the column to `YEAR` by executing the following query:

```
USE foraltering;
ALTER TABLE tableforaltering
CHANGE COLUMN yearID yearID YEAR;
```

The previous query gives you an `Error Code: 1264. Out of range value for column 'yearID' at row 6` error. This is because the `YEAR` data type ranges from `1901` to `2155`. Unfortunately, our data includes years that precede `1901`. Let's instead change it to `SMALLINT`, since you will probably never store years that have five numeric values, by executing the following query:

```
USE foraltering;
ALTER TABLE tableforaltering
CHANGE COLUMN yearID yearID SMALLINT;
```

You can see, in the following screenshot, that the table type changes you made are reflected in the column definitions:

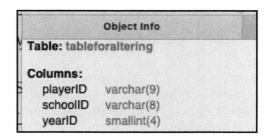

Next, you will learn how to add or change a column constraint.

Adding or changing a column constraint

When you created this table with the earlier scripts, only `playerID` was set to `NOT NULL`. Let's say you wanted the `schoolID` and `yearID` values to be `NOT NULL`. You can create a `NOT NULL` constraint by executing the following query:

```
USE foraltering;
ALTER TABLE tableforaltering
CHANGE COLUMN schoolID schoolID VARCHAR(8) NOT NULL,
CHANGE COLUMN yearID yearID SMALLINT NOT NULL;
```

The previous query fails with an `Error Code: 1138. Invalid use of NULL value` error. This error occurs because you have some `NULL` values in the table for `schoolID` and `yearID`. You have to fix them before proceeding to update the columns to `NOT NULL`, which you can do with the following query:

```
USE foraltering;
UPDATE tableforaltering
SET schoolID = 'rice', yearID = 2002
WHERE playerID = 'aardsda01' and yearID IS NULL;
```

Now, you can re-run `ALTER TABLE`, and changing the column constraint to `NOT NULL` for `schoolID` and `yearID` is successful.

To add a `CHECK` constraint for `yearID` to limit records to be from `1871` to `2155`, you can execute the following script:

```
USE foraltering;
ALTER TABLE tableforaltering
ADD CONSTRAINT check_yearID CHECK ((yearID >= 1871) and (yearID <= 2155));
```

The previous query makes it so that you can only enter values between and including `1871` to `2155` for `yearID`. If you had already included some ;yearID values that were outside that range, then the constraint would fail.

Let's now try inserting a value that's outside the date range for the `yearID CHECK` constraint. You can do this by executing the following query:

```
USE foraltering;
INSERT INTO tableforaltering
VALUES ('aardsda01','pennst',1850);
```

The previous query gives you an `Error Code: 3819. Check constraint 'check_yearID' is violated` error. This error occurs because you tried to insert the `1850` value for `yearID`, which is outside the allowed range.

Dropping a constraint, key, or index

To drop a CHECK constraint, you need to run the following query:

```
USE foraltering;
ALTER TABLE tableforaltering
DROP CHECK check_yearID;
```

The preceding query drops the CHECK constraint named check_yearID. Dropping CHECK constraints is different from dropping other constraints, such as foreign keys or primary keys. A foreign key constraint can be dropped using the following query:

```
ALTER TABLE tablename
DROP FOREIGN KEY FK_keyname;
```

Primary key constraints can be dropped using the following query:

```
ALTER TABLE tablename
DROP PRIMARY KEY;
```

An index can be dropped using the following query:

```
USE yourschema;
ALTER TABLE managers
DROP INDEX playerID_yearID_teamID_UNIQUE;
```

There are some differences in dropping constraints in other RDMS, which is covered in the following section.

Differences to other RDMS

In Oracle, PostgreSQL, and SQL Server, to drop a CHECK constraint, you instead use a query such as the following:

```
ALTER TABLE tableforaltering
DROP CONSTRAINT check_yearID;
```

Next, you will learn how to drop a table.

Dropping a table

To drop (delete) a table, you can execute the following query:

```
USE foraltering;
DROP TABLE tableforaltering;
```

This query deletes not only all the data in the table but also the table structure.

Summary

In this chapter, you learned how to gather information from a table to use it to `INSERT`, `UPDATE`, and `DELETE` data. You learned how to insert data using single- and multiple-row methods. You also learned how to create a new table and insert data from an existing table into it, as well as how to insert data from an existing table into another existing table.

You learned how to delete all the data from a table and how to delete only some data in a table. You also learned how to update all the data in a table and how to update only some of the data in a table. You learned what a transaction is and how to use it, including how to start a transaction and how to commit or roll back a transaction.

Finally, you learned how to modify the table structure, including how to add and drop columns, how to rename a column, how to change the data type of a column, how to add, change, and drop constraints, and how to drop a table.

In the next chapter, you will learn how to use expressions. By the end of the next chapter, you will understand what expressions are and how to use them, how to cast and convert data into different data types, how to use calculated fields, how to work with dates and times, how to carry out mathematical calculations, and how to use statistical functions.

Questions

1. How do you gather information about a table you want to insert, update, or delete data from?
2. How do you insert data into a new table from an existing table in MySQL?
3. How do you limit data to be deleted?
4. What's an alternative way to delete all the rows in a table?

5. How do you update data based on another table?
6. What is an SQL transaction?
7. How do you use transactions in MySQL?
8. How do you add a column to a table?
9. How do you change the data type of a column?
10. How do you rename a column?

Further reading

For more information:

- For an explanation of how to view table information in Oracle, visit `https://livesql.oracle.com/apex/livesql/file/tutorial_FIMJZ2NPQ4AWTCE0B329BW3GX.html`.
- For an explanation of how to view table information in PostgreSQL, visit `https://www.postgresql.org/docs/9.1/information-schema.html`.
- For an explanation of how to view table information in SQL Server, visit `https://docs.microsoft.com/en-us/sql/relational-databases/system-stored-procedures/sp-help-transact-sql?view=sql-server-ver15`.

Section 3: Advanced SQL Querying

3

With the foundations of basic SQL now under your belt, you will learn about more advanced SQL techniques, including how to use expressions, aggregate functions, flow control statements, error handling, subqueries, and common table expressions. You will also learn how to create programmable objects such as views, triggers, stored procedures, variables, and temporary tables.

This section comprises the following chapters:

- Chapter 9, *Working with Expressions*
- Chapter 10, *Grouping and Summarizing Data*
- Chapter 11, *Advanced Querying Techniques*
- Chapter 12, *Programmable Objects*

9

Working with Expressions

In this chapter, you will learn how to use expressions, including using literals, operators, columns, and built-in functions to create expressions. You will learn about the different types of built-in functions, including string, numeric, datetime, and advanced functions, which include casting and converting to other data types. You will learn how to use statistical functions, including how to get and use variance and standard deviation. Finally, you will learn how to create a generated column based on an expression.

In this chapter, we will cover the following topics:

- Using expressions
- Working with dates and times
- Using statistical functions
- Using generated columns

Technical requirements

You can refer to the code files of this chapter at the following GitHub link: `https://github.com/PacktPublishing/learn-sql-database-programming/tree/master/chapter-9`.

Using expressions

An expression is a combination of values that are interpreted by MySQL to produce another value. Expressions can be used in `SELECT` statement clauses, the `WHERE` clause, the `ORDER BY` clause, the `HAVING` clause (covered in `Chapter 10`, *Grouping and Summarizing Data*), or in a `SET` statement (covered in `Chapter 12`, *Programmable Objects*).

Expressions include column values, operators, literal values, built-in functions, NULL values, user-defined functions, and stored procedures. User-defined functions and stored procedures are covered in `Chapter 12`, *Programmable Objects*.

You can combine literals, operators, and built-in functions in countless ways to produce expressions. Your imagination may be the only limit on the ways you can combine these into expressions.

Literal values

A literal value is a constant value such as a `string`, a number, or a NULL value.

The following query shows an example of different literal values in a SELECT statement:

```
SELECT 'string', 1, 1.23, NULL;
```

The previous query has four literals: a `string`, a number, a floating-point or decimal number, and a NULL. The following screenshot shows the results:

string	1	1.23	NULL
string	1	1.23	NULL

As you can see in the previous screenshot, the column names are the values used in the query—that is, the column heading for **string** is **string**, **1** is **1**, and so on. If you want to name them differently, you can use aliases (covered in more detail in `chapter 7`, *Querying Multiple Tables*), as in the following query:

```
SELECT 'string' as stringvalue,
  1 as numbervalue,
  1.23 as floatdecimalvalue,
  NULL as 'nullvalue';
```

The previous query gives you the results shown in the following screenshot:

stringvalue	numbervalue	floatdecimalvalue	nullvalue
string	1	1.23	NULL

You will see that the column headings have the alias names you provided.

Operators

There are a few different types of operators: comparison, mathematical, and logical operators. Comparison and logical operators were covered in `Chapter 6`, *Querying a Single Table*.

Comparison operators

To recap what was covered in `Chapter 6`, *Querying a Single Table*, the following table lists comparison operators:

Symbol	Description	Examples
=	equal	`column = 'text'` `column = 1`
>=	greater than or equal to	`column >= 1`
>	greater than	`column > 1`
<=	less than or equal to	`column <= 1`
<	less than	`column < 1`
<>	does not equal	`column <> 'text'` `column <> 1`
!=	does not equal	`column != 'text'` `column != 1`

Some example use cases of comparison operators are listed here:

- `WHERE column = 100`—This will return all rows where a `column` value equals `100`.
- `WHERE column = 'string value'`—This will return all rows where a `column` value equals `'string value'`.
- `WHERE column != 1000`—This will return all rows where a `column` value does not equal `1000`.
- `WHERE column <> 'string value'`—This will return all rows where a `column` value does not equal `'string value'`.

Logical operators

To recap what was covered in `Chapter 6`, *Querying a Single Table*, here are the logical operators: `AND`, `OR`, `NOT`, `IN`, `LIKE`, and `BETWEEN`. Logical operators evaluate to `true` (or `1`), `false` (or `0`), or `NULL`.

Some example use cases of logical operators are listed here:

- `WHERE column1 <> 1 AND column2 = 2`—This will return all rows where `column` does not equal 1 and where `column2` equals 2.
- `WHERE column1 <> 1 OR column2 = 2`—This will return all rows where `column` does not equal 1 OR where `column2` equals 2.
- `WHERE column1 IN (1, 2, 3)`—This will return all rows where `column1` values are equal to 1, 2, or 3.
- `WHERE column1 BETWEEN 1 AND 4`—This will return all rows where `column1` values are between 1 and 4, including 1 and 4.
- `WHERE column1 NOT IN (1, 2, 3)`—This will return all rows where `column1` values are not equal to 1, 2, or 3.
- `WHERE column1 IS NOT NULL`—This will return all rows where `column1` values are not NULL.
- `WHERE column1 LIKE 'abc%'`—This will return all rows where `column1` values begin with `abc`.

You can also use string values with AND, OR, NOT, IN, and BETWEEN, and use numeric values with LIKE.

Mathematical operators

Mathematical operators perform math in your query. The mathematical operators are shown in the following table:

Symbol	Description	Examples
+	addition	`column + 1`
−	subtraction	`column - 1`
*	multiplication	`column * 1`
/	division	`column / 1`

Some example use cases of mathematical operators are listed here:

- `SELECT column1 + 2`: This returns a `column1` value with 2 added to it, so if the value of `column1` is 1, then it will display in the results as 3.
- `WHERE column1 + 2`: This returns all rows where `column1` values equal `column1` plus 2.

- SELECT 1 + NULL + 3: This returns NULL, as any of the mathematical operators will return when used with a NULL value, so if a column contains a NULL value and you use it with a mathematical operator, the result will be NULL.
- SELECT 0/0: This returns NULL since anything divided by zero is undefined.

By executing the following query, you can see what adding 2 to each value will result in:

```
SELECT 'string'+2 as stringvalue,
    1+2 as numbervalue,
    1.23+2 as floatdecimalvalue,
    NULL+2 as 'nullvalue';
```

The following screenshot shows you the results:

stringvalue	numbervalue	floatdecimalvalue	nullvalue
2	3	3.23	NULL

You can see that the string value became the number **2** since you can't add 2 to a string value. If you meant to add a 2 to the end of the string, you would need to change your query to use the CONCAT() function covered in the *Built-in functions* section later in this chapter.

Operator precedence

An important concept in mathematics is operator precedence, which means the order of operations. Precedence will perform higher-level mathematical operations first so that multiplication and division are done before addition and subtraction. You can add parentheses around calculations to impact the precedence—for example, 1+2*3 = 7, but if you meant to add 1 and 2 first, then multiply by 3, you would need to add parentheses, like so: (1+2)*3, which now equals 9 instead. The precedence of the mathematical operators we've covered is as follows: parentheses, multiplication/division, then addition/subtraction.

Column values

Column values can have comparison, mathematical, and logical operators used with them, as shown in the sections on each of those types of operators.

Built-in functions

Built-in functions allow you to modify data based on the function you use. There are a few different categories of built-in functions: `string`, `numeric`, and `date`. There are also some advanced built-in functions.

String built-in functions

String built-in functions allow you to manipulate string values. There are many different string functions. The commonly used string built-in functions are shown in the following list. Note that each of them can be used with a string value, a column with string values, or an expression that contains strings:

- `CHAR_LENGTH`: This returns the length of a string in characters.
  - `CHAR_LENGTH('string')`: This will return 6 since it's counting the number of characters in the string.
  - `CHAR_LENGTH(column1)`: This will return the string length in characters for the values in `column1` for each row.
- `LENGTH` : This returns the length of a string in bytes.
  - `LENGTH('string')`: This will return 6 since it's the length in bytes.
- `CONCAT` : This adds two or more expressions together.
  - `CONCAT('string1', 'string2')`: This concatenates `string1` and `string2` as `string1string2`.
  - `CONCAT (column1, " ", column2, column3)`: This concatenates three column values and places a space between the first and second values.
- `LEFT` : This extracts characters in a string starting from the left.
  - `LEFT('string', 3)`: This returns `str` because those are the first three characters.
- `RIGHT` —This extracts characters in a string starting from the right.
  - `RIGHT('string', 3)`: This returns `ing` because those are the last three characters.
- `LOWER`—This converts text to lowercase.
  - `LOWER('String')`: This returns `'string'` since it converts all letters to lowercase.

- UPPER : This converts text to uppercase.
  - UPPER('String'): This returns STRING since it converts all letters to lowercase.
- LTRIM —This removes leading spaces.
  - LTRIM('   String'): This returns String since it removes all the spaces at the beginning of the string .
- RTRIM —This removes trailing spaces.
  - RTRIM('String   '): This returns String since it removes all the spaces at the end of the string.
- TRIM : This removes leading and trailing spaces.
  - TRIM('   String   '): This returns String since it removes all the spaces at the beginning and the end of the string.
- LPAD : This left-pads a string to a certain length.
  - LPAD('string', 8, 'x'): This returns xxstring since it pads at the beginning of the string, and the middle parameter—8, in this case—is setting the length of the string after the padding.
- RPAD: This right-pads a string to a certain length.
  - RPAD('string', 8, 'x') : This returns stringxx since it pads at the end of the string, and the middle parameter— 8, in this case—is setting the length of the string after the padding.
- REPLACE : This replaces all occurrences of a substring within a string, with a new substring.
  - REPLACE('string', 'str', 'ing'): This returns inging.
    - The first parameter string is the entire string.
    - The second parameter str is what you want to replace.
    - The third parameter ing is what you want to replace str with.

- SUBSTRING: This extracts a substring from a string starting at any position.
  - SUBSTRING('string', 2, 3): This returns tri.
    - The first parameter string is the entire string.
    - The second parameter 2 is the start position. Counting starts at 0.
    - The third parameter 3 is the number of characters to extract.

- REVERSE : This reverses a string.
  - REVERSE('string'): This returns gnirts since this reverses the string.

Example usage with built-in string functions is shown in the following query:

```
USE lahmansbaseballdb;
SELECT UPPER(playerid) as playeridupper,
  playerid,
  LOWER(CONCAT(teamid, ' ', lgid)) as teamleague,
  teamid,
  lgid,
  LOWER(gameid) as gameidlower,
  gameid
FROM allstarfull;
```

The results of the previous query are shown in the following screenshot:

playeridupper	playerid	teamleague	teamid	lgid	gameidlower	gameid
AARONHA01	aaronha01	atl nl	ATL	NL	als197307240	ALS197307240
AARONHA01	aaronha01	atl nl	ATL	NL	nls197407230	NLS197407230
AARONHA01	aaronha01	ml4 al	ML4	AL	als197507150	ALS197507150
AASEDO01	aasedo01	bal al	BAL	AL	nls198607150	NLS198607150
ABREUBO01	abreubo01	phi nl	PHI	NL	nls200407130	NLS200407130
ABREUBO01	abreubo01	phi nl	PHI	NL	als200507120	ALS200507120
ABREUJO02	abreujo02	cha al	CHA	AL	als201407150	ALS201407150
ABREUJO02	abreujo02	cha al	CHA	AL	nls201807170	NLS201807170

- You can see that the UPPER function was used on playerid and resulted in the characters in playerid being capitalized.
- You can also see that teamid and lgid were concatenated with a space between them, which was nested inside a LOWER function.
- Also, gameid was put into a LOWER function, so the characters in gameid were in lowercase.

Differences in RDMS (Relational Database Management Systems)

The following are the differences in built-in string functions in Oracle (noted only where different):

- SUBSTR: Instead of SUBSTRING, LEFT, and RIGHT, use SUBSTR in Oracle the same way you used SUBSTRING in MySQL. Also, use SUBSTR instead of LEFT and RIGHT.
- LENGTHB: Instead of LENGTH, use LENGTHB in Oracle the same way you used LENGTH in MySQL.
- LENGTH: Instead of CHAR_LENGTH, use LENGTH in Oracle the same way you used CHAR_LENGTH in MySQL.
- CONCAT: This only allows the concatenation of two strings.

The following are the differences in built-in string functions in SQL Server (noted only where different):

- LEN: Instead of LENGTH.
- Not available in SQL Server: CHAR_LENGTH, LPAD, and RPAD.

Numeric built-in functions

Numeric built-in functions allow you to manipulate numeric values. There are many different numeric functions. Listed here are the commonly used numeric built-in functions. Note that each of them can be used with a column with numerical values or an expression that contains numerical values:

- AVG : This returns the average of an expression.
    - AVG(rating): This will return the average of all the values in a rating column.
    - NULL values are ignored.
- COUNT : This returns the number of records.
    - COUNT(column1): This will return the count of values in the column1 value, and column1 can contain either strings, dates, or numbers.
    - NULL values are ignored.

- MAX : This returns the maximum value in a set of values.
  - MAX(rating):This will return the maximum rating in a column of rating values.

- MIN: This returns the minimum value in a set of values.
  - MIN(rating): This will return the minimum rating in a column of rating values.

- ROUND: This rounds a number to a specified number of decimal places.
  - ROUND(123.456, 2): This will return 123.46 since the number will round to two decimal places.

- SUM: This is the sum of a set of values.
  - SUM(number): This will return the sum of the values in a column of number values.
  - NULL values are ignored.

- FORMAT: This formats decimal numbers to have commas for readability.
  - FORMAT(1234.4567, 2): This will return 1,234.46 since the number will round to two decimal places and a comma is added for readability.

Example usage with built-in numeric functions is shown in the following query:

```
USE lahmansbaseballdb;
SELECT ROUND(AVG(g_all),1) as average_g_all,
  MAX(g_all) as max_g_all,
  MIN(g_all) as min_g_all
FROM appearances;
```

The results of the previous query are shown in the following screenshot:

average_g_all	max_g_all	min_g_all
51.3	165	1

You can see that the AVG function was used on g_all and resulted in the average of all g_all fields being averaged, which was nested instead of the ROUND function with one decimal place. You can also see that the MAX and MIN functions were used on g_all, and respectively resulted in the maximum and minimum games played being displayed.

If you wanted to also include a `playerid` in this query, you could add it as in the following query:

```
USE lahmansbaseballdb;
SELECT playerid,
    ROUND(AVG(g_all),1) as average_g_all,
    MAX(g_all) as max_g_all,
    MIN(g_all) as min_g_all
FROM appearances;
```

The previous query will give you an error: `Error Code: 1140`. In an aggregated query without `GROUP BY`, expression #1 of `SELECT` list contains the `lahmansbaseballdb.appearances.playerID;` nonaggregated column. This is incompatible with `sql_mode=only_full_group_by`.

In order to add a column to a query that isn't a built-in function, you will need to use the `GROUP BY` clause, which is covered in more detail in `Chapter 10`, *Grouping and Summarizing Data*. The following query will resolve the error from the previous query:

```
USE lahmansbaseballdb;
SELECT playerid,
    ROUND(AVG(g_all),1) as average_g_all,
    MAX(g_all) as max_g_all,
    MIN(g_all) as min_g_all
FROM appearances
GROUP BY playerid
ORDER BY playerid;
```

The results of the previous query are shown in the following screenshot:

playerid	average_g_all	max_g_all	min_g_all
aardsda01	36.8	73	1
aaronha01	143.4	161	85
aaronto01	62.4	141	8
aasedo01	34.5	66	7
abadan01	5.0	9	1
abadfe01	40.3	69	18
abadijo01	6.0	11	1

You can see the `GROUP BY` clause, which is telling the query to group the `AVG`, `MIN`, and `MAX` functions by the `playerid`, gives us the average games by each `playerid` now, as well as the max and min games.

Differences in RDMS

You can't use the FORMAT built-in function in Oracle, PostgreSQL, or SQL Server.

Datetime built-in functions

Datetime built-in functions allow you to manipulate datetime values. There are many different datetime functions. The commonly used datetime built-in functions are listed next. Note that each of them can be used with a date value, a column with date values, or an expression that contains date values.

To get the current date or time, use the following:

- CURRENT_DATE: This returns the current date.
  - CURRENT_DATE(): This returns the date in YYYY-MM-DD format—that is, 2020-01-11.
- CURRENT_TIME—This returns the current time.
  - CURRENT_TIME(): This returns the time in HH:MM:SS format—that is, 21:09:27.
- CURRENT_TIMESTAMP: This returns the current date and time.
  - CURRENT_TIMESTAMP(): This returns the datetime in YYYY-MM-DD HH:MM:SS format—that is, 2020-01-11 21:10:23.
- NOW: This returns the current date and time in the same format as CURRENT_TIMESTAMP.
  - NOW(): This returns the datetime in YYYY-MM-DD HH:MM:SS format—that is, 2020-01-11 21:10:23.

To format dates and times, use the following:

- DATE_FORMAT: This formats a date into a specified format.
  - DATE_FORMAT(date, format): Here, date is a valid date value and format is the format you want the date in. For example, DATE_FORMAT(NOW(), %m-%d-%y') will return 01-12-20 (depending on the date you run it). To read about all the formats you can use, see the DATE_FORMAT information in the Further reading section of this chapter.

- `TIME_FORMAT`: This formats a time into a specified format.
  - `TIME_FORMAT(time, format)`: Here, `time` is a valid time value, and `format` is the format you want the time in. For example, `TIME_FORMAT(NOW(), '%T')` will return the current time in 24-hour format, `18:52:24` (depending on the time you run it). To read about all the formats you can use, see the TIME_FORMAT information in the Further reading section of this chapter.

To add or subtract dates and times, use the following:

- `ADDDATE` : This adds a date interval from a date and returns that date.
  - `ADDDATE(date, INTERVAL value addunit)`: Here, `date` is a valid date value, `INTERVAL` is a keyword that stays unchanged, `value` is a number, and `addunit` is the unit of time, such as `DAY`. For example, `ADDDATE('2020-01-01', INTERVAL 5 DAY)` will return `2020-01-06` because the ADDDATE function will add 5 days to the date specified. To read about all INTERVAL you can use, see the ADDDATE information in the Further reading section of this chapter.
- `ADDTIME`—This adds a date/time interval from a date and returns that date.
  - `ADDTIME(datetime, addtime)`—Here, `datetime` is a valid datetime value, and `addtime` is the amount of time to add (positive or negative). For example, `ADDTIME('2020-01-01 10:10:10', '8:10:5')` will return `2020-01-01 18:20:15` because the ADDTIME function will add 8 hours, 10 minutes, and 5 seconds to the date specified.
- `DATE_SUB`: This subtracts a date/time interval from a date and returns that date.
  - `DATE_SUB(date, INTERVAL value subunit)`—Here, `date` is a valid date value, `INTERVAL` is a keyword that stays unchanged, `value` is a number, and `subunit` is the unit of time, such as `DAY`. For example, `DATE_SUB('2020-01-01', INTERVAL 5 DAY)` will return **2019-12-27** because the `DATE_SUB` function will add 5 days to the date specified. `DATE_SUB INTERVAL` is the same as `ADDDATE INTERVAL`.
- `DATEDIFF`: This returns the number of days between two date values.
  - `DATEDIFF(date1, date2)`—Here, `date1` and `date2` are two valid datetimes. It will calculate the difference between `date1` and `date2`. For example, `DATEDIFF('2020-01-01', '2020-01-03')` results in `-2`.

To get pieces of the date or time returned, use the following:

- `DATE` : This returns the date part from the datetime expression.
  - `DATE('2019-06-10 12:12:12')` returns `2019-06-10`.
- `DAY`: This returns the day of the month for a date.
  - `DAY('2019-06-10 12:12:12')` returns `10`.
- `DAYNAME`: This returns the weekday for a date.
  - `DAYNAME('2019-06-10 12:12:12')` returns `Monday`.
- `DAYOFMONTH`: This returns the day of the month for a date.
  - `DAYOFMONTH('2019-06-10 12:12:12')` returns `10`.
- `DAYOFWEEK`: This returns the day of the week for a date.
  - `DAYOFWEEK('2019-06-10 12:12:12')` returns `2`, where Sunday is 1, so Monday is 2, and the rest of the week counts up.
- `DAYOFYEAR`—This returns the day of the year for a date.
  - `DAYOFYEAR('2019-06-10 12:12:12')` returns `161`.
- `HOUR`—This returns the hour part for a date.
  - `HOUR('2019-06-10 12:12:12')` returns `12`.
- `LAST_DAY`—This returns the last day of the month for a date.
  - `LAST_DAY('2019-06-10 12:12:12')` returns `2019-06-30`.
- `MINUTE`—This returns the minute for a date.
  - `MINUTE('2019-06-10 12:12:12')` returns `12`.
- `MONTH`—This returns the month for a date.
  - `MONTH('2019-06-10 12:12:12')` returns `6`.
- `MONTHNAME`—This returns the month name for a date.
  - `MONTHNAME('2019-06-10 12:12:12')` returns `June`.
- `SECOND`—This returns the second for a date.
  - `SECOND('2019-06-10 12:12:12')` returns `12`.
- `WEEK`—This returns the week number for a date
  - `WEEK('2019-06-10 12:12:12')` returns `23`.
- `WEEKDAY`—This returns a weekday number for a date.
  - `WEEKDAY('2019-06-10 12:12:12')` returns `0`, where Monday is 0 and the rest of the week counts up.
- `WEEKOFYEAR`—This returns the week number for a date.
  - `WEEKOFYEAR('2019-06-10 12:12:12')` returns `24`.

- YEAR—This returns the year part for a date.
  - YEAR('2019-06-10 12:12:12') returns 2019.
- YEARWEEK—This returns the year and week number for a date.
  - YEARWEEK('2019-06-10 12:12:12') returns 201923.

Example usage with built-in datetime functions is shown in the following query:

```
SELECT
DAYNAME('2019-06-10 11:12:13') as dayofweek,
MONTH('2019-06-10 11:12:13') as month,
DAY('2019-06-10 11:12:13') as day,
YEAR('2019-06-10 11:12:13') as year,
HOUR('2019-06-10 11:12:13') as hour,
MINUTE('2019-06-10 11:12:13') as minute,
SECOND('2019-06-10 11:12:13') as second
```

The results of the previous query are shown in the following screenshot:

dayofweek	month	day	year	hour	minute	second
Monday	6	10	2019	11	12	13

You can see that the **month**, **day**, **year**, **hour**, **minute**, and **second** built-in date functions were used on a date, and it resulted in those being extracted from the date. Also, the dayname was queried using the DAYNAME function.

Working with time zones

Since MySQL doesn't support storing time zone information with datetime data types, I recommend choosing a time zone that you will store your data in—for example, **Coordinated Universal Time (UTC)**, or the time zone that the server is in—and let the application handle any local time zones that need to be displayed. If a user is in New York and they are using the application, and they need to see the time in the Eastern time zone, the application will convert it on display from the time stored in the database to their time zone. If users are inserting data into the database, and an insert date is captured for that inserted data (which is good practice), then it will be inserted into the database in the database time zone (whichever you've selected). Then, if they want to view the data, it could either be displayed back in a portal to them as their time zone or the database's time zone, depending on preference. If they are directly querying the database without an application interface, they will see the data in the database's time zone.

Differences in RDMS

The following are the differences in built-in `datetime` functions in Oracle (noted only where different):

- `CURRENT_DATE` —Use without `()`
  - `SELECT CURRENT_DATE;`
- `CURRENT_TIME` —Use without `()`
  - `SELECT CURRENT_TIME;`
- `LAST_DAY`—Different formatting with literal
  - `LAST_DAY(DATE '2019-06-10')`
- `EXTRACT`—Use in place of `YEAR`, `MONTH`, `DAY`, `MINUTE`, `SECOND`
  - `EXTRACT( MONTH FROM TO_DATE('10-Jun-2019 12:12:12', 'DD-Mon-YYYY HH24:MI:SS'))` returns 6 for the month number. To learn more about the Oracle `EXTRACT` function, see the *Further reading* section in this chapter.

The rest of the MySQL `datetime` functions are not included in Oracle.

The following are the differences in built-in `datetime` functions in PostgreSQL (noted only where different):

- `CURRENT_DATE` —Use without `()`
  - `SELECT CURRENT_DATE;`
- `CURRENT_TIME`—Use without `()`
  - `SELECT CURRENT_TIME;`
- `NOW`—Use without `()`
  - `SELECT NOW;`
- `EXTRACT`—Use in place of `YEAR`, `MONTH`, `DAY`, `MINUTE`, and `SECOND`
  - `EXTRACT(MONTH FROM timestamp '10-Jun-2019 12:12:12')` returns 6 for the month number. To learn more about the PostgreSQL `EXTRACT` function, see the *Further reading* section in this chapter.
- `CURRENT_TIMESTAMP` and `DATE` work the same way.

The rest of the MySQL datetime functions are not included in PostgreSQL.

The following are the differences in built-in datetime functions in SQL Server (noted only where different):

- GETDATE—Use instead of NOW
    - GETDATE() returns the datetime in YYYY-MM-DD HH:MM:SS format—that is, 2020-01-11 21:10:23.
- CONVERT—Use instead of DATE_FORMAT and TIME_FORMAT
    - CONVERT (VARCHAR, GETDATE(), 110) returns a date in format mm-dd-yyyy. To learn more about converting dates into specific formats, see the *Further reading* section of this chapter.
- DATEADD—Use instead of ADDDATE, ADDTIME, and DATE_SUB. To learn more about DATEADD, see the *Further reading* section of this chapter.
- DATEDIFF('2020-01-01', '2020-01-03');: To learn more about DATEDIFF, see the *Further reading* section of this chapter.
- DATEPART — Use instead of DAYOFWEEK, DAYOFYEAR, HOUR, MINUTE, SECOND, and WEEK. To learn how to use DATEPART, see the *Further reading* section in this chapter.
- DATENAME—Use instead of WEEKDAY, MONTHNAME, WEEKOFYEAR. To learn how to use DATENAME, see the *Further reading* section in this chapter.
- DAY, MONTH, and YEAR can be used the same as in MySQL, but can also be used in DATEPART in SQL Server.
- CURRENT_TIMESTAMP works the same way.

The rest of the MySQL datetime functions are not included in SQL Server.

Advanced built-in functions

Advanced built-in functions allow you to do many different things, such as convert to different data types or get the current username or database name. The commonly used advanced built-in functions are listed next. Note that each of them can be used with a value, a column, or an expression.

To get information about the user or system, use the following:

- CURRENT_USER returns the username for the current connection.
    - SELECT CURRENT_USER(); returns root@% (depending on who you are logged in as).
- DATABASE returns the name of the active database.
    - SELECT DATABASE(); returns lahmansbaseballdb (depending on which database you are using).
- VERSION returns the current version of the MySQL database.

    SELECT VERSION(); returns 8.0.18 (depending on your MySQL version).

To explicitly convert/cast values, use the following:

- CAST converts a value into the specified data type.
    - CAST(value as datatype)
    - CAST can only use these data types:
        - DATE converts the value to a date in YYYY-MM-DD format.
        - DATETIME converts the value to a datetime in YYYY-MM-DD HH:MM:SS format.
        - TIME converts the value to a time in HH:MM:SS format.
        - CHAR converts the value to a char.
        - SIGNED converts the value to a signed int.
        - UNSIGNED converts the value to an unsigned int.
        - BINARY converts the value to a binary.
        - DECIMAL converts the value to a decimal.
    - For example:
        - SELECT CAST('2019-06-10 11:12:13' AS DATE); returns 2019-06-10.
        - SELECT CAST('2019-06-10 11:12:13' AS UNSIGNED); returns 2019.

- CONVERT converts a value into a specified data type or character set.
    - CONVERT(value, datatype)
    - Or CONVERT(value USING charset)
    - CONVERT can only use these data types:
        - DATE converts the value to date in YYYY-MM-DD format.
        - DATETIME converts the value to a datetime in YYYY-MM-DD HH:MM:SS format.
        - TIME converts the value to a time in HH:MM:SS format.
        - CHAR converts the value to a char.
        - SIGNED converts the value to a signed int.
        - UNSIGNED converts the value to an unsigned int.
        - BINARY converts the value to a binary.
        - DECIMAL converts the value to a decimal.
    - For example:
        - SELECT CONVERT('2019-06-10 11:12:13', DATE); returns 2019-06-10.
        - SELECT CONVERT('100.2', decimal(5,2)); returns 100.20/
        - SELECT CONVERT('2019-06-10 11:12:13', unsigned); returns 2019.
        - SELECT CONVERT('testing' USING latin1); returns a BLOB.
    - Execute SHOW CHARACTER SET to see a list of all the character sets available to convert to.

To work with data, use the following:

- IF returns a value if the condition is TRUE and another value if it's FALSE.
    - IF(condition, value if true, value if false)
        - SELECT IF(10<20, 1, 2); returns 1.
        - SELECT IF(10<20, 'true', 'false'); returns TRUE.
    - CASE goes through conditions and then returns a value once the condition is met. This is like an expanded IF function.
        - CASE
            ```
            WHEN condition1 THEN result1
            WHEN condition2 THEN result2
            WHEN conditionN THEN resultN
            ```

```
                        ELSE result
            END;
```

- For example:

  - USE lahmansbaseballdb;
    SELECT playerid, yearid,
    CASE
    WHEN g_all between 0 and 10 then 'barely any'
    WHEN g_all between 11 and 50 then 'some'
    WHEN g_all between 51 and 100 then 'many'
    ELSE 'tons'
    END
    FROM appearances; returns the case statements for g_all instead of the number value that is in the column.

- LAST_INSERT_ID returns the auto-increment ID that was last used on insert.

  - SELECT LAST_INSERT_ID(); —If the table has auto-increment enabled, it will return the last ID that was used on insert.

Working with NULL values

NULL is not an empty string or 0; it is unknown or undefined. NULL is not equal to anything, including itself.

To work with NULL values, use the following built-in functions:

- NULLIF compares two expressions and returns NULL if they are equal. If they are not equal, it returns the first expression.
  - SELECT NULLIF(1, 1); returns NULL.
  - SELECT NULLIF(1, 2); returns 1.
- IFNULL returns the specified value if the expression is NULL.
  - SELECT IFNULL(NULL, 'testing'); returns testing.
  - SELECT IFNULL(NULL, NULL); returns NULL.
- ISNULL returns **0** or **1** depending on whether the value is NULL.
  - SELECT ISNULL(NULL); returns 1.
  - SELECT ISNULL('testing'); returns 0.

Differences in advanced built-in functions in RDMS

The following are the differences in built-in advanced functions in Oracle (noted only where different):

- `USER` or `sys_context('USERENV', 'SESSION_USER')` instead of `CURRENT_USER`
  - `SELECT USER from dual;`
  - `SELECT sys_context('USERENV', 'SESSION_USER') from dual;`
- `sys_context('USERENV', 'CURRENT_SCHEMA')` instead of `DATABASE()`
  - `SELECT sys_context('USERENV', 'CURRENT_SCHEMA') from dual;` To learn more about the Oracle `sys_context` function, see the *Further reading* section in this chapter.
- `SELECT * FROM v$version WHERE banner LIKE 'Oracle%';` instead of `VERSION()`
- `CAST`—Oracle has different data types you can cast to and from. To learn more about the Oracle `CAST` function, see the *Further reading* section in this chapter.
- `CONVERT`—Oracle only allows the conversion of a string to another character set. To learn more about the Oracle `CONVERT` function, see the *Further reading* section in this chapter.
- `IF`—Oracle doesn't allow the same syntax as MySQLs `IF`. It requires `IF`, `ELSE`. To learn more about the Oracle `IF` function, see the *Further reading* section in this chapter.
- `COALESCE` instead of `IFNULL`
  - `SELECT COALESCE(NULL, 'testing');` returns `'testing'`
  - `SELECT COALESCE(NULL, NULL);` returns `NULL`

`LAST_INSERT_ID` and `ISNULL` are not included in Oracle.

The following are the differences in built-in advanced functions in PostgreSQL (noted only where different):

- `CURRENT_USER` no `()`
  - `SELECT CURRENT_USER;`
- `CURRENT_DATABASE` instead of `DATABASE`
  - `SELECT CURRENT_DATABASE;`
- `CAST`—The same syntax, but different types to cast to based on PostgreSQL data types, covered in more detail in `Chapter 3`, *Understanding Data Types*.

- Use the Data Type Formatting functions instead of CONVERT. To learn more about the PostgreSQL Data Type Formatting functions, see the *Further reading* section in this chapter.
- IF—different syntax with PostgreSQL. To learn more about the PostgreSQL IF function, see the *Further reading* section in this chapter.
- COALESCE instead of IFNULL
  - SELECT COALESCE(NULL, 'testing'); returns 'testing'
  - SELECT COALESCE(NULL, NULL); returns NULL

LAST_INSERT_ID and ISNULL are not included in PostgreSQL.

The following are the differences in built-in advanced functions in SQL Server (noted only where different):

- CURRENT_USER no ()
  - SELECT CURRENT_USER;
- DB_NAME instead of DATABASE
  - SELECT DB_NAME();
- @@VERSION instead of VERSION
  - SELECT @@VERSION;
- CAST works but has different data types. To learn more about the SQL Server CAST and CONVERT functions, see the *Further reading* section in this chapter.
- CONVERT has different data types. To learn more about the SQL Server CAST and CONVERT functions, see the *Further reading* section in this chapter.
- IF has a different syntax. To learn more about the SQL Server IF function, see the *Further reading* section in this chapter.
- SCOPE_IDENTITY instead of LAST_INSERT_ID
  - SELECT SCOPE_IDENTITY();
- COALESCE instead of IFNULL
  - SELECT COALESCE(NULL, 'testing'); returns 'testing'
  - SELECT COALESCE(NULL, NULL); returns NULL
- ISNULL has a different syntax. To learn more about the SQL Server ISNULL function, see the *Further reading* section in this chapter.

Built-in functions and indexing

When using a built-in function in your query, the query may not use the indexes on the table. For example, the following query needs to do a full scan of the table:

```
USE lahmansbaseballdb;
SELECT UPPER(playerid) as playeridupper, playerid
FROM allstarfull
WHERE upper(playerid) = 'AARONHA01';
```

The following screenshot shows the execution plan of the previous query:

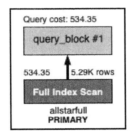

The following query can seek the rows that are needed:

```
USE lahmansbaseballdb;
SELECT playerid FROM allstarfull
WHERE playerid = 'aaronha01';
```

The following screenshot shows the execution plan of the previous query:

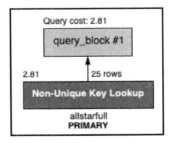

You can see that the query that doesn't use a built-in function in the WHERE clause performs much better than the one that does.

Reading and running execution plans are covered in more detail in Chapter 6, *Querying a Single Table*, and in Chapter 7, *Querying Multiple Tables*.

Using statistical functions

MySQL includes some built-in functions for calculating statistics. We covered SUM, AVG, MIN, and MAX earlier in the chapter. Let's learn about a couple of built-in functions that are helpful in calculating statistics.

Learning how to use built-in statistical functions

To calculate standard descriptive statistics, you can use the following built-in functions in addition to the ones previously learned:

- VARIANCE—This gives you the variance of your data, which calculates what the difference is for each point and the mean of all the points. If zero is returned, then all the data points are the same. A larger value returned means that individual data points are farther from the mean.
- STDDEV—This gives you the standard deviation, which helps you understand how spread out your data is, and how close each data point is to the mean (you calculate the mean by using the AVG built-in function). If 0 is returned, then all the data points are the same. A larger value returned means that individual data points are farther from the mean. Using the standard deviation gives you a standard way of knowing what is normal, and helps to find outlier values.

To learn more about variance and standard deviation, please see the *Further reading* section in this chapter.

You can execute the following query to return information on the statistics of hits:

```
USE lahmansbaseballdb;
SELECT COUNT(h) AS count,
  SUM(h) AS sum,
  AVG(h) AS mean,
  STDDEV(h) AS 'stddev',
  VARIANCE(h) AS 'variance',
  MIN(h) AS minimum,
  MAX(h) AS maximum
FROM batting;
```

The results from the previous query are shown in the following table:

count	sum	mean	stddev	variance	min	max
105861	3902204	36.8616	52.471012533351455	2753.2071562751253	0	262

In the previous table, the sum isn't useful with hits, but it's there to show you the different statistical functions you can run against the batting table. The count is the count of all the hits in the batting table. The mean is the average of all the hits, and you can see the minimum is **0** (meaning a player had no hits), and the maximum is **262**. More importantly, you can see that the standard deviation and the variance are both quite large, so this tells you that the individual data points are quite dissimilar to one another. This variance makes sense since there is a lot of variation in how many hits a baseball player gets.

Exploring differences in RDMS

In SQL Server, use STDEV instead of STDDEV, and use VAR instead of VARIANCE. The functions in SQL Server work the same way as in MySQL but just have a different function name.

Using generated columns

A generated column allows you to store data in a column based on an expression. Generated columns can be useful when you want to store something in a table based on other columns. For example, if you wanted to have the batting average stored, you would need to divide other fields in the batting table to do this. Generated columns can be helpful instead of having to calculate a value every time you execute a query. With a generated column, you will just put the generated column name in the query instead of having to calculate on the fly.

Types of generated columns

A generated column can either be virtual or stored. You can store a mix of virtual and stored columns in a table. Generated columns can refer to other generated columns, as long as the generated column you are referring to is earlier in the table definition.

- **Virtual**: Column values aren't stored on disk and therefore don't use any storage. They are evaluated when the rows are read with a query. They only support secondary indexes, so you can't place this column in a primary key. This is explained next, with the GENERATED ALWAYS AS syntax.
- **Stored**: Column values are stored on insert and update, and therefore take storage on disk. Stored generated columns can have indexes placed on them. This is explained next, with the GENERATED ALWAYS AS with STORED syntax.

Creating a generated column

Let's say you regularly need to get a player's batting average, so you want to store it in a generated column instead of calculating it each time with an expression. The following is a query that calculates the batting average:

```
USE lahmansbaseballdb
SELECT playerid, yearid, teamid,
  h, ab, h/ab AS batavg
FROM batting;
```

To create a virtual generated column with the batting average in the batting table, execute the following query:

```
USE lahmansbaseballdb;
ALTER TABLE batting
ADD COLUMN batavg DECIMAL(4,3) GENERATED ALWAYS AS (h/ab) AFTER lgID;
```

To create a stored generated column with the batting average in the batting table, execute the following query:

```
USE lahmansbaseballdb;
ALTER TABLE batting
ADD COLUMN batavgstored DECIMAL(4,3) GENERATED ALWAYS AS (h/ab) STORED
AFTER lgID;
```

The previous query results in an error: Error Code: 1365. To perform division by 0, you can use the NULLIF built-in function to avoid errors, as shown in the following query:

```
USE lahmansbaseballdb;
ALTER TABLE batting
ADD COLUMN batavg DECIMAL(4,3)
GENERATED ALWAYS AS (h/NULLIF(ab,0))
STORED AFTER lgID;
```

The column shows up in the column listing in MySQL Workbench, regardless of whether it's virtual or stored on disk. To see if it's a virtual or stored generated column, you will need to alter the table in MySQL Workbench to see the column definition. The column listing can be seen in the following screenshot:

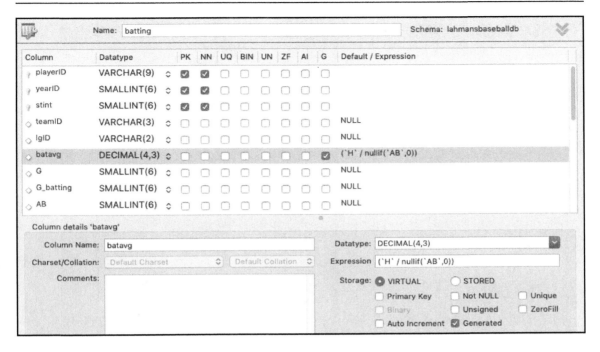

You can see in the preceding screenshot that the **batavg** column is a virtual generated column, in this case. If you specified **STORED** in the created or the generated column, then the **STORED** radio button would be selected instead.

Differences in RDMSes

Oracle only allows you to create virtual columns and does not allow you to add a column after a specific column, unlike in MySQL. You can create a virtual column in Oracle with the following code:

```
ALTER TABLE batting
ADD batavg GENERATED ALWAYS AS (h/ab);
```

PostgreSQL only allows you to create a generated column in version 12 or higher. You can create a virtual generated column in PostgreSQL with the following code:

```
ALTER TABLE batting
ADD batavg numeric GENERATED ALWAYS AS (h/ab) VIRTUAL;
```

You can create a stored generated column in PostgreSQL with the following code:

```
ALTER TABLE batting
ADD batavg numeric GENERATED ALWAYS AS (h/ab) STORED;
```

SQL Server allows you to create a computed column but doesn't allow you to add a column after a specific column. You can create a virtual computed column in SQL Server with the following code:

```
ALTER TABLE batting
ADD batavg AS (h/NULLIF(ab,0));
```

You can create a stored computed column in SQL Server with the following code:

```
ALTER TABLE batting
ADD batavg AS (h/NULLIF(ab,0)) PERSISTED;
```

Summary

In this chapter, you learned how to use expressions, including using literals, operators, columns, and built-in functions to create expressions. You learned how to use each and that you can use them all together to create expressions.

You learned about the different types of built-in functions, including string, numeric, datetime, and advanced functions, which include casting and converting to other data types. There are many different kinds of string, numeric, and datetime built-in functions. They help you to work with expressions to ensure they are in the format and data type that you want. You also learned how to work with NULL values. Additionally, you learned how indexing might be affected by built-in functions.

Next, you learned how to use statistical functions, including how to get and use variance and standard deviation with the STDDEV and VARIANCE functions. Finally, you learned how to create a generated column based on an expression, and what it means to store the column virtually or on disk.

In the next chapter, you will learn how to use aggregate functions to a group and summarize data. Aggregate functions include math functions such as AVG, SUM, COUNT, MIN, and MAX. You will also learn how to use the GROUP BY and HAVING clauses in conjunction with the aggregate functions.

Questions

1. What components can make up an expression?
2. What is a literal value?
3. What do mathematical operators do?
4. What is operator precedence?
5. What types of built-in functions exist?
6. What does LOWER return?
7. What does CAST allow you to do?
8. What happens with index usage when you use a built-in function in your WHERE clause?
9. How do you get the standard deviation on a table column?
10. What kinds of generated columns can you create?

Further reading

For more information:

- To learn more about the DATE_FORMAT built-in function, visit https://dev.mysql.com/doc/refman/8.0/en/date-and-time-functions.html#function_date-format.
- To learn more about the TIME_FORMAT built-in function, visit https://dev.mysql.com/doc/refman/8.0/en/date-and-time-functions.html#function_time-format.
- To learn more the ADDDATE built-in function INTERVALS, visit https://dev.mysql.com/doc/refman/8.0/en/expressions.html#temporal-intervals.
- To learn more about variance and standard deviation, visit https://www.khanacademy.org/math/probability/data-distributions-a1/summarizing-spread-distributions/v/range-variance-and-standard-deviation-as-measures-of-dispersion.
- To learn more about the Oracle EXTRACT function, visit https://docs.oracle.com/cd/B19306_01/server.102/b14200/functions050.htm.
- To learn more about the PostgreSQL EXTRACT function, visit https://www.postgresql.org/docs/11/functions-datetime.html#FUNCTIONS-DATETIME-EXTRACT.

- To learn more about converting dates into specific formats in SQL Server, visit `https://docs.microsoft.com/en-us/sql/t-sql/functions/cast-and-convert-transact-sql?view=sql-server-ver15#date-and-time-styles`.
- To learn more about the DATEPART function in SQL Server, visit `https://docs.microsoft.com/en-us/sql/t-sql/functions/datepart-transact-sql?view=sql-server-ver15`.
- To learn more about the DATENAME function in SQL Server, visit `https://docs.microsoft.com/en-us/sql/t-sql/functions/datename-transact-sql?view=sql-server-ver15`.
- To learn more about the DATEADD function in SQL Server, visit `https://docs.microsoft.com/en-us/sql/t-sql/functions/dateadd-transact-sql?view=sql-server-ver15`.
- To learn more about the DATEDIFF function in SQL Server, visit `https://docs.microsoft.com/en-us/sql/t-sql/functions/datediff-transact-sql?view=sql-server-ver15`.
- To learn more about the Oracle sys_context function, visit `https://docs.oracle.com/cd/B19306_01/server.102/b14200/functions165.htm`.
- To learn more about the Oracle CAST function, visit `https://docs.oracle.com/cd/B19306_01/server.102/b14200/functions016.htm`.
- To learn more about the Oracle CONVERT function, visit `https://docs.oracle.com/cd/B28359_01/server.111/b28286/functions027.htm#SQLRF00620`.
- To learn more about the Oracle IF function, visit `https://docs.oracle.com/cd/B19306_01/appdev.102/b14261/if_statement.htm`.
- To learn more about the PostgreSQL data type formatting functions, visit, `https://www.postgresql.org/docs/11/functions-formatting.html`.
- To learn more about the PostgreSQL IF function, visit `https://www.postgresql.org/docs/9.1/plpgsql-control-structures.html`.
- To learn more about the SQL Server CAST and CONVERT functions, visit `https://docs.microsoft.com/en-us/sql/t-sql/functions/cast-and-convert-transact-sql?view=sql-server-ver15#date-and-time-styles`.
- To learn more about the SQL Server IF function, visit `https://docs.microsoft.com/en-us/sql/t-sql/language-elements/if-else-transact-sql?view=sql-server-ver15`.
- To learn more about the SQL Server ISNULL function, visit `https://docs.microsoft.com/en-us/sql/t-sql/functions/isnull-transact-sql?view=sql-server-ver15`.

10
Grouping and Summarizing Data

In this chapter, you will learn how to use aggregate functions to group and summarize data. Aggregate functions include math functions such as AVG, SUM, COUNT, MIN, and MAX. You will also learn how to use the GROUP BY and HAVING clauses in conjunction with the aggregate functions. Finally, you will learn how MySQL executes your query clauses.

In this chapter, we will cover the following topics:

- Understanding aggregate functions
- Using the GROUP BY clause
- Using the HAVING clause
- Understanding SQL query order of execution

Let's get started!

Technical requirements

You can refer to the code files for this chapter by going to the following GitHub link: https://github.com/PacktPublishing/learn-sql-database-programming/tree/master/chapter-10.

Understanding aggregate functions

Aggregate functions include numeric and statistical built-in functions. These topics were covered in more detail in `Chapter 9`, *Working with Expressions*. The following is a recap from that chapter.

Numeric aggregate functions

Numeric built-in functions handle mathematical calculations. They can all operate on a numeric data type table column or an expression of a numeric data type. The following list shows a sample of these functions:

- `AVG`: Returns the average of an expression:
  - `AVG(rating)`: This will return the average of all the values in a rating column.
  - NULL values are ignored.
- `COUNT`: Returns the number of records:
  - `COUNT(column1)`: This will return the count of values in `column1` : `column1` can contain either strings, dates, or numbers.
  - NULL values are ignored.
- `MAX`: Returns the maximum value in a set of values :
  - `MAX(rating)`: This will return the maximum rating in a column of rating values.
- `MIN`: Returns the minimum value in a set of values:
  - `MIN(rating)`: This will return the minimum rating in a column of rating values.
- `ROUND`: Rounds a number to a specified number of decimal places:
  - `ROUND(123.456, 2)`: This will return `123.46` since the number will round to 2 decimal places.
- `SUM`: The sum of a set of values:
  - `SUM(number)`: This will return the sum of the values in a column of number values.
  - NULL values are ignored.

- FORMAT: Formats decimal numbers so that they have commas for readability:
  - FORMAT(1234.4567, 2): This will return 1,234.46 since the number will round to 2 decimal places. A comma has been added for readability.

Execute the following query to see each of the numeric aggregate functions in action:

```
USE lahmansbaseballdb;
SELECT
 ROUND(AVG(g_all),1) as average_g_all_rounded,
 MAX(g_all) as max_g_all,
 MIN(g_all) as min_g_all,
 FORMAT(COUNT(g_all), 0) as count_g_all_formatted,
 SUM(g_all) as sum_g_all
FROM appearances;
```

The previous query provides the results shown in the following table:

average_g_all_rounded	max_g_all	min_g_all	count_g_all_formatted	sum_g_all
51.3	165	1	105,789	5422767

The first column shows you the average of all games played. The second column shows you the maximum number of games played by a player. The third column shows you the minimum number of games played by a player. The fourth column shows you the count of all games formatted to have a comma and zero decimal places. The last column shows you the sum of all games played.

Statistical aggregate functions

In order to calculate standard descriptive statistics, you can use the following built-in functions:

- VARIANCE: This gives you the variance of your data, which calculates what the difference is for each individual point and the mean of all the points. If zero is returned, then all the data points are the same. A larger value returned means that individual data points are farther from the mean.

- STDDEV: This gives you the standard deviation, which helps you understand how spread out your data is, as well as how close each individual data point is to the mean (you calculate the mean by using the AVG built-in function). If zero is returned, then all the data points are exactly the same. A larger value returned means that individual data points are farther from the mean. Using the standard deviation gives you a *standard* way of knowing what is normal, and helps to find outlier values.

Execute the following query to see each of the statistical aggregate functions in action:

```
USE lahmansbaseballdb;
SELECT
 STDDEV(h) AS 'stddev',
 VARIANCE(h) AS 'variance'
FROM batting;
```

The previous query provides the results shown in the following table:

stddev	stddev
52.4710125	2753.20716

The first column shows you the stddev of all hits in the batting table. The second column shows you the variance of hits in the batting table.

Using the GROUP BY clause

The GROUP BY clause allows you to group rows that have the same values into summary rows. This clause is often used with aggregate functions, which were covered in the previous section of this chapter. It's an optional clause that can be used on a SELECT statement.

The following code shows the GROUP BY syntax, where the WHERE and ORDER BY clauses are optional:

```
SELECT column(s)
 FROM table
 WHERE condition(s)
 GROUP BY columns(s)
ORDER BY column(s);
```

Understanding how GROUP BY works without aggregate functions

Let's say you want to find the distinct list of player ID's and the teams they've played for. You can execute a query like the following:

```
USE lahmansbaseballdb;
SELECT playerid, teamid
FROM batting
GROUP BY teamid;
```

The previous query will give you this error: `Error Code: 1055. Expression #1 of SELECT list is not in GROUP BY clause and contains nonaggregated column 'lahmansbaseballdb.batting.playerID,' which is not functionally dependent on columns in GROUP BY clause; this is incompatible with sql_mode=only_full_group_by.`

This error means that you need to place `playerid` in the `GROUP BY` clause, as follows:

```
USE lahmansbaseballdb;
SELECT playerid, teamid
FROM batting
GROUP BY teamid, playerid;
```

The previous query will give you the results shown in the following screenshot:

playerid	teamid
aardsda01	SFN
aardsda01	CHN
aardsda01	CHA
aardsda01	BOS
aardsda01	SEA
aardsda01	NYA
aardsda01	NYN
aardsda01	ATL
aaronha01	ML1
aaronha01	ATL
aaronha01	ML4

Here, you can see that each player may have more than one row because they played for more than one team during their career.

Using WHERE with GROUP BY

You can also use the WHERE clause along with the GROUP BY clause. The GROUP BY clause will go after the WHERE clause like so:

```
USE lahmansbaseballdb;
SELECT playerid, teamid
FROM batting
WHERE playerid = 'aardsda01'
GROUP BY teamid, playerid;
```

The previous query returns the results shown in the following screenshot:

playerid	teamid
aardsda01	SFN
aardsda01	CHN
aardsda01	CHA
aardsda01	BOS
aardsda01	SEA
aardsda01	NYA
aardsda01	NYN
aardsda01	ATL

Here, you can see that you are now only getting the results for aardsda01.

As a comparison, if you execute the previous query without GROUP BY, the query will return one additional row:

```
USE lahmansbaseballdb;
SELECT playerid, teamid
FROM batting
WHERE playerid = 'aardsda01';
```

The following screenshot shows the results of running the previous query:

playerid	teamid
aardsda01	SFN
aardsda01	CHN
aardsda01	CHA
aardsda01	BOS
aardsda01	SEA
aardsda01	SEA
aardsda01	NYA
aardsda01	NYN
aardsda01	ATL

You can now see two rows containing style. This is because this player was on the Seattle team for 2 years, whereas he was only on the other teams for 1 year. You can view this information by executing the following query:

```
USE lahmansbaseballdb
SELECT playerid, teamid, yearid
FROM batting
WHERE playerid = 'aardsda01';
```

The following screenshot shows you the results of running the previous query:

playerid	teamid	yearid
aardsda01	SFN	2004
aardsda01	CHN	2006
aardsda01	CHA	2007
aardsda01	BOS	2008
aardsda01	SEA	2009
aardsda01	SEA	2010
aardsda01	NYA	2012
aardsda01	NYN	2013
aardsda01	ATL	2015

Here, you can see that teamid is not unique because there are 2 years for the SEA team ID. This shows us that GROUP BY is like using DISTINCT.

The following table shows a comparison between GROUP BY and DISTINCT:

GROUP BY query	DISTINCT query

`USE lahmansbaseballdb;`
`SELECT playerid, teamid`
`FROM batting`
`WHERE playerid = 'aardsda01'`
`GROUP BY teamid, playerid;`
	`USE lahmansbaseballdb;`
	`SELECT DISTINCT playerid, teamid`
	`FROM lahmansbaseballdb.batting`
	`WHERE playerid = 'aardsda01';`

GROUP BY query results	**DISTINCT query results**
playerid / teamid: aardsda01 SFN aardsda01 CHN aardsda01 CHA aardsda01 BOS aardsda01 SEA aardsda01 NYA aardsda01 NYN aardsda01 ATL	playerid / teamid: aardsda01 SFN aardsda01 CHN aardsda01 CHA aardsda01 BOS aardsda01 SEA aardsda01 NYA aardsda01 NYN aardsda01 ATL

Here, you can see that GROUP BY, without aggregate functions, produces the same results as DISTINCT.

Using ORDER BY with GROUP BY

You can also use the ORDER BY clause with GROUP BY. It will need to be placed after the GROUP BY clause, as shown in the following query:

```
USE lahmansbaseballdb;
SELECT playerid, teamid
FROM batting
WHERE playerid = 'aardsda01'
GROUP BY teamid, playerid
ORDER BY playerid, teamid;
```

The following screenshot shows the results of running the previous query:

playerid	teamid
aardsda01	SFN
aardsda01	CHN
aardsda01	CHA
aardsda01	BOS
aardsda01	SEA
aardsda01	NYA
aardsda01	NYN
aardsda01	ATL

Here, you can see that the results are now ordered by playerid and teamid.

Learning how to use the GROUP BY clause to group query results using aggregate functions

Using aggregate functions with GROUP BY can give you some interesting summarized results. We learned a bit about this already in Chapter 9, *Working with Expressions*. There are a couple of ways you can use aggregate functions in a query. One way requires a GROUP BY, while one doesn't.

If you want to summarize an entire table, you don't need to use GROUP BY, as shown in the following query:

```
USE lahmansbaseballdb;
SELECT sum(AB) AS sum_at_bats
FROM batting;
```

The results from running the previous query can be seen in the following table:

sum_at_bats
'14922240'

The previous result is the sum of all the **at-bats (AB)** for the entire table. That's the total for all the times every player came up to bat.

If you want to summarize data for specific columns in a table with aggregate functions, you will need to use a GROUP BY clause. Let's say you wanted to get some summarized information about each player's batting. You can execute the following query to do that:

```
USE lahmansbaseballdb;
SELECT playerid, teamid, sum(AB) AS sum_at_bats
FROM batting
GROUP BY playerid, teamid;
```

The following screenshot shows the results of running the previous query:

playerid	teamid	sum_at_bats
aardsda01	SFN	0
aardsda01	CHN	2
aardsda01	CHA	0
aardsda01	BOS	1
aardsda01	SEA	0
aardsda01	NYA	0
aardsda01	NYN	0
aardsda01	ATL	1
aaronha01	ML1	7080
aaronha01	ATL	4548
aaronha01	ML4	736

Here, we can see the sum of the **at-bats (AB)** for the combination of each player and the team they were on.

Learning how to use the ROLLUP modifier

The ROLLUP modifier allows you to get subtotal rows (also referred to as super-aggregate rows) and a grand total row. The ROLLUP modifier works by aggregating the grouping sets in a GROUP BY clause. A grouping set is the set of columns you group by. For example, with the following query, the grouping set is the sum of at-bats by playerid and teamid:

```
USE lahmansbaseballdb;
SELECT playerid, teamid, sum(AB) AS sum_at_bats
FROM batting
GROUP BY playerid, teamid;
```

To get a subtotal by grouping set and grand total, you will add the ROLLUP modifier, like so:

```
USE lahmansbaseballdb;
SELECT playerid, teamid, sum(AB) AS sum_at_bats
FROM batting
GROUP BY playerid, teamid WITH ROLLUP;
```

If you scroll down to the bottom of the results from running the previous query, you will see a grand total, as shown in the following screenshot:

playerid	teamid	sum_at_bats	
zuverge01	BAL	72	
zuverge01	CIN	2	
zuverge01	CLE	0	
zuverge01	DET	68	
zuverge01	NULL	142	⟵ subtotal
zwilldu01	CHA	87	
zwilldu01	CHF	1140	
zwilldu01	CHN	53	
zwilldu01	NULL	1280	⟵ subtotal
zychto01	SEA	0	
zychto01	NULL	0	⟵ subtotal
NULL	NULL	14922240	⟵ total

Here, you can see that each player and team combination has a sum_at_bats value and that playerid has a NULL teamid to show the total for each player (considered a subtotal of the results). At the bottom of the results, you can see a grand total of all at-bats for all players and team combinations.

You can also use WHERE and ORDER BY with the ROLLUP modifier on the GROUP BY clause.

Differences in RDBMSes

ROLLUP in Oracle, PostgreSQL, and SQL Server uses a different syntax, as shown in the following query:

```
USE lahmansbaseballdb;
SELECT playerid, teamid, sum(AB) AS sum_at_bats
FROM batting
GROUP BY ROLLUP (playerid, teamid)
ORDER BY playerid, teamid;
```

The following screenshot shows the results of running the previous query:

ᴬᴮᶜ playerid	ᴬᴮᶜ teamid	123 sum_at_bats
aardsda01	ATL	1
aardsda01	BOS	1
aardsda01	CHA	0
aardsda01	CHN	2
aardsda01	NYA	0
aardsda01	NYN	0
aardsda01	SEA	0
aardsda01	SFN	0
aardsda01	[NULL]	4
aaronha01	ATL	4,548
aaronha01	ML1	7,080
aaronha01	ML4	736
aaronha01	[NULL]	12,364

Oracle, PostgreSQL, and SQL Server ROLLUP subtotals and grand totals in the same way as MySQL. If you scroll to the bottom of the results, you will see a grand total with playerid and teamid set to NULL.

Using the HAVING clause

The HAVING clause is used to filter the GROUP BY results. The following code shows the HAVING syntax, where the WHERE and ORDER BY clauses are optional:

```
SELECT column(s)
 FROM table
WHERE condition(s)
 GROUP BY columns(s)
 HAVING condition(s)
 ORDER BY column(s);
```

Learning how to use the HAVING clause to limit query results

Let's say you needed to see the results of running the GROUP BY clause in the previous section, but where the sum of at-bats is greater than 100. This is when you would use a HAVING clause, as shown in the following query:

```
USE lahmansbaseballdb;
SELECT playerid, teamid, sum(AB) AS sum_at_bats
FROM batting
```

```
GROUP BY playerid, teamid
HAVING sum_at_bats > 100;
```

The following screenshot shows the results of running the previous query:

playerid	teamid	sum_at_bats
aaronha01	ML1	7080
aaronha01	ATL	4548
aaronha01	ML4	736
aaronto01	ML1	485
aaronto01	ATL	459
abbated01	PHI	102
abbated01	BSN	1856
abbated01	PIT	1086
abbeych01	WAS	1756
abbotfr01	CLE	385
abbotfr01	PHI	128

Here, you can see the results of GROUP BY, with only the sum of at-bats that are greater than 100.

Let's say you were using a WHERE clause for this instead, as shown in the following query:

```
USE lahmansbaseballdb;
SELECT playerid, teamid, sum(AB) AS sum_at_bats
FROM batting
WHERE sum(AB) > 100
GROUP BY playerid, teamid;
```

You will have two issues with the previous query:

- You won't be able to use a column alias in the WHERE clause. You have to use the function in the WHERE clause, so sum (AB) instead of sum_at_bats.
- Once you fixed the previous error, you will receive another error: Error Code: 1111. Invalid use of group function. You can't use a GROUP BY function in a WHERE clause and must instead use the HAVING clause.

You can also use multiple HAVING clauses, as shown in the following query:

```
USE lahmansbaseballdb;
SELECT playerid, teamid, sum(AB) AS sum_at_bats
FROM batting
GROUP BY playerid, teamid
HAVING sum_at_bats > 100
AND sum_at_bats < 400;
```

The following screenshot shows the results of running the previous query:

playerid	teamid	sum_at_bats
aaronha01	ML1	7080
aaronha01	ATL	4548
aaronha01	ML4	736
aaronto01	ML1	485
aaronto01	ATL	459
abbated01	PHI	102
abbated01	BSN	1856
abbated01	PIT	1086
abbeych01	WAS	1756
abbotfr01	CLE	385
abbotfr01	PHI	128

The previous results include any at-bats that are greater than 100 and less than 400.

You can use a BETWEEN clause like so:

```
USE lahmansbaseballdb;
SELECT playerid, teamid, sum(AB) AS sum_at_bats
FROM batting
GROUP BY playerid, teamid
HAVING sum_at_bats BETWEEN 100 AND 400;
```

The following screenshot shows the results of running the previous query:

playerid	teamid	sum_at_bats
abbated01	PHI	102
abbotfr01	CLE	385
abbotfr01	PHI	128
abbotku01	OAK	184
abbotku01	COL	357
abbotku01	NYN	157
abercre01	FLO	331
aberscl01	CHN	179
abnersh01	CAL	101
abnersh01	CHA	208
abramca01	BRO	228

The previous results will include the sum of at-bats that are between 100 and 400, including 100 and 400.

Any of the operators you can use in a WHERE clause, you can also use in a HAVING clause. The operators you can use in a WHERE clause were covered in more detail in Chapter 6, *Querying a Single Table*.

Understanding the difference between the HAVING and WHERE clauses

You can also use the WHERE and HAVING clauses in the same query, and each has its specific uses. The following table outlines each. side by side:

HAVING	WHERE
Filters on aggregated data	Filters on row data
Happens after aggregation	Happens before aggregation

For example, in a previous query of *Learning how to use the HAVING clause to limit query results* section, you were getting any aggregated at-bat results that were between 100 and 400. However, this would mean that MySQL is aggregating results that wouldn't even get summed, such as rows that have zero or NULL, so you would want to filter out those rows so they won't be counted. You can execute the following query to do that:

```
USE lahmansbaseballdb;
SELECT playerid, teamid, sum(AB) AS sum_at_bats
FROM batting
WHERE ab <> 0
AND ab IS NOT NULL
GROUP BY playerid, teamid
HAVING sum(AB) BETWEEN 100 and 400;
```

The previous query will give you the same results without the WHERE clause (which are the same results as in the previous section), but it should get you those results faster. Without the WHERE clauses, the query runs in 0.179 seconds, while with the WHERE clauses, it runs in 0.140 seconds.

That's not a huge difference, but the difference will become bigger and bigger the larger your dataset becomes. It's important to filter out as many of the rows with a WHERE clause as you can if you are going to be using a HAVING clause with GROUP BY.

Understanding SQL query order of execution

It's important to understand that there is a specific order you write SQL query clauses in, as well as a specific order that they are actually executed in by MySQL engine.

You write SQL query clauses in this order:

- SELECT
- FROM/JOIN
- WHERE
- GROUP BY
- HAVING
- ORDER BY
- LIMIT

The order that the clauses are run in by the MySQL engine is as follows:

- FROM/JOIN
- WHERE
- GROUP BY
- HAVING
- SELECT
- ORDER BY
- LIMIT

This is why you can only use column aliases from the SELECT clause in the ORDER BY clause. Understanding the order that MySQL actually runs your clauses in can help you to better understand how your query works or doesn't work.

There is a setting in MySQL that overrides this default behavior for the GROUP BY and HAVING clauses, which are enabled by default, so MySQL will allow you to use column aliases in them. The other RDBMSes, such as Oracle, PostgreSQL, and SQL Server, do not allow this.

Summary

In this chapter, you learned how to use aggregate functions to group and summarize data. Aggregate functions include math functions such as AVG, SUM, COUNT, MIN, and MAX. They also include statistical functions such as STDDEV and VARIANCE.

You learned how to use GROUP BY with and without aggregate functions to summarize data. You also learned how to filter summarized data with the HAVING clause. Then, you learned the difference between the HAVING and WHERE clauses.

Finally, you learned how MySQL actually executes your query clauses. It's not about the order you write the clauses in, but writing them in a different order that explains why you can't use aliases in all the clauses of the SQL statement.

In the next chapter, you will learn how to use advanced querying techniques. By the end of the next chapter, you will be able to understand what types of subqueries exist and how to use them, how flow control statements work and how to use them, when and how to use common table expressions, and how to implement error handling.

Questions

1. What does the GROUP BY clause allow you to do?
2. Do you use the WHERE clause before or after the GROUP BY clause?
3. What's the difference between a GROUP BY clause without aggregate functions and a DISTINCT query?
4. Do you use the ORDER BY clause before or after the GROUP BY clause?
5. What modifier can you use on the GROUP BY clause to get subtotals and grand totals?
6. What does the HAVING clause do?
7. What's the difference between the WHERE and HAVING clauses?
8. Can you use the WHERE and HAVING clauses together?
9. What order do you write query clauses in?
10. What order does MySQL execute query clauses in?

11
Advanced Querying Techniques

In this chapter, you will learn how to use advanced querying techniques and how to use two different kinds of subqueries, correlated and non-correlated. Then, you will learn about two different types of common table expressions, recursive and non-recursive. Next, you will learn about query hints and how to choose which index your query will use. Finally, you will learn about isolation levels and concepts related to how data is read from, and written to, tables.

In this chapter, we will cover the following topics:

- Using subqueries
- Using common table expressions
- Using query hints and transaction isolation levels

Let's get started!

Technical requirements

You can refer to the code files for this chapter by going to the following GitHub link: https://github.com/PacktPublishing/learn-sql-database-programming/tree/master/chapter-11

Using subqueries

A subquery is a query nested in another query with parentheses. A subquery can be used in SELECT, FROM, INSERT, DELETE, UPDATE, and WHERE clauses, and can also be nested inside another subquery. Subqueries can be beneficial when a query may require complex joins and unions. A subquery can return either a single value, row, column, or table.

A subquery is the inner query of another query, which is considered the outer query. The inner query is executed before the outer query so that the inner query results are passed to the outer query. For example, in the following code, the query inside parentheses is the inner query, while the query outside parentheses is the outer query:

```
SELECT col1
FROM table1
WHERE col1 IN
  (SELECT col1 FROM table 2 WHERE col1 = 'test')
```

Understanding the different types of subqueries and their usage

There are two types of subqueries, correlated and non-correlated. The following table outlines their differences:

Non-correlated	Correlated
The inner query doesn't depend on the outer query	Inner query depends on the outer query
Can run as a standalone query	Can't run as a standalone query
Executed only once	Executed once for each row selected in the outer query
Executed before the outer query	Executed after the outer query
Can't be used instead of JOIN on the outer query	Can be used instead of JOIN on the outer query, but will be slower than JOIN

The following sections will show examples of each to help you understand them better.

Using non-correlated subqueries

You can use a non-correlated subquery in a WHERE clause along with these operators:

- IN: This will return results in the outer query where the results are *in* the inner query. If the inner query returns even one NULL value, then there will be no outer query results. This is because IN can evaluate to either true, false, or NULL. The following code block shows some sample syntax:

```
SELECT column(s)
FROM tablea
WHERE col1 IN (SELECT col
               FROM tableb
                WHERE condition(s));
```

- NOT IN: This will return results in the outer query where the results are *not in* the inner query. If the inner query returns even one NULL value, then there will be no outer query results. This is because NOT IN can evaluate to either true, false, or NULL. The following code block shows some sample syntax:

```
SELECT column(s)
FROM tablea
WHERE col1 NOT IN (SELECT col
                   FROM tableb
                    WHERE condition(s));
```

- ANY: This will return results in the outer query where the results of the outer query satisfy *any* of the results of the inner query. The following code block shows some sample syntax:

```
SELECT column(s)
FROM tablea
WHERE col1 >= ANY (SELECT col
                   FROM tableb
                    WHERE condition(s));
```

- ALL: This will return results in the outer query where the results of the outer query satisfy *all* of the results of the inner query. The following code block shows some sample syntax:

```
SELECT column(s)
FROM tablea
WHERE col1 >= ALL (SELECT col
                   FROM tableb
                    WHERE condition(s));
```

- SOME: This is an alias for ANY and will return the same results as ANY. The following code block shows some sample syntax:

```
SELECT column(s)
FROM tablea
WHERE col1 >= SOME (SELECT col
                    FROM tableb
                        WHERE condition(s));
```

- =: This will return results in the outer query where the results are *equal* to the inner query result. This can only be used if the inner query returns one value. The following code block shows some sample syntax:

```
SELECT column(s)
FROM tablea
WHERE col1 = (SELECT col
                    FROM tableb
                        WHERE condition(s));
```

- >: This will return results in the outer query where the results are *greater than* the inner query result. This can only be used if the inner query returns one value. The following code block shows some sample syntax:

```
SELECT column(s)
FROM tablea
WHERE col1 > (SELECT col
                    FROM tableb
                        WHERE condition(s));
```

- <: This will return results in the outer query where the results are *less than* the inner query result. This can only be used if the inner query returns one value. The following code block shows some sample syntax:

```
SELECT column(s)
FROM tablea
WHERE col1 < (SELECT col
                    FROM tableb
                        WHERE condition(s));
```

- `>=`: This will return results in the outer query where the results are *greater than or equal to* the inner query result. This can only be used if the inner query returns one value. The following code block shows some sample syntax:

```
SELECT column(s)
FROM tablea
WHERE col1 >= (SELECT col
                FROM tableb
                 WHERE condition(s));
```

- `<=`: This will return results in the outer query where the results are *less than or equal to* the inner query result. This can only be used if the inner query returns one value. The following code block shows some sample syntax:

```
SELECT column(s)
FROM tablea
WHERE col1 <= (SELECT col
                FROM tableb
                 WHERE condition(s));
```

- `!=` or `<>`: This will return results in the outer query where the results are *not equal to* the inner query result. This can only be used if the inner query returns one value. The following code block shows some sample syntax:

```
SELECT column(s)
FROM tablea
WHERE col1 != (SELECT col
                FROM tableb
                 WHERE condition(s));
```

Using a non-correlated subquery in the WHERE clause

This section will help you better understand how to use a non-correlated subquery in the WHERE clause:

- Using IN: This will return results in the outer query where the results are *in* the inner query. If the inner query returns even one NULL value, then there will be no outer query results. This is because IN can evaluate to either true, false, or NULL. The IN operator allows you to use a subquery that returns zero or more rows.

You can execute the following query using a non-correlated subquery with IN:

```
USE lahmansbaseballdb;
SELECT playerid, yearid, g as GamesBatted
FROM batting
WHERE playerid IN (SELECT playerid FROM people WHERE birthcity =
'Boston');
```

The preceding query returns the results shown in the following screenshot:

playerid	yearid	GamesBatted
anderbi01	1925	2
bagweje01	1991	156
bagweje01	1992	162
bagweje01	1993	142
bagweje01	1994	110
bagweje01	1995	114
bagweje01	1996	162
bagweje01	1997	162
bagweje01	1998	147
bagweje01	1999	162
bagweje01	2000	159
bagweje01	2001	161

The preceding query will return the playerid, yearid, and
GamesBatted columns when playerid has birthcity as Boston in the people
table. This is because the WHERE clause has a non-correlated subquery that queries
the people table for all playerid that have birthcity equal to Boston, and
then queries the batting table to get the list of playerid with the corresponding
yearid and GamesBatted column.

- Using NOT IN: This will return results in the outer query where the results
  are *not in* the inner query. If the inner query returns even one NULL value, then
  there will be no outer query results. This is because NOT IN can evaluate to either
  true, false, or NULL. The NOT IN operator allows you to use a subquery that
  returns zero or more rows.

You can also use the same non-correlated subquery, but with NOT IN in the
WHERE clause instead, as shown in the following query:

```
USE lahmansbaseballdb;
SELECT playerid, yearid, g as GamesBatted
FROM batting
WHERE playerid NOT IN (SELECT playerid FROM people WHERE birthcity
= 'Boston');
```

The previous query returns the results shown in the following screenshot:

playerid	yearid	GamesBatted
aardsda01	2004	11
aardsda01	2006	45
aardsda01	2007	25
aardsda01	2008	47
aardsda01	2009	73
aardsda01	2010	53
aardsda01	2012	1
aardsda01	2013	43
aardsda01	2015	33
aaronha01	1954	122

The previous query will return the `playerid`, `yearid`, and
`GamesBatted` columns when `playerid` doesn't have `birthcity` as `Boston` in
the people table. This is because the `WHERE` clause has a non-correlated subquery
that uses `NOT IN` in the query of the people table for all `playerid` that have
`birthcity` equal to `Boston`, and then queries the batting table to get the list of
`playerid` with the corresponding `yearid` and `GamesBatted`columns.

> It's important to remember that if your non-correlated subquery returns
> any `NULL` values when you use `IN` or `NOT IN`, then the outer query will
> return no results.

- Using >= (greater than or equal to): This will return results in the outer query
  where the results are *greater than or equal to* the inner query result. This can only
  be used if the inner query returns one value. The >= operator allows you to use a
  subquery that returns zero or more rows.

You can also use comparison operators such as >= (greater than or equal to) with
a non-correlated subquery in the `WHERE` clause, as shown in the following query:

```
USE lahmansbaseballdb;
SELECT playerid, yearid, salary
FROM salaries
WHERE salary >=
 (SELECT AVG(salary)
 FROM salaries
 WHERE teamid = 'DET'
 GROUP BY teamid)
ORDER BY playerid, yearid;
```

The preceding query returns the results shown in the following screenshot:

playerid	yearid	salary
aardsda01	2010	2750000
aardsda01	2011	4500000
abbotji01	1994	2775000
abbotji01	1995	2775000
abbotpa01	2002	3425000
abreubo01	2000	2933333
abreubo01	2001	4983000
abreubo01	2002	6333333
abreubo01	2003	9100000
abreubo01	2004	10600000

The previous query will return the `playerid`, `yearid`, and `salary` columns if the salary of the player is greater than or equal to the average salary on the DET team.

It's important to remember that when using comparison operations such as =, >, <, >=, <=, or <>, your subquery can only return one row or you will receive an error: `Error Code: 1242. Subquery returns more than 1 row.`

- Using ANY: This will return results in the outer query where the results of the outer query satisfy any of the results of the inner query. The ANY operator allows you to use a subquery that returns zero or more rows.

You can also use comparison operators such as >= (greater than or equal to) with ANY and a non-correlated subquery in the WHERE clause, as shown in the following query:

```
USE lahmansbaseballdb;
SELECT playerid, yearid, salary
FROM salaries
WHERE salary >= ANY
  (SELECT AVG(salary)
  FROM salaries
  GROUP BY teamid)
ORDER BY playerid, yearid;
```

The preceding query returns the results shown in the following screenshot:

playerid	yearid	salary
aardsda01	2010	2750000
aardsda01	2011	4500000
aasedo01	1987	625000
aasedo01	1988	675000
abadfe01	2015	1087500
abadfe01	2016	1250000
abbotji01	1992	1850000
abbotji01	1993	2350000
abbotji01	1994	2775000
abbotji01	1995	2775000

The preceding query will return the playerid, yearid, and salary columns if the salary of the player is greater than or equal to ANY of the average salaries for each teamid.

- Using ALL: This will return results in the outer query where the results of the outer query satisfy all of the results of the inner query. The ALL operator allows you to use a subquery that returns zero or more rows.

You can also use comparison operators such as >= (greater than or equal to) with ALL and a non-correlated subquery in the WHERE clause, as shown in the following query:

```
USE lahmansbaseballdb;
SELECT playerid, yearid, salary
FROM salaries
WHERE salary >= ALL
  (SELECT AVG(salary)
  FROM salaries
  GROUP BY teamid)
ORDER BY playerid, yearid;
```

The preceding query returns the results shown in the following screenshot:

playerid	yearid	salary
aardsda01	2011	4500000
abreubo01	2001	4983000
abreubo01	2002	6333333
abreubo01	2003	9100000
abreubo01	2004	10600000
abreubo01	2005	13100000
abreubo01	2006	13600000
abreubo01	2007	15000000
abreubo01	2008	16000000
abreubo01	2009	5000000

The previous query will return the `playerid`, `yearid`, and `salary` columns if the salary of the player is greater than or equal to `ALL` of the average salaries for each `teamid`.

When using `ANY` or `ALL` with comparison operations such as =, >, <, >=, <=, or <>, your subquery can return more than one row.

Additionally, you can use any of the operators listed at the beginning of this section by following the rules for each of the operators.

Using a non-correlated subquery in the SELECT clause

To help you better understand how to use a non-correlated subquery in the `SELECT` clause, execute the following query:

```
USE lahmansbaseballdb;
SELECT playerid, yearid, salary,
 (SELECT ROUND(AVG(salary), 0)
 FROM salaries) AS average_salary,
 salary - (SELECT ROUND(AVG(salary), 0)
  FROM salaries) AS difference,
 (SELECT MAX(salary)
 FROM salaries) AS max_salary
FROM salaries
ORDER BY playerid, yearid;
```

The preceding query returns the results shown in the following screenshot:

playerid	yearid	salary	average_salary	difference	max_salary
aardsda01	2004	300000	2085634	-1785634	33000000
aardsda01	2007	387500	2085634	-1698134	33000000
aardsda01	2008	403250	2085634	-1682384	33000000
aardsda01	2009	419000	2085634	-1666634	33000000
aardsda01	2010	2750000	2085634	664366	33000000
aardsda01	2011	4500000	2085634	2414366	33000000
aardsda01	2012	500000	2085634	-1585634	33000000
aasedo01	1986	600000	2085634	-1485634	33000000
aasedo01	1987	625000	2085634	-1460634	33000000
aasedo01	1988	675000	2085634	-1410634	33000000

The previous query will return the `playerid`, `yearid`, `salary`, `average_salary`, `difference`, and `max_salary` columns for each row returned. `average_salary`, `difference`, and `max_salary` use a non-correlated subquery to return the results.

Using a non-correlated subquery in the FROM clause

To help you better understand how to use a non-correlated subquery in the FROM clause, execute the following query:

```
USE lahmansbaseballdb;
SELECT ROUND(AVG(average_salary), 0) AS average_of_all_teams_salaries
FROM
  (SELECT AVG(salary) average_salary
  FROM salaries
  GROUP BY teamid);
```

The preceding query will give you the following error:

```
Error Code: 1248. Every derived table must have an alias.
```

This means that we need to add an alias to the inner query contained in the FROM clause. The subquery used in a FROM clause is also referred to as a derived table. The following highlighted code shows you a proper derived table, along with its alias:

```
USE lahmansbaseballdb;
SELECT ROUND(AVG(average_salary), 0) as average_of_all_teams_salaries
FROM
    (SELECT AVG(salary) average_salary
    FROM salaries
    GROUP BY teamid) AS team_salary;
```

Subquery and derived table terminology are often used interchangeably.

When you execute the following query with a properly defined derived table, it will work without returning an error:

```
USE lahmansbaseballdb;
SELECT ROUND(AVG(average_salary), 0) AS average_of_all_teams_salaries
FROM
 (SELECT AVG(salary) average_salary
 FROM salaries
 GROUP BY teamid) AS team_salary;
```

The preceding query returns the result shown in the following screenshot:

average_of_all_teams_salaries
2078464

The preceding query will return the average of all the averages of the teams' salaries. This is accomplished via a non-correlated query in the FROM clause that gets each teams' average salary. By doing this, the outer query gets the average of those averages.

If you were to run the inner query on its own, you would see the listing of teams' average salaries. The inner query is highlighted in the following screenshot:

```
USE lahmansbaseballdb;
SELECT ROUND(AVG(average_salary), 0) as average_of_all_teams_salaries
FROM
    (SELECT AVG(salary) average_salary
    FROM salaries
    GROUP BY teamid) AS team_salary;
```

You can add `teamid` to the columns of the inner query to see the `teamid` column and make it more obvious what is happening with the inner query:

```
SELECT teamid, AVG(salary) average_salary
FROM salaries
GROUP BY teamid
```

The results from the inner query are shown in the following screenshot:

teamid	average_salary
ATL	2211176.3114754097
BAL	2028838.645744681
BOS	2968591.2033898304
CAL	739073.179347826
CHA	2168060.259009009
CHN	2353348.3900552485
CIN	1759986.7666666666
CLE	1651203.1548998947
DET	2386561.292410714
HOU	1788017.0908059024

The outer query then averages those team's salaries into one average for all the teams.

As an example of how you can exclude records from the derived table with a WHERE clause, you can execute the following query:

```
USE lahmansbaseballdb;
  SELECT ROUND(AVG(average_salary), 0) AS average_of_all_teams_salaries
FROM
  (SELECT AVG(salary) average_salary
  FROM salaries
  GROUP BY teamid) AS team_salary
WHERE team_salary.average_salary > 2000000;
```

The preceding query provides the results shown in the following screenshot:

average_of_all_teams_salaries
2537765

Here, you can see that `average_of_all_teams_salaries` is now higher than in the previous query since it has a derived table without a WHERE clause that filters data in the derived table, that is, 2537765 (with a WHERE clause on the derived table column) versus 2078464 (with a derived table only).

Using INSERT, UPDATE, and DELETE with non-correlated subqueries

To show you an example of inserting with a non-correlated subquery, execute the following query to create a new table to hold the data:

```
USE lahmansbaseballdb;
 CREATE TABLE salaries_avg (
 teamID varchar(3) NOT NULL,
 salaryavg double NOT NULL
 );
```

Once you've created the table with the preceding script, you can execute the following script to insert data into the table:

```
USE lahmansbaseballdb;
INSERT INTO salaries_avg
 SELECT teamid, average_salary
 FROM
 (SELECT teamid, AVG(salary) average_salary
 FROM salaries
 GROUP BY teamid) AS team_salary
 WHERE team_salary.average_salary > 2000000;
```

Here, you can see that the non-correlated subquery is actually in the SELECT clause of the INSERT query. This is how you can insert data by using a subquery in the same way you use it in a SELECT clause and then use that SELECT clause to query the data you want to insert. The following screenshot shows the results of what was inserted into the salaries_avg table:

teamid	salaryavg
ATL	2211176.3114754097
BAL	2028838.645744681
BOS	2968591.2033898304
CHA	2168060.259009009
CHN	2353348.3900552485
DET	2386561.292410714
LAN	2795033.524555904
NYA	3968910.44076841
NYN	2463019.7297592997

You can also update from a subquery, as shown in the following query:

```
USE lahmansbaseballdb;
UPDATE salaries_avg
SET
 teamid = (SELECT teamid
 FROM
 (SELECT teamid, AVG(salary) average_salary
 FROM salaries
 GROUP BY teamid) AS team_salary
 WHERE team_salary.average_salary > 2000000
 LIMIT 1);
```

After the previous update, salary_avg table will look as follows. It's showing all ATL because that's what the previous UPDATE query ultimately did:

teamid	salaryavg
ATL	2211176.3114754097
ATL	2028838.645744681
ATL	2968591.2033898304
ATL	2168060.259009009
ATL	2353348.3900552485
ATL	2386561.292410714
ATL	2795033.524555904
ATL	3968910.44076841

Additionally, you can delete with a subquery, as shown in the following query:

```
USE lahmansbaseballdb;
DELETE FROM salaries_avg
WHERE teamid IN (SELECT teamid
  FROM
  (SELECT teamid, AVG(salary) avgsalary
   FROM salaries
   GROUP BY teamid) AS team_salary
  WHERE team_salary.avgsalary > 2000000
AND teamid = 'ATL');
```

Now, there will be no rows in salaries_avg table.

Differences between non-correlated subqueries in other relational database management systems (RDMSes)

There is only one small difference in Oracle when using the subquery in a FROM clause: you can't use the AS keyword with the alias for the subquery. Instead, the query will look as follows:

```
USE lahmansbaseballdb;
SELECT ROUND(AVG(average_salary), 0) AS average_of_all_teams_salaries
FROM
 (SELECT AVG(salary) average_salary
 FROM salaries
 GROUP BY teamid) team_salary;
```

The original query had AS between the code snippets GROUP BY teamid) and team_salary, like this:

```
GROUP BY teamid) AS team_salary;
```

Using correlated subqueries

You can use a correlated subquery in a WHERE clause along with these operators:

- IN: This will return results in the outer query where the results are *in* the inner query. If the inner query returns even one NULL value, then there will be no outer query results. This is because IN can evaluate to either true, False, or NULL. The following shows some sample syntax:

```
SELECT column(s) FROM table a
WHERE a.col IN (SELECT b.col
                FROM table b
                WHERE a.col = b.col);
```

- NOT IN: This will return results in the outer query where the results are *not in* the inner query. If the inner query returns even one NULL value, then there will be no outer query results. This is because NOT IN can evaluate to either true, false, or NULL. The following shows some sample syntax:

```
SELECT column(s) FROM table a
WHERE a.col NOT IN (SELECT b.col
                FROM table b
                WHERE a.col = b.col);
```

- `EXISTS`: This will return results in the outer query where the results *exist* in the inner query. It evaluates to either `true` or `false`. The following shows some sample syntax:

```
SELECT column(s) FROM table a
WHERE EXISTS (SELECT 1 FROM table b
 WHERE a.col = b.col);
```

- `NOT EXISTS`: This will return results in the outer query where the results *do not exist* in the inner query. It evaluates to either `true` or `false`. The following shows some sample syntax:

```
SELECT column(s) FROM table a
WHERE NOT EXISTS (SELECT 1 FROM table b
                 WHERE a.col = b.col);
```

Using a correlated subquery in the WHERE clause

This section will help you better understand how to use a correlated subquery in the `WHERE` clause:

- Using `EXISTS`: This will return results in the outer query where the results *exist* in the inner query. It evaluates to either `true` or `false`. The `EXISTS` operator allows you to use a subquery that returns exactly one row.

  You can execute the following query using a correlated subquery with `EXISTS`:

```
USE lahmansbaseballdb;
SELECT f.playerid, f.yearid, f.teamid, pos
FROM fielding f
WHERE EXISTS(SELECT 1
 FROM salaries s
 WHERE salary < 200000
 AND salary IS NOT NULL
 AND (f.playerid = s.playerid
 AND f.teamid = s.teamid
 AND f.yearid = s.yearid))
ORDER BY f.playerid;
```

The preceding query returns the results shown in the following screenshot:

playerid	yearid	teamid	pos
abbotje01	1998	CHA	OF
abbotji01	1989	CAL	P
abbotji01	1990	CAL	P
abbotku01	1995	FLO	SS
abbotku01	1994	FLO	SS
abbotku01	1993	OAK	SS
abbotku01	1993	OAK	OF
abbotku01	1993	OAK	2B
abbotky01	1995	PHI	P
abbotky01	1992	PHI	P

The preceding query will return the `playerid`, `yearid`, `teamid`, and `pos` columns when `playerid` has `salary` less than `200000` in the `salaries` table. This is because the `WHERE` clause has a correlated subquery that queries the `salaries` table for all `playerid` that have a salary less than $200,000, and joins the `playerid`, `yearid` and, `teamid` combination in the `salaries` table to the `playerid`, `yearid`, and `teamid` combination in the `fielding` table. The inner query will run exactly once for each row in the outer table.

- Using `IN`: This will return results in the outer query where the results are *in* the inner query. If the inner query returns even one `NULL` value, then there will be no outer query results. This is because `IN` can evaluate to either `true`, `false`, or `NULL`. The `EXISTS` operator allows you to use a subquery that returns exactly one row.

You can execute the following query using a correlated subquery with `IN`:

```
USE lahmansbaseballdb;
SELECT f.playerid, f.yearid, f.teamid, pos
FROM fielding f
WHERE playerid IN (SELECT playerid
 FROM salaries s
 WHERE salary < 200000
 AND salary IS NOT NULL
 AND (f.playerid = s.playerid
 AND f.teamid = s.teamid
 AND f.yearid = s.yearid))
ORDER BY f.playerid;
```

The preceding query returns the same results as the previous query, as shown in the following screenshot:

playerid	yearid	teamid	pos
abbotje01	1997	CHA	OF
abbotje01	1998	CHA	OF
abbotje01	1999	CHA	OF
abbotje01	2000	CHA	OF
abbotje01	2001	FLO	OF
abbotji01	1999	MIL	P
abbotji01	1989	CAL	P
abbotji01	1990	CAL	P
abbotji01	1991	CAL	P
abbotji01	1992	CAL	P
abbotji01	1993	NYA	P
abbotji01	1994	NYA	P

The previous query will return the `playerid`, `yearid`, `teamid`, and `pos` columns when `playerid` has `salary` less than `200000` in the `salaries` table. This is because the `WHERE` clause has a correlated subquery that queries the `salaries` table for all `playerid` that have a salary less than $200,000, and joins the `playerid`, `yearid` and, `teamid` combination in the `salaries` table to the `playerid`, `yearid`, and `teamid` combination in the `fielding` table. The inner query will run exactly once for each row in the outer table.

Using a correlated subquery in the SELECT clause

You can execute the following query using a correlated subquery in the `SELECT` clause:

```
USE lahmansbaseballdb;
SELECT f.playerid, f.yearid, f.teamid, pos,
 (SELECT salary
 FROM salaries s
 WHERE (f.playerid = s.playerid
  AND f.teamid = s.teamid
  AND f.yearid = s.yearid)) AS salary
FROM fielding f
ORDER BY f.playerid;
```

The previous query returns the same results as the previous query in this section did, as shown in the following screenshot:

playerid	yearid	teamid	pos	salary
aardsda01	2004	SFN	P	300000
aardsda01	2006	CHN	P	NULL
aardsda01	2007	CHA	P	387500
aardsda01	2008	BOS	P	403250
aardsda01	2009	SEA	P	419000
aardsda01	2010	SEA	P	2750000
aardsda01	2012	NYA	P	500000
aardsda01	2013	NYN	P	NULL
aardsda01	2015	ATL	P	NULL
aaronha01	1954	ML1	OF	NULL
aaronha01	1955	ML1	2B	NULL
aaronha01	1955	ML1	OF	NULL

The previous query will return the `playerid`, `yearid`, `teamid`, `pos`, and `salary` columns. `salary` is obtained by querying the `salaries` table and joining it to the `fielding` table by `playerid`, `yearid`, and `teamid`. The inner query will run exactly once for each row in the outer table.

Using common table expressions

A **common table expression (CTE)** is a *container* for a single SQL statement that will allow you to query a temporary result set. A CTE allows you to create complex queries in a more readable way. It may be beneficial to use a CTE instead of subqueries because it's easier to read and understand later. CTEs can also be used instead of creating a view. To create a view, you need elevated permissions in a database, but you won't need any additional permissions to use a CTE. Views will be covered in more detail in Chapter 12, *Programmable Objects*. Additionally, CTEs can help you run recursive queries.

Using non-recursive CTEs

The syntax for a single non-recursive CTE is as follows:

```
WITH ctename (col1, col2, colN)
AS (SELECT col1, col2, colN FROM table)
SELECT col1, col2, colN FROM ctename;
```

The syntax for a non-recursive CTE with multiple CTEs is as follows:

```
WITH ctename1 (col1, col2, colN)
AS (select col1, col2, colN from table1),
ctename2 (col1, col2, colN)
AS (select col1, col2, colN from table2)
SELECT col1, col2, colN
FROM ctename1
JOIN ctename2
ON ctename1.col1 = ctename2.col1;
```

The following diagram will help you understand what each piece of the CTE is:

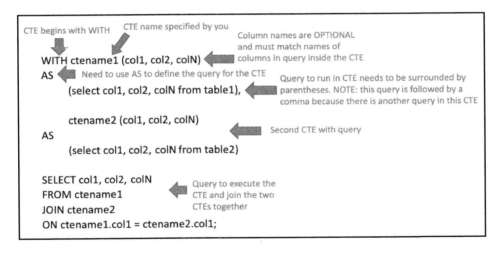

Non-recursive CTE with the SELECT statement

To help you understand a good use case for a CTE, let's work with a query from earlier in this chapter that uses a derived table:

```
USE lahmansbaseballdb;
 SELECT ROUND(AVG(average_salary), 0) AS average_of_all_teams_salaries
FROM
 (SELECT AVG(salary) average_salary
 FROM salaries
 GROUP BY teamid) AS team_salary
WHERE team_salary.average_salary > 2000000;
```

The preceding query will be rewritten into the following CTE:

```
USE lahmansbaseballdb;
WITH avgsalarycte
AS
(SELECT AVG(salary) AS average_salary
FROM salaries
GROUP BY teamid)

SELECT ROUND(AVG(average_salary), 0) AS average_of_all_teams_salaries
FROM avgsalarycte
WHERE average_salary > 2000000;
```

The CTE query will give you the same results as the derived table query (2537765), but may be a little bit easier to read and understand, especially if you aren't the one who wrote the query or if you are coming back to the query a long while after writing it. Of course, you would comment your code so that anyone can understand what you are trying to do, but it's still nice to make your code as simple as possible. This really comes into play when your derived tables get way more complicated than this example query, but still, the same concept applies.

Using recursive CTEs

The syntax for a recursive CTE is as follows:

```
WITH RECURSIVE ctename
AS (
 initial query
 UNION ALL
 recursive query
)
SELECT * FROM ctename;
```

The initial query is the base result set of your CTE. This is also referred to as an anchor member. The recursive query is the query that will be referencing the CTE name. It is joined to the anchor query by a UNION ALL. If you're doing a simple counting style CTE, then you will also use what's referred to as a termination condition so that your CTE stops when the recursive query stops returning rows.

A simple example of recursion is as follows:

```
WITH RECURSIVE cte (x) AS
(
 SELECT 1
 UNION ALL
 SELECT x + 1 FROM cte
 WHERE x < 10
)
SELECT x FROM cte;
```

The preceding CTE will return x as 1, and then keep adding 1 to x, as long as x is less than 10, as shown in the following results:

If you were to leave off the termination condition on the recursive query (WHERE x < 10), you would receive this error from MySQL:

```
Error Code: 3636. Recursive query aborted after 1001 iterations. Try
increasing @@cte_max_recursion_depth to a larger value.
```

Instead of changing @@cte_max_recursion_depth, you would need to add a termination condition. Some other examples of ways to use a recursive CTE could be with data series generation or hierarchical data, such as employee reporting structures.

Differences between CTEs in other RDMSes

In SQL Server and Oracle, remove the RECURSIVE keyword when running a recursive CTE. Non-recursive and recursive use the same syntax in SQL Server and Oracle.

Using query hints and transaction isolation levels

Query hints and isolation levels help you to have more control over how your query is executed by MySQL. Before we discuss these topics, let's go over what locking, blocking, and deadlocking mean.

Understand the concepts of locking, blocking, and deadlocking

Locking is what happens when a query runs against a database. There are read locks and write locks:

- **Read locks**: Allow other queries reading data (SELECT) to read as well.
- **Write locks**: Other queries can't read or write data until the write (INSERT, UPDATE, DELETE) query is complete.

Blocking can happen when one or more queries holds a lock on the same data. Deadlocking can happen when each query locks data that the other query needs.

For example, when you run a query, MySQL has to decide how to get the data from the table(s). If your table has no index, the query will need to scan through the entire table to find the data, much the same way you would have to scan through an entire book if it didn't have an index in the back. That would be very time-consuming, depending on how long the book is. The same thing goes for an index on a table. You might not notice any issues with your query running for a long time if the table is small, but once the table is large, scanning the entire table to get the results could take quite a while. Plus, if other people are also running queries on the same table, the results may never return since queries may block each other or deadlock.

Locking happens when you run a query. Locking isn't bad in itself. Locking becomes an issue when different queries interfere with each other and cause blocking. Blocking happens when more than one query is trying to read or write the same data. Sometimes, blocking happens and it's just for a short period of time, so blocking isn't necessarily bad, but if two or more queries request the same data for creating locks that won't be resolved, MySQL will decide which is easiest to kill (usually based on how long it will take to rollback any given query), and this is what is referred to as a deadlock. MySQL will need to roll back a query if it hasn't finished inserting, updating, or deleting data to keep the data in a consistent state.

If you create indexes and use them properly with your queries, you will have less blocking and deadlocking to deal with because the index will allow you to query data more quickly.

The main way indexes can speed up a query is by using the columns in the index when joining tables, when filtering results (that is, `yearid = 2017`), and when ordering results (that is, order by year descending).

Learning how to use index hints to improve queries

Generally speaking, MySQL will know how to choose the correct index for your queries. That being said, you can force it to choose which index to use with index hints on your query. `USE INDEX` keywords will allow you to specify the index you want your query to use. The following code block shows the syntax of an index hint:

```
SELECT columns
FROM tablename USE INDEX(indexname)
WHERE condition;
```

To follow along with the USE INDEX query later in this section, add the following index to the appearances table:

```
USE lahmansbaseballdb;
ALTER TABLE appearances
ADD INDEX NC_playerid_g_cols
(playerID ASC, G_all ASC, G_batting ASC, G_defense ASC) VISIBLE;
```

If you want to see a list of the indexes on your table, along with associated information about those indexes, execute the following query:

```
USE lahmansbaseballdb;
SHOW INDEXES FROM appearances;
```

The SHOW INDEXES query will give you the results shown in the following screenshot:

Table	Non_unique	Key_name	Seq_in_index	Column_name	Collation	Cardinality	Sub_part	Packed	Null	Index_type
appearances	0	PRIMARY	1	yearID	A	151	NULL	NULL		BTREE
appearances	0	PRIMARY	2	teamID	A	2827	NULL	NULL		BTREE
appearances	0	PRIMARY	3	playerID	A	105627	NULL	NULL		BTREE
appearances	1	NC_playerid_g_cols	1	playerID	A	19632	NULL	NULL		BTREE
appearances	1	NC_playerid_g_cols	2	G_all	A	97630	NULL	NULL	YES	BTREE
appearances	1	NC_playerid_g_cols	3	G_batting	A	99498	NULL	NULL	YES	BTREE
appearances	1	NC_playerid_g_cols	4	G_defense	A	102543	NULL	NULL	YES	BTREE

The previous screenshot gives you information about the indexes on the appearances table. This includes the name of the index, the columns in the index, and the order of the columns.

Then, execute this query without any index hints:

```
USE lahmansbaseballdb;
EXPLAIN SELECT playerid FROM appearances;
```

You will see that it will choose the index you just added to the key column, as shown in the following screenshot:

id	select_type	table	partitions	type	possible_keys	key	key_len	ref	rows	filtered	Extra
1	SIMPLE	appearances	NULL	index	NULL	NC_playerid_g_cols	47	NULL	105627	100.00	Using index

Let's say you wanted to ensure it used the primary key index. Here, you can add an index hint to the query, as shown in the following example:

```
USE lahmansbaseballdb;
EXPLAIN SELECT playerid FROM appearances USE INDEX (PRIMARY);
```

The following screenshot shows that the query is now using the PRIMARY index instead:

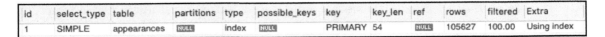

id	select_type	table	partitions	type	possible_keys	key	key_len	ref	rows	filtered	Extra
1	SIMPLE	appearances	NULL	index	NULL	PRIMARY	54	NULL	105627	100.00	Using index

The query does run slightly faster in this case, but it may not always do so, depending on the system specifications and the query that is being executed, as shown in the following screenshot, the **Action Output** window shows the **Duration/Fetch Time**:

Action Output			
	Time	Action	Response	Duration / Fetch Time
1	17:13:03	SELECT playerid FROM appearances USE INDEX (PRIMARY)	105789 row(s) returned	0.161 sec / 0.443 sec
2	17:13:22	SELECT playerid FROM appearances	105789 row(s) returned	0.222 sec / 0.442 sec

It's mainly best to let MySQL engine choose the best index for your query, but index hints are an option if you really want to choose the specific index to use.

Learning how to use transaction isolation levels

You learned about isolation briefly in Chapter 8, *Modifying Data and Table Structures*, as part of the four properties of database transactions: **Atomicity**, **Consistency**, **Isolation**, and **Durability (ACID)**.

There are a few key terms to understand before learning about isolation levels:

- **Dirty read**: Let's say that one transaction (T1) is running and updating some data, and another transaction (T2) comes along to select data from that same table and returns the data, but then T1 rolls back. Now, the user who was running T2 thinks this data is how T1 would have left it, had it not rolled back.
- **Non-repeatable read**: Like the previous example, we have two transactions executing (T1 and T2). T1 is executing the update, while T2 is selecting from the same table, but this time, T2 gets a snapshot of the data when it starts running, so it won't see T1's data in-progress. However, if T2 were to run again after T1 is done, it would return different results.

- **Phantom read**: Like the previous examples, we have two transactions executing (T1 and T2). T1 is executing the insert, while T2 is selecting from the same table, but this time, T2 gets a snapshot of the data when it starts running, so it won't see T1's data in-progress. However, in this case, the same results would be used throughout T2's execution, whenever the select query is re-executed as part of that transaction. It won't take into account any of the changes that T1 made, even if they are already committed. Phantom reads happen when rows are returned that weren't in the previous results.

To sum up the differences between dirty reads, non-repeatable reads, and phantom reads, you can think of dirty reads as reading uncommitted data, non-repeatable reads occur when a transaction reads committed updates from another transaction, and phantom reads occur when a transaction reads from another transaction committing inserts or deletes.

There are four different kinds of isolation levels in MySQL (in order of least isolation to most isolation, and also fastest to slowest):

- READ UNCOMMITTED: There is very little isolation in this isolation level. With this isolation level, transactions can see data that hasn't been committed in other transactions yet. This is what is considered a dirty read. It can be highly performant, but it's the isolation level with the most issues when it comes to getting the correct data returned. It could even return data that won't be there anymore after another concurrently running transaction is running.
- READ COMMITTED: Unlike READ UNCOMMITTED, more isolation exists in this isolation level. READ COMMITTED solves the dirty read problem and introduces a non-repeatable read. This isolation level ensures that only committed data is read.
- REPEATABLE READ: This is the default for MySQL. With this isolation level, the problem of dirty reads and non-repeatable reads are eliminated, but the risk of phantom reads is introduced.
- SERIALIZABLE: This isolation level takes it one step farther than REPEATABLE READ and completely isolates transactions from one another. You won't encounter dirty reads, non-repeatable reads, or phantom reads. With this isolation level, transactions appear to be executed in a serial order. If you set this as the default in MySQL, then everything will run much slower. This is best in environments where accuracy is most important, and transactions aren't long-running.

To summarize when different issues with each isolation level occur, refer to the following table:

Isolation level	Dirty reads	Non-repeatable reads	Phantom reads
READ UNCOMMITTED	Maybe	Maybe	Maybe
READ COMMITTED	No	Maybe	Maybe
REPEATABLE READ	No	No	Maybe
SERIALIZABLE	No	No	No

The isolation level can be set globally (this affects all queries), can be set for each transaction (set of queries), or you can set it for the session. If you set the transaction isolation level to something different than the global setting, it will override the isolation for just that one transaction or session.

To set the isolation level for the session, you add the following before starting a transaction or query:

```
SET SESSION TRANSACTION isolationlevel;
```

In the previous query, `isolationlevel` is changed to the isolation level you want to set.

To set the isolation level for the transaction, you add the following before starting a transaction:

```
SET TRANSACTION isolationlevel;
```

In the previous query, `isolationlevel` is changed to the isolation level you want to set.

Generally speaking, changing the isolation level isn't something you want to do, but let's say you want to ensure that your SELECT statement won't lock any data. Here, you can execute the following query:

```
USE lahmansbaseballdb;
SET TRANSACTION ISOLATION LEVEL READ UNCOMMITTED;
SELECT * FROM appearances;
```

The previous query would only return dirty reads if another transaction was actually changing data in the appearances table at the same time you were querying it.

Summary

In this chapter, you learned how to use advanced querying techniques. First, you learned how to use subqueries, which includes non-correlated subqueries and how to use each with the SELECT, FROM, and WHERE clauses, and also how to use them in INSERT, UPDATE, and DELETE queries. You also learned about correlated subqueries and how to use them with the SELECT, FROM, and WHERE clauses.

Next, you learned about the different kinds of CTEs and how to use them, including recursive and non-recursive. Then, you learned about query hints and how to choose which index your query will use. Finally, you learned about isolation levels, which include four levels and what happens during each level. You also learned how to set your queries to use a specific isolation level.

In the next chapter, you will learn how to create programmable objects. By the end of the next chapter, you will be able to understand what types of views exist and how to use them, as well as when and how to use variables, procedures (and the components of procedures, such as error handling and flow control), functions, triggers, and temporary tables.

Questions

1. What type of subqueries can you use?
2. What's the difference between correlated and non-correlated subqueries?
3. Where can you use a non-correlated subquery?
4. Where can you use a correlated subquery?
5. What is CTE?
6. What types of CTEs exist?
7. What is locking?
8. How can you make a query use a specific index?
9. What transaction isolation levels exist?
10. What is a phantom read?

Further reading

For more information on Oracle isolation levels, visit https://blogs.oracle.com/ oraclemagazine/on-transaction-isolation-levels.

12
Programmable Objects

In this chapter, you will learn how to create programmable objects, including how to create and use views, which includes selecting data from views and inserting, updating, and deleting data using views. You will learn how to create and use variables, which includes how to declare and assign values to variables. You will also learn how to create and use stored procedures, including how to use variables and parameters in stored procedures, as well as how to control flow and error handling. Finally, you will learn how to create and use functions, triggers, and temporary tables.

In this chapter, we will cover the following topics:

- Creating and using views
- Creating and using variables
- Creating and using stored procedures
- Creating and using functions
- Creating and using triggers
- Creating and using temporary tables

Let's get started!

Technical requirements

You can refer to the code files for this chapter by going to the following GitHub link: https://github.com/PacktPublishing/learn-sql-database-programming/tree/master/chapter-12.

Creating and using views

A **view** is a stored query. You can select data from a view to return the results of the query. You can also think of a view as a virtual table. A view can be created from one or more tables and can contain all or just some of the rows from one or more tables.

Views can be important for allowing certain users to have access to only specific fields in a table. If you had sensitive data in some of the columns and you didn't want everyone to be able to view that data, then you could provide them with the view instead. Also, you can use a view to make column names more intuitive by using column aliases in the view definition. You could also summarize data in a view to generate reports.

Learning how to create and query a view

In this section, we will learn how to create a view when writing queries. To create a view, use the following syntax:

```
CREATE VIEW nameofview AS
SELECT col1, col2, coln
FROM tablename
WHERE condition;
```

Let's take a query and place it into a view with the following code:

```
USE lahmansbaseballdb;
CREATE VIEW playergameinfo AS
SELECT p.playerid, birthyear,
       a.yearid, a.teamid,
        G_defense AS defensegames,
        H AS numberofhits
FROM appearances AS a
JOIN people AS p
ON p.playerid = a.playerid
JOIN batting AS b
ON a.playerid = b.playerid
AND a.yearid = b.yearid
AND a.teamid = b.teamid
WHERE b.yearid = 2017
AND H <> 0;
```

Once this view is created, you will be able to query data from the view, as shown in the following query:

```
USE lahmansbaseballdb;
SELECT * FROM playergameinfo;
```

The following screenshot shows the results of the previous query:

playerid	birthyear	yearid	teamid	defensegames	numberofhits
abreujo02	1987	2017	CHA	139	189
adamsla01	1989	2017	ATL	41	30
adamsma01	1988	2017	ATL	72	79
adamsma01	1988	2017	SLN	9	14
adducji02	1985	2017	DET	26	20
adlemti01	1987	2017	CIN	30	3
adriaeh01	1989	2017	MIN	61	43
aguilje01	1990	2017	MIL	78	74
ahmedni01	1990	2017	ARI	48	42

You can also specify the columns you want to be returned from the view, as shown in the following query:

```
USE lahmansbaseballdb;
SELECT playerid, birthyear, yearid, teamid, defensegames
FROM playergameinfo
WHERE teamid = 'CHA'
ORDER BY defensegames DESC;
```

The previous query will give you the results shown in the following screenshot:

playerid	birthyear	yearid	teamid	defensegames
anderti01	1993	2017	CHA	145
abreujo02	1987	2017	CHA	139
garciav01	1991	2017	CHA	132
sanchca01	1992	2017	CHA	130
engelad01	1991	2017	CHA	96
cabreme01	1984	2017	CHA	92
narvaom01	1992	2017	CHA	84
garcile02	1991	2017	CHA	83

You can see that the previous query specifies the columns you want to be returned, as well as that it uses the WHERE and ORDER BY clauses. You can do this with a view in exactly the same way as you would with a regular query.

You can see the views that are created in MySQL Workbench in the **SCHEMAS** panel for each database, right below the **Tables** listing:

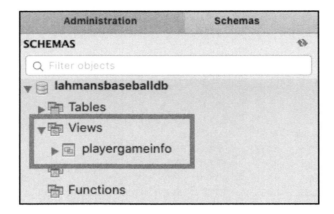

If you don't see the view you just created listed under **Views**, then right-click **Views** and choose **Refresh All**.

Learning how to modify data returned in a view

You can insert, update, and delete data with the help of a view. You just have to use the view name in your INSERT, UPDATE, or DELETE statements instead of a table name.

 Whatever permissions a user has to the underlying table(s) will determine if they can insert, update, or delete via a view.

In order to insert and update records via a view, there is one more thing to know about view creation. There is WITH CHECK OPTION, which ensures that any data that's inserted or updated via a view conforms to the conditions specified in the view. Before you add a new view, you should create a copy of the parks table to ensure you don't update the original table. We are only doing this for this test case, but if you really want to update the parks table, you could create the view on that table instead. You can execute the following query to create a copy of the parks table:

```
USE lahmansbaseballdb;
CREATE TABLE parks_copy
SELECT * FROM parks
```

Now, you can create another view by using WITH CHECK OPTION on parks_copy with the following code:

```
USE lahmansbaseballdb;
CREATE VIEW parksalias AS
SELECT parkalias, parkkey, parkname,
       city, state, country
FROM parks_copy
WHERE parkalias IS NOT NULL
WITH CHECK OPTION;
```

If you query the parksalias view in the following query, you will see that the parkalias column doesn't have any NULL values:

```
USE lahmansbaseballdb;
SELECT * FROM parksalias;
```

The following screenshot shows the results of the parksalias view:

parkalias	parkkey	parkname	city	state	country
Edison Field; Anaheim Stadium	ANA01	Angel Stadium of Anaheim	Anaheim	CA	US
The Ballpark in Arlington; Ameriquest Fl	ARL02	Rangers Ballpark in Arlington	Arlington	TX	US
American League Park	BAL09	Oriole Park IV	Baltimore	MD	US
Oriole Park V	BAL10	Terrapin Park	Baltimore	MD	US
Walpole Street Grounds	BOS01	South End Grounds I	Boston	MA	US
Union Park	BOS02	Dartmouth Grounds	Boston	MA	US
Bee Hive	BOS08	Braves Field	Boston	MA	US
Federal League Park	BUF04	International Fair Association Grounds	Buffalo	NY	US

Updating data using a view

To update parkalias to NULL where parkkey = 'ANA01', you can execute the following query:

```
UPDATE parksalias
SET parkalias = NULL
WHERE parkkey = 'ANA01';
```

You will receive the following error:

```
Error Code: 1369. CHECK OPTION failed 'lahmansbaseballdb.parksalias'
```

You can't update `parkalias` to NULL because NULL is filtered out in the WHERE clause of the view, and the view has WITH CHECK OPTION defined.

Now, let's create a view as shown in the following code:

```
USE lahmansbaseballdb;
CREATE VIEW parksalias AS
SELECT parkalias, parkkey, parkname,
       city, state, country
FROM parks_copy
WHERE parkalias IS NOT NULL;
```

You will be able to update a `parkalias` value that is NULL, even though the WHERE clause filters to IS NOT NULL. This is because you didn't specify WITH CHECK OPTION in your view definition.

Updating data using a view that has multiple tables

You can update data via a view that has multiple tables. First, you need to set up a copy of an existing table so you don't update the data in the original table. You can do that with the following query:

```
USE lahmansbaseballdb;
DROP TABLE IF EXISTS collegeplaying_copy;
CREATE TABLE collegeplaying_copy
SELECT * FROM collegeplaying;
```

Next, you can create a view with this new table in it with the following query:

```
USE lahmansbaseballdb;
DROP VIEW IF EXISTS collegeplayingbyname;
CREATE VIEW collegeplayingbyname AS
SELECT namefirst, namelast, schoolid, yearid
FROM collegeplaying_copy c
INNER JOIN people p
ON p.playerid = c.playerid;
```

You can see what the view contains by executing the following query:

```
USE lahmansbaseballdb;
SELECT * FROM collegeplayingbyname;
```

The previous query returns the results shown in the following screenshot:

namefirst	namelast	schoolid	yearid
David	Aardsma	rice	2003
David	Aardsma	rice	2002
David	Aardsma	pennst	2001
Andy	Abad	gamiddl	1993
Andy	Abad	gamiddl	1992
Bert	Abbey	vermont	1892

`namefirst` and `namelast` come from the `people` table, while `schoolid` and `yearid` come from the `collegeplaying_copy` table. Let's update a value in the `collegeplaying_copy` table with the following query:

```
USE lahmansbaseballdb;
UPDATE collegeplayingbyname
SET schoolid = 'testing', yearid = 2004
WHERE (namefirst = 'David' and namelast = 'Aardsma')
and (schoolid = 'rice' and yearid = 2003);
```

Execute the following query again:

```
USE lahmansbaseballdb;
SELECT * FROM collegeplayingbyname;
```

Now, you will see that the `collegeplaying_copy` table has been updated, as shown in the following screenshot:

namefirst	namelast	schoolid	yearid
David	Aardsma	testing	2004
David	Aardsma	rice	2002
David	Aardsma	pennst	2001
Andy	Abad	gamiddl	1993

You can also update the people table from this view, but this shows you how you can update fields in one table via a view that has multiple tables joined. You can't update more than one table at a time in a view. Execute the following query, which tried to update both tables at the same time, via the view:

```
USE lahmansbaseballdb;
UPDATE collegeplayingbyname
SET schoolid = 'testing', yearid = 2004, namefirst = 'Peter'
WHERE (namefirst = 'David' and namelast = 'Aardsma')
and (schoolid = 'rice' and yearid = 2003);
```

The preceding query will give you an error:Error Code: 1393. Can not modify more than one base table through a join view 'lahmansbaseballdb.collegeplayingbyname'. You will need to do use update statements instead of one to get to the end results that you want, but to show you this, you need to create a copy of the people table first to ensure that you don't update the original table:

```
USE lahmansbaseballdb;
DROP TABLE IF EXISTS people_copy;
CREATE TABLE people_copy
SELECT * FROM people;
```

You will also need to update the view so that it includes the `people_copy` table instead of the people table:

```
USE lahmansbaseballdb;
DROP VIEW IF EXISTS collegeplayingbyname;
CREATE VIEW collegeplayingbyname AS
SELECT namefirst, namelast, schoolid, yearid
FROM collegeplaying_copy c
INNER JOIN people_copy p
ON p.playerid = c.playerid;
```

Now, we can update the school information with the following query:

```
USE lahmansbaseballdb;
UPDATE collegeplayingbyname
SET schoolid = 'testing', yearid = 2004
WHERE (namefirst = 'David' and namelast = 'Aardsma')
and (schoolid = 'rice' and yearid = 2003);
```

You can see that it updated the school information with the following query:

namefirst	namelast	schoolid	yearid
David	Aardsma	testing	2004
David	Aardsma	rice	2002
David	Aardsma	pennst	2001
Andy	Abad	gamiddl	1993

Then, update the player name with the following query:

```
USE lahmansbaseballdb;
UPDATE collegeplayingbyname
SET namefirst = 'Peter'
WHERE (namefirst = 'David' and namelast = 'Aardsma')
and (schoolid = 'rice' and yearid = 2003);
```

Here, you can see that it didn't just update the one row contained the new player's name. It updated them all because the `people_copy` table holds the player name, not the `school` table, so when you updated the player's name, it updated it for all the rows in the view, as shown in the following screenshot:

namefirst	namelast	schoolid	yearid
David	Aardsma	testing	2004
David	Aardsma	rice	2002
David	Aardsma	pennst	2001

You need to be very careful when updating multiple tables at the same time in a view to avoid updating data you didn't intend to update.

Inserting data using a view

To insert data into a view that has WITH CHECK OPTION, you can execute the following query:

```
USE lahmansbaseballdb;
INSERT INTO parksalias
VALUES (NULL,
  'TST01',
  'testing park name',
  'Seattle',
  'WA',
  'US');
```

The preceding query will return the following error:

```
Error Code: 1423. Field of view 'lahmansbaseballdb.parksalias' underlying
table doesn't have a default value.
```

The preceding error has to do with the fact that the ID field in the `parks_copy` table isn't auto-incremented, and your view doesn't include it. This brings up an interesting point about inserting data via a view because this could happen to you if an ID field isn't auto incremented or another field doesn't allow a NULL to be inserted. If those fields aren't in the view, then your INSERT statement using that view will fail. To fix this issue on the `parks_copy` table, execute the following query:

```
USE lahmansbaseballdb;
ALTER TABLE parks_copy
CHANGE COLUMN ID ID SMALLINT NOT NULL AUTO_INCREMENT,
ADD PRIMARY KEY (ID);
```

If you re-execute the INSERT statement shown in the preceding query, you will get a different error, but an error that will be similar to the one you received when you tried to update to a NULL value. This time, the error will be as follows:

```
Error Code: 1369. CHECK OPTION failed 'lahmansbaseballdb.parksalias'
```

You can't insert parkalias as NULL because NULL is filtered out in the WHERE clause of the view, and the view has WITH CHECK OPTION defined.

Let's say we create a view like this with the following code instead:

```
USE lahmansbaseballdb;
CREATE VIEW parksalias AS
SELECT parkalias, parkkey, parkname,
       city, state, country
FROM parks_copy
WHERE parkalias IS NOT NULL;
```

By doing this, you will be able to insert a parkalias value that is NULL, even though the WHERE clause filters to IS NOT NULL. This is because you didn't specify WITH CHECK OPTION in your view definition.

Inserting data using a view that has multiple tables

You can insert data via a view that has multiple tables. First, you need to set up a copy of an existing table so you don't insert data into the original table. You can do that with the following query:

```
USE lahmansbaseballdb;
DROP TABLE IF EXISTS collegeplaying_copy;
CREATE TABLE collegeplaying_copy
SELECT * FROM collegeplaying;
```

Next, you can create a view with this new table in it with the following query:

```
USE lahmansbaseballdb;
DROP VIEW IF EXISTS collegeplayingbyname;
CREATE VIEW collegeplayingbyname AS
SELECT namefirst, namelast, schoolid, yearid
FROM collegeplaying_copy c
INNER JOIN people p
ON p.playerid = c.playerid;
```

You can see what the view contains by executing the following query:

```
USE lahmansbaseballdb;
SELECT * FROM collegeplayingbyname;
```

The preceding query returns the results shown in the following screenshot:

namefirst	namelast	schoolid	yearid
David	Aardsma	rice	2003
David	Aardsma	rice	2002
David	Aardsma	pennst	2001
Andy	Abad	gamiddl	1993
Andy	Abad	gamiddl	1992
Bert	Abbey	vermont	1892

The `namefirst` and `namelast` columns come from the people table, while the `schoolid` and `yearid` columns come from the `collegeplaying_copy` table. Let's insert a row into the view with the following query:

```
USE lahmansbaseballdb;
INSERT INTO collegeplayingbyname (namefirst, namelast, schoolid, yearid)
VALUES ('David', 'Aardsma', 'rice', 2004);
```

The preceding query will give you an error:

```
Error Code: 1393. Can not modify more than one base table through a join
view 'lahmansbaseballdb.collegeplayingbyname'.
```

You will need to insert the school information via this view, but there's a problem – you can't update who the school information will belong to, so you will need to update the view so that it includes `playerid` from the `schoolplaying_copy` table:

```
USE lahmansbaseballdb;
DROP VIEW IF EXISTS collegeplayingbyname;
CREATE VIEW collegeplayingbyname AS
SELECT c.playerid, namefirst, namelast, schoolid, yearid
FROM collegeplaying_copy c
INNER JOIN people_copy p
ON p.playerid = c.playerid;
```

Execute the following query to see the fields in the view:

```
USE lahmansbaseballdb;
SELECT * FROM collegeplayingbyname;
```

Now, you can see that `playerid` is in the view, as shown in the following screenshot:

playerid	namefirst	namelast	schoolid	yearid
aardsda01	David	Aardsma	rice	2003
aardsda01	David	Aardsma	rice	2002
aardsda01	David	Aardsma	pennst	2001
abadan01	Andy	Abad	gamiddl	1993
abadan01	Andy	Abad	gamiddl	1992
abbeybe01	Bert	Abbey	vermont	1892

Now, you will be able to insert college information for a player with the following query:

```
INSERT INTO collegeplayingbyname (playerid, schoolid, yearid)
VALUES ('aardsda01', 'rice', 2004);
```

Execute the following query:

```
USE lahmansbaseballdb;
SELECT * FROM collegeplayingbyname
WHERE playerid = 'aardsda01';
```

Now, you will see that the `collegeplaying_copy` table has a new row, as shown in the following screenshot:

playerid	namefirst	namelast	schoolid	yearid
aardsda01	David	Aardsma	rice	2004
aardsda01	David	Aardsma	rice	2003
aardsda01	David	Aardsma	rice	2002
aardsda01	David	Aardsma	pennst	2001

You wouldn't want to insert items into the people table from this view because you would be missing a lot of data related to the person you are inserting. This because you can only insert the first and last names from this view. The best way to avoid having someone try to insert a first and last name from this view is to ensure that there is a primary key on the `playerid` field in the people table so that if someone tried to insert from this view, it would fail as they didn't add a `playerid` to the `people` table.

Deleting data using a view

To delete the row in the `parksalias` view that corresponds to `parkkey = 'ALB01'`, you can execute the following query:

```
USE lahmansbaseballdb;
DELETE from parksalias
WHERE parkkey = 'ALB01';
```

You won't receive an error, but it won't delete that row because it doesn't exist in the view. It exists in the underlying table, but since the view doesn't contain that row, a `DELETE` statement via the view won't be able to delete it.

The **Output** panel shows that zero rows were deleted, as shown in the following screenshot:

Action Output ⌃			
	Time	Action	Response
✓ 1	11:57:42	USE lahmansbaseballdb	0 row(s) affected
✓ 2	11:57:42	DELETE from parksalias WHERE parkkey = 'ALB01'	0 row(s) affected

Let's try to delete the row you just inserted via the view with the help of the following query:

```
USE lahmansbaseballdb;
DELETE from parksalias
WHERE parkkey = 'TST01';
```

Again, you won't receive an error, but it won't delete that row because it doesn't exist in the view. The **Output** panel shows that zero rows were deleted, as shown in the following screenshot:

Action Output ⌃			
	Time	Action	Response
✓ 1	11:58:28	USE lahmansbaseballdb	0 row(s) affected
✓ 2	11:58:28	DELETE from parksalias WHERE parkkey = 'TST01'	0 row(s) affected

Even though you could insert it via the view, now that it's in the underlying table with a `NULL` value in `parkalias`, it's not available to the view to be deleted. This is an important reason to use `WITH CHECK OPTION` on your views.

Deleting data using a view that has multiple tables

To see if you can delete data via a view that has multiple tables, you need to set up a copy of an existing table so that you don't delete the data in the original table. You can do that with the following query:

```
USE lahmansbaseballdb;
DROP TABLE IF EXISTS collegeplaying_copy;
CREATE TABLE collegeplaying_copy
SELECT * FROM collegeplaying;
```

Next, you can create a view with this new table in it with the following query:

```
USE lahmansbaseballdb;
DROP VIEW IF EXISTS collegeplayingbyname;
CREATE VIEW collegeplayingbyname AS
SELECT namefirst, namelast, schoolid, yearid
FROM collegeplaying_copy c
INNER JOIN people p
ON p.playerid = c.playerid;
```

Let's delete a value using the view we just created with the following query:

```
USE lahmansbaseballdb;
DELETE FROM collegeplayingbyname
WHERE (namefirst = 'David' AND namelast = 'Aardsma')
    AND (schoolid = 'rice' AND yearid = 2003);
```

You will receive an error:

```
Error Code: 1395. Can not delete from join view
'lahmansbaseballdb.collegeplayingbyname'
```

This shows that you can't delete from a view that includes multiple tables.

Learning how to update or delete a view

If you want to update a view (change the view definition), you can execute the following query:

```
USE lahmansbaseballdb;
ALTER VIEW parksalias AS
SELECT parkalias, parkkey, parkname, city, state, country
FROM parks_copy
WHERE parkalias IS NOT NULL
WITH CHECK OPTION;
```

The difference is that you use ALTER VIEW instead of CREATE VIEW.

If you want to delete a view, you can execute the following query:

```
USE lahmansbaseballdb;
DROP VIEW playergameinfo;
```

By dropping the view, it has been deleted from the database.

Differences between views in other relational database management systems (RDBMSes)

Oracle and PostgreSQL don't have the same functionality as the ALTER keyword. In order to change the view definition, you will need to use CREATE OR REPLACE VIEW, as shown in the following query:

```
CREATE OR REPLACE VIEW parksalias AS
SELECT parkalias, parkkey, parkname, city, state, country
FROM parks_copy
WHERE parkalias IS NOT NULL
WITH CHECK OPTION;
```

The preceding query will replace the view if it already exists or create it if it doesn't.

Creating and using variables

A variable lets you store a single data value that can be used during your session's queries. You can only store a limited set of data types in a variable. These include string, integer, decimal, float, or NULL. If you use a different type in your variable, it will be converted into one of the permitted types listed previously.

Learning how to create and assign values to variables

In order to create and assign a value to a variable, you use the SET statement. There are two variations of assigning a value to a variable:

- SET @varname = value;
- SET @varname := value;

You can also set a variable with a SELECT statement, as shown in the following code sample:

```
SELECT @varname := column1 FROM tablename;
```

You can name your variable what you like. Variable names are not case-sensitive. You can name it @varname and then use @VARname in a query when referencing the variable name, and it will work.

Learning how to use variables in SQL statements

In order to use a variable in a SQL statement, you need to place the variable name into the query, as shown in the following example:

```
USE lahmansbaseballdb;
SET @varname := 'ALB01';
SELECT * FROM parks_copy
WHERE parkkey = @varname;
```

The preceding query produces the following results:

ID	parkalias	parkkey	parkname	city	state	country
1	NULL	ALB01	Riverside Park	Albany	NY	US

This was a simple example that shows how to use a variable – they can be quite powerful.

Differences between variables in other RDBMSes

The differences between variables in each of the RDMSes are outlined as follows:

- **Oracle:** In Oracle, there is a different syntax for using variables, as shown in the following query:

```
DECLARE
    var_parkname varchar2(100);
    var_parkkey varchar2(5) := 'ALB01';
BEGIN
SELECT parkname INTO var_parkname FROM parks_copy
WHERE parkkey = var_parkkey;
DBMS_OUTPUT.PUT_LINE(var_parkname);
END;
```

The query has you declare a variable for `parkkey` (`var_parkkey`), as well as for the output of the query with the variable in it, which is named `var_parkname`. Then, you output `var_parkname` to get the results.

- **PostgreSQL**: You can't use variables outside of functions.
- **SQL Server**: In SQL Server, you can't use `:=` to set a variable, only `=`. Also, you need to declare the variable before setting it, as shown in the following code snippet:

```
DECLARE @varname varchar(5);
```

You can also declare and set the variable in one line, as shown in the following code snippet:

```
DECLARE @varname varchar(5) = 'ALB01';
```

The first `DECLARE` statement will require you to use a `SET` statement to set the value, but the second `DECLARE` statement won't.

Creating and using stored procedures

A stored procedure is a set of SQL statements stored in a database. It could be just one SQL statement or many statements. With the help of this, you can reuse certain pieces of code. This can particularly be helpful when you are grouping business logic into a set of queries that will need to be run over and over again.

Creating a stored procedure

Let's learn how to create a stored procedure. First, we'll go through the following syntax, which is used to create a stored procedure:

```
DELIMITER $$
CREATE PROCEDURE storedprocname()
 BEGIN
 your sql statments go here;
 END $$
DELIMITER ;
```

In the previous code sample, we have the following:

- DELIMITER lets MySQL know that there may be lines in-between the delimiter statements that end in a semicolon.
- If you don't put DELIMITER around a stored procedure, you will get an error when MySQL hits the semicolon in your first SQL query, inside the stored procedure.

Let's work through an example of how to create a stored procedure. The following code will help you create a stored procedure:

```
USE lahmansbaseballdb;
DELIMITER $$
CREATE PROCEDURE getplayergameinfo()
BEGIN
  SELECT p.playerid, birthyear, a.yearid,
         a.teamid, G_defense AS defensegames,
         H AS numberofhits
  FROM appearances AS a
  JOIN people AS p ON p.playerid = a.playerid
  JOIN batting AS b ON a.playerid = b.playerid
  AND a.yearid = b.yearid
  AND a.teamid = b.teamid
  WHERE b.yearid = 2017 AND H <> 0
  ORDER BY p.playerid, a.yearid, a.teamid,
         G_defense, H;
END $$
DELIMITER ;
```

With that, you have created a stored procedure.

In order to call the stored procedure that you just created, execute the following code:

```
USE lahmansbaseballdb;
CALL getplayergameinfo();
```

The call to the stored procedure will return the results shown in the following screenshot:

playerid	birthyear	yearid	teamid	defensegames	numberofhits
abreujo02	1987	2017	CHA	139	189
adamsla01	1989	2017	ATL	41	30
adamsma01	1988	2017	ATL	72	79
adamsma01	1988	2017	SLN	9	14
adducji02	1985	2017	DET	26	20
adlemti01	1987	2017	CIN	30	3
adriaeh01	1989	2017	MIN	61	43
aguilje01	1990	2017	MIL	78	74
ahmedni01	1990	2017	ARI	48	42

You can view the stored procedures that were created in MySQL Workbench in the **SCHEMAS** panel for each database, right below the **Views** listing:

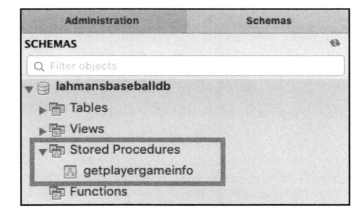

If you don't see the stored procedure you just created listed under **Stored Procedures**, then right-click **Stored Procedures** and choose **Refresh All**.

Learning how to alter and drop stored procedures

In order to alter a store procedure, you will need to drop it and then recreate it. Let's try to alter the stored procedure that we just created in the previous section. First, drop it with the following query:

```
DROP PROCEDURE getplayergameinfo;
```

You can now recreate it with any modifications that you want to make. Be careful when dropping a stored procedure because you can't restore the same without having a database backup. You can do this in MySQL Workbench by right-clicking on **Stored Procedures** in the **Schemas** panel, then choosing **Send to SQL Editor**, and then choosing **Create Statement**, as shown in the following screenshot:

Make sure to script out the stored procedure before dropping it.

Using variables and parameters in stored procedures

Earlier in this chapter, you learned how to use variables outside of stored procedures. Variables can also be used inside a stored procedure, mainly with flow control statements. When working with stored procedures, you may want to pass in a value to use inside the stored procedure. This is called a **parameter**. The main difference between a variable and a parameter is that parameters are static throughout the procedure, but a variable can be changed during the stored procedure. IN parameters allow you to provide a value or values to the stored procedure. OUT parameters allow you to receive output from the stored procedure.

IN parameter

Let's begin by dropping the procedure that we created in the previous section with the help of the following code:

```
USE lahmansbaseballdb;
DROP PROCEDURE IF EXISTS getplayergameinfo;
```

In the preceding code, there is an IF EXISTS in the DROP PROCEDURE statement. This will drop the procedure if it exists, but won't throw an error after dropping it if it doesn't exist.

Next, you will create the procedure, but this time it will have a couple of parameters so that you can change the WHERE clause values:

```
USE lahmansbaseballdb;
DELIMITER $$
CREATE PROCEDURE getplayergameinfo
(
IN yearid_in year,
IN hits_in smallint
)
BEGIN
SELECT p.playerid, birthyear, a.yearid,
       a.teamid, G_defense AS defensegames,
       H AS numberofhits
FROM appearances AS a
JOIN people AS p ON p.playerid = a.playerid
JOIN batting AS b ON a.playerid = b.playerid
AND a.yearid = b.yearid
AND a.teamid = b.teamid
WHERE b.yearid = yearid_in AND h > hits_in
ORDER BY p.playerid, a.yearid,
       a.teamid, G_defense, H;
END $$
DELIMITER ;
```

By doing this, you will have two parameters inside the parentheses after the procedure name: yearid_in and hits_in. They are declared with IN at the beginning, the name of the parameter, the data type of the parameter, and separated by a comma.

Then, you can call the procedure with the parameters shown in the following code:

```
USE lahmansbaseballdb;
CALL getplayergameinfo(2016, 0);
```

The preceding code will return the results shown in the following screenshot:

playerid	birthyear	yearid	teamid	defensegames	numberofhits
abreujo02	1987	2016	CHA	152	183
ackledu01	1988	2016	NYA	22	9
adamecr01	1991	2016	COL	68	49
adamsma01	1988	2016	SLN	86	74
adlemti01	1987	2016	CIN	13	4
adriaeh01	1989	2016	SFN	25	16
ahmedni01	1990	2016	ARI	88	62
alberha01	1992	2016	TEX	29	8
alberma01	1983	2016	CHA	58	1

The call to the stored procedure allows you to put in any valid year for `yearid_in` and any `smallint` for `hits_in`. This will put those values into the `WHERE` clause and return the results based on those values.

OUT parameter

Let's begin by dropping the procedure that you created in the preceding section with the following code:

```
USE lahmansbaseballdb;
DROP PROCEDURE IF EXISTS getplayergameinfo;
```

Next, you will create the procedure, but this time, it will also have an `OUT` parameter:

```
USE lahmansbaseballdb;
DELIMITER $$
CREATE PROCEDURE getplayergameinfo
(
IN yearid_in year,
IN h_in smallint,
OUT countplayers smallint
)
BEGIN
  SELECT COUNT(p.playerid)
  INTO countplayers
  FROM appearances AS a
  JOIN people AS p ON p.playerid = a.playerid
  JOIN batting AS b ON a.playerid = b.playerid
  AND a.yearid = b.yearid
  AND a.teamid = b.teamid
  WHERE b.yearid = yearid_in AND h > h_in
```

```
    ORDER BY p.playerid, a.yearid, a.teamid, G_defense, H;
END $$
DELIMITER ;
```

You will see a couple of new things in the stored procedure. First, there's an OUT parameter. You will see that we now have another parameter inside the paratheses after the procedure name, countplayers. This is declared with OUT at the beginning, the name of the parameter, the data type of the parameter, and separated by a comma. The query also had to be changed to get the count of the playerid field and then select countplayers.

In order to call the stored procedure, you will need to execute the following query:

```
USE lahmansbaseballdb;
CALL getplayergameinfo(2015, 10, @countplayers);
SELECT @countplayers;
```

The preceding query will return the results shown in the following screenshot:

Next, we will cover flow control statements in stored procedures.

Using flow control statements

Flow control statements help you to loop through the logic in SQL queries inside of a stored procedure, such as in LOOP, REPEAT, and WHILE. They also allow you to apply conditions to values, such as in CASE statements.

Understanding the different types of flow control statements

There are several different MySQL keywords to control the flow of queries:

- IF: Returns a value if the condition is TRUE and another value if it's FALSE.
- CASE: Goes through conditions and then returns a value once the condition is met. This is like an expanded IF function (IF-THEN-ELSE).
- LOOP: Executes a statement repeatedly. If you don't specifically terminate this, it can run infinitely.

- REPEAT: Repeats a statement until a condition is true. It always runs at least once.
- WHILE: Repeats a statement while a condition is true.
- ITERATE: Starts the statement again. It can appear in LOOP, REPEAT, or WHILE statements.
- LEAVE: Exits the statement. It can appear in LOOP, REPEAT, or WHILE statements.
- RETURN: Used to return a value.

Understanding the difference between the IF and CASE statements and how to use them

The IF and CASE statements are similar but do have some differences, as outlined in the following table:

IF	CASE
Accepts three parameters	Accepts multiple parameters
Accepts one condition	Accepts multiple conditions

The following shows the syntax of IF:

```
IF(condition, value if true, value if false);
```

Here's an example of an IF statement that will return 'barely any' for g_all between 0 and 10, and 'some more' for any games not between 0 and 10 instead of the number value that is in the column:

```
USE lahmansbaseballdb;
SELECT playerid, yearid,
IF(g_all between 0 and 10, 'barely any', 'some more') as gamecount
FROM appearances
WHERE yearid = 1990;
```

The previous query returns the results shown in the following screenshot:

playerid	yearid	gamecount
averyst01	1990	some more
bellmi01	1990	some more
berroge01	1990	barely any
blausje01	1990	some more
boevejo01	1990	some more
cabrefr01	1990	some more
castito02	1990	some more
claryma01	1990	some more
davisjo02	1990	some more
esaskni01	1990	barely any

Now, let's go through the syntax of the CASE statement:

```
CASE
     WHEN condition1 THEN result1
     WHEN condition2 THEN result2
     WHEN conditionN THEN resultN
     ELSE result
  END;
```

The following query is an example of the CASE statement:

```
USE lahmansbaseballdb;
SELECT playerid, yearid,
CASE
WHEN g_all between 0 and 10 then 'barely any'
WHEN g_all between 11 and 50 then 'some'
WHEN g_all between 51 and 100 then 'many'
ELSE 'tons'
END
FROM appearances
WHERE yearid = 1990;
```

The preceding query returns the case statements for `g_all` instead of the number value that is in the column, as shown in the following screenshot:

playerid	yearid	gamecount
averyst01	1990	some
bellmi01	1990	some
berroge01	1990	barely any
blausje01	1990	tons
boevejo01	1990	some
cabrefr01	1990	many
castito02	1990	many
claryma01	1990	some
davisjo02	1990	some
esaskni01	1990	barely any

As you can see, the CASE statement is much more flexible and powerful than the IF statement.

Understanding how to loop through statements

You can loop through statements with LOOP, WHILE, and REPEAT:

- Using the LOOP statement: LOOP allows you to execute a statement repeatedly. If you don't specifically terminate a LOOP statement, it can run infinitely. The following shows you an example of the LOOP syntax:

```
[beginlabel:] LOOP
 sql statements
END LOOP [endlabel];
```

beginlabel and endlabel are optional, and you can name them whatever makes sense for the loop. You use the label when executing an ITERATE or LEAVE statement. The SQL statements will execute once, each time LOOP executes. You can terminate a LOOP with either a LEAVE or RETURN statement. You should use a LOOP statement when you aren't certain how many times it may need to run.

You can execute the following code to test out an example loop:

```
DELIMITER $$
CREATE PROCEDURE forloopexample()
BEGIN
 DECLARE n INT;
 DECLARE loopreturn VARCHAR(25);
```

```
SET n = 1;
SET loopreturn = '';

looplabel: LOOP
   IF n > 14 THEN
   LEAVE looplabel;
END IF;

SET n = n + 1;
IF (n mod 2) THEN
   ITERATE looplabel;
ELSE
   SET loopreturn = CONCAT(loopreturn,n,',');
END IF;
END LOOP;
SELECT loopreturn;
END$$
DELIMITER ;
```

You can execute the following code to call the loop stored procedure:

```
CALL forloopexample();
```

The previous code returns the results shown in the following screenshot:

The stored procedure loops through until it's at 14 and stores those numbers in the string variable (loopreturn). Then, the string variable is returned. You will also notice that the way a variable is declared and set is different than in the creating and using variables section of this chapter. In a stored procedure, you have to declare the variable (with the DECLARE keyword) and set its data type. Then, you separately set the variable's value.

- Using the REPEAT statement: REPEAT allows you to repeat a statement until a condition is true. It always runs at least once. The following shows you an example of the REPEAT syntax:

```
[beginlabel:] REPEAT
    sql statements
UNTIL condition
END REPEAT [endlabel]
```

beginlabel and endlabel are optional, and you can name them whatever makes sense for the repeat loop. The SQL statements will execute once for each time REPEAT executes. You can use a REPEAT statement when you aren't certain how many times it may need to run, but know you need it to run at least once. You use UNTIL to terminate the loop once the condition of UNTIL is met. You can execute the following code to test out an example repeat loop:

```
USE lahmansbaseballdb;
DELIMITER $$
CREATE PROCEDURE repeatexample()
BEGIN
    DECLARE count INT DEFAULT 1;
    DECLARE result VARCHAR(30) DEFAULT '';
    REPEAT
        SET result = CONCAT(result,count,',');
        SET count = count + 1;
    UNTIL count > 10
    END REPEAT;
    SELECT result;
END$$
DELIMITER ;
```

You can execute the following code to call the repeat stored procedure:

```
CALL repeatexample();
```

The preceding code returns the results shown in the following screenshot:

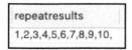

The stored procedure repeats until it's at 10 and stores those numbers in the string variable (repeatreturn). Then, the string variable is returned. You will also notice that the way a variable is declared and set is different than in the creating and using variables section of this chapter. In a stored procedure, you have to declare the variable (with the DECLARE keyword) and set its data type. Then, you separately set the variable's value.

- Using the WHILE statement: The WHILE statement is executed repeatedly till a condition is true. The following shows you an example of the WHILE syntax:

```
[beginlabel:]
WHILE condition DO
sql statements
```

```
END WHILE
[end_label]
```

`beginlabel` and `endlabel` are optional, and you can name them whatever makes sense for the WHILE loop. The SQL statements will execute once while the condition is true. You can execute the following code to test out an example WHILE loop:

```
USE lahmansbaseballdb;
DELIMITER $$
CREATE PROCEDURE whileexample()
BEGIN
  DECLARE count INT;
  DECLARE whileresult Varchar(50);
  SET count = 1;
  SET whileresult = '';
  WHILE count <=10 DO
    SET whileresult = CONCAT(whileresult, count, ',');
    SET count = count + 1;
  END WHILE;
  SELECT whileresult;
END $$
DELIMITER ;
```

You can execute the following code to call the while stored procedure:

```
CALL whileexample();
```

The previous code returns the results shown in the following screenshot:

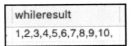

The stored procedure loops while it's equal to or less than 10 and stores those numbers into the string variable (whilereturn). Then, the string variable is returned. You will also notice that the way a variable is declared and set is different than as shown in the creating and using variables section of this chapter. In a stored procedure, you have to declare the variable (with the DECLARE keyword) and set its data type. Then, you separately set the variable's value.

Using error handling

When you encounter an error in SQL code, you want to make sure you handle it properly by continuing or exiting the current query and issuing a useful error message.

Understanding error handling syntax and how to implement error handling

In order to handle errors, you can use special error handling. The syntax for that is as follows:

```
DECLARE action HANDLER FOR condition statement;
```

When a condition matches the condition specified in the handler, MySQL will execute the statement specified in the handler and either continue or exit based on the action specified. This statement can be a single statement or multiple statements surrounded by BEGIN and END.

The action specified in the handler can be one of two values:

- Continue: Execution of the code will continue
- Exit: Execution of the code will terminate

The condition specified in the handler can be one of the following:

- **A MySQL error code**: This will be an integer value for a specific error, such as 1051. More information on error codes can be found in the *Further reading* section.
- **A standard SQLSTATE value**: This will be a five-character string value, such as 42S01. This could also be SQLWARNING, NOTFOUND, or SQLEXCEPTION. More information on these can be found in the *Further reading* section.

Let's look at an example, for ease of understanding. You can execute the following to create a stored procedure with error handling:

```
USE lahmansbaseballdb;
DELIMITER $$
CREATE PROCEDURE insertallstarfull(
IN inplayerid varchar(9),
IN inyearid smallint,
IN ingamenum smallint
)
BEGIN
```

```
DECLARE EXIT HANDLER FOR 1062
BEGIN
SELECT CONCAT('Duplicate key (',inplayerid,',',inyearid,',',ingamenum,')
occurred') AS message;
END;

INSERT INTO allstarfull (playerid, yearid, gamenum)
VALUES (inplayerid, inyearid, ingamenum);

SELECT count(*)
FROM allstarfull
WHERE playerid = inplayerid;
END$$
DELIMITER ;
```

The previous stored procedure will allow us to insert values into `allstarfull` by passing in `playerid`, `yearid`, and `gamenum` as parameters.

You can call it with the following query:

```
CALL insertallstarfull('aaronha01', 1958, 0);
```

The preceding call will produce an error, as follows:

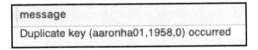

Unlike if you didn't have error handling in your stored procedure, it won't throw an error and show that error in the **Output** area of MySQL Workbench. In this case, it shows you the error you custom coded into the stored procedure in your query window and gracefully exits the stored procedure.

Instead, if we call the stored procedure with different parameter values, as shown in the following query, we won't receive an error message:

```
CALL insertallstarfull('aaronha01', 1954, 0);
```

We now get the `count(*)` results from the query that follows in the insert in the stored procedure, as shown in the following screenshot:

Declaring and handling errors is considered catching errors. With this method, you have more control over how errors are handled instead of just letting a stored procedure fail and having to find the error message in the output panel. This can be especially beneficial if you want to continue with an error or capture the errors to write them to a table.

Differences between stored procedures in other RDBMSes

Each RDBMS and its differences will be explained in more detail here.

Oracle

Oracle has a different syntax to create and call a stored procedure. It also has different syntax for flow control and error handling. The syntax for how to create and call a stored procedure is outlined in the *Creating and calling a stored procedure in Oracle* section. The flow control and error handling differences will be covered in the *Flow control in Oracle* and *Error handling in Oracle* sections, respectively.

Creating and calling a stored procedure in Oracle

To create a stored procedure, you can execute the following query:

```
CREATE OR REPLACE PROCEDURE getplayergameinfo(data OUT varchar2)
IS
BEGIN
 SELECT p.playerid
 INTO data
 FROM appearances a
 JOIN people p ON p.playerid = a.playerid
 JOIN batting b ON a.playerid = b.playerid
 AND a.yearid = b.yearid
 AND a.teamid = b.teamid
 WHERE b.yearid = 2017 AND H <> 0
 FETCH FIRST 1 ROWS ONLY;
END;
```

To call a stored procedure, you can execute the following query:

```
DECLARE
   results VARCHAR2(4000);
BEGIN
   getplayergameinfo(results);
```

```
    DBMS_OUTPUT.PUT_LINE(results);
END;
```

The preceding query will return the results of the getplayergameinfo stored procedure.

Flow control in Oracle

Oracle has IF/ELSE, CASE, and LOOP and WHILE statements for flow control options.

The LOOP statement in Oracle is similar to the REPEAT statement in MySQL and uses the following syntax:

```
[label]
LOOP
sql statements go here;
EXIT [label] WHEN condition;
END LOOP;
```

The WHILE statement in Oracle, which is very similar to the WHILE statement in MySQL, uses the following syntax:

```
[label]
WHILE condition LOOP
sql statements go here;
END LOOP [label];
```

For more information about Oracle flow control, take a look at the *Further reading* section.

Error handling in Oracle

Oracle does error handling with the EXCEPTION statement. The following syntax is an example of how Oracle handles errors:

```
DECLARE
err_num NUMBER;
err_msg VARCHAR2(200);
BEGIN
sql statements go here
EXCEPTION
conditions for exception go here
WHEN OTHERS THEN
err_num := SQLCODE;
err_msg := SUBSTR(SQLERRM, 1, 200);
INSERT INTO errors VALUES (err_num, err_msg);
END;
```

To learn more about error handling in Oracle, take a look at the *Further reading* section.

PostgreSQL

PostgreSQL has a different syntax for creating stored procedures. It also has different syntax for flow control and error handling. Generally speaking, you won't use stored procedures in PostgreSQL; instead, you'll use functions.

Creating a stored procedure in PostgreSQL

In PostgreSQL, you can't return data via a stored procedure. If you need to return data, you will need to use a function instead. If you want to create a stored procedure to insert, update, or delete data, you can use the following syntax:

```
CREATE OR REPLACE PROCEDURE procedurename()
LANGUAGE plpgsql
AS $$
BEGIN
    -- update, insert, or delete sql statements go here
END
$$;
```

To create a stored procedure with IN parameters, you can use the following syntax:

```
CREATE OR REPLACE PROCEDURE procedurename
(
    varname vartype,
    varname2 vartype
)
LANGUAGE plpgsql
AS $$
BEGIN
    INSERT INTO tablename (col1, col2)
    VALUES (varname, varname2);

END
$$;
```

Since no results can be returned from a PostgreSQL stored procedure, there are no OUT parameters.

Flow control in PostgreSQL

PostgreSQL has IF/ELSE, CASE, and LOOP and WHILE statements for flow control options. For the IF/ELSE example we used in MySQL, you would need to use a CASE statement in PostgreSQL.

The LOOP statement in PostgreSQL is similar to the REPEAT statement in MySQL and uses the following syntax:

```
[looplabel]
LOOP
sql statements go here;
EXIT [looplabel] WHEN condition;
END LOOP;
```

The WHILE statement in PostgreSQL, which is very similar to the WHILE statement in MySQL, uses the following syntax:

```
[whilelabel]
WHILE condition LOOP
sql statements go here;
END LOOP;
```

For more information about PostgreSQL flow control, take a look at the *Further reading* section.

Error handling in PostgreSQL

PostgreSQL does error handling with the RAISE statement. Any errors will be caught in the RAISE statement when it's used.

The following query will try to insert values into the allstarfull table and use RAISE to output the error:

```
DO $$
BEGIN
INSERT INTO allstarfull
(playerid, yearid, gamenum)
VALUES ('aaronha01', 1958, 0);

exception when others then
RAISE notice '% %', SQLERRM, SQLSTATE;

END $$;
```

You will receive an error with those variables set as-is because there is a primary key violation:

```
duplicate key value violates unique constraint
"allstarfull$index_2bd68208_c8b4_4347" 23505
```

To learn more about error handling in PostgreSQL, take a look at the *Further reading* section.

SQL Server

SQL Server has a different syntax for creating and calling stored procedures. It also has different syntax for flow control and error handling. The syntax for how to create and call a stored procedure is outlined in the *Creating and calling a stored procedure in SQL Server* section. The flow control and error handling differences will be covered in the *Flow control in SQL Server* and *Error handling in SQL Server* sections, respectively.

Creating and calling a stored procedure in SQL Server

To create a stored procedure, you can execute the following query:

```
CREATE or ALTER PROCEDURE getplayergameinfo
AS
SELECT p.playerid, birthyear,
 a.yearid, a.teamid,
 G_defense AS defensegames,
 H AS numberofhits
FROM appearances AS a
JOIN people AS p
ON p.playerid = a.playerid
JOIN batting AS b
ON a.playerid = b.playerid
AND a.yearid = b.yearid
AND a.teamid = b.teamid
WHERE b.yearid = 2017 AND H <> 0
ORDER BY p.playerid, a.yearid,
 a.teamid, G_defense, H;
```

To call a stored procedure, execute the following query:

```
EXEC getplayergameinfo;
```

To create a stored procedure with IN parameters, execute the following query:

```
CREATE or ALTER PROCEDURE getplayergameinfo
    @yearid_in smallint,
```

```
        @hits_in smallint
AS
SELECT p.playerid, birthyear,
        a.yearid, a.teamid,
        G_defense AS defensegames,
        H AS numberofhits
FROM appearances AS a
JOIN people AS p
ON p.playerid = a.playerid
JOIN batting AS b
ON a.playerid = b.playerid
AND a.yearid = b.yearid
AND a.teamid = b.teamid
WHERE b.yearid = @yearid_in
AND H > @hits_in
ORDER BY p.playerid, a.yearid, a.teamid, G_defense, H;
```

To call the stored procedure with IN parameters, execute the following query:

```
EXEC getplayergameinfo
@yearid_in = 2017, @hits_in = 0;
```

To create a stored procedure with OUT parameters, execute the following query:

```
CREATE or ALTER PROCEDURE getplayergameinfo
      @yearid_in smallint,
      @hits_in smallint,
      @countplayers smallint OUT
AS
SELECT COUNT(p.playerid)
FROM appearances AS a
JOIN people AS p
ON p.playerid = a.playerid
JOIN batting AS b
ON a.playerid = b.playerid
AND a.yearid = b.yearid
AND a.teamid = b.teamid
WHERE b.yearid = @yearid_in
AND H > @hits_in;
```

To call the stored procedure with OUT parameters, execute the following query:

```
DECLARE @countplayers smallint
EXEC getplayergameinfo
@yearid_in = 2017,
@hits_in = 0,
@countplayers = @countplayers OUT;
SELECT @countplayers;
```

The previous query will return the count of players.

Flow control in SQL Server

SQL Server has IF/ELSE, CASE, and WHILE statements for flow control options. For the IF/ELSE example we used in MySQL, you would need to use a CASE statement in SQL Server.

The WHILE has different syntax, as shown in the following query:

```
DECLARE @counter INT = 1;
WHILE @counter <= 10
BEGIN
    PRINT @counter;
    SET @counter = @counter + 1;
END
```

The WHILE loop will print 1 through 10.

Also, in SQL Server, you can use a WHILE statement in any query, and it doesn't have to be contained in a stored procedure.

Error handling in SQL Server

SQL Server does error handling with the TRY and CATCH statements. The syntax for this is shown in the following code:

```
BEGIN TRY
    --sql statements
END TRY
BEGIN CATCH
    --sql statements
END CATCH
```

Anything you want to execute goes in the TRY statement, and if there is an error, the CATCH statement will run. If there is no error, the TRY statements are successfully executed, and the CATCH statement is never used.

The following query will try to insert values into the allstarfull table using the TRY and CATCH statements:

```
DECLARE @inplayerid varchar(9) = 'aaronha01';
DECLARE @inyearid smallint = 1958;
DECLARE @ingamenum smallint = 0;
BEGIN TRY
```

```
INSERT INTO allstarfull
(playerid, yearid, gamenum)
VALUES
(@inplayerid, @inyearid, @ingamenum);
END TRY
BEGIN CATCH
SELECT
 ERROR_NUMBER() AS ErrorNumber
 ,ERROR_MESSAGE() AS ErrorMessage;
END CATCH;
```

You will receive an error with those variables set as-is because there is a primary key violation, as shown in the following screenshot:

To learn more about the `TRY` and `CATCH` statements in SQL Server, take a look at the *Further reading* section.

Creating and using functions

You can create user-defined functions in MySQL. These are used to extend the functionality of MySQL, and they work much the same as other built-in functions work. As you may recall, built-in functions are things such as `SUM()` or `AVG()`.

Understanding the difference between a function and a stored procedure

A function differs from a stored procedure in many ways, as shown in the following table:

Function	Stored procedure
Returns only one mandatory value	Can return zero, one, or multiple values
Doesn't allow transactions	Allow transactions
Can be used in `SELECT`, `WHERE`, and `HAVING` clauses	Can't be used in `SELECT`, `WHERE`, and `HAVING` clauses
Only allows input parameters	Allows input and output parameters
Can't use error handling	Can use error handling

Each is powerful in their own way, and you need to keep in mind how each works to ensure you choose the right one for your use case. Generally speaking, a function is used to compute a value, while a stored procedure is used to execute business logic.

Learning how to create and use functions

The syntax to create a function is quite similar to creating a stored procedure:

```
DELIMITER $$
 CREATE FUNCTION functionname(
 parameter1,
 parameter2,...
 )
 RETURNS datatype
 [NOT] DETERMINISTIC
 BEGIN
 -- put sql statements here
 END $$
 DELIMITER ;
```

`DELIMITER` lets MySQL know that there may be lines in-between the delimiter statements that end in a semicolon. If you don't put `DELIMITER` around a function, you will get an error when MySQL hits the semicolon in your first SQL query, inside the stored procedure.

A function can be deterministic or non-deterministic. Deterministic always returns the same result for the same input parameters, whereas non-deterministic doesn't.

Let's walk through an example. You can execute the following query to create a function:

```
USE lahmansbaseballdb;
DELIMITER $$
 CREATE FUNCTION hittinglevel(
 g_all smallint
 )
 RETURNS VARCHAR(10)
 DETERMINISTIC
 BEGIN
 DECLARE hitlevel VARCHAR(10);
 IF g_all BETWEEN 0 and 10 THEN
 SET hitlevel = 'barely any';
 ELSEIF g_all BETWEEN 11 and 50 THEN
 SET hitlevel = 'some';
 ELSEIF g_all BETWEEN 51 and 100 THEN
 SET hitlevel = 'many';
 ELSEIF g_all > 100 THEN
 SET hitlevel = 'tons';
```

```
END IF;
RETURN (hitlevel);
END$$
DELIMITER ;
```

The function you just created will set `hitlevel` for the `g_all` parameter and we will use this in a function.

Now, you can call the function in a `SELECT` query, as follows:

```
USE lahmansbaseballdb;
 SELECT playerid, yearid, teamid,
        hittinglevel(ab) AS hits
 FROM batting
 WHERE yearid = 2017;
```

The function we used in the previous query was used to pass in the `g_all` parameter. It returns the results shown in the following screenshot:

playerid	yearid	teamid	hits
abadfe01	2017	BOS	barely any
abreujo02	2017	CHA	tons
adamecr01	2017	COL	some
adamsau02	2017	WAS	barely any
adamsla01	2017	ATL	tons
adamsma01	2017	SLN	some
adamsma01	2017	ATL	tons

You could also use this function for any `smallint` type value that's passed into it, even if it has nothing to do with baseball hits.

You can see the functions that have been created in MySQL Workbench in the **SCHEMAS** panel for each database, right below the **Stored Procedures** listing:

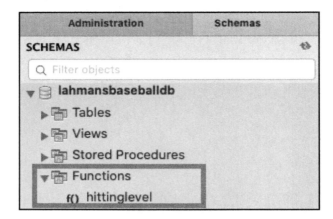

If you don't see the function you just created listed under **Functions**, then right-click **Functions** and choose **Refresh All**.

Learning how to alter or delete functions

In order to alter a function, you will need to drop it, then recreate it. If you wanted to alter the function you just created in the previous section, you would drop it with the following query:

```
DROP FUNCTION hittinglevel;
```

Then, you would have to recreate it with any modifications you wanted to make. Be careful when dropping because you can't restore the function without having a database backup. You can do this in MySQL Workbench by right-clicking on the function in the **SCHEMAS** panel, then choosing **Send to SQL Editor**, and then choosing **Create Statement**, as shown in the following screenshot:

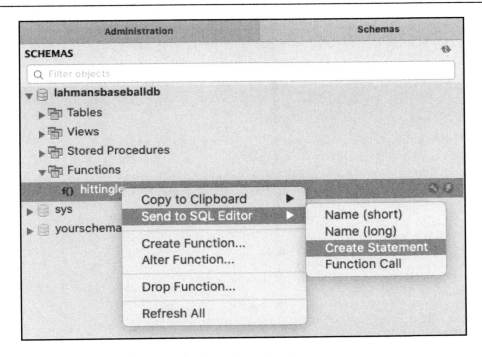

Make sure to script out the function before dropping it.

Differences between functions in other RDBMSes

Each RDBMS and its differences will be explained in more detail in this section.

Oracle

Oracle has a different syntax from MySQL for creating a function, but generally works the same way, as shown in the following query:

```
CREATE FUNCTION hittinglevel(g_all IN NUMBER)
    RETURN VARCHAR AS
    hitlevel VARCHAR(10);
BEGIN
 hitlevel := CASE
 WHEN g_all BETWEEN 0 and 10 THEN 'barely any'
 WHEN g_all BETWEEN 11 and 50 THEN 'some'
 WHEN g_all BETWEEN 51 and 100 THEN 'many'
 ELSE 'tons'
 END;
```

```
RETURN hitlevel;
END;
```

You can call the function and drop the function the same way that you do in MySQL.

PostgreSQL

PostgreSQL has a different syntax from MySQL for creating a function, but generally works the same way, as shown in the following query:

```
CREATE FUNCTION hittinglevel(g_all SMALLINT)
RETURNS VARCHAR(10)
AS $hitlevel$
DECLARE hitlevel varchar(10);
BEGIN
IF g_all BETWEEN 0 and 10 THEN
SET hitlevel = 'barely any';
ELSEIF g_all BETWEEN 11 and 50 THEN
SET hitlevel = 'some';
ELSEIF g_all BETWEEN 51 and 100 THEN
SET hitlevel = 'many';
ELSEIF g_all > 100 THEN
SET hitlevel = 'tons';
END IF;
RETURN hitlevel;
END;
$hitlevel$
LANGUAGE plpgsql;
```

You can call the function and drop the function the same way that you do in MySQL.

SQL Server

SQL Server has a different syntax for creating a function, but it works quite similarly to MySQL. The following query shows you how to create a function in SQL Server:

```
CREATE FUNCTION hittinglevel
(@g_all SMALLINT)
RETURNS VARCHAR(10)
AS
BEGIN
    DECLARE @hitlevel varchar(10);
    IF @g_all BETWEEN 0 and 10
    SET @hitlevel = 'barely any'
    IF @g_all BETWEEN 11 and 50
```

```
        SET @hitlevel = 'some'
        IF @g_all BETWEEN 51 and 100
        SET @hitlevel = 'many'
        IF @g_all > 100
        SET @hitlevel = 'tons'
        RETURN @hitlevel;
    END;
```

The function you just created in SQL Server will work the same way as in MySQL, and you can drop it the same way as well.

Creating and using triggers

A trigger is a set of actions that run after you insert, update, or delete data. Triggers are created on tables. You can use triggers to enforce business rules for data, audit data, or validate data.

There are a few different types of DML triggers:

- BEFORE INSERT: This causes the trigger to run some logic before you insert data into the table.
- AFTER INSERT: This causes the trigger to run some logic after you insert data into the table.
- BEFORE UPDATE: This causes the trigger to run some logic before you update data in the table.
- AFTER UPDATE: This causes the trigger to run some logic after you update data in the table.
- BEFORE DELETE: This causes the trigger to run some logic before you delete data from the table.
- AFTER DELETE: This causes the trigger to run some logic after you delete data from the table.

Additionally, you can create multiple triggers on a table. You can have the triggers in a specific order from the same insert/update/delete on a table.

Learning how to create and use a trigger

Let's take a look at the following syntax for creating a trigger:

```
CREATE TRIGGER triggername
{BEFORE | AFTER} {INSERT | UPDATE| DELETE }
ON tablename FOR EACH ROW
triggerbody;
```

You can choose either BEFORE or AFTER, and either INSERT, UPDATE, or DELETE. You can name the trigger with a descriptive name, and you choose the table for your trigger in place of tablename. Finally, you put the logic in triggerbody.

Creating and using a trigger with one statement

Let's create a copy of a table and an audit table:

1. We'll start by creating a copy of the allstarfull table:

    ```
    USE lahmansbaseballdb;
    CREATE TABLE allstarfull_copy
    SELECT * FROM allstarfull;
    ```

2. Then, we'll create an audit table for the allstarfull_copy table with the following query:

    ```
    USE lahmansbaseballdb;
     CREATE TABLE allstarfull_audit (
     id INT AUTO_INCREMENT PRIMARY KEY,
     playerID varchar(9) NOT NULL,
     yearID smallint(6) NOT NULL,
     gameNum smallint(6) NOT NULL,
     gameID varchar(12) NULL,
     teamID varchar(3) NULL,
     lgID varchar(2) NULL,
     GP smallint(6) NULL,
     startingPos smallint(6) NULL,
     changedate DATETIME NOT NULL,
     actiontype VARCHAR(50) NOT NULL);
    ```

3. You can create a `BEFORE UPDTE` trigger on the `allstarfull_copy` table, which will write changes to the audit table using the following query. The `OLD` keyword signifies that you want to capture the value before it was changed. The other option you can use is `NEW`, which would capture the value after it was changed:

```
USE lahmansbaseballdb;
 CREATE TRIGGER before_allstar_update
 BEFORE UPDATE ON allstarfull_copy
 FOR EACH ROW
 INSERT INTO allstarfull_audit
 SET actiontype = 'update',
 playerid = OLD.playerid,
 yearid = OLD.yearid,
 gamenum = OLD.gamenum,
 gameid = OLD.gameid,
 teamid = OLD.teamid,
 lgid = OLD.lgid,
 gp = OLD.gp,
 startingpos = OLD.startingpos,
 changedate = NOW();
```

4. You can update some data in the `allstarful_copy` table with the following query:

```
USE lahmansbaseballdb;
 UPDATE allstarfull_copy
 SET
 yearID = 2015,
 gameNum = 1,
 gameID = 'NLS201507170',
 teamID = 'CHI',
 lgID = 'AL',
 GP = 1,
 startingPos = 9
 WHERE playerid = 'arrieja01';
```

5. Select from `allstarfull_copy` with the following query:

```
USE lahmansbaseballdb;
 SELECT * FROM allstarfull_copy
 WHERE playerid = 'arrieja01';
```

You will see that the rows have been updated to the values you specified in the preceding UPDATE statement, as shown in the following screenshot:

playerID	yearID	gameNum	gameID	teamID	lgID	GP	startingPos
arrieja01	2015	1	NLS201507170	CHI	AL	1	9

6. Select from `allstarfull_audit` with the following query:

```
USE lahmansbaseballdb;
SELECT * FROM allstarfull_audit;
```

You will see that a row has been inserted into the `allstarfull_audit` table with the OLD values, as shown in the following screenshot:

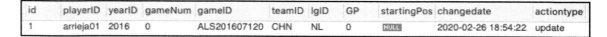

id	playerID	yearID	gameNum	gameID	teamID	lgID	GP	startingPos	changedate	actiontype
1	arrieja01	2016	0	ALS201607120	CHN	NL	0	NULL	2020-02-26 18:54:22	update

You can also see that `changedate` and `actiontype` have been updated accordingly with the current datetime of the `allstarfull_copy` update and the `actiontype` update.

Creating and using a trigger with multiple statements

If you want to run multiple statements inside your trigger, you will need to use DELIMITER statements around your SQL statements, much the same way you use them in a stored procedure. The syntax for this is as follows:

```
DELIMITER $$

CREATE TRIGGER before_allstar_update
 BEFORE UPDATE ON allstarfull_copy
 FOR EACH ROW
BEGIN
 IF OLD.playerid <> NEW.playerid THEN
 INSERT INTO allstarfull_audit
 SET actiontype = 'update',
 playerid = OLD.playerid,
 yearid = OLD.yearid,
 gamenum = OLD.gamenum,
 gameid = OLD.gameid,
 teamid = OLD.teamid,
 lgid = OLD.lgid,
 gp = OLD.gp,
 startingpos = OLD.startingpos,
```

```
    changedate = NOW();
  END IF;
END$$
DELIMITER ;
```

The preceding code will only insert into the `allstarfull_audit` table if the new `playerid` doesn't equal the old `playerid`.

Creating and using multiple triggers on the same table

You can create multiple triggers on a table and have them precede or follow one another by adding the `PRECEDES` or `FOLLOWS` keywords to the trigger definition. The following code sample shows you the placement of these keywords:

```
CREATE TRIGGER triggername
 {BEFORE | AFTER} {INSERT | UPDATE| DELETE }
 ON tablename FOR EACH ROW
 {FOLLOWS | PRECEDES} anothertriggername
triggerbody;
```

You can add an additional trigger for `BEFORE UPDATE` to the `allstarfull_copy` table with the following code:

```
USE lahmansbaseballdb;
 CREATE TRIGGER before_allstar_update2
 BEFORE UPDATE ON allstarfull_copy
 FOR EACH ROW
 FOLLOWS before_allstar_update
 INSERT INTO allstarfull_audit
 SET actiontype = 'update',
 playerid = OLD.playerid,
 yearid = OLD.yearid,
 gamenum = OLD.gamenum,
 gameid = OLD.gameid,
 teamid = OLD.teamid,
 lgid = OLD.lgid,
 gp = OLD.gp,
 startingpos = OLD.startingpos,
 changedate = NOW();
```

Notice that this new trigger is also an update trigger, and it will follow `before_allstar_update`.

You can also have a delete or insert trigger on the same table, but they won't have to precede or follow because they aren't of the same type. If you wanted to have more than one insert or delete trigger on the same table, then you would also define them with precedes or follows.

Deleting a trigger

In order to delete a trigger, execute the following query:

```
USE lahmansbaseballdb;
DROP TRIGGER before_allstar_update;
```

Differences between triggers in other RDBMSes

Each RDBMS and its differences are explained as follows:

- **Oracle**: Oracle has a similar syntax to MySQL for creating triggers. For more information about Oracle triggers, take a look at the *Further reading* section.
- **PostgreSQL**: In PostgreSQL, you need to create a function and a trigger function. The trigger function contains the logic for the trigger, and the trigger placed on the table calls the trigger function. For more information about PostgreSQL triggers, take a look at the *Further reading* section.
- **SQL Server**: In SQL Server, the syntax is different, and you can't do BEFORE triggers, only AFTER triggers. SQL Server creates two virtual tables to store the data before and after the changes. Those tables are referred to as INSERTED and DELETED. The following table shows you which of these tables holds for INSERT, UPDATE, and DELETE actions:

Action	INSERTED table	DELETED table
INSERT	Rows to be inserted	Empty
UPDATE	Rows to be updated	Existing rows modified
DELETE	Empty	Rows to be deleted

To help you understand this, here is the BEFORE trigger that you created earlier in this chapter and modified for use in SQL Server:

```
CREATE TRIGGER after_allstar_update
ON allstarfull_copy
AFTER UPDATE
AS
BEGIN
```

```
INSERT INTO allstarfull_audit(
playerid, yearid,
gamenum, gameid,
teamid, lgid,
gp, startingpos,
changedate, actiontype
)
SELECT playerid, yearid,
gamenum, gameid, teamid,
lgid, gp, startingpos,
GETDATE(), 'update'
FROM inserted i
UNION ALL
SELECT playerid, yearid,
gamenum, gameid, teamid,
lgid, gp, startingpos,
GETDATE(), 'delete'
FROM deleted d;
END
```

This trigger inserts a row into the audit table for the new data (FROM inserted i) and a row for the old data (FROM deleted d). If you just wanted to get the old data in the audit table, you could remove the section of the trigger that inserts from the inserted table, as shown in the following code:

```
SELECT playerid, yearid,
gamenum, gameid, teamid,
lgid, gp, startingpos,
GETDATE(), 'update'
FROM inserted i
UNION ALL
```

To learn more about SQL Server triggers, take a look at the *Further reading* section.

Creating and using temporary tables

Temporary tables allow you to store temporary query results that can be used during a query session. A temporary table can only be used in your current session. No one else can use them except you. These kinds of tables are useful when you have a complicated or long-running query whose results you want to use in a session. This way, you won't have to keep running the same query over and over, but instead, store the results and query that table.

Learning how to create and use a temporary table

To create a temporary table, you can use the same syntax that we used for creating a permanent table, except we will add the TEMPORARY keyword. You can either create a temporary table with a definition or create one from an existing permanent table. Let's have a look at the syntax that's used to create temporary tables:

- **Explicit creation of a temporary table**:

  Use the following syntax to create a temporary table schema explicitly:

  ```
  CREATE TEMPORARY TABLE temptablename(
    col1 col1type,
    col2 col2type);
  ```

  You will define each column name, data type, and any constraints on it, such as NOT NULL, the same as you would when you create a permanent table.

- **Implicit creation of a temporary table**:

  Use the following syntax to create a temporary table schema implicitly from one or more tables via a query:

  ```
  CREATE TEMPORARY TABLE temptablename
  SELECT * FROM permanenttable
  LIMIT 0;
  ```

  Setting LIMIT to 0 means it will only create the schema, but if you want the data as well, you can leave off LIMIT, or you can set it to a different LIMIT of your choosing.

When you create a temporary table with the following query, you will have a blank table with the columns specified in the query:

```
USE lahmansbaseballdb;
CREATE TEMPORARY TABLE tempplayerinfo
SELECT p.playerid, birthyear,
a.yearid, a.teamid,
G_defense AS defensegames,
H AS numberofhits
FROM lahmansbaseballdb.appearances AS a
JOIN lahmansbaseballdb.people AS p
ON p.playerid = a.playerid
JOIN lahmansbaseballdb.batting AS b
ON a.playerid = b.playerid
AND a.yearid = b.yearid
```

```
AND a.teamid = b.teamid
WHERE b.yearid = 2017
AND H <> 0
LIMIT 0;
```

After creating the preceding temporary table, you can execute the following query to get information about the columns in the temporary table:

```
USE lahmansbaseballdb;
DESCRIBE tempplayerinfo;
```

The following screenshot shows the results of running the preceding query:

Field	Type	Null	Key	Default	Extra
playerid	varchar(255)	YES		NULL	NULL
birthyear	int(11)	YES		NULL	NULL
yearid	smallint(6)	NO		NULL	NULL
teamid	varchar(3)	NO		NULL	NULL
defensegames	smallint(6)	YES		NULL	NULL
numberofhits	smallint(6)	YES		NULL	NULL

You can see that each of the columns listed in the SELECT portion of the query has been placed into the temporary table, along with any specification of the columns that exist in the permanent tables that those columns refer to.

When you execute the following query, you will see that the table is empty:

```
USE lahmansbaseballdb;
SELECT * FROM tempplayerinfo;
```

This previous query returns no results because the original creation was set to LIMIT 0.

 You won't see a temporary table listed with the other tables in MySQL Workbench.

If you set LIMIT to another number or leave LIMIT off when creating the temporary table, the table will have data in it, so you will have to drop it first and then recreate it.

Learning how to delete a temporary table

In order to delete a temporary table, you can execute the following query:

```
USE lahmansbaseballdb;
DROP TEMPORARY TABLE tempplayerinfo;
```

This will delete the temporary table. Then, you can recreate it with different specifications. Also, if you close your session, your temporary table will be automatically deleted.

Differences between temporary tables in other RDBMSes

The differences between each RDBMS are outlined as follows:

- **Oracle**: You need to specify either a GLOBAL or PRIVATE temporary table when creating a temporary table. You also need the AS keyword after the temporary table name, as shown in the following query:

```
CREATE GLOBAL TEMPORARY TABLE tempplayerinfo AS
 SELECT p.playerid, birthyear,
 a.yearid, a.teamid,
 G_defense AS defensegames,
 H AS numberofhits
 FROM appearances a
 JOIN people p
 ON p.playerid = a.playerid
 JOIN batting b
 ON a.playerid = b.playerid
 AND a.yearid = b.yearid
 AND a.teamid = b.teamid
 WHERE b.yearid = 2017
 AND H <> 0
```

Additionally, you drop a temporary table slightly differently in Oracle than in MySQL, as shown in the following query:

```
DROP TABLE tempplayerinfo;
```

For more information about Oracle temporary tables, please take a look at the link provided in the *Further reading* section.

- **PostgreSQL**: The difference in PostgreSQL when creating a temporary table from a query is that you need to use AS after the temporary table name, as shown in the following query:

```
CREATE TEMPORARY TABLE tempplayerinfo AS
SELECT p.playerid, birthyear,
       a.yearid, a.teamid,
       G_defense AS defensegames,
       H AS numberofhits
FROM appearances AS a
JOIN people AS p
ON p.playerid = a.playerid
JOIN batting AS b
ON a.playerid = b.playerid
AND a.yearid = b.yearid
AND a.teamid = b.teamid
WHERE b.yearid = 2017
AND H <> 0
LIMIT 0;
```

Additionally, you drop a temporary table slightly differently in PostgreSQL than in MySQL, as shown in the following query:

```
DROP TABLE tempplayerinfo;
```

Otherwise, PostgreSQL temporary tables work the same way as they do in MySQL.

- **SQL Server**: SQL Server doesn't use the TEMPORARY keyword to create temporary tables. SQL Server has two types of temporary tables, as outlined in the following table:

Local	Global
Available to the current session	Available to all sessions
Deleted once the current session is closed or with a DROP statement	Deleted after all sessions are closed or with a DROP statement
Table name starts with #	Table name starts with ##

Similar to MySQL, you can create a table first, then insert data into it or select a temporary table with SQL Server.

To show you how this works in SQL Server, execute the following query. This will create a temporary table from a query:

```
SELECT TOP 0 p.playerid, birthyear,
             a.yearid, a.teamid,
             G_defense AS defensegames,
             H AS numberofhits
INTO #tempplayerinfo
FROM appearances AS a
JOIN people AS p
ON p.playerid = a.playerid
JOIN batting AS b
ON a.playerid = b.playerid
AND a.yearid = b.yearid
AND a.teamid = b.teamid
WHERE b.yearid = 2017
AND H <>;
```

This is the same temporary table we created earlier in MySQL, but there is a slightly different syntax for SQL Server.

Also, to drop a temporary table in SQL Server, execute the following query:

```
DROP TABLE #tempplayerinfo;
```

To learn more about SQL Server temporary tables, take a look at the *Further reading* section.

Summary

In this chapter, you learned how to create programmable objects, including how to create and use views, which included selecting data from views and inserting, updating, and deleting data using views. Additionally, you learned how to alter and drop views. You learned how to create and use variables, which included how to declare and assign values to variables. This also included how to use variables in a query.

Then, you learned how to create and use stored procedures, including how to alter and drop stored procedures. This included learning how to use variables and parameters in stored procedures, as well as how to control flow in stored procedures using IF, CASE, LOOP, REPEAT, and WHILE. Finally, you learned how to handle errors in stored procedures.

After that, you learned how to create and use functions, including how to alter and drop functions. You learned how to create and use triggers, including how to create triggers with one statement, triggers with multiple statements, and multiple triggers on one table. Finally, you learned how to create and use temporary tables, either explicitly or implicitly, as well as how to drop temporary tables.

In the next chapter, you will learn how to explore and process data. By the end of the next chapter, you will be able to understand how to get to know the data by creating a statistical identity, learn how to detect and fix anomalous and missing values, learn how to formalize strings via functions, and use regular expressions to match data value patterns.

Questions

1. What is a view?
2. Can you update, insert, and delete via a view?
3. What is a variable?
4. How do you set the value of a variable?
5. What is a stored procedure?
6. What is the difference between a parameter and a variable?
7. What types of flow control statements are available?
8. What is a function?
9. What is a trigger?
10. What is a temporary table?

Further reading

- For more information on MySQL error codes, visit `https://dev.mysql.com/doc/refman/8.0/en/server-error-reference.html`.
- For more information on MySQL SQL states in error handling, visit `https://dev.mysql.com/doc/refman/5.6/en/declare-handler.html`.
- For more information on Oracle flow control statements, visit `https://docs.oracle.com/cd/E18283_01/appdev.112/e17126/controlstatements.htm`.
- For more information on PostgreSQL flow control statements, visit `https://www.postgresql.org/docs/11/plpgsql-control-structures.html#PLPGSQL-CONTROL-STRUCTURES-LOOPS`.

- For more information on Oracle error handling, visit `https://docs.oracle.com/cd/E11882_01/timesten.112/e21639/exceptions.htm#TTPLS195`.

- For more information on PostgreSQL error handling, visit `https://www.postgresql.org/docs/11/plpgsql-errors-and-messages.html`.

- For more information on SQL Server `TRY CATCH` statements, visit `https://docs.microsoft.com/en-us/sql/t-sql/language-elements/try-catch-transact-sql?view=sql-server-ver15`.

- For more information on Oracle triggers, visit `https://docs.oracle.com/cd/B19306_01/server.102/b14200/statements_7004.htm`.

- For more information on PostgreSQL triggers, visit `https://www.postgresql.org/docs/11/sql-createtrigger.html`.

- For more information on SQL Server triggers, visit `https://docs.microsoft.com/en-us/sql/t-sql/statements/create-trigger-transact-sql?view=sql-server-ver15`.

- For more information on SQL Server temporary tables, visit `https://docs.microsoft.com/en-us/sql/t-sql/statements/create-table-transact-sql?view=sql-server-ver15#temporary-tables`.

- For more information on Oracle temporary tables, visit `https://docs.oracle.com/en/database/oracle/oracle-database/18/admin/managing-tables.html#GUID-6EB347F0-64BA-4B15-8182-41BA7D5A876F`.

Section 4: Presenting Your Findings

This section will outline how you can present your findings. This will include providing an explanation of exploring and processing your data. By doing this, you will be able to tell a story with the data you've collected. By the end of this section, you will be able to understand and clean your data, as well as present it to your audience.

This section comprises the following chapters:

13
Exploring and Processing Your Data

In this chapter, you will learn how to explore and process data. By the end of this chapter, you will understand how to get to know the data by creating a statistical identity, learn how to detect and fix anomalous and missing values, and use regular expressions to match data value patterns.

In this chapter, we will cover the following topics:

- Exploring your dataset
- Processing your dataset

Let's get started!

Technical requirements

You can refer to the code files for this chapter by going to the following GitHub link: https://github.com/PacktPublishing/learn-sql-database-programming/tree/master/chapter-13.

Exploring your dataset

Exploring your dataset is vital so that you can get acquainted with and learn more about your data. You can do this by checking the statistical identity of your data and checking for rare, missing, and duplicate values. Additionally, you can either consult the expert or become the expert on the dataset.

Getting to know your data using statistical identities

Getting to know your data is vital so you can understand how to analyze and tell a story with it. There are a few built-in functions in MySQL that you can use to get to know your data, including the following:

- AVG: Returns the average of an expression
- COUNT: Returns the number of records
- MAX: Returns the maximum value in a set of values
- MIN: Returns the minimum value in a set of values
- ROUND: Rounds a number to a specified number of decimal places
- SUM: The sum of a set of values
- VARIANCE: Gives you the variance of your data
- STDDEV: Gives you the standard deviation of your data

Each of these was covered in more detail in Chapter 9, *Working with Expressions*. Please refer to that chapter if you need additional information on the built-in functions included here.

If you want to get some general idea of hits in the batting table, you can execute the following query:

```
USE lahmansbaseballdb;
SELECT AVG(h) AS mean,
STDDEV(h) AS stddev,
VARIANCE(h) AS variance,
MIN(h) AS minimum,
MAX(h) AS maximum
FROM batting;
```

The results from the preceding query are shown in the following table:

mean	stddev	variance	min	max
36.8616	52.4710125	2753.20716	0	262

In the preceding table, the mean is the average of all the hits, and we can see that the minimum is 0 and that the maximum is 262. More importantly, we can see that the standard deviance and the variance are both quite large, so this tells us that the individual data points are very dissimilar to one another. This information makes sense since there is quite a lot of difference in how many hits a player may get in any given year.

Maybe you would like to see the statistical identity based on each player. If so, you can execute the following query:

```
USE lahmansbaseballdb;
SELECT playerid,
AVG(h) AS mean,
STDDEV(h) AS stddev,
VARIANCE(h) AS variance,
MIN(h) AS minimum,
MAX(h) AS maximum
FROM batting
GROUP BY playerid;
```

The preceding query will give you a list of all the players, along with their mean, stddev, variance, minimum, and maximum hits over all the years they played, as shown in the following screenshot:

playerid	mean	stddev	variance	minimum	maximum
aardsda01	0.0000	0	0	0	0
aaronha01	163.9565	39.70486582914487	1576.4763705103962	62	223
aaronto01	30.8571	27.51845391955095	757.265306122449	3	77
aasedo01	0.0000	0	0	0	0
abadan01	0.6667	0.9428090415820634	0.888888888888889	0	2
abadfe01	0.1111	0.3142696805273545	0.09876543209876545	0	1
abadijo01	5.5000	4.5	20.25	1	10
abbated01	77.2000	62.31982028215421	3883.7599999999998	0	170
abbeybe01	6.3333	3.4480268109295333	11.888888888888888	1	12

Maybe you would like to see the statistical identity based on each year. If so, you can execute the following query:

```
USE lahmansbaseballdb;
SELECT yearid,
AVG(h) AS mean,
STDDEV(h) AS stddev,
VARIANCE(h) AS variance,
MIN(h) AS minimum,
MAX(h) AS maximum
FROM batting
GROUP BY yearid;
```

The preceding query will give you a list of all the years the player's played and the `mean`, `stddev`, `variance`, `minimum`, and `maximum` hits over all the years they played, as shown in the following screenshot:

yearid	mean	stddev	variance	minimum	maximum
2004	33.0773	52.80202141332675	2788.0534653334166	0	262
2006	32.7328	52.70350916804687	2777.6598786264008	0	224
2007	32.4744	52.91470788468406	2799.9663105214454	0	238
2008	31.7487	50.870690179533604	2587.8271193420965	0	213
2009	31.3573	50.56072300834159	2556.3867111262425	0	225
2010	31.3820	49.48379640741829	2448.6461068908234	0	214
2012	29.8743	48.14048414779622	2317.5062139842194	0	216
2013	29.8744	48.45953998617647	2348.3270156718368	0	199
2015	28.3351	47.48300756005938	2254.636006948656	0	205

Maybe you would like to see the statistical identity based on each team's hits. If so, you can execute the following query:

```
USE lahmansbaseballdb;
SELECT teamid,
AVG(h) AS mean,
STDDEV(h) AS stddev,
VARIANCE(h) AS variance,
MIN(h) AS minimum,
MAX(h) AS maximum
FROM batting
GROUP BY teamid;
```

The preceding query will give you a list of all the teams and their `mean`, `stddev`, `variance`, `minimum`, and `maximum` hits over all the years they played, as shown in the following screenshot:

teamid	mean	stddev	variance	minimum	maximum
SFN	34.6597	49.723618668352444	2472.438253475728	0	208
CHN	38.7813	52.90249138611787	2798.6735948582755	0	229
CHA	37.1048	52.77147268378825	2784.8283292158094	0	224
BOS	38.1086	55.085629471992824	3034.4265743256847	0	240
SEA	32.3567	51.57954201225256	2660.449154193727	0	262
NYA	37.7133	55.02322842740567	3027.5556665744634	0	238
NYN	31.4877	45.889666160965	2105.861460364816	0	227
ATL	33.3161	50.67764177905283	2568.2233762860005	0	219
ML1	39.0728	55.567917134036385	3087.7934146151347	0	223

The general idea is to look at as many tables and their columns as you can to get a good idea of what your data looks like. Then, you need to determine what it means so that you can tell a story with your data.

Detecting rare and outlier values

Detecting rare and outlier values can help you determine if you have bad or irrelevant data. The terms *rare* and *outlier* can be subjective. Different people might define *rare* and *outlier* data standards differently. Knowing this can help you prepare for possible disagreements in a business situation.

To see the distinct values in a table, execute the following query:

```
USE lahmansbaseballdb;
SELECT DISTINCT h as hits, COUNT(h) as count
FROM batting
GROUP BY hits
ORDER BY count;
```

The preceding query will give you a list of each distinct value in the h (hits) column and a count of those hits, as shown in the following two screenshots. This first screenshot shows you the beginning rows of the results:

hits	count
248	1
235	1
229	1
233	1
253	1
257	1
246	1
242	1
262	1

This second screenshot shows you the last rows of the results:

hits	count
8	1638
7	1845
6	2054
5	2282
4	2638
3	3225
2	4248
1	6928
0	28067

Here, we can see that the values at the top of the results are rare or outlier results because they only have one value with that number of hits, but this doesn't mean that they are erroneous. If you saw a result that was way beyond any other values, such as 400, for example, then you should research that value more because it may need to be fixed to the correct value. Of course, the value that may seem erroneous will depend on the column's values, so this is why you need to check for rare and outlier values, as well as view all the other distinct values to determine what rare and outlier values mean for your data.

Detecting missing values

Another important thing to look for is missing values to determine whether you need to fix the values or remove the data points. To see the count of NULL versus NON NULL values in a table, execute the following query:

```
USE lahmansbaseballdb;
SELECT
SUM(!ISNULL(h)) AS hits_count,
SUM(ISNULL(h)) AS null_hits_count
FROM batting;
```

The results from the preceding query can be seen in the following table:

hits_count	null_hits_count
105861	0

Looking at the results in the preceding table, you can see that there aren't any NULL values for hits since null_hits_count is 0.

Let's try a different column in our preceding query, as follows:

```
USE lahmansbaseballdb;
SELECT
SUM(!ISNULL(ibb)) AS ibb_count,
SUM(ISNULL(ibb)) AS null_ibb_count
FROM batting;
```

The results from the preceding query are shown in the following table:

ibb_count	null_ibb_count
69210	36651

Looking at the results in the preceding table, you can see that there are a lot of NULL values for ibb since `null_ibb_count` is 36651. In case you don't know, **ibb** is **intentional base on balls** (or intentional walks), which means the batter was thrown four balls in a row to allow them to walk to first base without the opportunity to swing at the ball. It may be the case that there are a lot of NULL values. Maybe there wasn't data available, or maybe the baseball rules changed at some point to allow intentional walks, so players in years before this rule was changed would show up as NULL.

You can confirm this theory by executing the following query:

```
USE lahmansbaseballdb;
SELECT MIN(yearid) as minyear,
MAX(yearid) as maxyear
FROM batting
WHERE ibb IS NULL;
```

The preceding query will give you the following results:

minyear	maxyear
1871	1954

Here, you can see that only the years from 1871 to 1954 have NULL values in the ibb column, so it seems to indicate that maybe a rule changed in 1955 that allows intentional base on balls. If you do an internet search for the intentional base on balls, you will see that official tracking data for this baseball statistic started in 1955, but it was allowed before then. This is why it's essential to follow through to a proper conclusion before assuming anything about your data.

Detecting duplicate and erroneous values

To see duplicate values in a table, execute the following query:

```
USE lahmansbaseballdb;
SELECT name_full
FROM schools
GROUP BY name_full
HAVING count(*) >= 2;
```

The preceding query gives you the results shown in the following screenshot:

name_full
Bethel College
"University of California
"California Polytechnic State University
Southwestern College
"Long Island University
"Miami-Dade College
Butler County Community College
Lincoln University
"Minnesota State University
"Community College of Baltimore County
"St. Louis Community College

These are possible duplicates. If you execute the following query, you will see be able all the fields in the table to see if they are genuinely duplicates:

```
USE lahmansbaseballdb;
SELECT * FROM schools
WHERE name_full = 'Bethel College';
```

The preceding query gives you the results shown in the following screenshot:

schoolID	name_full	city	state	country
betheltn	Bethel College	McKenzie	TN	USA
inbethel	Bethel College	Mishawaka	IN	USA

You can see that these aren't duplicates since they each have a unique `schoolID` and are in different locations. You can also search for duplicates based on the combination of multiple columns with the following query:

```
USE lahmansbaseballdb;
SELECT name_full, city
FROM schools
GROUP BY name_full, city
HAVING count(*) >= 2;
```

The preceding query will return no results because there aren't any duplicates with the school name and city combination.

Checking for duplicates on this table brought up something interesting, though. There are some double quotes (") at the front of some of the school names. Let's take a look at that data more closely with the following query:

```
USE lahmansbaseballdb;
SELECT * FROM schools
WHERE name_full = '"California Polytechnic State University';
```

The preceding query returns the results shown in the following screenshot:

schoolID	name_full	city	state	country
calpoly	"California Polytechnic State University	San Luis Obispo"	San Luis Obispo	CA,USA
calpolypom	"California Polytechnic State University	Pomona"	Pomona	CA,USA

You can see from the results that there is a double quote at the start of the name_full column and a double quote ending the city column. This error must have occurred when the data was inserted. We will go through cleaning up erroneous data later in this chapter.

Consulting with experts or becoming the expert

It may be possible that an expert on the data you are using is available for you to speak with directly, or has already written documentation that you can refer to. If not, you may need to become the expert on the data yourself. We've already gone through some ways you can acquaint yourself with the data you are using. Additionally, you can create documentation for your data so that you have it for future reference and so that you can provide it to someone else if they need to understand the data better. One way to become an expert on the data you are working with is to follow the information provided in the preceding sections of this chapter. Another way is to create a data dictionary to document the data.

Creating a data dictionary

A data dictionary is a document that helps you understand what is in your database. It includes things such as the names of all the objects, tables, and column names, what the data type of each column is, and any constraints on table columns. The data dictionary can also include any notes about the tables you think would be necessary for people to know about the data.

To create a data dictionary in MySQL for free, you will need to install a Python plugin into your MySQL Workbench installation. The Python file you will need for this can be found in the code files you downloaded in the *Technical requirements* section of this chapter. Follow these steps to install the plugin:

1. In MySQL Workbench, click **Scripting** from the menu and click **Install Plugin/Module...**:

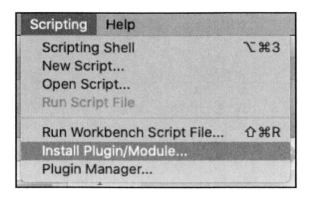

2. Navigate to the location of the `chapter-13` files, choose the `mysql-workbench-plugin-doc-generating.py` file, and click **Open**. For more information about this Python plugin, visit `https://github.com/letrunghieu/mysql-workbench-plugin-doc-generating/blob/master/LICENSE`:

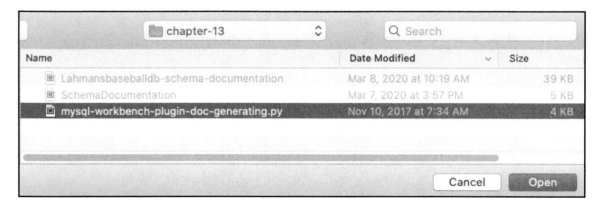

3. A popup will appear, letting you know that the plugin has been installed and that you need to restart MySQL Workbench to use it. Click **OK** on the popup and close and reopen MySQL Workbench:

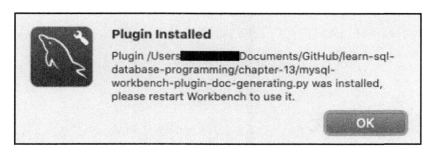

4. Once you have installed the plugin, you will need to create an **Entity-Relationship Diagram (ERD)**. The steps to create this were covered in `Chapter 7`, *Querying Multiple Tables*. To recap how to start the ERD process, you click on the **Database** menu item and click **Reverse Engineer**. Then, you follow the steps provided to get the objects you want into the ERD. We will start the data dictionary creation process after the ERD has been created.

Once you have generated your ERD, click **Tools** in the menu, then **Utilities**, and then **Generate documentation (Markdown)**:

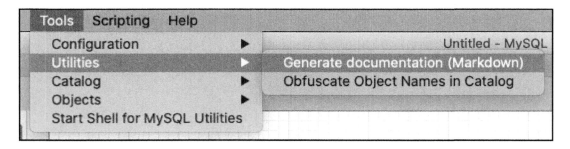

Once you've done that, you will have the documentation in the clipboard on your computer so that you can paste it into the file of your choosing.

You could just paste it into a text file, but it works best for readability purposes when it's in a Markdown editor. There are many free markdown editors. I use Typora, but you can install any one of your choosing.

You will need to open your markdown editor and make sure that you have a blank markdown file before pasting the markdown from MySQL Workbench into the file. Then, you will have something that looks similar to the following:

Schema documentation

Generated by MySQL Workbench Model Documentation v1.0.0 - Copyright (c) 2015 Hieu Le

Table: `allstarfull`

Description:

Columns:

Column	Data type	Attributes	Default	Description
playerID	VARCHAR(9)	PRIMARY, Not null		
yearID	SMALLINT	PRIMARY, Not null		
gameNum	SMALLINT	PRIMARY, Not null		
gameID	VARCHAR(12)		NULL	
teamID	VARCHAR(3)		NULL	
lgID	VARCHAR(2)		NULL	
GP	SMALLINT		NULL	
startingPos	SMALLINT		NULL	

Indices:

Name	Columns	Type	Description
PRIMARY	playerID, yearID, gameNum	PRIMARY	

This markdown file will contain each table, along with its columns and their types, attributes, and constraints. You can also add a description for each table and a description for each column if needed. There will also be a section for each table to show its indexes.

You can add all the objects from your database into your data dictionary, not just tables, depending on whether you want to add an explanation for each of those objects.

You can use the description column on the tables to add explanations. For example, some of the columns in the batting table may need more explanations as to what they mean; for example, G means Games, while AB means At-bats. The data dictionary allows you to explain further, as shown in the following screenshot:

Table: `batting`

Description:

Columns:

Column	Data type	Attributes	Default	Description
playerID	VARCHAR(9)	PRIMARY, Not null		
yearID	SMALLINT	PRIMARY, Not null		
stint	SMALLINT	PRIMARY, Not null		
teamID	VARCHAR(3)		NULL	
lgID	VARCHAR(2)		NULL	
G	SMALLINT		NULL	Games
G_batting	SMALLINT		NULL	Games batted
AB	SMALLINT		NULL	At-bats
R	SMALLINT		NULL	Runs scored
H	SMALLINT		NULL	Hits
2B	SMALLINT		NULL	

There is a complete data dictionary in the code files you downloaded in the *Technical requirements* section of this chapter.

Using regular expressions

Regular expressions (REGEXP) help you search for string patterns in your data. REGEXP expands upon the patterns you can use in the LIKE operator, which we covered in Chapter 6, *Querying a Single Table*. LIKE allowed you to use the percent sign (%) wildcard to represent zero or more characters or the underscore (_) wildcard to represent one or more characters to match patterns on strings in the WHERE clause. Regular expressions have far more wildcard characters, thereby giving you far more options for matching patterns. The downside to regular expressions is that they can be complicated and hard to understand. Regular expressions can also reduce query performance, depending on how complex they get.

The following table outlines some of the commonly used regular expression characters:

Character	How it works
^	Matches the beginning of a string
$	Matches the end of a string
.	Matches any character
[. . .]	Matches any character inside square brackets
[^ . . .]	Matches any character not inside square brackets
p1|p2|p3	Matches any of the patterns specified
+	Matches a sequence of characters one or more times

To use REGEXP in a MySQL query, you need to add the REGEXP keyword to a WHERE clause, as shown in the following code sample:

```
SELECT col1, col2, col3
FROM tablename
WHERE stringcolumn REGEXP pattern;
```

You can also use NOT REGEXP to search for the opposite of the pattern. Let's go through some examples of how to use the REGEXP characters:

- **Caret** (^): Use this to match at the beginning of a string. This can be seen in the following query, which will return any playerid starting with a or A:

```
USE lahmansbaseballdb;
SELECT playerid
FROM people
WHERE playerid REGEXP '^a';
```

- **Dollar sign** ($): Use this to match at the end of a string. This can be seen in the following query, which will return any `birthcity` values ending with `y` or `Y`:

```
USE lahmansbaseballdb;
SELECT birthcity
FROM people
WHERE birthcity REGEXP 'y$';
```

- **Period** (.): Use this to match any character in a string, as shown in the following query:

```
USE lahmansbaseballdb;
SELECT birthyear
FROM people
WHERE birthyear REGEXP '199.';
```

The preceding query will return any `birthyear` values that start with `199`. It will return values such as 1990 through 1999.

- **Square brackets** ([...]): Use this to match any character placed inside the square brackets, as shown in the following query:

```
USE lahmansbaseballdb;
SELECT playerid
FROM people
WHERE playerid REGEXP '^[C]'
ORDER BY playerid;
```

The preceding query will return any `playerid` values that start with `C` or `c`.

Use the following query to match any character not placed inside the square brackets:

```
USE lahmansbaseballdb;
SELECT playerid
FROM people
WHERE playerid REGEXP '^[^C]'
ORDER BY playerid;
```

The preceding query will return any `playerid` values that don't start with `C` or `c`.

- **Pipe delimiter** (|): Use this to match any of the patterns specified, as shown in the following query:

```
USE lahmansbaseballdb;
SELECT playerid
FROM people
WHERE playerid REGEXP '^[C|D|E]'
ORDER BY playerid;
```

The preceding query will return any `playerid` values that start with C or c, D or d, and E or e.

- **Plus sign** (+): Use this to match any of the patterns specified, as shown in the following query:

```
USE lahmansbaseballdb;
SELECT birthcity
FROM people
WHERE birthcity REGEXP 'son+';
```

The preceding query will return any `birthcity` values that have the string, son, in them.

Combining regular expression characters

You can mix the characters to get even more complicated search patterns, as shown in the following query:

```
USE lahmansbaseballdb;
SELECT DISTINCT birthcity
FROM people
WHERE birthcity REGEXP '^[abc].{3}on$'
ORDER BY birthcity;
```

The preceding query will return any `birthcity` that starts with a, b, or c, then has three characters in the middle, then ends with on, as shown in the following screenshot:

Regular expressions can be powerful, but you need to be careful when using them because they may not use the indexes of the table you are querying, and then your query can become quite slow, depending on the size of the table.

Processing your dataset

After you've gotten to know your data, you may need to fix issues residing in it. This section will do a walkthrough of some methods you can use to address the problems you may encounter in your dataset.

Fixing rare and outlier values

Detecting rare and outlier values can help you determine if you have bad or irrelevant data. To proceed from where we left off in the detecting rare and outlier values section, execute the following query:

```
USE lahmansbaseballdb;
SELECT DISTINCT h as hits, COUNT(h) as count
FROM batting
GROUP BY hits
ORDER BY count;
```

The preceding query will give you a list of each distinct value in the h (hits) column and a count of those hits, as shown in the following two screenshots. This first screenshot shows you the beginning rows of the results:

hits	count
248	1
235	1
229	1
233	1
253	1
257	1
246	1
242	1
262	1

Here, we can see that the values at the top of the results could be rare or outlier results because they only have one value with that number of hits, but it doesn't mean that they are erroneous. Let's just say, for the sake of showing you how to fix an outlier or rare value that is erroneous, that you think the 248 hits value is incorrect. You would need to do some more research to fix it. To get more information about the player that this hit count relates to, execute the following query:

```
USE lahmansbaseballdb;
SELECT b.playerid, namefirst, namelast,
       yearid, teamid, g, ab, h
FROM batting b
INNER JOIN people p
ON p.playerid = b.playerid
WHERE h = 248;
```

The preceding query gives you the results shown in the following screenshot:

playerid	namefirst	namelast	yearid	teamid	g	ab	h
cobbty01	Ty	Cobb	1911	DET	146	591	248

Here, you can see that this hit count relates to Ty Cobb, who is a very famous baseball player, and he did likely have that many hits in a year, but let's just double-check that number by going to a baseball reference site: https://www.baseball-reference.com/. You can look him up in there and go to the year in question. You can find the specific page at: https://www.baseball-reference.com/players/split.fcgi?id=cobbty01year=1911t=b.

What you will discover is that he did have 248 hits that season, but if you found that that number was wrong, you would have to run an UPDATE statement against that table with the following query:

```
USE lahmansbaseballdb;
UPDATE batting
SET h = whatevernumberiscorrect
WHERE playerid = 'cobbty01'
AND yearid = 1911
AND teamid = 'DET';
```

The preceding query won't work because you can't set the hits to a non-numeric value, but that's just to show you how you would fix an erroneous value, and since this isn't an incorrect value, you shouldn't fix it. This is how you would handle a rare or outlier value that is erroneous.

There could also be cases where the value is erroneous, but you can't find the correct value. In this case, you would need to decide whether you want to remove the data from your dataset.

Fixing missing values

Another essential thing to look for is missing values to determine if you need to adjust the values or remove the data points. A row may be complete except for one column, so you may need to fix that one column of missing data. To see the count of NULL versus NON NULL values in a table, execute the following query:

```
USE lahmansbaseballdb;
SELECT
SUM(!ISNULL(birthyear)) AS birthyear_count,
SUM(ISNULL(birthyear)) AS null_birthyear_count
FROM people;
```

The results from the preceding query are shown in the following table:

birthyear_count	null_birthyear_count
19497	120

Looking at the results in the preceding table, you can see that there are some NULL values for birthyear. It may be valid that there are some NULL values in this case. Maybe there wasn't data available for those players. You can find out more information about these players by executing the following query:

```
USE lahmansbaseballdb;
SELECT playerid, namefirst, namelast, debut
FROM people
WHERE birthyear is NULL;
```

The preceding query will give you the results shown in the following screenshot:

playerid	namefirst	namelast	birthyear	debut
barre01	John	Barrett	NULL	1872-09-18 00:00:00
barrebi01	Bill	Barrett	NULL	1871-07-08 00:00:00
besti01	William	Bestick	NULL	1872-06-20 00:00:00
bolan01	NULL	Boland	NULL	1875-09-04 00:00:00
booth01	NULL	Booth	NULL	1875-05-01 00:00:00
boothed01	Eddie	Booth	NULL	1872-04-26 00:00:00
brown01	Robert	Brown	NULL	1874-07-29 00:00:00
browned01	Ed	Brown	NULL	1882-08-19 00:00:00
burkeja01	James	Burke	NULL	1882-06-10 00:00:00
burnsji01	Jim	Burns	NULL	1888-09-25 00:00:00

Here, you can see that players with a missing birthyear started playing baseball in the 1870s. It may be that this data is missing for them because no one knows when they were born.

Let's look up John Barrett in the baseball reference website. You can do that by going to: https://www.baseball-reference.com/players/b/barre01.shtml.

You can see that his birthdate is unknown, but let's say you discovered that they did have a birthdate listed for him. You could update his information by executing the following query:

```
USE lahmansbaseballdb;
UPDATE people
SET birthyear = whateverbirthyeariscorrect
WHERE playerid = 'barre01';
```

The preceding query won't work because you can't set the birthyear to a non-numeric value, but that's just to show you how you would fix a missing value.

There could also be cases where the missing value is significant, but you can't find the correct value. In this case, you would need to decide whether you want to remove the data from your dataset.

Removing or fixing duplicates

There are a couple of ways to remediate duplicates, either by removing them or fixing them. We will go through each way in the following sections.

Removing duplicates

To remove a duplicate, let's do some setup first with the following queries:

1. Let's create a copy of the `schools` table with the following query:

```
USE lahmansbaseballdb;
DROP TABLE IF EXISTS schools_copy;
CREATE TABLE schools_copy
SELECT *
FROM schools
WHERE 1=0;
```

2. Now, let's insert some data into the `schools_copy` table with the following query:

```
USE lahmansbaseballdb;
INSERT INTO schools_copy VALUES
('adelphi','Adelphi University','Garden City','NY','USA'),
('adelphi1','Adelphi University','Garden City','NY','USA'),
('akron','University of Akron','Akron','OH','USA'),
('alabama','University of Alabama','Tuscaloosa','AL','USA'),
('alabamast','Alabama State University','Montgomery','AL','USA');
```

3. Now that we have a table set up so that we can remove duplicates, execute the following query:

```
USE lahmansbaseballdb;
SELECT name_full
FROM schools_copy
GROUP BY name_full
HAVING count(*) >= 2;
```

The preceding query gives you the results shown in the following screenshot:

name_full
Bethel College
"University of California
"California Polytechnic State University
Southwestern College
"Long Island University
"Miami-Dade College
Butler County Community College
Lincoln University
"Minnesota State University
"Community College of Baltimore County
"St. Louis Community College

`Bethel College` is a possible duplicate.

4. If you execute the following query, you will see all the fields in the table to tell whether they are genuinely duplicates:

```
USE lahmansbaseballdb;
SELECT * FROM schools_copy
WHERE name_full = 'Bethel College';
```

The preceding query gives you the results shown in the following screenshot:

schoolID	name_full	city	state	country
betheltn	Bethel College	McKenzie	TN	USA
inbethel	Bethel College	Mishawaka	IN	USA

Here, we can see that `Bethel College` truly is a duplicate value, even though `schoolID` is different. It's just that the `schoolID` column can't have duplicates, so maybe someone inserted it with a different `schoolID` at some point, not realizing that it already existed with another `schoolID`. You can delete one of these rows based on `schoolid`, as shown in the following query:

```
USE lahmansbaseballdb;
DELETE FROM schools_copy
WHERE schoolid = 'inbethel';
```

Execute this query again:

```
SELECT name_full
FROM schools_copy
GROUP BY name_full
HAVING count(*) >= 2;
```

You will see that you no longer have any duplicates in the `school_copy` table.

Execute this query again:

```
USE lahmansbaseballdb;
SELECT * FROM schools_copy
WHERE name_full = 'Bethel College';
```

The preceding query gives you the results shown in the following screenshot:

schoolID	name_full	city	state	country
betheltn	Bethel College	McKenzie	TN	USA

Now, you only have the one result for `Bethel College` since you removed the duplicate.

If you didn't have a unique ID for each row, then this will become much more difficult. This is why it's crucial to design tables so that you have a unique identifier for each row or a combination of values, or make a unique identifier enforced by a primary key.

Fixing duplicates

Next, let's look at fixing a duplicate value. To fix a duplicate, let's do some setup first with the following queries:

1. Let's create a copy of the `schools` table with the following query:

```
USE lahmansbaseballdb;
DROP TABLE IF EXISTS schools_copy;
CREATE TABLE schools_copy
SELECT *
FROM schools
WHERE 1=0;
```

2. Now, let's insert some data into the `schools_copy` table with the following query:

```
INSERT INTO schools_copy VALUES
('adelphi','Adelphi University','Garden City','NY','USA'),
('adrianmi','Adelphi University','Garden City','NY','USA'),
('akron','University of Akron','Akron','OH','USA'),
('alabama','University of Alabama','Tuscaloosa','AL','USA'),
('alabamast','Alabama State University','Montgomery','AL','USA');
```

3. Now that we have a table set up to fix duplicates, execute the following query:

```
USE lahmansbaseballdb;
SELECT name_full
FROM schools_copy
GROUP BY name_full
HAVING count(*) >= 2;
```

The preceding query gives you the results shown in the following screenshot:

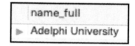

`Adelphi University` is a possible duplicate. If you execute the following query, you will be able to view all the fields in the table to see if they are genuinely duplicates:

```
USE lahmansbaseballdb;
SELECT * FROM schools_copy
WHERE name_full = 'Adelphi University';
```

The preceding query gives you the results shown in the following screenshot:

schoolID	name_full	city	state	country
adelphi	Adelphi University	Garden City	NY	USA
adrianmi	Adelphi University	Garden City	NY	USA

Here, we can see that `Adelphi University` doesn't look like a duplicate value because `schoolID` is very different, as if it should have been a different school altogether. We have the `schools` table as a reference point in this case, but if you didn't have that, maybe you could figure out what `adrianmi` is with a Google search. The Google search results for this are shown in the following screenshot:

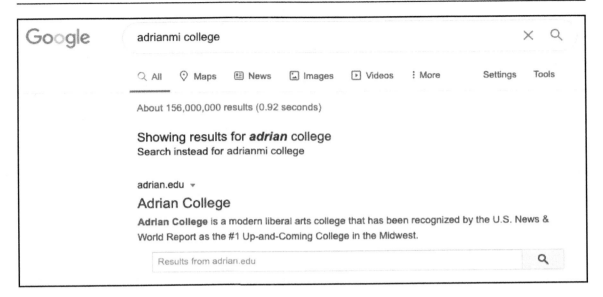

4. From the information provided online about the college, you can execute the following query to fix the record:

```
USE lahmansbaseballdb;
UPDATE schools_copy
SET name_full = 'Adrian College',
    city = 'Adrian',
    state = 'MI',
    country = 'USA'
WHERE schoolid = 'adrianmi';
```

Execute this query again:

```
SELECT name_full
FROM schools_copy
GROUP BY name_full
HAVING count(*) >= 2;
```

5. You will see that you no longer have any duplicates in the `school_copy` table.

Execute this query again:

```
USE lahmansbaseballdb;
SELECT * FROM schools_copy
WHERE name_full = 'Adelphi University';
```

The preceding query gives you the results shown in the following screenshot:

schoolID	name_full	city	state	country
adelphi	Adelphi University	Garden City	NY	USA

Now, you only have the one result for `Adelphi University` since you fixed the duplicate.

Fixing erroneous data

Checking for duplicates on the `schools` table in the *Detecting duplicate and erroneous values* section brought up something interesting: there are some double quotes (") at the front of some of the school names. Let's take a look at that data more closely with the following query:

```
USE lahmansbaseballdb;
SELECT * FROM schools
WHERE name_full = '"California Polytechnic State University';
```

The preceding query returns the results shown in the following screenshot:

schoolID	name_full	city	state	country
calpoly	"California Polytechnic State University	San Luis Obispo"	San Luis Obispo	CA,USA
calpolypom	"California Polytechnic State University	Pomona"	Pomona	CA,USA

Here, you can see that there is a double quote to start the `name_full` column and a double quote to end the `city` column. This error must've happened when inserting the data. To fix this, you will need to run an `UPDATE` statement to set the values correctly, as shown in the following query:

```
USE lahmansbaseballdb;
UPDATE schools
SET name_full = 'California Polytechnic State University',
 city = 'San Luis Obispo',
 state = 'CA',
 country = 'USA'
WHERE schoolid = 'calpoly';
```

The preceding query will fix the issues we saw earlier with one row, that is, `'"California Polytechnic State University"`.

Execute this query again:

```
USE lahmansbaseballdb;
SELECT * FROM schools
WHERE name_full = '"California Polytechnic State University';
```

You will see that you have one more erroneous value to fix, as shown in the following screenshot:

schoolID	name_full	city	state	country
calpolypom	"California Polytechnic State University	Pomona"	Pomona	CA,USA

This can also be fixed in the same way you fixed the preceding erroneous value.

Summary

In this chapter, you learned how to explore your dataset and get to know your data with statistical identities. You also learned how to detect rare and outlier values, missing values, and duplicate values.

Then, you learned how to become an expert of your dataset by creating a data dictionary. You also learned how to use regular expressions to match data patterns. Finally, you learned how to process your dataset by fixing or removing rare or outlier values, missing values, and duplicate values.

In the next chapter, you will learn how to tell a story with your data. You will learn how to find a narrative, including what types of stories are told with data. This includes how to use the statistical identity of your data to determine a story. You will also learn how to know your audience, including determining who they are and what would be an effective presentation for them. Additionally, you will learn how to determine a presentation framework, including explaining the question, answer, and methodology, as well as how to use visualizations in your presentations.

Questions

1. How do you detect rare or outlier values?
2. How do you detect missing values?
3. How do you detect duplicate values?
4. How can you become an expert on your data?
5. What is a data dictionary?
6. How can you create a data dictionary from MySQL Workbench?
7. What is a regular expression?
8. What does the caret (^) regular expression do?
9. What does the pipe delimiter (|) regular expression do?
10. Can you combine multiple regular expressions?

Telling a Story with Your Data **14**

In this chapter, you will learn how to tell a story with your data. You will learn how to find a narrative, including what types of stories you can tell with data and how to use the statistical identity of your data to determine a story. You will also learn how to *know your audience*, including deciding who they are and what would be a compelling presentation for them. You will then learn how to identify a presentation framework, including explaining the question, answer, and methodology. Finally, you will learn how to use visualizations in your presentations.

In this chapter, we will cover the following topics:

- Finding a narrative
- Knowing your audience
- Determining a presentation framework
- Using visualizations

Let's get started!

Technical requirements

You can refer to the code files for this chapter by going to the following GitHub link: `https://github.com/PacktPublishing/learn-sql-database-programming/tree/master/chapter-14`.

Finding a narrative

To tell a good story, you will need to find a narrative for your data. A narrative is all about telling the story of your data. A good narrative will draw the reader or listener into the story of your data and make them feel engaged with the topic at hand. People may not feel compelled to listen to or act on your findings if you present them in a dull or overly complicated way.

Types of data stories

There are many different types of stories that you can tell with data:

- **Reporting**: Tells a story about the past. For example, this could be a batting report for all the players on a specific baseball team.
- **Explanatory**: Tells a story about what people or things are up to and may include asking people questions via surveys. For example, this could be votes cast by fans for players to appear in the Allstar game.
- **Predictive**: Tells a story about the future; for example, how many runs will score based on how many outs there are and the number of players on base.
- **Correlation**: Tells a story about how variables relate to one another. For example, it could be that a player with more walks also has more hits than other players.
- **Causation**: Tells a story about how one variable caused another one to change. For example, it could be that a team with more home runs has more wins.

 Correlation doesn't imply causation. For example, you may find that just because a player with the most walks has the most hits, it doesn't mean that having a lot of walks causes them to have a lot of hits.

You can also combine these types of stories and tell stories such as the following:

- **How something changed over time**. For example, how many wins a team has year over year.
- **Go from the big picture to a narrow focus**. For example, going from how many hits there are in 1 year in baseball to how many hits were on each team for that year, to how many hit each player got in any given year for each team.
- **Start narrow and go to the big picture**. For example, going from how many hits each player got in any given year for each team, to how many hits were on each team for that year, to how many hits there are in one year in baseball.
- **Comparing and contrasting**. Comparing or contrasting one team's or player's statistics for any given year to another team's or player's statistics.

Asking questions to find your narrative

A lot of times, you won't get a clear-cut question handed to you that you can quickly solve, so you will need to talk with people having problems and figure out the question that they lack an answer to. You then need to be able to translate the question into an actionable issue.

Let's say you were trying to solve a baseball problem while working for a major league baseball team who's trying to decide which players they may want to add to or remove from their team. You are going to need to ask a lot of good questions to get to the question or questions that need to be answered. Maybe some of these questions would be good to ask:

- Who is performing well on the current team, and who isn't?
- What are some factors you would look for in a new player?
- How much money are you spending on current players?
- How much money are you willing to spend to get new players?

Once you've asked enough questions to find the problem that can be solved, you will be able to come up with a story to tell.

Of course, there may not be a problem to solve, if you are just gathering data to tell a story. For example, with a reporting story, you are only showing what's happened in the past. It may be that you can use that to also come up with a predictive story or a correlation story.

Using the statistical identity of your data to determine a narrative

In `Chapter 13`, *Exploring and Processing Your Data*, we covered how to determine the statistical identity of your data. The general idea is to look at as many tables and their columns as you can to get a good idea of what your data looks like and what it means so that you can tell a story about your data.

To give you an idea of something you could look for to determine a narrative, you can execute the following query:

```
USE lahmansbaseballdb;
SELECT f.pos, FORMAT(AVG(salary),0) as averagesalary
FROM salaries s
INNER JOIN fielding f
ON f.playerid = s.playerid
AND f.yearid = s.yearid
GROUP BY pos
ORDER BY averagesalary;
```

The preceding query returns the results shown in the following screenshot:

position	averagesalary
C	1,415,324
2B	1,467,949
SS	1,588,975
3B	1,667,332
P	1,939,988
OF	2,157,168
1B	2,374,374

This query shows you the average salary based on a position across all of major league baseball for the entire history of the league. The query results show you a way you could start from a big picture and bring that down a narrow focus. Starting with the average salary of each position, you can work your way into a story of why the average salary looks the way it does.

Don't feel frustrated if your story doesn't pop out at you right away, or it takes time to build. Telling a story with data isn't always easy. Usually, it is pretty tricky, especially if you want to tell a story that's worth reading or listening to, or if you need to find the right solution to the problem you are trying to solve.

Knowing your audience

Information regarding who will be viewing your presentation and findings will be necessary for deciding how to present your findings. You will need to determine who your audience is so that you can provide your results in the proper manner.

Determining who your audience is

Your audience can include many people or a specific subset of people. When you are telling a story with business data, some of your audience may be as follows:

- **Decision-makers**: This could include your manager or the executives at your organization. Your direct manager may want or need more information than an executive, who would like a more high-level, less-detailed presentation.
- **Colleagues**: This could be people who are on your team or members of other teams in your organization. Your team members may want additional information about how you came to your conclusions. In contrast, members of other groups may not understand the details and will need a more high-level, less-detailed presentation.
- **General public**: You may need to create a presentation for a broader audience, and in this case, it may make sense to create a presentation that isn't quite as detailed.

Creating a compelling presentation for your audience

When creating a presentation, it's important to remember that you need to think about whether your audience is a beginner, intermediate, or advanced in their knowledge of the topic. You may need to create different presentations for different audiences. It will be beneficial to have at least a couple of different versions of the presentation: a detailed one and a less detailed one. You may even need to create different presentations for different formats or purposes, such as for a website or compliance reasons.

For baseball data storytelling, your audience will most likely be people who are familiar with and interested in baseball. Still, it can't hurt to include some information about the basics if you want to add people who don't know as much about baseball. It can be essential to show your presentation to someone who doesn't know the topic matter well to see if they understand what you are trying to explain.

Determining a presentation framework

A presentation framework consists of a few things, including the following:

- Creating a structure for your presentation. This structure will tell your audience what you will cover in your presentation, what the objectives are, and what they will learn.
- Determining the level of information presented, such as how detailed or high-level you want to make your presentation.

To have a proper presentation framework, you will need to ensure that your audience understands what question you are asking, what the answer is, and how you got to the answer.

Explaining the question

You need to begin your presentation by explaining the question you are trying to answer. It's essential to keep your focus on one question and not get distracted by other questions. If you decide to answer too many questions in a presentation (that is, telling too many stories), the story will become lost in too much data and explanations.

For example, let's say you were trying to determine why individual players or types of players make more than other players; you would want to keep the focus on that question only. You don't want to suddenly throw in statistics about manager salaries or details about why a team moved to another city. Even if you are providing a big picture of this and narrowing down the focus, you still don't want your big picture to include everything and anything. Your big picture needs to focus on the specific question you are trying to answer.

An example question could be: *Why do certain baseball player positions make more than others?*

Explaining the answer

After making sure you've explained the question clearly, you will need to explain the answer clearly. Again, you can start with the big picture and work your way down to a narrow focus if that's the story you've chosen to tell. As you explain the answer, make sure to give context along the way and don't wait to answer everything until the end.

To explain the answer to the question, *Why do certain baseball player positions make more than others?*, you could go first through the high-level salary information showing the average salary for each type of player in a graph. Next, you could go through batting information for each of the positions to see if there is a correlation between batting and salary. Additionally, you could look at pitching or fielding statistics to get to the full detailed story of why certain positions make more than others.

Explaining your methodology

Make sure that you describe your methodology so that it gives your presentation context. You may need to go through a long process to get to the question's answer, but most audiences won't want or need that much explanation. Long explanations of the methodology are best left to colleagues that share your love of diving into the data to tell stories.

Using visualizations

Creating a visualization means taking query results and making graphic representations of the data, such as graphs or charts. The visualizations tell your story, and your words will add the required context, which follows along with the expression that a picture is worth a thousand words. You don't want your audience to sit there reading or watching you read from dry slides of paragraphs or tables, describing your data in great detail. Of course, the detail can and should be available to those who want or need to see it, but your presentation should be mostly visualizations, along with some context, for your findings to shine through.

Common mistakes to avoid in visualizations

There are several things to avoid in visualizations:

- **Jumping to conclusions**: Just because a baseball player's hits keep going up year after year doesn't mean that they will continue to do so the next year.
- **Switching colors**: Don't use one color in one chart for Player A and a different color in another chart for Player A.
- **Not labeling your charts**: Always label your chart's components and give them a descriptive title so that people don't have to draw their own conclusions regarding what you are trying to show.

- **Not providing context**: You may say that something increased 500%, but what are the actual numbers? 400% increase from 1 to 5 may seem like a lot or not very much, depending on the thing you are measuring. If a player had one hit last year and has five hits this year, that's a 400% increase, but it's still not very good, depending on how many times they batted in a year. Maybe they only batted in one game each year, which means they did a lot better from one year to the next, but if they batted in a lot of games, then five hits isn't that great.
- **Cherry-picking data**: Instead of using all the data to show the real story, maybe a player's batting average would look a lot better if you removed the games where they didn't get any hits. However, if you do this, you aren't giving the full picture.
- **Not properly formatting numbers for readability**: For example, it's hard to tell the scale of each of these numbers:

123456789.1234
1234.567891234

In this case, use a comma to make this a bit more obvious and do some rounding to make it easier to read:

123,456,789.12
1,234.57

- **Arbitrary scale**: Having your scale start at something other than zero to try to make the numbers seem better, worse, or just different than they are.

Using data visualization tools

There are many different and powerful visualization tools available, depending on your operating system and how much you want to pay for them. Some of these data visualization tools are as follows:

- **Microsoft Office** (https://www.office.com/): You can use Excel and PowerPoint to make your presentation with visualizations.
- **Google Documents** (https://about.google/products/): Free Google option with Google account signup.
- **OpenOffice** (https://www.openoffice.org/): Free version of Microsoft Office products.

- **Tableau** (https://www.tableau.com/): A custom visualization tool for building dashboards and data stories. You can get a 14-day free trial of their enterprise product, Tableau Desktop. There is also a free option you can install called Tableau Public, but it doesn't allow MySQL connections, and all your visualizations are published publically.
- **Power BI** (https://powerbi.microsoft.com/en-us/): A custom visualization tool for building dashboards and data stories. PowerBI is not available on Mac.

I will be using Google Sheets for the visualizations in this section, but you should be able to achieve similar results in the other visualization options listed previously. If you don't have a Google account, you can do something very similar in OpenOffice, which is the free version of Microsoft Excel.

To get started with visualizations in Google Sheets, you will need to execute the queries in MySQL first, then copy the data into Google Sheets to get the charts you will need for your visualizations. Let's get started:

1. You can execute the following query in MySQL Workbench:

```
USE lahmansbaseballdb;
SELECT f.pos as position, FORMAT(AVG(salary),0) as averagesalary
FROM salaries s
INNER JOIN fielding f
ON f.playerid = s.playerid
AND f.yearid = s.yearid
GROUP BY position
ORDER BY averagesalary;
```

2. Then, you can take the results of the query and place them into Google Sheets, as shown in the following screenshot:

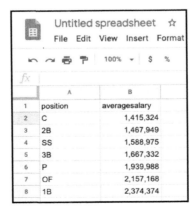

3. From there, you can create a bar chart to use as your visualization, as shown in the following screenshot:

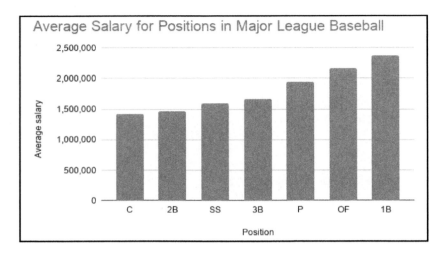

Here, we can see that catchers (**C**) get paid the least overall, while first basemen (**1B**) get paid the most overall.

4. To understand the possible reasons why this is the case, let's take a look at the batting average for each position by executing the following query:

```
USE lahmansbaseballdb;
SELECT f.pos as position, avg(h/ab) as battingaverage
FROM fielding f
INNER JOIN batting b
ON f.playerid = b.playerid
AND f.yearid = b.yearid
GROUP BY position
ORDER BY battingaverage;
```

5. After placing the data from the preceding query into Google Sheets, you can generate the following chart of batting averages for each position:

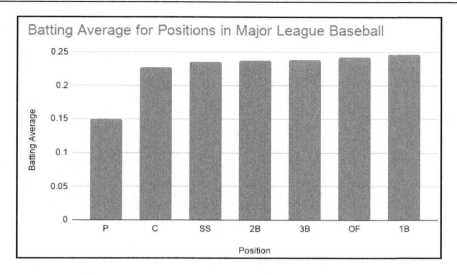

Here, from the last two charts, we can that when the player has a higher batting average, they get paid more, with a couple of exceptions. The pitcher (**P**) position has the lowest batting average but the second-highest pay. The main takeaway from this is that you don't hire a pitcher because of their exceptional batting skills – you hire them because they're a good pitcher. Another exception is that second baseman (**2B**) and shortstops (**SS**) are reversed in terms of pay and batting, with **SS** having a lower batting average than **2B** but higher pay.

6. This difference in pay may be able to be explained by fielding skills. Let's take a look at those by executing the following query:

```
USE lahmansbaseballdb;
SELECT f.pos as position, avg(innouts) as inningouts,
FROM fielding f
WHERE f.pos IN ('2B', 'SS')
GROUP BY position;
```

7. After placing the data from the preceding query into Google Sheets, you can generate the following chart of outs per inning for the **2B** and **SS** positions:

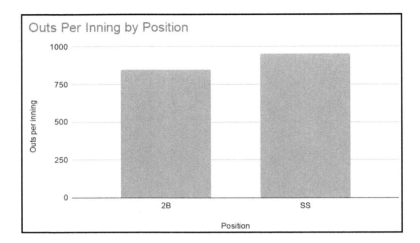

Looking at the preceding chart, we can see that shortstops have more outs per inning, which could account for why they get paid more than second basemen, even though they have a lower batting average than second basemen. Since we are looking at salary and understanding why certain positions make what they do, we could take this a step farther to understand why pitchers make the money they do. We can see that the salary isn't based on fielding or batting.

8. Execute the following query to look at the pitcher's earned runs:

```
USE lahmansbaseballdb;
SELECT format(avg(salary),0) as avgsalary,
CASE WHEN round((er/(ipouts/3))*9, 2) < 4.6
then 'ERA less than average runs scored per game'
ELSE 'ERA more than average runs scored per game'
END as eracalc
FROM pitching p
INNER JOIN salaries s
ON p.playerid = s.playerid
GROUP BY eracalc
ORDER BY avgsalary;
```

9. After placing the data from the preceding query into Google Sheets, you can generate the following chart of average salary by **earned run average** (**ERA**):

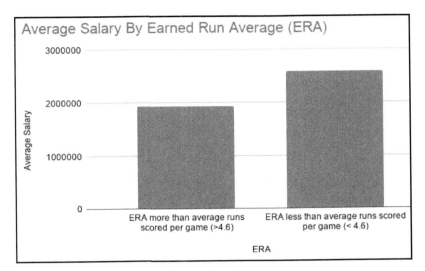

Let's take a look at how we got these numbers. The most crucial statistic in pitching is the ERA. The ERA is the average number of runs allowed by a pitcher per nine innings of pitching. So, first, you would need to determine the average number of runs per game with the following query:

```
USE lahmansbaseballdb;
SELECT avg(r/g) as avgrunspergame FROM teams;
```

The preceding query returns `4.60267536`. This is why we use greater than or less than `4.6` in our `CASE` calculation, as shown in the following query:

```
CASE WHEN round((er/(ipouts/3))*9, 2) < 4.6
then 'ERA less than average runs scored per game'
ELSE 'ERA more than average runs scored per game'
```

Plus, the formula for the ERA is (earned runs divided by innings pitched) x 9. Since we only have `ipouts` columns available to us, we need to calculate the inning pitched by dividing `ipouts` by three since there are three outs in an inning.

Here, we can see that the pitcher is paid based on their ERA, but there is possibly no accounting for why they have a lower salary than the first basemen.

10. You could extend your question to include the pay of managers and why they are paid how much they are. Your question would then become something like, *Why are all the members of baseball paid the amount they are?* Here's a query you can execute to get the winning ratio of managers and their average salary:

```
USE lahmansbaseballdb;
SELECT CASE WHEN w/g > .5 then 'winning record'
else 'losing record'
END as winratio,
FORMAT(AVG(salary), 0) as avgsalary
FROM managers m
INNER JOIN salaries s
ON s.playerid = m.playerid
GROUP BY winratio;
```

11. After placing the data from the preceding query into Google Sheets, you can generate the following chart of average salary by winning record versus losing record:

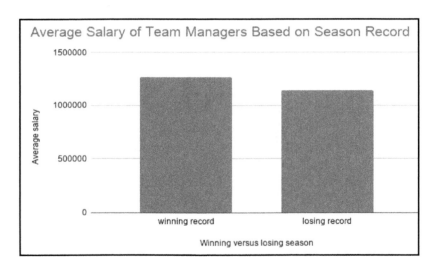

Here, we can see that, on average, a team manager will make more money if they have a winning season. You can see this in the following query, where the manager's average salary is compared to the position players in baseball:

```
USE lahmansbaseballdb;
SELECT 'manager' as position, FORMAT(AVG(salary), 0) as
averagesalary
FROM managers m
INNER JOIN salaries s
ON s.playerid = m.playerid
UNION
SELECT f.pos as position, FORMAT(AVG(salary),0) as averagesalary
FROM salaries s
INNER JOIN fielding f
ON f.playerid = s.playerid
AND f.yearid = s.yearid
GROUP BY position
ORDER BY averagesalary;
```

12. After placing the data from the preceding query into Google Sheets, you can generate the following chart of average salary by all positions in baseball, including the manager:

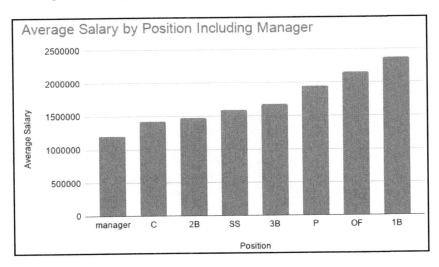

The findings are as follows:

- First basemen have the highest salary of any position player because they have the best batting statistics.
- Shortstops have a higher salary than second basemen because they have better fielding statistics.
- Pitchers have a higher salary when their ERA is less than the average runs scored in a baseball game.
- Managers have a higher salary based on having a winning record.

These charts, data, and findings have been placed in a Google Slides presentation, which you can find in the code files for this chapter.

Summary

In this chapter, you learned how to tell a story with your data. You learned how to find a narrative, including what types of stories can be told with data, including reporting, explanatory, predictive, correlation, and causation stories. You also learned about combining these types of stories to tell stories about how something changed over time, how to go from a big picture to a narrow focus and vice versa, and comparing and contrasting data. You then learned how to ask questions to get to the question or problem you want to solve. After, you learned how to use the statistical identity of your data to determine a story.

Then, you learned how to know your audience, including determining who they are and what would be a compelling presentation for them. Some of your audience may include decision-makers, colleagues, and the general public. You learned that different types of audiences require different presentations.

Next, you learned how to determine a presentation framework, including explaining the question, answer, and methodology. You learned to keep your question focused on one topic and not try to answer too many questions in one story. You also learned that, when answering a question, you need to stay focused on the question you are answering and not get distracted by unrelated data. After that, you learned that you need to explain your methodology, but different audiences will want or need different levels of explanation of your methodology.

Finally, you learned how to use visualizations in your presentations, as well as what types of visualization tools are available to use. You also learned about common mistakes to avoid in your visualizations.

In the next chapter, some best practices will be outlined regarding the topics we discussed in the previous chapters. We will also show you how to quickly reference best practices instead of having to go through each chapter.

Questions

1. What are the types of stories that we can tell with data?
2. How can you combine these stories to tell additional stories?
3. What kinds of people will your audience include?
4. Should you create more than one presentation to accommodate different audiences?
5. How do you determine a presentation framework?
6. How should you go about figuring out the question you want to answer?
7. How should you go about telling the answer to your question?
8. How do you explain your methodology?
9. What are some common mistakes to avoid in your visualizations?
10. What are some common visualization tools you can use?

Section 5: SQL Best Practices

5

This section will outline the best practices for database design, indexing, and querying and modifying data. and it will also provide an appendix of SQL syntax, so you can refer to it later without having to go through each chapter.

This section comprises the following chapters:

- Chapter 15, *Best Practices for Design and Querying*
- Chapter 16, *SQL Appendix*

15

Best Practices for Designing and Querying

In this chapter, you will learn about database best practices, including database design, indexing, and querying and modifying data. You learned about these topics throughout the previous chapters. This chapter will summarize and give additional tips regarding the best practices. This chapter will also provide a way for the more experienced among you to quickly reference best practices instead of having to go through each chapter.

In this chapter, we will cover the following topics:

- Best practices for database design
- Best practices for indexing
- Best practices for querying and modifying data

Technical requirements

You can refer to the code files of this chapter at `https://github.com/PacktPublishing/learn-sql-database-programming/tree/master/chapter-15`.

Best practices for database design

To implement the best design for your database, you will need to follow some basic guidelines and ensure that you have proper data integrity by implementing keys and constraints, naming your database objects correctly, and using the correct data types. Always remember to document the database with a data dictionary, an **entity-relationship diagram** (**ERD**), or both.

Understanding data integrity

Data integrity refers to the consistency and accuracy of data. In RDMS, keys enforce data integrity. A key forces values in a table to conform to a standard that you specify in the key. It's essential to enforce data integrity in your database so that you have accurate and consistent data. You want to ensure that incorrect values don't wind up in the database. You also want to ensure that data isn't in the wrong format. You don't want users to be able to delete information from one table that another table relies on.

There are many types of keys to ensure data integrity and enforce table relationships or referential integrity, as shown in the following list. For more detail about this topic, go to Chapter 1, *Introduction to Relational Database Management Systems.*

- **Entity integrity**: This is used to ensure that each row in a table is identifiably unique. Entity integrity is accomplished with a few different types of keys or constraints, including unique, not null, and primary key constraints:
    - **Unique constraint**: This is used to ensure that all values in a column or columns are different from each other.
    - **Not null constraint**: This is used to ensure that all values in a column are not null.
    - **Primary key**: This is used to ensure that all values in a column are not null and are unique. Each table can have only one primary key. There are two types of primary key: natural and surrogate. With a natural key, you are using unique columns, and the data in those columns exists outside the database (that is, in the business world). With a surrogate key, you are creating a column to hold a unique value for each row, and that value isn't used anywhere outside the database. If there was an obvious choice for a primary key (bearing in mind that this is unique and non-null), we could use that column. For instance, we could use an obvious primary key if one of these tables contained information about books. Each book has a unique, non-null ISBN. This natural key would be an excellent choice for a primary key. Still, when your tables contain multiple columns that are unique and not null to make a composite primary key, then it's better to have one column that uniquely identifies each row. You can then still have a unique, not null composite key on those columns that uniquely identify a row. Nevertheless, you should always ensure that the easiest way to identify a row with one column is with a surrogate primary key.

- **Referential integrity**: This refers to the consistency and accuracy between tables that can be linked together. Referential integrity is achieved by having a primary key on the parent table and a foreign key on the child table. When a foreign key is present, it must reference a valid, existing primary key in the parent table. A lack of referential integrity leads to incomplete data being returned without an indication of an error. It's basically as if your records are lost in the database, since they may never show up in reports or query results. It can cause all kinds of problems, such as strange results, lost orders, and in certain use cases, potentially life-and-death situations, such as patients not receiving proper treatments. The foreign key constraint can maintain three types of table relationships:
  - **One-to-one**: This type of relationship is created when one table has just one corresponding row in another table. An example of this could be a table with employees and computers; each employee has one computer.
  - **One-to-many**: This type of relationship is created when one table has none, one, or many corresponding rows in another table. An example of this could be a table with adults and children; an adult table row may have none, one, or many rows in the child table.
  - **Many-to-many**: This type of relationship is created when many rows in one table correspond to many rows in another table. An example of this could be customers and product tables; customers can purchase many products, and many products can be bought by many customers.
- **Domain integrity**: This is used to ensure that data values follow defined rules for the format, range, and value using check and default constraints:
  - **Check constraint**: This is used to ensure that all values in a column are within a range of values. A check constraint is enforced with user-defined conditions and is evaluated as either true or false.
  - **Default constraint**: This is used to ensure that all rows in a column have a value. A default constraint assigns a default value to a field.

You should always have a primary key on a table to ensure uniqueness, preferably with a natural key, but a surrogate key can be used if there is no apparent natural key. Use foreign keys and constraints as they are needed since you don't want to rely on developers to enforce database integrity via an application.

Naming conventions of database objects

Naming conventions are important for multiple reasons. You must ensure that you name things accurately and descriptively, while at the same time avoiding keywords that might add any kind of confusion to the naming. You must avoid adding spaces in the names, choose a proper case, and stick to one naming convention. You should also make sure that you only use permitted characters when naming a database object. You can read about this topic in more detail in `Chapter 4`, *Designing and Creating a Database*. The following list shows the object-naming conventions that you should follow:

- **Avoiding keywords**: There are lots of keywords or reserved words in MySQL. You should avoid naming your database and database objects with keywords. For instance, you wouldn't want to name your table `DATETIME` because this is a keyword reserved for the `datetime` data type.

- **Avoiding spaces**: If you use spaces in a database name or database object, you will always need to use backticks around that name when querying.

- **Using descriptive and accurate names**: Try to use full words when you can as abbreviations may be misunderstood. Name a table as accurately and descriptively regarding its purpose as possible so that it's easy to understand what's in the table just by looking at its name. For example, it may be hard to understand what's inside a table named `tblName`; it uses the abbreviation `tbl` for table and `Name`, which doesn't help you know what's inside it. If the table contains cat breeds, then you could name the table `CatBreeds`, and that will make it pretty clear what might be inside that table. An important decision regarding naming database objects is whether you should name them so that you know that it is a table, view, or stored procedure. You could name a table as `tblCatBreeds`, but it's best to leave the type of the object out of the name, so you would instead name the table `CatBreeds`.

- **Case and separating words**: There are different ideas behind how to use cases and how to separate words in database object names. You shouldn't use spaces to separate words, but you can use cases or underscore. The different types of case naming are as follows:

  - **lowercase naming**: This means that the entire object name is lowercase—for example, `catbreeds` or `dogbreeds` are table names with lowercase naming.

  - **UPPERCASE naming**: This means that the entire object name is in uppercase—for example, `CATBREEDS` or `DOGBREEDS` are table names with uppercase naming.

  - **camelCase naming**: This means that the name starts with a lowercase letter, and each new word starts with uppercase—for example, `catBreeds` and `dogBreeds` are table names with camelCase naming.

- **PascalCase naming**: This means that the first letter in each word is capitalized—for example, `CatBreeds` and `DogBreeds` are table names with PascalCase naming.

 Since MySQL doesn't support anything but lowercase naming by default, I would recommend using underscores (_) between words in database object naming systems if some of the names are long to avoid confusion with an all-lowercase naming system.

- **Allowed characters when naming database objects**: When creating a database object, you can't just use any character. You need to use the permitted characters, which include numbers (`0–9`), lowercase letters (`a–z`), uppercase letters (`A–Z`), dollar signs (`$`), and underscores (`_`).

Understanding what data types to use

Data types define the type of value that can be stored in a column. To decide which data type a column should be, you need to know what kind of data will be stored in that column. In MySQL, there are three main data types: string, numeric, and datetime.

Each data type has different characteristics based on the amount of space it takes up, the kind of values that can be stored, whether the values can be indexed, and how the values are compared to each other. It's best to choose the most precise type to optimize storage.

For example, don't store the first name in a column with `varchar(max)`, but instead store the first name in a column that would accommodate a long first name, such as `varchar(20)`; this way, you use much less storage for your first-name column. It's also vital to use numeric data types for numerical values and datetime data types for datetime values so that you don't have to convert these values from strings if you store numerical or datetime values in a string instead. Data types are covered in more detail in `Chapter 3`, *Understanding Data Types*.

Here are some reasons why you need to choose wisely:

- If you choose a data type that is too large for the data that it will hold, it will cause extra stress for your database because you will be using additional storage. The less storage you use, the more data you can have in memory (RAM). This will increase your database's performance.
- If you choose a data type that is too small for the data it will hold, this will cause your data to be truncated have failures upon insertion because the data type won't allow those sizes of data to be inserted.

The following table takes you through some examples of how to choose data types. It also helps you understand the reasoning behind why you would choose each data type:

Value(s) or type of data	Type in MySQL
State abbreviations that are always two letters, such as CA, CO—we would use CHAR here instead of VARCHAR because these values will always be the same length	CHAR(2)
State names such as California or Colorado—we would use VARCHAR here because there is a variable length, and we would set the VARCHAR to the longest length string, which in this case would be South or North Carolina.	VARCHAR(14)
Primary key, autoincremented column for a table.	Unsigned INT with auto_increment
Large amounts of text—consider putting TEXT columns in a separate table to optimize table performance. Database and table design will be covered in more detail in Chapter 4, *Designing and Creating a Database*.	TEXT
Storing files, including images—for the most part, you should use the filesystem for what it was intended for—storing files—and you should *not store them in the database*. If you do store them in the database, then store them in a separate table to avoid performance problems.	BLOB
Enumerated and set values—you should avoid these data types because if you ever decide to add something else to the ENUM or SET declaration, then MySQL will have to rebuild the table, and if you have a lot of rows, this could be very time consuming. In addition, developers can use logic on the application side to handle this much better than a MySQL table can.	ENUM or SET
Storing 0 and 1 values, such as whether a value is true or false.	BIT
Storing zip codes (such as 11155)	TINYINT

Storing money values (such as $115.25)	DECIMAL
Social security numbers (123-45-6789)—these are numbers, but you won't be doing calculations on them, and you may want to store the hyphens for proper formatting.	VARCHAR
Dates with time—don't use string types to store dates.	DATETIME
Scientific data or data where you don't need exact precision	Float or Double

The preceding table took you through some examples of how to choose data types. It also helped you understand the reason for selecting each data type.

Best practices for indexing

Indexing is a method of optimizing database performance by reducing the amount of disk usage when running a query against the database. Indexes are placed on column(s) in a table. Tables can have more than one index, but there tends to be an optimal number of indexes that you can have before indexes start hurting performance instead of helping it. The optimal number can vary depending on the table; this is why index tuning can be an art as well as a science. To properly index a table, you need to have a good understanding of how the data in the table is being used.

It's good to plan out the indexing that you will need in advance of adding data, if possible. When you add an index to a blank table, it adds it pretty much instantaneously. If you add an index later, it can take quite a while depending on how much data you have, especially when adding certain kinds of indexes that reorder the data in the table.

Understanding when to create indexes

You should create indexes for regularly used queries. Don't create indexes that don't have a use case for the queries being executed against a table. Don't guess at what indexes a table needs. Instead, you need to know the queries that are being executed, how often they are executed, and how important they are. Then you can decide how to create indexes based on the conditions used in the WHERE clause and by the columns used in the ORDER BY and GROUP BY clauses.

There is no right number of indexes on a table or columns in your indexes. Generally speaking, too few or too many indexes can make the performance of your database worse. This is why it's important to know what queries are being executed on the table so that you can understand best what would help the performance. Having only one index might work for some tables, but maybe some tables need five indexes. Try to keep the number of columns in an index to the minimum number required—for example, you don't want to add all the columns of your table to an index. An exception to this could be if a table only has a few columns.

Here are some important things to note about indexing:

- You should create indexes for uniqueness (primary key) and referential integrity (foreign keys). This will help ensure your database's data integrity.
- Indexing doesn't speed up everything that happens in a database table. It won't speed up writes (the insertion, updating, and deletion of data); it only speeds up reading (querying data from the database), so you need to be careful that you don't add an index for reads that then slows down writes too much. Indexing slows down writes because the index has to be updated each time data is written.
- The order of the columns in indexes matters. If you have the columns in the index written as `managerid` then `yearid`, and you want to filter on just `yearid`, then your query filtering on `yearid` might not even use the index. You may need an index that has `yearid` first or maybe as the only column in the index. Also, just filtering on `managerid` would give you good performance even if you didn't use `yearid` in the filter, since the query would use the `managerid` then the `yearid` indexes.
- Indexes can take a lot of storage. A clustered index shouldn't take upspace on disk since it's an ordering of the data that is already sitting on disk, but nonclustered indexes can take up quite a bit of room depending on the size of the table and the number of columns in the index.
- Indexing columns that contain a lot of nonunique values may not provide much performance improvement. If you have to decide between the columns to index, then you should choose a column with more variability, such as the first name rather than state names.

Best practices for querying and modifying data

To query and modify data appropriately, you will need to follow some basic guidelines—including the following guidelines for writing clean code—to make your queries fast.

Understanding how to write clean code

It's important to write clean code for readability and ease of use so that you and others can easily understand what your code is trying to do. This can be done by following these tips:

- Formatting your SQL code for readability is important so that you and others can easily understand your SQL code. SQL ignores whitespace, making it easy to format for readability. You can write SQL code all on one line, but it's much easier to read if you place different parts of the SQL on separate lines.

  For example, say that you wrote some code like the following query, which has all the code on one line and wraps around:

  ```
  CREATE TABLE `managers` (`managerkey` smallint NOT NULL, `playerid`
  varchar(9) NOT NULL, `yearid` year(4) NOT NULL, `teamid` char(3) NOT
  NULL);
  ```

  Instead, think about writing it so that it's easier to read, as is shown in the following query, where each piece is on a separate line:

  ```
  CREATE TABLE `managers` (
  `managerkey` smallint NOT NULL,
  `playerid` varchar(9) NOT NULL,
  `yearid` year(4) NOT NULL);
  ```

  When writing queries, you can use the beautify button in MySQL Workbench to make your code nicely formatted. The beautify button is shown in the following screenshot:

The following screenshot shows a query before the beautify button is used:

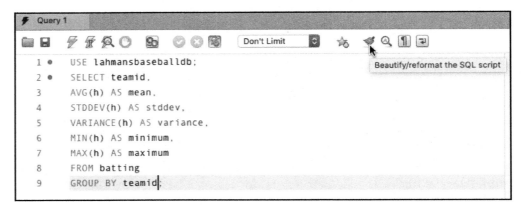

The following screenshot shows you the same query after using the beautify button:

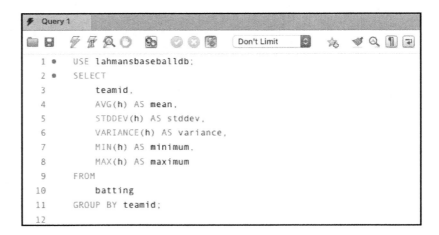

- Use uppercase for keywords and lowercase for everything else. This way, it's easier to see the keywords in a query or script.
- Add comments to your SQL code to ensure that it's clear to you and others what is being done in the script. You may want to save this script for later or share it with others, and it will make a lot of difference if you comment your code with explanations. When creating comments, it's important to note a few things, such as who created the code, when the code was created, who last modified the code, the date of the modification, and an explanation of why it was created or modified. More details are provided in Chapter 6, *Querying a Single Table*.

Understanding query optimization

To make sure your queries are optimized and run as quickly as they can, you want to ensure that they are correctly using the indexes on the table you are querying. If you use indexes properly with your queries, then you will have less blocking and deadlocking to deal with because the index will allow you to query data more quickly.

There is a simple way to see how MySQL will run your query, and that is to append `EXPLAIN` to the front of your query. For example, you can see `EXPLAIN` being used in the following query:

```
USE lahmansbaseballdb;
EXPLAIN SELECT playerid, g_all, g_batting, g_defense
FROM appearances;
```

What `EXPLAIN` will do is give you a table of information about how it's going to run the query. The preceding query will provide you with the results shown in the following screenshot:

id	select_type	table	partitions	type	possible_keys	key	key_len	ref	rows	filtered	Extra
1	SIMPLE	appearances	NULL	ALL	NULL	NULL	NULL	NULL	105113	100.00	NULL

Let's look at an example query that uses some more clauses to see some more information in our `EXPLAIN` result:

```
USE lahmansbaseballdb;
EXPLAIN SELECT distinct playerid, g_all, g_batting, g_defense
FROM appearances
WHERE playerid LIKE 'a%'
ORDER BY playerid;
```

The preceding query gives us the results shown in the following screenshot:

id	select_type	table	partitions	type	possible_keys	key	key_len	ref	rows	filtered	Extra
1	SIMPLE	appearances	NULL	ALL	NULL	NULL	NULL	NULL	105113	11.11	Using where; Using temporary; Using filesort

Now we can see some more interesting information with our `EXPLAIN` results. The **filtered** column shows us that we are only getting approximately 11.11% of the rows returned. It also shows that we are using a `WHERE` clause, that the query needs a temporary table, and that MySQL had to use an extra pass to sort the records. In this specific case, since it's such a small table and it won't be growing quickly, you could get away with not changing anything, but if this table were to become much larger, then you would need to account for these issues.

Let's say that we knew this table will soon grow much larger. How could we fix these issues that we are seeing? Let's take a step back and examine how this query could be changed to use an index. Let's say that we ran the following query instead:

```
USE lahmansbaseballdb;
EXPLAIN SELECT distinct playerid
FROM appearances
WHERE playerid LIKE 'a%'
ORDER BY playerid;
```

In the following screenshot, we can see the results from the preceding query:

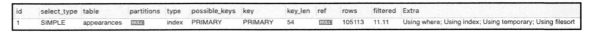

id	select_type	table	partitions	type	possible_keys	key	key_len	ref	rows	filtered	Extra
1	SIMPLE	appearances	NULL	index	PRIMARY	PRIMARY	54	NULL	105113	11.11	Using where; Using index; Using temporary; Using filesort

Since we removed the g_all, g_batting, and g_defense columns from the SELECT query, we can see that the query is now using the PRIMARY key (which is the clustered index on this table), so this will make the query faster, but it doesn't have all the columns that we may need in our query. This is when we need to think about whether we need those columns that we've removed, and if so, then we may need to add a new index to account for this. This is called adding an index to cover a query. Addressing similar concerns as we did previously in this section, this is a small table that isn't going to grow, so it may not be necessary to change anything. Still, if we were going to account for a table that might become significantly larger, and we are planning to run this query frequently, we could add a nonclustered index to cover the additional columns in the query. You also need keep in mind that when you add indexes you will affect other queries, possibly making them less efficient, and you will slow down insertions, updates, and deletions.

You can also use a graphical interface for the query execution plan. To do this, you will need to run your query first:

```
USE lahmansbaseballdb;
SELECT distinct playerid, g_all, g_batting, g_defense
FROM appearances
WHERE playerid LIKE 'a%'
ORDER BY playerid;
```

Then click **Query** in the MySQL Workbench menu, then **Explain Current Statement**, as shown in the following screenshot:

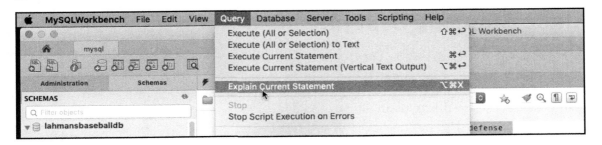

This will bring up a **Visual Explain** plan panel below the query window and above the output window, as shown in the following screenshot:

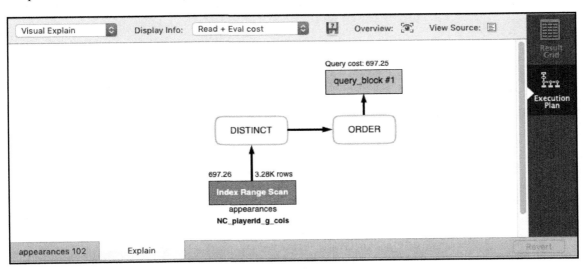

The preceding screenshot shows that the query is using the `NC_playerid_g_cols` index, and it only has to use a range of the index, which is good since it does not have to scan the entire index. It gives you the approximate row count and the time it will take to return the query, which is **3.28K** rows and **697.26** milliseconds, respectively. It also tells you the table it will be using, **appearances**. You can then see that it checks for distinct values and orders them, and then returns the query results.

Understanding best practices when querying data

To build fast queries, you need to follow some best practices when querying data. First, it's important to understand that you have to write the clauses in a specific order or your query will fail, as shown in the following list:

- SELECT statement best practices:
  - Use SELECT fields instead of SELECT *. This is taxing on database resources, especially if a table has a lot of columns. It's best to write a query just to select the columns that you know you will need instead of selecting them all with SELECT *.
  - Use column aliases, especially when using functions. When you use a function in the WHERE clause, it will put the function as the name of the column instead of a more useful name. While giving the column an alias doesn't speed up your query, it will make it easier to know what you see in the results—for example, if you execute SELECT UPPER('ab'), the column in the results will be displayed as shown in the following screenshot:

Whereas if you give the function an alias such as SELECT UPPER('ab') in uppercase, then the results will have a better column name, as shown in the following screenshot:

- Avoid using SELECT DISTINCT. You can use DISTINCT to remove duplicates from query results, but this can be an intensive process that uses a lot of database resources depending on the size of the table. It may be better just to add more columns to your SELECT statement to ensure the distinctiveness of the results. One exception to this can be if you are trying to get a list of distinct values in one column only.

- WHERE clause best practices:
  - Only use wildcards at the end of a string. Wildcards, such as the percent sign (%) and underscore (_), at the beginning of a string are slower to process because the user won't be able to use any indexes on the table.
  - Use an underscore (_) wildcard instead of a percent sign (%) when possible. This is because the underscore will perform faster than the percent sign since the underscore matches on one character and the percent sign matches on one or more characters.
  - Avoid WHERE clauses with functions. Functions in the WHERE clause can cause the query to be a lot slower because the query won't be able to use any indexes on the table. For example, the following query will be slow:

    ```
    SELECT column WHERE UPPER(column) = 'ab';
    ```

    However, the following query will be faster:

    ```
    SELECT column WHERE column = 'ab';
    ```

- Use WHERE instead of HAVING to filter, when possible. HAVING is used to filter query results in a GROUP BY. WHERE can filter those results before it even gets to the GROUP BY, which makes your query less expensive to run. For example, if you are trying to filter by a count in a grouping, then you will need to use a HAVING clause, but if you are also trying to filter by a date range, then you should use a WHERE clause first.
- Use lookup tables instead of IN clauses.
- JOIN clause best practices:
  - Use table aliases. It's more human-readable to use table aliases when joining tables together. Look at the following query:

    ```
    SELECT tablea.col, tableb.col
    FROM tablea
    INNER JOIN tableb
    ON tablea.id = tableb.id;
    ```

    Instead, you should use this query:

    ```
    SELECT a.col, b.col
    FROM tablea a
    INNER JOIN tableb b
    ON a.id = b.id;
    ```

- ORDER BY clause best practices:
    - Avoid using column numbers in the ORDER BY clause. It can be confusing if you use column numbers instead of the column names in the ORDER BY clause. In addition, if you change the columns in the SELECT statement, you will have no idea what the column numbers in the ORDER BY clause corresponded to.

      For example, you should execute the following query:

      ```
      SELECT col1, col2 FROM tablename ORDER BY col1, col2;
      ```

      You should not execute the following query :

      ```
      SELECT col1, col2 FROM tablename ORDER BY 1, 2;
      ```

- Don't order by too many columns. If you order by all the columns in the table, then there will be a performance impact on your query, so you need to be careful when choosing which and how many columns to use in your ORDER BY clause.
- LIMIT clause best practices:
    - Use LIMIT when running a query for the first time. This can help you to see a subset of your query results to check whether you are on the right track without returning a lot of results that may be too taxing on the database system.
- Other best practices:
    - Use transactions and error handling in stored procedures and functions. You want to be able to group functionality and have it roll back as one if something fails. It's essential to understand what error happened so that you can troubleshoot how to fix any issues that come up.
    - Avoid subqueries when you can. They are more intensive than a JOIN—for example, the following query will be more intensive:

      ```
      SELECT a.col,
       (SELECT b.col
       FROM tableb b
       WHERE b.id = a.id) AS colname
      FROM tablea a;
      ```

      The following query will be less intensive:

      ```
      SELECT a.col, b.col
      FROM tablea a
      LEFT JOIN tableb b
      ON b.id=a.id;
      ```

- When running intensive analytical queries, run them during nonpeak hours, or if there is a secondary readable database, execute them there. Intensive queries include queries that will return a lot of results or query large tables. You may be able to schedule them to execute at nonpeak hours so that you don't have to work at strange hours to execute them.
- Don't take user input to build a query. Instead, use a stored procedure or function to take values via variables, but with the caveat that if an application is passing through values into the stored procedure or function, then it should check values before they are passed in to avoid attacks on your database.
- Use stored procedures, functions, or views for queries that are used repeatedly. This ensures that the queries are more easily maintained. It can also ensure that similar functionality is stored together. It's also possible to limit access at a more granular level by granting user access to just one view or stored procedure.

Understanding best practices when modifying data

To build fast queries, you need to follow some best practices when modifying data.

- `INSERT` statement best practices:
  - Always use column names in `INSERT`. To avoid confusion, it's best to specify column names in your `INSERT` statements. For example, the following query may work fine:

    ```
    INSERT INTO tablename VALUES (1, 'testing', 100);
    ```

  - The previous query may encounter an error if the column types change or another column is added, so it's better to use the following query instead:

    ```
    INSERT INTO tablename (id, name, value) VALUES (1, 'testing', 100);
    ```

- Use small batches when running large `INSERT`, `UPDATE`, and `DELETE` statements. This will avoid issues with the `INSERT`, `UPDATE`, or `DELETE` queries blocking other queries that are trying to execute concurrently. You can use a loop to limit the number of rows that will be inserted, updated, or deleted until you reach the total number of rows you need to affect.

- DELETE statement best practices:
    - If you are deleting all the data in a table, then you should use TRUNCATE instead. TRUNCATE is a fast option for deleting all data from a table. The following syntax shows an example of its use:

```
TRUNCATE TABLE tablename;
```

Summary

In this chapter, you learned about the best practices for databases. You also learned about the best practices for database design, including which data types to use.

You also learned about the best practices for indexing, including indexing naming conventions, how indexes relate to data integrity with primary and foreign keys, how indexing impacts performance, and when to create indexes. You also learned about the best practices for querying and modifying data, including how to write clean code. You also learned about the best practices for querying data, with specific tips on SQL statements and clauses, as well as tips on best practices when modifying data.

In the next chapter, the SQL commands discussed in this book will be outlined for quick reference. The syntax for querying data, modifying data, and designing databases and tables will also be included. This will help you by providing a quick reference guide so that you won't need to go back through all the chapters of this book to check your syntax.

Questions

1. Why is data integrity important for your database?
2. Why is it important to name your database objects by following naming standards?
3. Why is it important to choose the right data types for your data?
4. Is there a right number of indexes or columns in an index on a table?
5. How do you see which indexes a query is using?
6. How do you write clean code?
7. What are some best practices when writing SQL statements?
8. What are some best practices when using the WHERE clause?
9. What are some best practices when using an INSERT statement?
10. What are some best practices when using a DELETE statement?

16
SQL Appendix

In this chapter, the SQL commands that are mentioned in this book will be outlined for quick reference. This includes the syntax for querying data, modifying data, and designing databases and tables. This chapter will help you by providing a quick reference guide so that you won't have to go back through all the chapters to check the syntax, but if you require more details regarding how the syntax works, you can refer to the specific chapter for that information.

In this chapter, we will cover the following topics:

- SQL for designing databases
- SQL for selecting data
- SQL for modifying data
- SQL expressions
- Advanced query techniques
- Programmable objects

SQL for designing databases

This section takes you through some example syntax for creating and altering databases in MySQL. For more details on this syntax, visit Chapter 4, *Designing and Creating a Database*, and Chapter 8, *Modifying Data and Table Structures*. These chapters will also outline the differences in syntax for Oracle, PostgreSQL, and SQL Server.

Syntax for creating a database

In order to create a database, you can use the following sample syntax:

```
CREATE DATABASE yourschema;
```

Syntax for creating and altering tables

In order to create a table, you can use the following sample syntax. The items in square brackets are optional:

```
CREATE TABLE schemaname.tablename (
col1name datatype [constraintinfo] [AUTO_INCREMENT],
col2name datatype [constraintinfo],
...
colNname datatype [constraintinfo]
[PRIMARY KEY (col1name),]
[UNIQUE KEY uniquekeyname (col1name),]);
```

You can alter a table in several different ways, as follows:

- Altering a table to add a column:

```
ALTER TABLE tablename
ADD COLUMN colname datatype [constraintinfo] [AFTER othercolname];
```

- Altering a table to add multiple columns:

```
ALTER TABLE tablename
ADD COLUMN col1name datatype [constraintinfo] [AFTER othercolname],
ADD COLUMN col2name datatype [constraintinfo] [AFTER
othercolname1],
```

- Altering a table to drop a column:

```
ALTER TABLE tablename
DROP COLUMN colname;
```

- Altering a table to drop multiple columns:

```
ALTER TABLE tablename
DROP COLUMN col1name,
DROP COLUMN col2name;
```

- Altering a table to rename a column:

```
ALTER TABLE tablename
CHANGE COLUMN oldcolname newcolname datatype;
```

- Altering a table to change the data type of a column:

```
ALTER TABLE tablename
CHANGE COLUMN colname colname newdatatype;
```

- Altering a table to change a column constraint:

```
ALTER TABLE tablename
CHANGE COLUMN colname colname datatype newconstrainttype;
```

- Altering a table to add a column constraint:

```
ALTER TABLE tablename
ADD CONSTRAINT constraintname constraintinfo;
```

- Altering a table to drop a check constraint:

```
ALTER TABLE tablename
DROP CHECK constraintname;
```

- Altering a table to drop a foreign key constraint:

```
ALTER TABLE tablename
DROP FOREIGN KEY fkname;
```

- Altering a table to drop a primary key constraint:

```
ALTER TABLE tablename
DROP PRIMARY KEY;
```

- Dropping a table:

```
DROP TABLE tablename;
```

Syntax for creating and altering indexes

To see what index a query has, you can use the following sample syntax:

```
EXPLAIN SELECT statement;
```

To create an index, you can use the following sample syntax:

```
ALTER TABLE tablename
ADD INDEX indexname (columnnames);
```

To change an index in MySQL, you need to drop it and then add it back again using the following sample syntax:

```
ALTER TABLE tablename
DROP INDEX indexname;
```

SQL for selecting data

This section takes you through some example syntax for selecting data in MySQL. For more details on this syntax, visit Chapter 6, *Querying a Single Table*; Chapter 7, *Querying Multiple Tables*; and Chapter 10, *Grouping and Summarizing Data.* These chapters will also outline the differences in syntax for Oracle, PostgreSQL, and SQL Server.

Syntax for selecting data

To select all columns from one table, you can use the following sample syntax:

```
SELECT * FROM tablename;
```

To select one or more columns from one table, you can use the following sample syntax:

```
SELECT col1, col2, col3 FROM tablename;
```

To select from a specified database, you can use the following sample syntax:

```
USE databasename;
SELECT col1, col2, col3 FROM tablename;
```

To select distinct records from a table, you can use the following sample syntax:

```
SELECT DISTINCT col1, col2 FROM tablename;
```

To limit and offset the number of records that are returned, you can use the following sample syntax:

```
SELECT col1, col2 FROM tablename
LIMIT 500 OFFSET 1000;
```

To comment on your SQL query, you can use the following sample syntax:

```
# this is single line comment

/*
this is a
multi line
comment
*/
```

Syntax for filtering data

To limit results using WHERE, you can use the following sample syntax:

```
SELECT col1, col2
FROM tablenameWHERE condition(s);
```

To limit results using AND with WHERE, you can use the following sample syntax:

```
SELECT col1, col2
FROM tablename
WHERE condition AND condition;
```

To limit results using OR with WHERE, you can use the following sample syntax:

```
SELECT col1, col2
FROM tablename
WHERE condition OR condition;
```

To limit results using IN with WHERE, you can use the following sample syntax:

```
SELECT col1, col2
FROM tablename
WHERE col1 IN (values);
```

To limit results using NOT IN with WHERE, you can use the following sample syntax:

```
SELECT col1, col2
FROM tablename
WHERE col1 NOT IN (values);
```

To limit results using BETWEEN with WHERE, you can use the following sample syntax:

```
SELECT col1, col2
FROM tablename
WHERE col1 BETWEEN value and anothervalue;
```

To limit results using NOT BETWEEN with WHERE, you can use the following sample syntax:

```
SELECT col1, col2
FROM tablename
WHERE col1 NOT BETWEEN value and anothervalue;
```

To limit results using the percent sign (%) with WHERE, you can use the following sample syntax:

```
SELECT col1, col2
FROM tablename
WHERE col1 LIKE 'value%';
```

To limit results using the underscore (_) with WHERE, you can use the following sample syntax:

```
SELECT col1, col2
FROM tablename
WHERE col1 LIKE 'value_';
```

Syntax for ordering results

To order results by one column using ORDER BY, you can use the following sample syntax. The WHERE clause is optional:

```
SELECT col1, col2, col3
FROM table
WHERE condition(s)
ORDER BY col1;
```

To order results by multiple columns using ORDER BY, you can use the following sample syntax. The WHERE clause is optional:

```
SELECT col1, col2, col3
FROM table
WHERE condition(s)
ORDER BY col2, col1;
```

To order results in descending order using ORDER BY, you can use the following sample syntax. The WHERE clause is optional:

```
SELECT col1, col2, col3
FROM table
WHERE condition(s)
ORDER BY col2 DESC, col1 DESC;
```

Syntax for joining tables

To join tables using an inner join, you can use the following sample syntax:

```
SELECT column(s)
FROM table1 AS a
JOIN table2 AS b
ON a.id = b.id
```

To create a join using the left outer join, you can use the following sample syntax:

```
SELECT column(s)
FROM table1 AS a
LEFT OUTER JOIN table2 AS b
ON a.id = b.id
```

To create a join using the right outer join, you can use the following sample syntax:

```
SELECT column(s)
FROM table1 AS a
RIGHT OUTER JOIN table2 AS b
ON a.id = b.id
```

Syntax for grouping results

To group data using GROUP BY, you can use the following sample syntax. WHERE and ORDER BY are optional:

```
SELECT column(s)
FROM table
WHERE condition(s)
GROUP BY columns(s)
ORDER BY column(s);
```

To get subtotals and totals with GROUP BY and ROLLUP, you can use the following sample syntax:

```
SELECT col1, col2, col3
FROM table
GROUP BY col2, col1, WITH ROLLUP;
```

Syntax for filtering grouped results

To limit results in GROUP BY using HAVING, you can use the following sample syntax. WHERE and ORDER BY are optional:

```
SELECT column(s)
FROM table
WHERE condition(s)
GROUP BY columns(s)
HAVING condition(s)
ORDER BY column(s);
```

Syntax for using aggregate functions

For numeric functions, you can use the following sample syntax:

```
SELECT
 ROUND(AVG(col1),1) AS rounded_average,
 MAX(col1) AS maximum,
 MIN(g_all) AS minimum,
 FORMAT(COUNT(col1), 0) AS count_formatted,
 SUM(col1) AS sum
FROM tablename;
```

For statistical functions, you can use the following sample syntax:

```
SELECT
     STDDEV(col1)      AS 'standard_deviation',
     VARIANCE(col1)    AS 'variance'
FROM tablename;
```

SQL for modifying data

This section takes you through some example syntax for modifying data in MySQL. For more details on this syntax, visit Chapter 8, *Modifying Data and Table Structures*. This chapter will also outline the differences in syntax for Oracle, PostgreSQL, and SQL Server.

Syntax for inserting data

To INSERT a single row, you can use the following sample syntax:

```
INSERT INTO tablename (col1, col2, col3)
VALUES ('value1','value2',value3);
```

To INSERT multiple rows, you can use the following sample syntax:

```
INSERT INTO tablename (col1, col2, col3)
VALUES ('value1','value2',value3),
       ('value5','value6',value7),
       ('value8','value9',value10);
```

To create a table and insert data from another table into the new table, you can use the following sample syntax:

```
CREATE TABLE newtablename
SELECT * FROM existingtablename
```

To insert data from one table into another, you can use the following sample syntax:

```
INSERT INTO existingtable
SELECT * FROM anotherexistingtable
```

Syntax for updating data

To UPDATE certain data in a table, you can use the following sample syntax:

```
UPDATE tablename
SET col1 = 'value1', col2 = value2
WHERE col1 = 'value3';
```

To UPDATE all the data in a table, you can use the following sample syntax:

```
UPDATE tablename
SET col1 = 'value1';
```

To UPDATE data in a table based on a query, you can use the following sample syntax:

```
UPDATE tablename tn
INNER JOIN anothertablename atn
ON tn.col1 = atn.col1
SET tn.col2 = atn.col2;
```

Syntax for deleting data

To DELETE data from a table, you can use the following sample syntax:

```
DELETE FROM tablename
WHERE col1 = 'value1';
```

To DELETE all the data from a table, you can use the following sample syntax:

```
DELETE FROM tablename;
```

For a faster way to delete all the data from a table, you can use the following sample syntax:

```
TRUNCATE TABLE tablename;
```

Syntax for SQL transactions

To put a SQL query in a TRANSACTION and COMMIT the transaction, you can use the following sample syntax:

```
START TRANSACTION;
UPDATE tablename
SET col1 = 'value1';
COMMIT;
```

To put a SQL query in a TRANSACTION and ROLLBACK the transaction, you can use the following sample syntax:

```
START TRANSACTION;
UPDATE tablename
SET col1 = 'value1';
ROLLBACK;
```

To put a SQL query in a TRANSACTION using savepoints to ROLLBACK the transaction, you can use the following sample syntax:

```
START TRANSACTION;
SAVEPOINT firstsavepoint;
INSERT INTO tablename
SELECT * FROM anothertablename
WHERE col1 = 'value1';
SAVEPOINT secondsavepoint;
DELETE FROM tablename
WHERE col1 = 'value2';
ROLLBACK TO firstsavepoint;
```

SQL expressions

This section takes you through some example syntax for using expressions in MySQL. For more details on this syntax, visit Chapter 9, *Working with Expressions*. That chapter also outlines the differences in syntax for Oracle, PostgreSQL, and SQL Server.

Types of expressions

To use literal values in expressions, you can use the following sample syntax:

```
SELECT 'string', 1, 1.23, NULL;
```

To use **comparison operators**, you can use the following examples:

- SELECT column FROM table WHERE column = 100: This is an example of equal to.
- SELECT column FROM table WHERE column = 'value': This is an example of equal to.
- SELECT column FROM table WHERE column != 1000: This is an example of not equal to.

- `SELECT column FROM table WHERE column != 'value'`: This is an example of not equal to.
- `SELECT column FROM table WHERE column <> 1000`: This is an example of not equal to.
- `SELECT column FROM table WHERE column <> 'value'`: This is an example of not equal to.
- `SELECT column FROM table WHERE column >= 1`: This is an example of greater than or equal to.
- `SELECT column FROM table WHERE column > 1`: This is an example of greater than.
- `SELECT column FROM table WHERE column < 1`: This is an example of less than.
- `SELECT column FROM table WHERE column <= 1`: This is an example of less than or equal to.

To use **logical operators**, you can use the following examples:

- `SELECT column FROM table WHERE column1 <> 1 AND column2 = 2`: This is an example of the `AND` operator.
- `SELECT column FROM table WHERE column1 <> 1 OR column2 = 2`: This is an example of the `OR` operator.
- `SELECT column FROM table WHERE column1 IN (1, 2, 3)`: This is an example of the `IN` operator.
- `SELECT column FROM table WHERE column1 BETWEEN 1 AND 4`: This is an example of the `BETWEEN` with `AND` operator.
- `SELECT column FROM table WHERE column1 NOT IN (1, 2, 3)`: This is an example of the `NOT IN` operator.
- `SELECT column FROM table WHERE column1 IS NOT NULL`: This is an example of the `IS NOT NULL` operator.
- `SELECT column FROM table WHERE column1 LIKE 'abc%'`: This is an example of the `LIKE` operator.

To use **mathematical operators**, you can use the following examples:

- `SELECT column FROM table WHERE column + 2`: This is an example of addition.
- `SELECT column FROM table WHERE column - 2`: This is an example of subtraction.

- `SELECT column FROM table WHERE column * 2`: This is an example of multiplication.
- `SELECT column FROM table WHERE column / 2`: This is an example of division.

For **string functions**, you can use the following examples:

- `CHAR_LENGTH('string')`: This will return 6 since it's counting the number of characters in the string.
- `LENGTH('string')`: This will return 6 since it's the length in bytes.
- `CONCAT('string1', 'string2')`: This concatenates `string1` and `string2`; for example, `string1string2`.
- `LEFT('string', 3)`: This returns `str` because those are the first three characters.
- `RIGHT('string', 3)`: This returns `ing` because those are the last three characters.
- `LOWER('String')`: This returns string since it converts all letters into lowercase.
- `UPPER('String')`: This returns `STRING` since it converts all letters into lowercase.
- `LTRIM('    String')`: This returns `string` since it removes all the spaces at the beginning of the string.
- `RTRIM('String    ')`: This returns `string` since it removes all the spaces at the end of the string.
- `TRIM('    String    ')`: This returns `string` since it removes all the spaces at the beginning and the end of the string.
- `LPAD('string', 8, 'x')`: This returns `xxstring` since it pads at the beginning of the string. The middle parameter – 8, in this case – is setting the length of the string after the padding.
- `RPAD('string', 8, 'x')` : This returns `stringxx` since it pads at the end of the string. The middle parameter – 8, in this case – is setting the length of the string after the padding.
- `REPLACE('string', 'str', 'ing')`: This returns `inging`.
- `SUBSTRING('string', 2, 3)`: This returns `tri`.
- `REVERSE('string')`: This returns `gnirts` since this reverses the string.

For **numeric functions**, you can use the following examples:

- AVG(rating): This will return the average of all the values in a rating column.
- COUNT(column1): This will return the count of values in column1. column1 can contain either strings, dates, or numbers.
- MAX(rating): This will return the maximum rating in a column of rating values.
- MIN(rating): This will return the minimum rating in a column of rating values.
- ROUND(123.456, 2): This will return 123.46 since the number will be rounded up to two decimal places.
- SUM(number): This will return the sum of the values in a column of number values.
- FORMAT(1234.4567, 2): This will return 1,234.46 since the number will be rounded up to two decimal places. A comma is added for readability.

For date or time functions, you can use the following examples:

- CURRENT_DATE(): Returns date in YYYY-MM-DD format, that is, 2020-01-11.
- CURRENT_TIME(): Returns time in HH:MM:SS format, that is, 21:09:27.
- CURRENT_TIMESTAMP(): Returns datetime in YYYY-MM-DD HH:MM:SS format, that is, 2020-01-11 21:10:23.
- NOW(): Returns datetime in YYYY-MM-DD HH:MM:SS format, that is, 2020-01-11 21:10:23.
- DATE_FORMAT(date, format): Here, date is a valid date value and format is the format you want the date in. For example, DATE_FORMAT(NOW(), %m-%d-%y'), will return 01-12-20.
- TIME_FORMAT(time, format): Here, time is a valid time value and format is the format you want the time in.

For **advanced functions**, you can use the following examples:

- SELECT CURRENT_USER();: Returns root@% (depending on who you are logged in as).
- SELECT DATABASE();: Returns lahmansbaseballdb (depending on which database you are using).
- SELECT VERSION();: Returns 8.0.18 (depending on your MySQL version).
- CAST(value as datatype): Converts the value from one datatype into another datatype.

- `CONVERT(value, datatype)`: Similar to the `cast` function.
- `IF(condition, value if true, value if false)`: Returns the result based on the result of the condition.
- `CASE`

```
    WHEN condition1 THEN result1
    WHEN condition2 THEN result2
    WHEN conditionN THEN resultN
        ELSE result
```

`END;`: The result is shown based on the condition that returns true.

To work with **NULL values**, you can use the following examples:

- `SELECT NULLIF(1, 1)`: Returns `NULL`.
- `SELECT NULLIF(1, 2)`: Returns `1`.
- `SELECT IFNULL(NULL, 'testing')`: Returns `'testing'`.
- `SELECT IFNULL(NULL, NULL)`: Returns `NULL`.
- `SELECT ISNULL(NULL)`: Returns `1`.
- `SELECT ISNULL('testing')`: Returns `0`.

Syntax for using generated columns

To create a virtual generated column, you can use the following sample syntax:

```
ALTER TABLE tablename
ADD COLUMN columnname datatype GENERATED ALWAYS AS (expression) AFTER
column;
```

To create a stored generated column, you can use the following sample syntax:

```
ALTER TABLE tablename
ADD COLUMN columnname datatype GENERATED ALWAYS AS (expression) STORED
AFTER column;
```

Advanced query techniques

This section takes you through some example syntax for advanced query techniques in MySQL. For more details on this syntax, visit `Chapter 11`, *Advanced Query Techniques*. This chapter will also outline the differences in syntax for Oracle, PostgreSQL, and SQL Server.

Syntax for subqueries

In the following code, the query inside parentheses is the inner query, while the query outside parentheses is the outer query.

To use a subquery, you can follow the following sample syntax:

```
SELECT col1
FROM table1
WHERE col1 IN
     (SELECT col1 FROM table 2 WHERE col1 = 'test')
```

For a non-correlated subquery in WHERE with multiple values being returned, you can follow the following sample syntax. The square brackets indicate you could use any one of those options in place of those listed options:

```
SELECT column(s)
FROM tablename
WHERE column [IN | NOT IN | ANY | ALL | SOME]
             (SELECT col1 from tablename WHERE condition(s));
```

For a non-correlated subquery in WHERE with a single value being returned, you can follow the following sample syntax. The square brackets indicate you could use any one of those options in place of those listed options:

```
SELECT column(s)
FROM tablename
WHERE column [= | > | >= | < | <= | != |<>]
             (SELECT col1 from tablename WHERE condition(s));
```

For a non-correlated subquery in SELECT, you can follow the following sample syntax:

```
SELECT col1, col2,
  (SELECT col from tablename)
FROM tablename;
```

For a non-correlated subquery in FROM, you can follow the following sample syntax:

```
SELECT col1, col2
FROM(SELECT col from tablename);
```

For a correlated subquery in WHERE, you can follow the following sample syntax. The square brackets indicate you could use any one of those options in place of those listed options:

```
SELECT column(s)
FROM tablename1 a
WHERE column [IN | NOT IN |EXISTS | NOT EXISTS]
            (SELECT col1 from tablename2 b WHERE a.id = b.id);
```

For a correlated subquery in SELECT, you can follow the following sample syntax:

```
SELECT col1, col2,
        (SELECT col3 FROM tablename2 b WHERE a.id = b.id)
FROM tablename1 a;
```

Syntax for common table expressions

For a single non-recursive CTE, you can use the following sample syntax:

```
WITH ctename (col1, col2, colN)
AS (SELECT col1, col2, colN FROM table)
SELECT col1, col2, colN FROM ctename;
```

For a non-recursive CTE with multiple CTEs, you can use the following sample syntax:

```
WITH ctename1 (col1, col2, colN)
AS (select col1, col2, colN from table1),
ctename2 (col1, col2, colN)
AS (select col1, col2, colN from table2)
SELECT col1, col2, colN
FROM ctename1
JOIN ctename2
ON ctename1.col1 = ctename2.col1;
```

For a recursive CTE, you can use the following sample syntax:

```
WITH RECURSIVE ctename
AS (
  initial query
  UNION ALL
  recursive query
)
SELECT * FROM ctename;
```

Syntax for query hints

For an index hint, you can use the following sample syntax:

```
SELECT column(s)
FROM tablename USE INDEX(indexname)
WHERE condition(s);
```

Syntax for transaction isolation level

To set the isolation level for the session, you can use the following sample syntax:

```
SET SESSION TRANSACTION isolationlevel;
```

To set the isolation level for the transaction, you can use the following sample syntax:

```
SET TRANSACTION isolationlevel;
```

Programmable objects

This section takes you through some example syntax for modifying data in MySQL. For more details on this syntax, visit Chapter 12, *Programmable Objects.* This chapter will also outline the differences in syntax for Oracle, PostgreSQL, and SQL Server.

Syntax for views

To create a view, you can use the following sample syntax:

```
CREATE VIEW nameofview AS
SELECT col1, col2, co1n
FROM tablename
WHERE condition(s);
```

To create a view that will be used to modify data, you can use the following sample syntax:

```
CREATE VIEW nameofview AS
SELECT col1, col2, co1n
FROM tablename
WHERE condition(s)
WITH CHECK OPTION;
```

Syntax for variables

To use a variable in your SQL statement, you can use the following sample syntax:

```
SET @varname := 'value';
SELECT * FROM tablename
WHERE col1 = @varname;
```

Syntax for stored procedures

To create a stored procedure, you can use the following sample syntax:

```
DELIMITER $$
CREATE PROCEDURE storedprocname()
 BEGIN
 your sql statments go here;
 END $$
DELIMITER ;
```

To call the stored procedure that you just created, you can use the following sample syntax:

```
CALL storedprocname ();
```

To use IN parameters in a stored procedure, you can use the following sample syntax:

```
DELIMITER $$
CREATE PROCEDURE storedprocname
(
IN in_varname vartype,
IN in_varname2 vartype
)
 BEGIN
 SELECT * FROM tablename
 WHERE col1 = in_varname AND col2 = in_varname2
 END $$
DELIMITER ;
```

To call your stored procedure with IN parameters, you can use the following sample syntax:

```
CALL storedprocname('value', value);
```

To use IN parameters in a stored procedure, you can use the following sample syntax:

```
DELIMITER $$
CREATE PROCEDURE storedprocname
(
IN in_varname vartype,
IN in_varname2 vartype,
OUT out_varname vartype
)
 BEGIN
 SELECT * FROM tablename
 WHERE col1 = in_varname AND col2 = in_varname2
 END $$
DELIMITER ;
```

To call your stored procedure with the IN and OUT parameters, you can use the following sample syntax:

```
CALL storedprocname ('value', value, @out_varname);
SELECT @out_varname;
```

To alter the stored procedure, you need to delete it and recreate it with the following sample syntax:

```
DROP PROCEDURE storedprocname;
```

Syntax for flow control statements

To loop through data in a stored procedure with LOOP, you can use the following sample syntax:

```
[beginlabel:] LOOP
 sql statements
 END LOOP [endlabel];
```

To loop through data in a stored procedure with REPEAT, you can use the following sample syntax:

```
[beginlabel:] REPEAT
    sql statements
UNTIL condition
END REPEAT [endlabel]
```

To loop through data in a stored procedure with WHILE, you can use the following sample syntax:

```
[beginlabel:]
WHILE condition DO
sql statements
END WHILE
[end_label]
```

Syntax for error handling

To handle errors in a stored procedure, you can use the following sample syntax:

```
DECLARE action HANDLER FOR condition statement;
```

Syntax for functions

To create a function, you can use the following sample syntax:

```
DELIMITER $$
 CREATE FUNCTION functionname(
 parameter1,
 parameter2,...
 )
 RETURNS datatype
 [NOT] DETERMINISTIC
 BEGIN
 -- put sql statements here
 END $$
 DELIMITER ;
```

To call the function in a SELECT query, you can use the following sample syntax:

```
SELECT col1, col2,
        functionname(col3)
FROM tablename;
```

To alter the function, you need to delete it and recreate it with the following sample syntax:

```
DROP FUNCTION functionname;
```

Syntax for triggers

To create a trigger, you can use the following sample syntax. The square brackets indicate you could use any one of those options in place of those listed options:

```
CREATE TRIGGER triggername
[BEFORE | AFTER] [INSERT | UPDATE| DELETE]
ON tablename FOR EACH ROW
triggerbody;
```

To create multiple triggers, you can use the following sample syntax. The square brackets indicate you could use any one of those options in place of those listed options:

```
CREATE TRIGGER triggername
[BEFORE | AFTER] [INSERT | UPDATE| DELETE]
ON tablename FOR EACH ROW
[FOLLOWS | PRECEDES] anothertriggername
triggerbody;
```

To delete a trigger, you can use the following sample syntax:

```
DROP TRIGGER triggername;
```

Syntax for temporary tables

To explicitly create a temporary table, you can use the following sample syntax:

```
CREATE TEMPORARY TABLE temptablename(
col1definition,
col2definition,
colndefinition);
```

To implicitly create a temporary table schema from one or more tables via a query, you can use the following sample syntax:

```
CREATE TEMPORARY TABLE temptablename
SELECT * FROM permanenttable
LIMIT 0;
```

To delete a temporary table, you can use the following sample syntax:

```
DROP TEMPORARY TABLE temptablename;
```

Summary

In this book, you learned many things about the SQL programming language and how to use it in MySQL Workbench. This included creating databases, creating and alerting tables, and creating and altering indexes.

You learned how to select data with SQL syntax using the SELECT, WHERE, ORDER BY, JOIN, GROUP BY, and HAVING clauses. We also provided information about the aggregate functions you can use in the GROUP BY clause. You also learned how to modify data with SQL syntax including INSERT, UPDATE, and DELETE. This included how to use SQL transactions to commit and rollback SQL statements.

Then, you learned about advanced query techniques, including how to create and use subqueries, common table expressions, query hints, and transaction isolation level syntax. You learned about programmable objects, including creating and using views, variables, stored procedures, functions, triggers, and temporary tables.

Finally, you learned about the best practices for database design and querying, how to explore and process your data, and how to tell a story with your data. You now have the necessary skills to successfully query a SQL database and tell a story with the data.

Assessments

Chapter 1

1. Structured Query Language, or SQL (pronounced see-quel), is the language used for querying and manipulating data, and defining structures in databases.
2. **Data definition language (DDL)**, **data manipulation language (DML)**, and **data control language (DCL)**
3. Queries, clauses, predicates, expressions, statements, and white space.
4. To avoid redundant data, optimize database performance, and ensure data integrity.
5. First normal form, second normal form, and third normal form.
6. Ensuring consistency and accuracy of data.
7. Entity, referential, and domain integrity.
8. The top four are Oracle, MySQL, SQL Server, and PostgreSQL.
9. It's available for free, it offers a lot of functionality for system and database administrators, it's easy to use and implement, and it's fast and stable.
10. Licensing is expensive, and it may require significant database administrator resources after installation to maintain it.

Chapter 2

1. Windows and Mac.
2. Open the **System Preferences**, then click **MySQL**; then, you can see the status and configuration options.
3. Click the + sign next to **MySQL Connections** in **MySQL Workbench**, then fill in the connection information.
4. By using the **Data Import/Restore** in the **Administration** tab.
5. After executing a query, it will be in the **Action Output** panel.
6. By clicking on the table name in the **Schemas** panel, then the columns will appear in the **Information** panel.

7. By using the **View** menu and clicking **Panels**, then **Hide Secondary Sidebar**.
8. In the **Output** panel in the **Action** column.
9. In the **Output** panel in the **Message** column.
10. By right-clicking the table, then choosing **Select Rows - Limit 1000**.

Chapter 3

1. CHAR, VARCHAR, BINARY, VARBINARY, BLOB, TEXT, ENUM, SET.
2. They make your database size much larger and hurt query performance.
3. INT, FLOAT, DOUBLE, DECIMAL, BIT.
4. Use this when you are concerned about the upper bounds of the range on your INT.
5. DATE, TIME, DATETIME, TIMESTAMP, YEAR.
6. Oracle, PostgreSQL, and SQL Server.
7. JSON and spatial data types.
8. You want to pick the smallest data type that will hold your data so that you can have the fastest query performance.
9. TINYINT.
10. VARCHAR.

Chapter 4

1. Keywords and spaces.
2. Numbers (0-9), lowercase letters (a-z), uppercase letters (A-Z), the dollar sign ($), and the underscore (_).
3. CREATE DATABASE yourschema;
4. The **Output** panel.
5. With a natural key, you are using unique columns, and the data in those columns exists outside the database (that is, in the business world). With a surrogate key, you are creating a column to hold a unique value for each row, and that value isn't used anywhere outside the database.

6. `# this is a single line comment`

7. ```
/*
this is a
multi line
comment
*/
```

8. Clustered indexes sort the data in order on disk and nonclustered indexes don't.

9. If two or more queries are requesting the same data, creating locks that won't be resolved, MySQL will decide which is easiest to kill (usually based on how long it will take to roll back any given query).

10. Yes.

# Chapter 5

1. Table Data Import and Export, SQL Data Import and Export, Result Data Export, and SQL syntax.

2. Right-click a table, then choose **Table Data Import Wizard**.

3. You use the **Configure Import Settings** page to map the columns.

4. Right-click a table and choose **Table Data Export Wizard**.

5. Go into the **Management** or **Administration** panel in MySQL Workbench, then select **Data Import/Restore**.

6. Go into the **Management** or **Administration** panel in **MySQL Workbench**, then select **Data Export**.

7. Select rows from a table, then click the **Export recordset to an external file** button.

8. ```
LOAD DATA INFILE '/pathtoyourfiles/baseballdatabank-csv/csv-
files/Teams.csv'
INTO TABLE yourschema.teams
FIELDS TERMINATED BY ',';
```

9. ```
SELECT * INTO OUTFILE 'teams-export.csv'
FIELDS TERMINATED BY ';' OPTIONALLY ENCLOSED BY '"'
LINES TERMINATED BY '\n'
FROM yourschema.teams;
```

10. `secure-file-priv`
```

Chapter 6

1. The semicolon (;).
2. SELECT and FROM.
3. Since this selects all columns in a table, it is considered more expensive than if you specify the columns you need.
4. It helps to limit the results of your queries.
5. Percent (%) and underscore (_).
6. It helps you to sort your results.
7. ASC or DESC.
8. EXPLAIN.
9. Right-click a table and choose **Alter Table** or you can execute a SQL query to alter the table.
10. Click the **Query** menu in MySQL Workbench, then choose **Explain Current Statement**.

Chapter 7

1. INNER, OUTER, cross, natural, and self joins.
2. Returns only matching records from each joined table.
3. dbname.tablename AS a
4. LEFT, RIGHT, FULL, right excluding, and left excluding.
5. Includes all rows from the right table that don't match records in the left table.
6. Associates columns of the same name in the joined tables with each other. It's similar to an inner join or left outer join.
7. It returns a combination of every row from two tables.
8. UNION removes duplicates and UNION ALL doesn't.
9. By using DISTINCT in SELECT clause and an INNER JOIN.
10. By ensuring you use the indexes that are on the tables or by adding indexes to the tables.

Chapter 8

1. `USE yourschema;`
   `describe managers;`
2. `CREATE TABLE newtablename`
   `SELECT * FROM existingtablename`
3. By using a `WHERE` clause.
4. `TRUNCATE TABLE tablename;`
5. `UPDATE table1 t1`
   `INNER JOIN table2 t2`
   `ON t1.id = t2.id`
   `SET t1.col1 = t2.col1`
6. A grouping of one or more changes to the database.
7. To start a transaction in MySQL, use the `START TRANSACTION` or `BEGIN` keywords. To commit the transaction, you use the `COMMIT` keyword. To roll back a transaction, use the `ROLLBACK` keyword.
8. `ALTER TABLE table1`
   `ADD COLUMN col2 datatype constraint AFTER col1;`
9. `ALTER TABLE table1`
   `CHANGE COLUMN col1 col1 newdatatype;`
   `ALTER TABLE table1`
10. `CHANGE COLUMN col1 col1a datatype;`

Chapter 9

1. You can combine literals, operators, and built-in functions in countless ways to produce expressions.
2. A constant value such as a string, a number, or a NULL value.
3. Perform math in your query.
4. An important concept in mathematics is operator precedence, which means the order of operations. Precedence means that higher-level mathematical operations will be performed first so that multiplication and division are done before addition and subtraction. You can add parentheses around calculations to impact the precedence.

5. String, numeric, and date.
6. Converts text to lowercase.
7. Converts a value into the specified data type.
8. The query may no longer use the indexes on the table.
9. STDDEV(column)
10. Virtual and stored.

Chapter 10

1. To group rows that have the same values into summary rows.
2. Use the WHERE clause before the GROUP BY clause.
3. They wind up returning the same results.
4. Use ORDER BY clause after the GROUP BY clause.
5. ROLLUP.
6. To filter the GROUP BY results.
7. Yes.
8. SELECT
   FROM/JOIN
   WHERE
   GROUP BY
   HAVING
   ORDER BY
   LIMIT
9. FROM/JOIN
   WHERE
   GROUP BY
   HAVING
   SELECT
   ORDER BY
   LIMIT

Chapter 11

1. Correlated and non-correlated.
2.

Non-correlated	Correlated
The inner query doesn't depend on the outer query.	Inner query depends on the outer query.
Can run as a standalone query.	Can't run as a standalone query.
Executed only once.	Executed once for each row selected in the outer query.
Executed before the outer query.	Executed after the outer query.
Can't be used instead of JOIN on the outer query.	Can be used instead of JOIN on the outer query, but will be slower than a JOIN.

3. SELECT, WHERE, FROM, INSERT, UPDATE, and DELETE clauses.
4. SELECT and WHERE clauses.
5. A container for a single SQL statement that will allow you to query a temporary result set.
6. Recursive and non-recursive.
7. Locking is what happens when a query runs against a database.
8. With an index hint.
9. READ UNCOMMITTED, READ COMMITTED, REPEATABLE READ, and SERIALIZABLE.
10. Phantom reads happen when rows are returned that weren't in the previous results.

Chapter 12

1. A stored query.
2. Yes, depending on the query in the view. You can update, insert, and delete from a view if it queries one table. You can insert and update from a view if queries multiple tables, but you can't delete.

3. It lets you store a single data value that can be used during your session's queries.
4. One of two ways:

   - `SET @varname = value;`
   - `SET @varname := value;`

5. A set of SQL statements stored in the database.
6. The main difference between a variable and parameter is that parameters are static throughout the procedure, but a variable can be changed during the stored procedure.
7. `IF`, `CASE`, `LOOP`, `REPEAT`, `WHILE`, `ITERATE`, and `LEAVE`.
8. These are a way to extend the functionality of MySQL, and they work much the same other built-in functions work.
9. A set of actions that run after you insert, update, or delete data in a table.
10. Allow you to store temporary query results that can be used during a query session.

Chapter 13

1. By listing the distinct values in a table.
2. By querying for `NULL` values in a table.
3. By querying the table with a `GROUP BY` and a `HAVING count(*) > 2`.
4. Acquaint yourself with the data and create a data dictionary.
5. A document that helps you to understand what is in your database.
6. First, you will need to install a Python plugin into your MySQL Workbench installation, then create an ERD. Next, you can use the Python plugin to create the data dictionary to paste into a text or markdown editor of your choice.
7. They help search for string patterns in your data.
8. Matches the beginning of a string.
9. Matches any of the patterns specified.
10. Yes. `WHERE column REGEXP '^[abc].{3}on$'`

Chapter 14

1. Reporting, Explanatory, Predictive, Correlation, Causation.
2. How something changed over time, go from the big picture to a narrow focus, start narrow and go to the big picture, and comparing and contrasting.
3. Decision-makers, colleagues, and the general public.
4. Yes, depending on how many audiences you might have.
5. Explaining the question, answer, and methodology.
6. It's essential to keep your focus on one question.
7. As you go through explaining the answer, make sure to give context along the way, and don't wait to answer everything until the end.
8. Make sure to describe your methodology so that it gives your presentation context. You may have a long process to get to the question's answer, but most audiences won't want or need that much explanation.
9. Jumping to conclusions, switching colors, not labeling your charts, not providing context, cherry-picking data, not properly formatting numbers for readability, arbitrary scale.
10. Microsoft Office, Google Documents, OpenOffice, Tableau, and PowerBI.

Chapter 15

1. It helps to ensure your data is consistent, accurate, and in the right format.
2. You must ensure that you name things accurately, descriptively, and at the same time avoiding keywords that will add any kind of confusion to the naming. You must avoid adding spaces in the names, choose the right case, and stick to one convention. You should make sure that you use only permitted characters when naming a database object.
3. If the data type is too large, it takes up too much space on disk. If the data type is too small, then it doesn't fit your data.
4. There is no right number of indexes on a table or columns in your indexes. Generally speaking, too few or too many indexes can make the performance of your database worse. This is why it's important to know what queries are being executed on the table to understand best what would help the performance.

5. The EXPLAIN keyword with your query or in the MySQL Workbench menu under **Query**, then **Explain Current Statement**.

6. Steps to write clean code are as follows:

   - Format it for readability.
   - Using uppercase for keywords and lowercase for everything else.
   - Adding comments.

7. Some best practices when writing SQL statements are as follows:

   - Use SELECT fields instead of SELECT *.
   - Use column aliases, especially when using functions.
   - Avoid using SELECT DISTINCT.

8. Some best practices when using the WHERE clause are as follows:

   - Only use wildcards at the end of a string.
   - Use an underscore (_) wildcard instead of a percent sign (%) when possible.
   - Avoid WHERE clauses with functions.
   - Use WHERE instead of HAVING to filter when possible.

9. Always use column names in INSERT.

10. If you are deleting all the data in a table, use TRUNCATE instead.

Other Books You May Enjoy

If you enjoyed this book, you may be interested in these other books by Packt:

SQL for Data Analytics
Upom Malik, Matt Goldwasser, Et al

ISBN: 978-1-78980-735-6

Learn how to clean your data and ready it for analysis

- Use SQL to summarize and identify patterns in data
- Apply special SQL clauses and functions to generate descriptive statistics
- Use SQL queries and subqueries to prepare data for analysis
- Perform advanced statistical calculations using the window function
- Analyze special data types in SQL, including geospatial data and time data
- Import and export data using a text file and PostgreSQL
- Debug queries that won't run
- Optimize queries to improve their performance for faster results

Advanced MySQL 8
Eric Vanier, Birju Shah, Et al

ISBN: 978-1-78883-444-5

- Explore new and exciting features of MySQL 8.0
- Analyze and optimize large MySQL queries
- Understand MySQL Server 8.0 settings
- Master the deployment of Group Replication and use it in an InnoDB cluster
- Monitor large distributed databases
- Discover different types of backups and recovery methods for your databases
- Explore tips to help your critical data reach its full potential

Leave a review - let other readers know what you think

Please share your thoughts on this book with others by leaving a review on the site that you bought it from. If you purchased the book from Amazon, please leave us an honest review on this book's Amazon page. This is vital so that other potential readers can see and use your unbiased opinion to make purchasing decisions, we can understand what our customers think about our products, and our authors can see your feedback on the title that they have worked with Packt to create. It will only take a few minutes of your time, but is valuable to other potential customers, our authors, and Packt. Thank you!

Index

D

Printed in Great Britain
by Amazon

78150487R00323